NATIVE AMERICAN WHALEMEN AND THE WORLD

NATIVE AMERICAN WHALEMEN AND THE WORLD

Indigenous Encounters and the Contingency of Race

NANCY SHOEMAKER

THE UNIVERSITY OF NORTH CAROLINA PRESS

Chapel Hill

© 2015 The University of North Carolina Press
All rights reserved

Set in Miller
by Westchester Publishing Services
Manufactured in the United States of America

The paper in this book meets the guidelines
for permanence and durability of the Committee on
Production Guidelines for Book Longevity
of the Council on Library Resources.

The University of North Carolina Press has been a
member of the Green Press Initiative since 2003.

Jacket illustration: Detail of harbor traffic at Cape Horn; courtesy
of the New Bedford Whaling Museum. Whale image from the log of the
Abraham Barker; Nicholson Whaling Collection, Providence Public Library
Special Collections, Providence, RI.

Library of Congress Cataloging-in-Publication Data

Shoemaker, Nancy, 1958–
    Native American whalemen and the world : indigenous encounters and the
contingency of race / Nancy Shoemaker. — First edition.
        pages cm
    Includes bibliographical references and index.
    ISBN 978-1-4696-2257-6 (cloth : alk. paper)
    ISBN 978-1-4696-2258-3 (ebook)
    1. Indians of North America—New England—History—19th century.
2. Indian whalers—New England—History.   3. Whaling—New England—
History—19th century.   4. Indians of North America—Fishing—New England.
5. Indians of North America—New England—Ethnic identity.   6. Whaling—
Social aspects—New England—History.   7. Whites—New England—Relations
with Indians.   8. New England—Race relations.   9. New England—Ethnic
relations.   I. Title.
    E78.N5S48 2015
    974.004'97—dc23

                                                                2014034897

Contents

Tables, Maps, and Figures

Acknowledgments

I am very grateful for the support this project received from the National Endowment for the Humanities, the American Antiquarian Society, the University of Connecticut Humanities Institute, and the University of Connecticut Research Foundation. I am hugely indebted to the University of Connecticut Libraries' interlibrary loan team for all they have done to help me over the years. And I thank the staff of the many archives I visited for their knowledge and patience. Especially gracious given the number of questions and demands I placed on them were Michael Dyer, Laura Pereira, and Mark Procknik at the New Bedford Whaling Museum; Paul O'Pecko at the G. W. Blunt White Library, Mystic Seaport Museum; and the many staff members who assisted me at the U.S. National Archives at Boston and the National Archives of the Fiji Islands.

Many other individuals helped in a variety of ways. At the University of Connecticut, I thank several who received their doctorates in history and anthropology and have since moved on—Patrick Blythe, Elliotte Draegor, Brian Carroll, Jason Mancini, Timothy Ives, Cedric Woods, Meredith Vasta, and Blaire Gagnon; my colleagues in the History Department, especially Helen Rozwadowski, Cornelia Dayton, Altina Waller, Richard Brown, Matthew McKenzie, Micki McElya, Janet Watson, and Shirley Roe; and the community of fellows during my year at the UConn Humanities Institute. Researchers affiliated with the Mashantucket Pequot Museum and Research Center, a fantastic resource to have nearby, generously shared research findings and responded to questions: Kevin McBride, Paul Grant-Costa (now at the Yale Indian Papers Project), Jason Mancini, and Russell Handsman. Jason and I, in particular, have had many conversations, especially after he also developed an interest in New England natives' maritime world. During my year at the American Antiquarian Society, I received much useful feedback and encouragement from Caroline Sloat, Jim Moran, Robert Bonner, Seth Rockman, Jenny Anderson, Jeffrey Sklansky, and others who belonged to the community of fellows that year. Formal and informal conversations in response to my queries, while at conferences or in discussions following presentations I gave, also had an impact on this book, for which I thank David Silverman, Susan Lebo, Edward Gray, Judith Lund, Christina Snyder, Lisa Norling, Martha Hodes, Daniel Mandell, Ann Fabian, and Joshua Reid. For my New Zealand research, I received invaluable aid from Betty Apes, Angela Wanhalla, Lachy Paterson, Mark Seymour, Tony Ballantyne, Michael Stevens, and David Haines. In Fiji, I greatly appreciated advice received from Ian Campbell and David Routledge.

In the final stages of writing this book, I began another project, which has ended up appearing in print first: *Living with Whales: Documents and Oral Histories of Native New England Whaling History*, published in 2014 by the University of Massachusetts Press. A wonderful afternoon spent with Ramona Peters at Mashpee, when she told me of her family's whaling history and what it meant to her, inspired the oral history project, and I learned much from the other people who contributed oral histories: Elizabeth James Perry and Jonathan Perry of the Aquinnah Wampanoag tribe and, at the Shinnecock Indian Nation on Long Island, Elizabeth Haile, Holly Haile Davis, and David Bunn Martine. Early on, Linda Coombs offered guidance on how to proceed with the oral histories, and later she organized opportunities for me to present my research at the Aquinnah Cultural Center. Ramona Peters also invited me to talk at Mashpee and gave me a tour of the Mashpee meetinghouse. While these individuals' suggestions and willingness to share their vast knowledge on Wampanoag, Shinnecock, and New England native history more generally has infused both books, the perspective presented here is entirely my own (meaning that none of them should be held responsible for anything I say).

Chapter 8, "Race and Indigeneity in the Life of Elisha Apes," was previously published in *Ethnohistory* (Winter 2013, volume 60, pp. 27–50). In Appendix B, table 4, a list of native-authored logbooks and journals, appeared first as the appendix in *Living with Whales*, which also reprints some of the documents analyzed in *Native American Whalemen and the World*. My article "Mr. Tashtego: Native American Whalemen in Antebellum New England," in the *Journal of the Early Republic* (Spring 2013, volume 33, pp. 109–32), gives an overview of nineteenth-century native whaling using some material from this book, mostly drawn from chapters 1–3.

NATIVE AMERICAN WHALEMEN AND THE WORLD

Introduction

Years ago, while whizzing through a microfilm reel of whaling logbooks, I saw a familiar name flash across the screen, Joel G. Jared. With incredulity, I reeled back to the first page of the volume, and there it was: "Joel G. Jared, Belonging to Ship Amethyst of New Bedford." If I needed confirmation, midway through the journal, he had signed his name again, this time adding "born Gay head Chillmark." Jared was indeed a Native American whaleman, one of many hundreds of native men whose voyages on nineteenth-century American whaleships took them around the world. In his journal, he diligently recorded the events of the day for over five years beginning with his second whaling voyage, aboard the *Amethyst* from 1846 to 1850, and continuing while on the bark *Samuel & Thomas* of Mattapoisett from 1850 to 1852. Traces of another, later voyage on the bark *Mary Frances* of Warren, Rhode Island, fill up the journal's few remaining pages.[1]

The volume itself resides in the New Bedford Whaling Museum Research Library collections and is in sad condition, its binding collapsed, the pages splotched and age-worn. Otherwise, it looks and reads much like any other of the thousands of extant logbooks and private journals inspired by the nineteenth-century American whaling industry (figure 1). In daily entries, Jared described the weather, sail handling, and latitude and longitude and recorded life aboard ship: lowering boats to chase whales, boiling whales into oil, stowing oil down below decks, eating plum duff and salt horse, gamming (socializing) with other whaleships while at sea, sighting the Azores and Galapagos Islands, anchoring at Paita and Maui, a "Portugee" and other men dying aboard ship, knife fighting, and floggings. Although nearly all entries follow the style of an official logbook, the doodles, sentimental sailor song lyrics, aborted letters ("Dear Brother I take this opertunity to inform you that i am well"), and birthday observances ("Joel G. Jared, 20 years ould this day of march 12th AD 1847") indicate that this is a private journal and, as it turned out, not so rare in its native authorship as I had first thought.[2]

Jared's doodles give us some insight into who he was and what he cared about. Amid the block-cut stamps of whales, drawings of scrolls and pointing hands, and plays on his name ("Gershom J Joel," "Jared J. Gershom," "Joel J. Gershom") that clutter the journal's first page, he listed three women: Sarah Gershom, Anstress Gershom, and Temperance Gershom. Sarah was

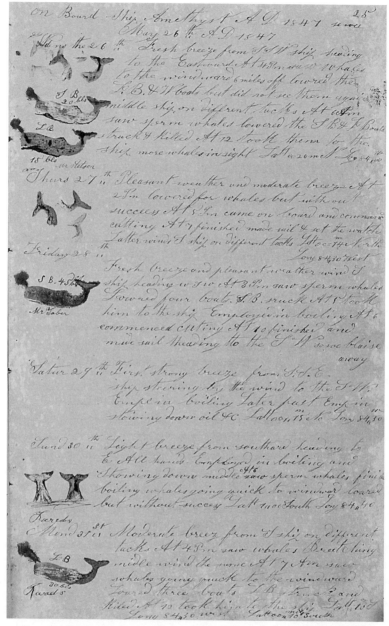

Figure 1. *This page from Joel G. Jared's journal covers May 26th through May 31st, 1847, while he was on the ship* Amethyst *of New Bedford. The crew caught four sperm whales in this period. Jared "raised" (sighted) the whale they caught on May 31st and the two whales that got away the day before. Courtesy of the New Bedford Whaling Museum.*

his mother, Anstress and Temperance her sisters, his aunts.[3] A second page of miscellanea follows, much of which is taken up by a list of names:

Joel G. Jared	do	Cannot Findanny
William S. James	do	" "
Samel Haskins	do	Druzilla Salsbury
George E. James	do	Mary H. Simmon
Abraham Jared	do	Almira Johnson
Zachues Cooper	do	Sophia Peters
William Belain	do	Mary A. Chamblin
Thomas Jeffers	do	Hannah Cuff
Johannas Salsbury	do	Alace Jeffers
George W. Degrass	do	Emily Salsbury
Alfred Peters	do	Lucretia Belain
John Tomson	[do]	Winford S. Howwaswee

As a boatsteerer on the *Amethyst*, nineteen-year-old Jared would have shared quarters in steerage with the other boatsteerers, one of whom was sixteen-year-old William S. James, who hailed from the Wampanoag community of Christiantown, just a few miles from Gay Head (Aquinnah) on Martha's Vineyard.[4] Sometime early on in the voyage, the two young whalemen must have been commiserating about romantic futures with a wife named "Cannot Findanny," made bleaker by how all their male acquaintances of about their age could be matched up with the women listed on the right. Jared eventually did marry a woman from Gay Head, later writing in his journal "Rosenah Dear Dearest Wife" as though about to draft a letter to her. Even the sentimental song lyrics of "The Haymaker" that he wrote into his journal tell of love, courtship, and marriage, with a description of a man coming upon a beautiful woman making hay in a field and ending with "Together we'll make hay."[5] Thus interspersed amid the routine and technical descriptions of weather, sail handling, and ship's duties typical of whaling logbooks, something of the person Joel G. Jared can be discerned. Young and hopeful, he set out on the *Amethyst* to earn his living and make his mark on the world as a professional whaleman. (Why else would he have taken such pains to produce a journal so faithful to the genre's expectations?) An affectionate son and brother, he wanted also to be a loving husband. Sailing over the world's oceans for three or four years at a time never meant that he had left home behind.

For all the journal reveals about Jared's aspirations and personality, it is silent on the issue of race. It says nothing about the economic hardships that the everyday racism of New England society imposed on Indians and other people of color, nothing about the dependency assumed by Massachusetts in regulating Indian affairs, and nothing about the slights and slurs New England's native people faced from white neighbors. Nowhere in his journal did Jared identify himself or anyone else by racial labels common in his day. There are no references to Indian, native, black, "colored," or white people at all. The closest Jared came to identifying by race was by referencing not a racial category but a native place, Gay Head, one of the largest of Massachusetts's native communities. A reader of the journal unfamiliar with Gay Head would undoubtedly assume that Jared was a white Yankee, someone like Herman Melville but with less literary ability and more tolerance for the demands of whaling labor. That Jared did not overtly state a racial identity in his journal seems unusual only because the Native American authors we can think of usually did write about Indians in one way or another. But race does not come up much in whaling logbooks and journals generally. A partial journal from the same voyage of the *Amethyst*, kept by Captain Gorham B. Howes, makes no mention of race either.[6] The absence of explicit references to race in Jared's journal shows how fully he committed himself to the whaling industry by keeping to the norms of the logbook genre.

More fundamentally, Jared's silence on race illustrates an important aspect of it, its contingency. Studies of race often treat it as a fixed and singular idea that originated in the past, changed over time, and varied from place to place.[7] But race has also fluctuated in a more fleeting way by the situation.[8] Recently, historians have turned their sights to "the mercurial nature of race," as Martha Hodes termed it. Her account of a marriage between a white woman in antebellum New England and a "colored" man from the Cayman Islands explores the geography of "different racial systems" and what happened when individuals from one part of the world moved to another.[9] As Hodes and others have shown, however, even within one cultural system of race, baffling inconsistencies permeate racial categorization schemes. A close look at the decennial U.S. federal census, for example, exposes peculiar shifts in the rise and fall of "mulattoes," "quadroons," and "octoroons" in the nineteenth century, the twentieth century's indecision about how best to count people of "Spanish origins," and the twenty-first century's acknowledgment of multiracialism. Census enumerators and other local bureaucrats tasked with assigning individuals to a racial category and individuals asked to identify themselves by race add more idiosyncrasies, each to the logic of the moment.[10] That people intermarry and reproduce across racial lines muddles efforts to categorize by race even more.[11]

The situation accounts for how people experience race as much as, if not more than, chronological and geographical variability. Gloria Anzaldúa pointed out some underlying causes for race's contingency in her classic autobiographical reflection, *Borderlands/La Frontera*. Social expectations about race, gender, and sexuality can clash with one's sense of self and are inept at allowing people to occupy multiple social categories simultaneously.[12] That Jared's journal does not address Indian issues current in his time does not mean that he did not think about those issues nor that he did not identify as Indian. It means only that through the medium of the whaling journal he expressed one part of himself, his occupation as a whaleman. Another source of race's contingency arose from its function. Race was an ideological system put in place by the white race to exert political control over others; to amass wealth by appropriating other people's land, resources, and labor; and to enjoy social privileges and prestige. But to make race work to one's advantage, it had to be adaptable to the context. In consequence, the lived experience of race is full of exceptions, contradictions, and unpredictability: race has never functioned like a well-oiled machine but more like a Rube Goldberg contraption with quick-fix patches, roundabout mechanisms, and clattering, wild movements. Individuals could encounter shifts in expectations not only over a lifetime but even in the course of a single day.

One example of contradictions embedded in race comes from transatlantic slave trade history. In *Slave Ship Sailors and Their Captive Cargoes*, Emma Christopher ruminates on the paradox of free black seamen laboring on behalf of slave trade ventures. Racist depictions of blacks served to legitimate the brutal treatment of Africans as cargo, but at the same time white and black sailors commingled with little racial conflict or differentiation in treatment. Despite the employment of black sailors on the slavers' side, ships' crews were often referred to collectively as "whites" in opposition to the "blacks" on shore or the "blacks" in chains below.[13] Black sailors were not, as in the historiography on Irish and Italian immigrants, aspiring to whiteness to ascend the racial hierarchy, nor were they regarded as white by their fellow crew members.[14] Instead, the position they then held, their utility toward some specific purpose, shaped how the variety of ideas about blacks in circulation bore on individual experiences with race.

Slavery justifications fed European diminishment of African capacity while processes of colonization presumed the cultural inferiority of "Indians." Narratives of colonization prescribed certain roles for each race (white = settler = civilized; Indian = native = savage), which were destined to produce inconsistencies and confusions. Who was who when natives from one place and at one stage of colonization explored, harvested resources, came to trade, and settled in another place? Joel Jared and other native whalemen contradicted nineteenth-century ideas about Indians by traveling the world, mastering ocean navigation, and accumulating knowledge of the globe's great diversity in language, custom, and environment. They were "unexpected Indians" somewhat like those in Philip Deloria's *Indians in Unexpected Places*. With photographs of Plains Indians in powwow regalia driving cars or having their nails manicured, Deloria jars us, forcing us to notice how popular images of Indians enable white claims to modernity—to progress, technology, and economic and cultural achievement.[15] In the nineteenth century, Plains Indian iconography had not yet come to dominate the American imagination. Instead, narratives of Europeans arriving by ship at a new world and displacing its savage inhabitants molded popular images of Indians.

This book explores the variable configurations of race that nineteenth-century New England whalemen encountered, the uneven and often contrary application of racial assertions in different settings, and the consequent disjunctures between racial ideas and lived experience. The book's four parts—"The Ship," "The Beach," "Islands," and "The Reservation"—emphasize that the particular setting and the roles assumed by individuals in those settings continually reconfigured the content of racial ideas and how race impinged on social relations. These four social settings align metaphorically with stages in the colonization process. In each of these situations that native whalemen found themselves in, the circumstances dictated how much race mattered and, if it mattered, how so.

Part 1 explains why and how Native American men became laborers in the global workforce of the extractive economy that opened up the Pacific and Arctic to European and American colonization. The whaling industry needed labor. The discovery and exploitation of natural resources spearheaded expansion into distant seas, but such expansion was possible only because, wherever whaleships ventured, new sources of labor were found. The ship engrossed men from all over the world in the same endeavor, resulting in a unique social community that operated by its own rules. Native American whalemen lived and worked alongside white and black Americans, Portuguese-speaking white Azoreans and black Cape Verdeans, Pacific Islanders, Africans, Asians, Latin Americans, Arctic peoples, and Europeans mainly from Britain, Germany, and France. New England natives were one segment of this global workforce. They had their own particular relationship to the whaling industry, but they also belonged to the ship, as all in the polyglot crew did, and they abided by its rules. On the ship, rank reigned supreme. Intent on profit, the whaling industry relied on rank to organize labor into an occupational hierarchy that designated where men worked and slept and that dictated who deferred to whom. Rank predominated because whaleship owners, captains, and government supporters of industry believed that an orderly crew facilitated profitable voyages. Other social hierarchies had some impact on shipboard culture. Whaling crews' great diversity in race, culture, and nationality intersected with rank to influence notions about what each man brought to the job and could spontaneously erupt during a voyage to disrupt the chain of command. Gender also informed relations aboard ship by transcending the distances created by rank, race, nationality, and culture to bind whalemen around a common identity as men.

In part 2, the situation is the beach, where crews from foreign ships met indigenous inhabitants at whaleship landfalls. These culturally distinct peoples came to know each other through amicable, mutually beneficial exchanges interrupted by bouts of violence. In his history of European encroachment at the Marquesas, the historian Greg Dening configured the beach as a classic cultural encounter narrative. Europeans bearing metal trade goods, diseases, and a sense of cultural superiority came by ship to the island abodes of darker, culturally inscrutable natives.[16] As popular in the nineteenth century as it is today, the cultural encounter narrative provided a powerful framework for drawing racial distinctions between the civilized and the savage, a polarity that allotted no clear role for the Native American whaleman nor for the other natives (Hawaiians, Tahitians, Maoris, and so on) swept up by maritime trades into colonization's workforce. Cultural encounters involving whaleships were messy affairs with "Indians" on ships and on shore. The position of native New England whalemen was especially fraught with ambiguity. The memory of European expansion into North America acted as a template for the cultural encounter narrative and heavily influenced ideas about what an Indian was. Two hundred years before native New Englanders' work brought them to the Pacific, Indian, and Arctic Oceans, their ancestors had experienced similar encounters with foreign ships. Thus, they experienced colonization from two opposing angles. Long accustomed to foreign usurpations of their land and culture, living in New England under a colonial state, they simultaneously stood on the front lines for the early stages of foreign intrusion in other parts of the world.

Islands provide the setting for part 3. Its form is plural to convey how different local constructions of race developed as whalemen settled in foreign lands. Beachcombers, typically runaway sailors or convicts who chose to live on a Pacific island and often married native women with whom they had children, constituted the first wave of foreign settlers. Then came Christian missionaries and a generation or two later a more numerous and purposeful class of European and American emigrants intent on replicating their own societies and pushing native inhabitants aside. Beachcombers straddled the shift in colonizing interests from resource extraction and trade to land acquisition. They may have come to their new homes by happenstance, but along with missionaries, they found themselves well situated to become landowners when foreign zeal for native land picked up in earnest. There were a few Native American beachcombers who lived out their lives in some Pacific locale. In Fiji and New Zealand, where racial categories emerged directly from the process of European colonization, Native American men, indigenous to the Americas only, were foreigners. By definition, a native to one place could not be native to another. Whatever racial expectations these native men faced back home in the United States had little bearing when their role now seemed more like colonizer than colonized. New England had beachcombers, too. Foreigners from Cape Verde, Hawai'i, St. Helena, and other stops along whaling routes married New England natives. They had the opposite experience from Pacific beachcombers, however. Their origins outside of the United States were inconsequential. Race in the United States drew more on the legacy of African slavery than on the history of colonization, and local constructions of race in New England had a category already in place for most of the foreigners who married natives: people of color.

The reservation, part 4, is shorthand for native life under a colonial regime in which foreigners have successfully acquired control over land and governance; claimed cultural supremacy in print culture, schools, and churches; and relegated native people to the economic and social margins. This is the stage of colonization scholars call "settler colonialism," when the new transplants wish only for the demise of the native in all but nostalgic memory.[17] "The Reservation," containing a single chapter, acts as an epilogue, an ironic counterpoint, for it shows how native New Englanders' lives at home contrasted completely with their experiences abroad. In nineteenth-century southern New England, the racial infrastructure portrayed local Indians as remnants of the exotic savage first encountered on the beach. Reading a newspaper, negotiating with a state-appointed Indian guardian for services, or making purchases at a store, native New Englanders routinely encountered the deeply entrenched and widely held belief that they were social derelicts, a degraded, abject, dependent people who barely even counted as Indians, so far had they fallen from the original archetype of the naive savage one might encounter on a beach. Even though the New England whaling industry valued native men's labor so highly as to promote them into positions of authority on the ship, the respect native whalemen earned at sea and in foreign ports did not ameliorate the disrespect they had to contend with at home in New England.

: : :

Nineteenth-century American culture envisioned Indians on the edges of an expansionist United States and gave little notice to the several thousand Wampanoags, Narragansetts, Pequots, Mohegans, Shinnecocks, and other peoples of southern New England and eastern Long Island (which I include in New England for its historical and cultural connections). English colonists had subjugated them long ago in a series of wars culminating in King Philip's War of 1675. Many found refuge as Christian converts in native communities called praying towns as the English squeezed the dwindling native population onto small plots of land and assigned Protestant missionaries and state- or town-appointed overseers, guardians, and trustees to act as a regulating, "civilizing" force. New England natives adapted to these initiatives in their own way. By the nineteenth century, they dressed much like their non-Indian neighbors, lived for the most part in frame houses, and spoke English. They had become Christian but on their terms and challenged the missions that supported their churches and schools by choosing their own faith to become Methodists, Baptists, or Adventists. They not only accepted school education but became strident advocates for longer school terms, better trained teachers, and more substantial school buildings. By the nineteenth century, New England's native communities had become fully integrated in the region's economy but at its hardscrabble periphery, earning a meager income as subsistence farmers, farm laborers, domestic servants, and peddlers of home-manufactured brooms and baskets.[18]

Even their ministers and teachers, who were paid much lower salaries than their white counterparts, struggled to attain a sufficiency on the salaries allowed them.[19] Following the sea usually paid more. In the mid-eighteenth century, unable to support a family on a minister's salary and hounded by creditors, Solomon Briant of Mashpee left his pulpit to go whaling.[20] Although the whaling industry was implicated in the processes of capitalism and colonization that brought hardship to New England's native population, it simultaneously offered coastal native communities the best means to survive these changes. The largest federally recognized tribes in southern New England and Long Island today are those with ancient ties to an ocean-based economy and a long history of laboring in the whaling industry. The lands of the Wampanoag Tribe of Gay Head (Aquinnah) and the Shinnecock still border the ocean. The Mashpee Wampanoag Tribe on Cape Cod has ocean nearby to the north and south, while the Narragansetts in Rhode Island and the Pequots and Mohegans in Connecticut live slightly inland from Long Island Sound (map 1).

New England native men had been important laborers in the American whaling industry since its inception in the mid-seventeenth century on the eastern end of Long Island. Inspired by frequent whale strandings, English colonists in Southampton and East Hampton formed shore whaling companies and contracted with Montaukett, Shinnecock, and other native men to provide the bulk of the labor. The English on Cape Cod soon started similar shore whaling operations, as did those on the island of Nantucket. In each locale, natives did much of the actual manning of the lookout towers and the whaleboats, splitting the blubber and whalebone from a successful catch with the English colonists who had helped capture the whale and the increasingly wealthy few English entrepreneurs who owned the whaling equipment: the lookout towers, whaleboats, harpoons, lances, and try-pots for boiling the blubber into oil. As Daniel Vickers has shown for Nantucket, John Strong for Long Island, and David Silverman for Martha's Vineyard, the political economy of early New England made natives vulnerable to English control of their labor. English colonists accumulated capital and built up a legal system that partnered debt with indenture, and many, but not all, natives who whaled in the seventeenth and eighteenth centuries did so through coercion.[21]

Shore whaling targeted slow-moving right whales, which conveniently floated when dead. The thick blubber that made them buoyant was boiled into oil and the plasticlike "whalebone" (baleen) was stripped from whales' mouths. Within a century, right whales became scarce off of southern New England, and the American whaling industry moved offshore. Loading their whaleboats onto larger sailing vessels, descendants of the earliest English colonists headed off to the North and South Atlantic Ocean and took Native American and African American laborers with them. By the middle of the eighteenth century, Nantucket surpassed all other whaling ports. Even after a mysterious epidemic decimated the island's native population in 1763, Nantucket whaling still relied on native labor and recruited native men from Cape Cod and Martha's Vineyard and from merchants, farmers, and mariners in the region who held Indians as bond servants.[22]

Despite disruptions during the Revolutionary War and the War of 1812, the American whale fishery flourished, and American whaleships breached the Cape of Good Hope and Cape Horn in search of new prey. The Indian Ocean's trade in luxury goods had early on drawn Europe's seafarers, and as the English colonized New England, the Spanish had made inroads on the Pacific. British, French, and Russian ships of exploration followed. The

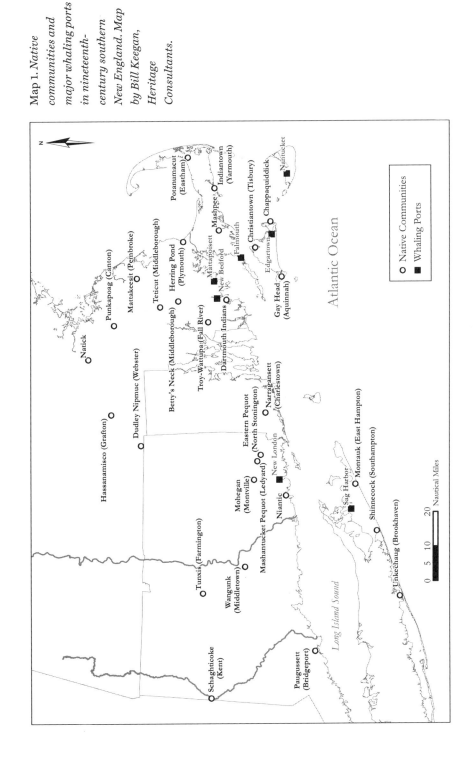

Map 1. Native communities and major whaling ports in nineteenth-century southern New England. Map by Bill Keegan, Heritage Consultants.

most famous had James Cook as commander. He departed on his first voyage of exploration in 1768 to observe the transit of Venus at Tahiti, and on his third voyage, after a fruitless search for the Northwest Passage, was killed by Hawaiians at Kealakekua Bay in 1779.[23] Cook's observations of North America's northwest coast spawned a transpacific fur trade, which New Englanders joined. They sold guns and cloth for furs on the northwest coast, transported the pelts to China to exchange for cargoes of tea, silk, and porcelain wares, and stopped for provisions along the way at the Hawaiian Islands. Soon, American ships began harvesting other Pacific resources: seals, sandalwood, bêche-de-mer, tortoise shell, and, most important for the size of the industry, whales.[24] In the early 1790s, the *Beaver* of Nantucket, the *Rebecca* of New Bedford, and a half dozen other New England whaleships rounded Cape Horn to become the first American whalers in Pacific waters.[25] The British and French operated whaling industries, too, but at a scale nowhere near New England's.

Pacific whaling grew exponentially over the next several decades in a boom targeting sperm whales. More dangerous to hunt than right whales, sperm whales moved fast and had teeth instead of baleen. Besides a body of valuable whale blubber, sperm whales carried a waxy substance in their heads, spermaceti, which burned cleanly and made superior candles. In the 1830s, as whaling vessels increased in tonnage and quantity, New Bedford, on the southeastern coast of the Massachusetts mainland, replaced Nantucket as the world's largest whaling port. At the industry's peak in 1851 (the same year that Herman Melville published *Moby-Dick*), 137 whalers departed from New Bedford, half of them bound for the Pacific Ocean.[26] The Hawaiian Islands became the primary servicing hub and supply depot for whaling traffic in the 1840s and 1850s, visited by hundreds of whaling vessels annually, most on seasonal respites from hunting bowhead whales in the icy waters of the far North Pacific.[27] Although headquartered in New England, the American whale fishery had become a fully global enterprise.

Ship owners, usually a consortium of shareholders, owned the sloops, brigs, schooners, and ships that dominated whaling early in the century and the barks that became more common later in the century. ("Ship" refers both to a particular rigging and more generically to any large sailing vessel.) By the end of the century, steam whalers came into vogue but never fully replaced sailing vessels in the American whale fishery. Agents outfitted the whaler to make it seaworthy, stocked it with provisions, and hired twenty to forty men to go on the voyage. The size of whaling crews varied by the number of whaleboats that would be lowered to chase whales. Each whaleboat carried six men: a boatheader, boatsteerer, and four foremast hands to pull the oars. A large vessel would lower four whaleboats, perhaps five, and have an equal number of officers (also called mates) who, along with the captain if he so chose, each had charge of a whaleboat as its boatheader. Second in command in each whaleboat was the boatsteerer, whose duties included harpooning whales. Foremast hands made up the largest contingent aboard ship. Typically over half were greenhands who had never been to sea and never seen a whale. Whaling crews had in addition several men who stayed on the ship while others lowered the boats to chase whales. The cooper manufactured barrels. Sometimes a carpenter or blacksmith was aboard. The cook fed the crew, and the steward waited on the captain and officers. There might also be a cabin boy and a steerage boy. If the cooper or cook was unable to manage the ship while all the boats were off chasing whales, then a shipkeeper would also be put on board. Before signing the shipping articles, each member of the crew negotiated his lay (share of the profits) with the agent. Lays ranged from about 1/15 for captains to as low as 1/250 or worse for cabin boys.[28]

Over the course of the nineteenth century, American whalemen scraped clean the baleen from the mouths of right whales and bowheads and cut the blubber from right whales, bowheads, sperm whales, pilot whales, humpback whales, California grays, and the occasional porpoise, seal, sea elephant, and walrus. They melted the blubber into oil over a hot fire burning in a tryworks built on deck. The oil arrived back in New England in casks, which local manufacturers purchased to make lamp fuel, lubricants, candles, soap, and paint. The firm but pliable baleen was cut and molded to become corset stays, luggage ties, fishing rods, and umbrella ribs.

Living on shrinking reservations or dispersed among other New Englanders and with a small population of about 2,000 at midcentury, southern New England natives were not proportionally as large a presence in the whaling industry as they had been in the seventeenth and eighteenth centuries, but they were still a presence.[29] In the nineteenth century, on average one of six whaleships from the New Bedford area had at least one Native American aboard, often two or three, sometimes as many as six or seven on a single voyage. They made up more of the crew earlier in the century, when nearly half of all whaling voyages had at least one native whaleman aboard. When the industry began its rapid expansion in the 1830s, owners of whaling enterprises had to reach farther away to find enough laborers to fill their ships. Young men from New York State and Pennsylvania and foreign labor from whaling ports of call soon outnumbered all coastal New Englanders, not just New England's native whalemen. In the 1850s, at the industry's peak, only one out of ten whaleships had an American native among the crew, but with more skill and experience than the raw recruits, there was a good chance that that one native whaleman served as an officer (figure 2).[30] When the American whaling industry shifted to the West Coast at the turn of the twentieth century, New England natives made the transition, too, and could be found on ships out of San Francisco as well as New Bedford.[31] Native whalemen continued to serve on American whalers into the twentieth century, as the American industry dwindled away, victim to the falling demand for whale oil and baleen and the rise of other whaling nations, such as Norway.[32] New Bedford's last completed whaling voyage was by the *John R. Manta* in 1925.[33]

The proportion of native men in the whaling industry may have declined over time, but whaling figured large in certain native communities. Throughout the nineteenth century, the majority of native men living near the southern New England coast went on at least one whaling voyage in their lifetime. Many were career whalemen who spent twenty to thirty years at sea. They went on long voyages, usually leaving home for three or four years at a time, returning briefly only to go out again on another lengthy voyage. Nearly overwhelmed by three centuries of intensive European settlement, the native people living along the coast from Cape Cod to eastern Long Island had suffered from dramatic population declines caused by foreign diseases, warfare, and environmental changes. Yet, they survived, in part because whaling offered young men a livelihood and a sense of self-respect that sustained families and communities in hard times.

: : :

In American history, whaling has undeservedly been relegated to a quaint past beloved by antiquarians but studied by few scholars. Museums of the highest caliber—the New Bedford Whaling Museum, Mystic Seaport, Nantucket Historical Association—keep the memory alive as do the remnant New England mansions turned bed-and-breakfast, whaling themed cafés and shops, and sperm-whale-shaped weather vanes visible along the southern New England coastline. For many Americans today, whaling evokes a folkloric portrait of the whaleman as a kind of cowboy at sea, an American innocent spinning yarns and singing sea shanties, who with daring and grit risked his life to chase down the world's largest mammals, all for little or no pecuniary reward. This sense of whaling as archaic and ephemeral obscures whaling's significance to the U.S. political economy and to Americans' relationships within an increasingly interconnected world. In the first half of the nineteenth century, American expansion was not only westward across the continent to the Mississippi or California but

Figure 2. *A typical native whaleman of the late nineteenth century, Samuel G. Mingo of Christiantown is shown here with his wife Lucina (Jeffers) at around the time of their marriage on 15 November 1885 (Tisbury, MAVR). Mingo had recently returned from a voyage as fourth officer on the ship* California *of New Bedford. In July 1886, he embarked again on the* California, *now second officer, for a three-year voyage (crew lists, WSL, 24 May 1881, 20 July 1886). Reproduced by permission from the Collections of the Martha's Vineyard Museum.*

beyond. Nineteenth-century American maritime expansion, especially out of New England ports, rippled into the twentieth and twenty-first centuries with a myriad of consequences from atom bomb tests on Bikini Atoll to Alaska oil drilling to the Hawaiian sovereignty movement. For much of the world's coasts, tracing their histories back a century or two would uncover the presence of American whalers and United States exploring expeditions, warships, and consuls sent out to protect American whalers.

Whaling was not only important economically and politically to the interests of many Americans. The world of the nineteenth-century whaleman was a fascinating place for its unique geographic vision and the diverse human community that fell within its reach. A map of the nineteenth-century American whaleman's world would start with the home port of the vessel. The whaling cities of Nantucket, New Bedford, and Edgartown in Massachusetts, New London in Connecticut, and Sag Harbor on Long Island derived wealth and reputations as specialists in the whale fishery. New York and Boston sent out an occasional whaler as did smaller ports such as Mattapoisett, Massachusetts, and New Haven, Connecticut, ports whose diverse maritime interests included fishing, trading, shipbuilding, and a few whaling ventures. Drawing on the local community for investors and crews, their efforts kept to a smaller scale than the large, corporate structures found in whaling cities.

The other places central to whaling history were the whaling grounds, each opened up to whaling in its turn and hunted to extremes until discovery of another ground, when the cycle began all over again. These whaling grounds had their own names and distinct characteristics: the Brazil Banks in the South Atlantic, Offshore Ground west of the Galapagos Islands, Japan Ground, Okhotsk Sea, Northwest Coast, and dozens of others. Vast expanses of open water, these were the places whalemen knew the best, for they spent months at a time cruising back and forth, with men stationed at the mastheads, eyes primed to detect a whale spout or breach.[34]

Then, of course, there were the world's watering holes—the human communities located on islands and alongshore on which American whalers depended, not just for water but for all their needs: wood, food, labor, and—debatably not a "need"—women. Like the merchant vessels that came earlier and the U.S. naval vessels that came later, American whaleships could not have mined the Pacific's resources if not for the sustenance and relief provided by the island chains that interrupted their ocean workscape. A three- to four-year whaling voyage out of New England typically headed first to the "Western Islands" (Azores) in the Atlantic Ocean, south to the "Cape de Verds" (Cape Verde Islands), further south to St. Helena or Tristan d'Acunha, and then rounded either cape to pass into the Pacific or Indian Oceans. Nearly all Cape Horn whalers stopped at one or more of the coastal cities of Chile and Peru—Talcahuano, Valparaiso, Paita, Callao, Tumbes. American whaleships made landfall nearly everywhere that there was land, from the Seychelles to Hobart Town to the Bay of Islands to Hakodate, to Hawaiʻi, Tonga, and Samoa—or as an American whaleman might say, the Sandwich, Friendly, and Navigators Isles—to the coldest nether regions of the planet, further south than South America and further north than North America.[35]

The whaling industry gave the United States a global presence from the beginning, and the thousands of Americans involved in that industry left a wide, deep trail of their activities in the documentary record, including many firsthand impressions of foreign places and peoples. Much of this voluminous literature appeared in print, as memoirs and newspaper stories, or as unpublished logbooks, private journals, and correspondence.[36] This tremendously rich material embraces the perspectives of people representing different cultures, nationalities, races, occupations, social classes, and genders. The authors of the thousands of extant whaling logbooks, journals, and memoirs were nearly all men, but for several dozen captains' wives. And most of them were white—that is, they likely thought of themselves as white and were regarded by others as belonging to the white race. But people of color recorded their experiences, too. Most important for this project, Native American whalemen contributed to the documentary record by writing private journals aboard ship, keeping official logbooks when first mates, and having their experiences published in as-told-to memoirs (see Appendix B). African Americans also produced logbooks, journals, and memoirs.[37] Rarer are the voices of Pacific Islanders and other peoples around the world who became caught up in the whaling enterprise.[38] I wish this project could accommodate the perspectives of everybody and truly study the dynamics of race, nation, and indigeneity in all their complexities, but that would be overwhelming. Having a single group of people at the center raises larger issues applicable to all those involved but in a manageable way.

The American whalemen, whose writings provided much of the raw material for this book, were ordinary people. They were not trying to formulate ideas about race like the scientists and physical anthropologists of the late eighteenth and nineteenth centuries who so energetically and often absurdly charted racial geographies to account for differences between Africans and Asians, Slavs and Pygmies, Polynesians and Melanesians.[39] They were just trying to make a living by catching whales. But as ordinary people who traveled the world, they had a remarkable vantage point from which to observe and think about human difference, and they contributed their ideas and stories about their experiences to an international conversation.

As I explain in Appendix A, I collected data on over 600 Native American whalemen who collectively went on several thousand voyages. In most cases, when more than one document labeled a person Indian or by a tribal designation, such as Narragansett or Pequot, I included them in my database. Through genealogical research, I also tried to discern how people were related and identified themselves. Many native whalemen had white and black ancestry as well as Indian. (Chapter 9 is where readers will find my discussion of intermarriage in New England.) In their own writings, native whalemen rarely reflected on their identities, and so nearly all identifications of them as Indians were made by others. If the men I have identified as native whalemen had been asked more often to speak for themselves and state their identity for the record, I expect most would have chosen "Indian" because of their native ancestry and residence or familial connections to Indian communities long recognized as such, the histories of which can be traced back to long before European contact.

However, when I classify an individual as native, I do not claim to speak for that individual. I mean that they appear in the historic record as people who self-identified or were, more than once, identified by others as being Indian or of Indian descent. And when I refer to an individual as native, white, African American, Cape Verdean, or something else, I am not asserting that that individual consistently and solely identified as such. As the book progresses, it should become clear that I am not trying to pigeonhole individuals into a single category but am instead interested in what racial categories, and especially the category "Indian," meant in different contexts.

Each of these situations, or sites of interaction that organized social relationships in a particular way—the ship, the beach, islands, and the reservation—generated a unique configuration of racial expectations. Assumptions fitting one situation did not mesh with others. Shifts in the meaning and relative significance of race inside and outside the nation's borders reveal that the racial category Indian in nineteenth-century America was inherently contradictory and just as mobile as the Indians themselves.

PART I : THE SHIP

1 : The Gay Head Harpooner

Native American whalemen's motivations and working life underwent a notable shift in the 1830s as the American whaling industry rapidly expanded. The number of whaling voyages doubled from the 1810s to 1820s, doubled again in the 1830s, and peaked at midcentury, with over 2,000 departures per decade in the 1840s and 1850s.[1] The concomitant rise in labor demand placed new value on native whalemen's skills and commitment. Because whaling was a relentlessly dismal occupation that drove most white men away, a niche opened for native men to fill the need for capable officers. How race informed native New England men's participation in the whaling industry evolved, too, as employers in search of a large, flexible workforce drew on racial presuppositions selectively.[2]

At the start of the nineteenth century, whaling crews consisted almost entirely of white, African American, and Native American men local to coastal New England, and ship owners overtly used race in hiring by treating men of color as an undifferentiated racial underclass. Whaling records from the first few decades of the nineteenth century usually included native men among the "Black Hands," "blacks," or "coloureds" at the end of crew lists as though race was equivalent to rank and a low rank at that.[3] Notions of Indians as childlike dependents added another racial dimension, since men living on reservations fell under the authority of state-appointed, white guardians. These guardians often helped whaling agents acquire labor. One notorious instance occurred in 1799, when Barnstable County authorities kidnapped two Pocknett brothers with the approval of a Mashpee guardian under the claim, or pretense, of debt. Transmitted to a Nantucket whaleship, where they refused to sign the shipping articles, the Pocknetts had no recourse but to go the length of the two-year voyage.[4] Such machinations led to native complaints that their "men are sent [on] Long voiages to sea by those who practice in a more soft manner that of Kidnaping who when they Return with ever so great success they are still In debt."[5]

Coercive hiring practices were on their way out in the 1820s, but middlemen found new ways to glean a profit and often targeted men of color. Gideon Hawley, missionary at Mashpee and frequently also guardian, called these middlemen "Indian speculators." They bought and traded shares in a whaleman's potential earnings, claiming the prerogative to place him on a vessel of their choosing.[6] In an 1820 agreement between seventeen-year-old Aaron Keeter of Mashpee and Percival Freeman, Keeter's mother signed the contract because he was under age, and then, because he was a Mashpee Indian, the tribe's guardians signed also. Percival Freeman received half of Keeter's anticipated profits on a three-year voyage by paying Keeter $100 and his outstanding debts. Freeman shipped Keeter on the Nantucket whaler *Dauphin*.[7] The need for immediate income may have driven the impoverished to accept unfavorable terms when selling profits in advance but not without negotiation. A traveler on Martha's Vineyard reported how Indian whalemen held out for cash advances or gifts of clothing and food before signing a contract.[8] By receiving cash or goods up front, whalemen let middlemen assume the monetary risk, but they still shouldered the greatest risk in the high rates of death, disablement, and abandonment in a foreign port, fates endemic to the whaling occupation.

By the 1830s, these middlemen also faded from the scene. One class of middlemen remained, whaling outfitters, who advanced clothing and supplies to nearly all whalemen, no matter their race, but did not trade in voyage shares. And there were no more complaints about guardians helping whaling agents extort labor. In 1828, the Massachusetts legislature passed a law endorsing the Christiantown and Chappaquiddick guardian's authority to "bind out" for the length of a voyage any who were "habitual drunkards, vagabonds, and idlers."[9] However, guardians seem not to have exercised this power, and there is no evidence of native men being shipped against their will after this law passed. Guardians continued to act as intermediaries, however. They collected and disbursed whaling earnings, which native whalemen must have considered both a bureaucratic nuisance and humbling reminder of their status as government wards.[10] But guardians could also advocate for them in disputes with employers, as Leavitt Thaxter did in a lawsuit against Lawrence Grinnell for the earnings of Samuel P. Goodridge. A Wampanoag of Chappaquiddick, Goodridge had died in 1836 in the Galapagos Islands while serving aboard the *Euphrates* of New Bedford. Thaxter had purchased on outfit for Goodridge from a local vendor, but so did Grinnell as agent for the *Euphrates*. After Goodridge's death, Grinnell retained Goodridge's earnings to pay for the outfit. Thaxter lost his suit on behalf of Goodridge's heirs, and the judge reprimanded him for expecting the ship owners to discern that Goodridge was a Chappaquiddick Indian with a legal guardian.[11] The native community at Chappaquiddick defended Thaxter. Hearing a rumor that "our white neighbours" were trying to eliminate the guardianship system, they appealed to the legislature to keep it in place because "most of our Young men are employed in the Whale fishing and often need assistance in settling their voyages."[12] Thaxter's defeat in court and the mounting critique of the 1828 law as inhumane reflected the rise of a free-labor ideology in antebellum America that celebrated voluntary participation in the labor marketplace as a man's right.[13]

In the 1830s, native whalemen began to benefit from opportunities that white men had always had. In 1816, seventeen-year-old Elemouth Howwoswee of Gay Head would not have presumed as he boarded the *Martha* that he might advance up the ranks as could his shipmate Walter Hillman, of the same age and also from Martha's Vineyard but white. The two went out again on the *Martha* the following year, Hillman as third mate. By 1822, Hillman had risen to first mate and the year after that to master of the *Maria Theresa*. Howwoswee was on the *Maria Theresa*, too, and served under Hillman's command off and on over the next few years, by chance or because of some personal bond between them. After sixteen whaling voyages, Howwoswee died at sea at age forty-two still a boatsteerer, whereas Hillman had captained seven voyages.[14] A generation later, native men's prospects had turned around. Joel Jared started whaling at age sixteen on the *Adeline* in 1843, where he worked alongside six other Gay Head men, including first mate George Belain and third mate Jonathan Cuff. Immediately upon the *Adeline*'s return to port, Jared shipped as boatsteerer on the *Amethyst* and subsequently as third mate on the *Samuel & Thomas* in 1850. He ended his career as second mate on the *Anaconda* in 1856–1860. He might have gone further had he not died at Gay Head the year after the *Anaconda*'s return.[15] Many had similar career trajectories, including the Belains, Goodridges, and Goulds from Chappaquiddick; George and James W. DeGrass from Christiantown; the Jeffers, Johnsons, and Cooks from Gay Head; Jesse Webquish's sons Nathan, Jesse Jr., Levi, and William from Chappaquiddick and Mashpee; Asa and Rodney Wainer from Westport, Massachusetts; the Ammons brothers, Joseph and Gideon, from the Narragansett reservation in Charlestown, Rhode Island; and Milton, Ferdinand, and William Garrison Lee, belonging to a Shinnecock family on eastern Long Island.[16]

As the industry declined in the latter half of the nineteenth century, agents and captains continued to place Native American men in positions of authority. For example, Francis F. Peters and Alonzo Belain of Gay Head, both seventeen years old, embarked on their first voyage together on the *Sunbeam* of New Bedford in 1868.[17] When the *Sunbeam* returned three years later, they advanced to boatsteerer on their next voyage, Belain on the *Kathleen*, Peters on the *Atlantic*.[18] They then shipped on their third and final voyages, Belain as third mate on the *Triton* and Peters once again on the *Atlantic* but now as fourth mate.[19] Belain died from consumption while at sea in 1877, at just twenty-six years of age.[20] Peters was promoted to third mate during his voyage but died a year later when the *Atlantic* lost two boats crews at sea while whaling.[21] Each voyage elevated the men another notch up the ranks, and if they had not died young, they might have made it as far as second or first mate.

Native Americans thrived in the whaling industry but only up to a point. Few became captains or investors. Most of those who did had connections to the mixed Wampanoag and African American families of Cuffes and Wainers in Westport, Massachusetts, and Bostons of Nantucket. In the 1790s, Paul Cuffe and his brother-in-law Michael Wainer bought their first whaler, the *Sunfish*. Wainer's son Paul served as captain on the *Protection* in 1821 as Cuffe's son William did in 1837 on the *Rising States*. This last excursion ended quickly and poorly, with Cuffe dead and the vessel condemned.[22] On Nantucket, Absalom Boston commanded the Nantucket ship *Industry* in 1822, but it also failed to turn a profit.[23]

Otherwise, in the entire nineteenth century, only three native men—Amos Haskins, Ferdinand Lee, and Joseph G. Belain—reached whaling master. Amos Jeffers of Gay Head almost made a fourth. Returning to New Bedford in 1847 as first mate on the *Mary*, Jeffers agreed to take the vessel out again as captain, but while waiting for the vessel's outfitting, he drowned in a fishing accident off of Gay Head.[24] Amos Haskins encountered misfortune, too (figure 3). As first mate, he took over for a sick captain left at Fayal and brought the bark *Elizabeth* safely home to Mattapoisett in 1850 with 1,060 barrels of sperm whale oil aboard, an impressive cargo for a seventeen-month voyage. The following year, Haskins took command of the *Massasoit* but made a disastrous showing of only 325 barrels. One more venture on the *Massasoit*, cut short by a fever among his crew that killed four and downed seven others, returned a mere sixty barrels.[25] Haskins continued whaling, as first mate, and died on the *March*, lost at sea in 1861.[26] First mate Ferdinand Lee similarly gained the confidence of shipping agents when the *Eliza Adams* arrived at New Bedford in 1871 with a "splendid catch."[27] Given the command of the *Callao* for four years, he generated a mediocre cargo that proved a financial loss for its owners.[28] Lee did not give up on whaling either. He died a second mate, along with first mate Moses Walker and several other Shinnecock men, when the *Amethyst* was crushed by Arctic ice in 1885.[29]

According to one study, perhaps as many as 40 percent of whaling masters from New Bedford made only one voyage, so Haskins's and Lee's brief

Figure 3. *Amos Haskins, captain of the bark* Massasoit *of Mattapoisett on its 1851–1852 and 1852–1853 voyages. Courtesy of the New Bedford Whaling Museum.*

tenures were not unusual.[30] But because so many native whalemen became officers while so few realized that final step to become captains, clearly the color line had not disappeared. It merely shifted to allow Indians to serve as officers. Hired as first mate on the *Palmetto* in 1875 at age twenty-five, Joseph G. Belain held that rank for decades except when he replaced the captain of the San Francisco-based whaler *Eliza* for the 1890 Arctic season.[31] Other native first mates took charge of vessels upon the illness or death of captains without official recognition as captain.[32]

African American whalemen were equally rare in the highest echelons of the industry. Among those few who became whaling masters were two men connected by marriage to native families. Pardon Cook, Paul Cuffe's son-in-law, headed five whaling voyages in the 1840s, all out of Westport, the Cuffe family's home port.[33] William A. Martin married Sarah Brown of the Chappaquiddick community, where the couple resided. Martin later became captain of the *Golden City* in 1878, the *Emma Jane* in 1883, and the *Eunice H. Adams* in 1887.[34]

Although native seafarers mostly worked as whalemen, some opted to stay closer to home on small trading vessels. Solomon Attaquin of Mashpee went whaling in his youth but in 1837 transported wood to Nantucket as captain of the newly built sloop *Native of Marshpee*.[35] Solomon Webquish, whose brothers rose to prominence in the whale fishery, preferred coastal trading also, with Plymouth as his home port.[36] And Aaron Cuffee—the only native whaleman I know of with scrimshaw attributed to him in a museum collection (an "ivory swift," or yarn winder, in the Sag Harbor Whaling Museum)—was captain of a New London–Sag Harbor steamship later in life.[37]

Native ownership of whaling vessels was rare as well, if not by choice then because of its great cost. Not only did owners have to invest several thousand dollars in the purchase of a vessel; they had the expense of outfitting it for a lengthy voyage. Missionary Dwight Baldwin obtained specifics on cost and profitability on his way to Hawai'i on the whaleship *New England* in 1831. Built originally for the China trade, the *New England* cost its whaling investors $17,500, with an additional $12,500 put toward outfitting it, for a total investment of $30,000. Larger than most whalers at 376 tons, the *New England* carried enough casks for 3,800 barrels of oil. A sufficiency of 3,200 barrels, reaping $60,000, would make the trip worthwhile.[38] From this, the crew had to be paid, each according to his lay. Back in the days of shore whaling, whalemen had divvied up the oil and whalebone. In the nineteenth century, they usually took their earnings in cash from the owners, but technically their lay still referred to their share of oil and baleen: a greenhand with a lay of 1/180 owned one barrel for every 180 barrels taken. Crew members never received the full value of each barrel because their share of pilot, wharf, medicine chest, insurance, and other fees cut into their final profits as did their advances and slop chest expenses.[39] A captain with a lay of 1/15 might make $4,000 per voyage while a boatsteerer at a lay of 1/80 might expect several hundred dollars. To invest in one-sixteenth of the *New England* would have cost $1,875. Only captains, perhaps first officers, could hope to accumulate enough of a surplus to enter the business as an investor.

The few native whalemen who bought shares of whalers met with poor luck. When a consortium of Mattapoisett merchants purchased the *Massasoit* to convert it into a whaler for Amos Haskins in 1851, he owned one-eighth of the bark. By 1854, he had sold his shares, probably forced to after the failure of his two voyages.[40] George Belain, Haskins's first officer on the *Massasoit*'s 1852 voyage, acquired a one-sixty-fourth share in it ten years later, just in time for its last whaling voyage.[41] By 1841, Asa Wainer had risen to first mate on the *Elizabeth* of Westport under Captain Pardon Cook and bought shares in the brig for what was also its last whaling voyage.[42] Another active whaling investor of color was African American John Mashow of Dartmouth, whose wife, Hope Amos, was a Mashpee Wampanoag. A shipbuilder highly regarded for the quality of his work, Mashow owned shares in several whalers through his partnership Matthews, Mashow, & Company. Earnings of the Mashow family reveal the scale of owners' advantage over ordinary crew members. Boatsteerer Isaac H. Mashow cleared $152 in the final settlement of the 1855–1859 voyage of the *Benjamin Cummings*, built by his father's company, which made $2,199 from one-sixteenth ownership in the bark. Whaling was a speculative risk for all, however, and even this respected firm hit a rough patch and closed, after contributing many of the finest whalers to the New Bedford fleet.[43]

Beginning in the 1830s, the door widened to allow more native men into officer positions than previously but did not open all the way. Native men remained skilled workers who did not control wealth or wield influence in the industry, and they saw that, even though they could go further than their fathers and grandfathers, race still imposed barriers. George E. James of Christiantown complained to state commissioners investigating Indian reservation conditions in 1848 that he had "risen to be second mate; but had come home discouraged, disheartened, with ambition quenched" because, as James reportedly told them, "'The prejudice against our color keeps us down. I may be a first rate navigator, and as good a seaman as ever walked a deck . . . but I am doomed to live and die before the mast. I might get to be second, first mate, and, when at sea, I should be treated as such, because I deserved it; but the moment we fall in company with other vessels, or arrive in port, and our captain invites other captains and mates to dine, I am banished from the cabin to the forecastle.'"[44] That James felt the sting of racial prejudice most intensely in settings of elite sociability shows that the bar of race had receded only so far as to place a high value on native whalemen's labor skills.

: : :

When whaling became less coercive and more of an appealing opportunity for native men in the 1830s, their reasons to choose whaling were much the same as those for white, coastal New Englanders: the legacy of whaling as a tradition running in families, the need to make a living somehow, and the ambition to earn others' respect. They shipped with purpose by reading newspapers, perusing wharves, or pursuing good prospects mentioned by previous employers, former shipmates, and neighbors. And they knew to negotiate rank and lay before signing shipping articles. The number of coastal New England men familiar with whaling were not enough to fill up a forecastle, however, and whaleships increasingly relied on green landsmen found by recruiters who prowled Philadelphia and New York streets and boarding houses for guileless, runaway farm boys to send on to New Bedford, New London, and Sag Harbor.[45] If more white recruits had found whaling worthwhile, native men would have had little chance to become officers. Native whalemen were not just filling slots left open by whites with higher aspirations, however. They proved themselves valuable laborers. They mastered seafaring skills and showed a tolerance for whaling's risks and drudgery. Although many white men took pride in their success as whalemen, especially those who stuck with it to become captains, native men needed this job even more.[46] They appreciated the industry's scant rewards because they had few options and low expectations.

Since the beginning of the New England whaling industry in the mid-seventeenth century, native men from Long Island to Cape Cod would have grown up hearing plenty of whaling stories passed down in families. Because of surnames changing over time and superficial record keeping about Indian whaling in the eighteenth century, the long genealogy of native whaling cannot be charted for all but are obvious in some cases. For example, Chappaquiddick whalemen Laban, Levi, and Joseph Corduddy very likely descended from Corduda, who in the eighteenth century did his whale hunting from shore stations strung along the Nantucket shore. A hundred years later, Corduda's Chappaquiddick descendants used the same technology of whaleboats, harpoons, lances, and trypots, but on three- to four-year voyages on larger vessels that took them to the Pacific Ocean. Even after Laban and others belonging to the crew of the Nantucket whaleship *Oeno* were shipwrecked and killed at Fiji in 1825 and after Levi's ship, the *Meridian* of Edgartown, was lost at sea in a typhoon off of New Zealand in 1836, their younger brother Joseph still gambled his life on a whaling voyage.[47] Whaling was the obvious path for boys to follow as they came of age. This was especially the case for Wampanoag men on Martha's Vineyard, who in the first half of the century nearly all went whaling, usually starting between the ages of fourteen and seventeen.[48] They may not even have asked themselves whether they should go whaling, instead assuming that of course they would.

Whaling was foremost a job, and though few native whalemen stated out-right how much the economy of whaling mattered relative to other motivations, they did talk about it in economic terms. Narragansett Gideon Ammons retired from whaling in 1852 because it no longer paid well, he said. At forty years of age, Ammons had approached the end of the typical whaleman's working years anyhow. If he had been a younger man, he might have deemed his best option to try one more voyage, but he took up stone masonry instead while also farming his five acres of land.[49] James F. Pells of Mashpee also expressed concerns about money. As his voyage on the *Barclay* of Nantucket came to end, he complained in his journal on June 9, 1838, "no Whales all the way from the line and dull prospecks all around us a wife And child at home now," and on June 24 noted, "No whales in sight My Boys and dull prospecks Ahead for it is calm and if we git eney whales they must swim to us." After a slow and tedious homeward passage, when just a month from home, his thoughts turned to what the market would bring: "oil is now 125 cts A gallon at home."[50] One way to end a voyage profitably was to keep expenses down. When asked for advice by a novice whaleman about to embark on his first voyage in 1907, Joseph G. Belain recommended to Napoleon Bonaparte Madison of Gay Head, "'Take enough money with you so that you will not be stranded, penniless, far from home. Be sure to take your own boots, foul weather gear and heavy clothes, too. . . . If you have to buy these things from the slop chest aboard ship, they'll cost you three or four times as much as they do at home and, at the end of the voyage, you'll find your purchases have swallowed up your entire pay.'"[51] For whaling to provide a living for them and their families, native whalemen had to guard against frivolous expenditures and hope for a good lay, full cargo, and high prices for their products when the vessel returned to port.

Native men had to make a living somehow, and whaling offered the chance of a better livelihood for themselves and their families than other employments open to them—subsistence farming, day labor, handicraft peddling, and domestic servitude.[52] In their whaling journals, Gideon Ammons's brother Joseph, from Charlestown, Rhode Island, and Thaddeus W. Cook of Gay Head recorded personal financial accounts for other kinds of labor. When not whaling, they took up odd jobs. In 1847 and 1848, Ammons chopped and carted wood, mowed, weeded, and dug a well. The work was occasional—not day in and day out, seven days a week, as with whaling—and rates of pay ranged from $0.50 to $1.00 a day.[53] In the 1860s and 1870s on Martha's Vineyard, Cook cleared a better daily wage for similar kinds of work: digging peat for $2 a day, plowing and carting for $3 another day, cutting corn stalks and mowing for $1.50 a day.[54] As physically demanding as whaling, if not more so, these activities were not any more remunerative. If whaling paid an equivalent $1.50 a day, a three-year voyage (not counting liberty days nor taking into account daily food provisions) would add up to $1,642.50, a large sum but within range of an officer's whaling earnings. The daily wage for farm labor and whaling may have been about the same, but the work otherwise was not at all comparable. Native men undertaking voyages had to weigh the three to four years of constant labor far from home and family at great risk of impoverishment or death with the chance for a windfall against the drudgery and peripatetic income of farm labor, which allowed one to stay home.

Those who stuck with whaling discovered that it could be profitable. Greenhands could expect little or no pay, but even if a man's first voyage proved a loss, it had value as an apprenticeship that could be bartered into a higher rank and more generous lay on the next voyage.[55] Starting out as a greenhand on the *Hesper* in 1831 at age fourteen, James W. DeGrass of Christiantown made only $43 for three years spent at sea (see Table 1). However, his rank, lay, and income increased over six voyages, and as second mate of the *Draco*, he brought home nearly $1,000, an extraordinary sum for any young, laboring man, but especially for a Native American, in 1850s America. This must have seemed to him a sufficient nest egg, for he retired from whaling early, when only thirty-four years old. William A. Vanderhoop, Gay Head Wampanoag, also stopped whaling after a highly successful voyage on the *Abraham Barker* in 1866. As the bark pulled away from New Bedford for a four-year voyage, he wrote optimistically in his journal, "Every thing this far seems to be quite pleasent Shipmates agreeable and all bids Fair for a prosperous and pleasent voyage."[56] His optimism paid off, earning him a final payment of over $2,000, a remarkable return considering that he was only fourth mate with a lay of 1/58. His Wampanoag shipmate Joseph S. Anthony, an eighteen-year-old foremast hand with a poor lay of 1/180, took home over $500.[57] Vanderhoop, at thirty years of age, made this his last voyage. He returned to Gay Head for good, built a house, married a Wampanoag woman from Herring Pond on Cape Cod, was elected Gay Head town selectman and town clerk, and turned to fishing and farming to make his living.[58]

The earnings whalemen took home at the conclusion of a voyage are deceptive since many supported family members while at sea. Agents deducted these charges before the final settlement. Agent account books document periodic $10, $20, or $50 payments made to fathers, mothers, and wives. A year into the *Abigail*'s voyage, DeGrass's wife received $20 from whaling agent Charles W. Morgan, who also paid Tisbury storekeeper W. A. May-

Table 1

Earnings of James W. DeGrass of Christiantown

Age	Ship	Voyage	Rank	Lay	Final Pay
14	*Hesper*	1831–1834	greenhand	1/160	$43.15
17	*Pioneer*	1834–1837	boatsteerer	1/80	$246.45
20	*Cherokee*	1837–1838			
22	*Abigail*	1839–1843	boatsteerer	1/85	$0.00?
26	*Draco*	1843–1847	third mate	1/57	$536.52
30	*Draco*	1847–1850	second mate	1/45	$949.67

Sources: Final Pay from Indian Guardian Accounts for 1834, Dukes County Probate Records, microfilm rl. 1, MSA; and for 1837, 1847, and 1850, Indian Guardian Papers, rl. 2, MSA. For age on bark *Hesper* of New Bedford, 1831–1834, see DPT; and for rank and lay, see SHP, Charles Waln Morgan Papers, NBW. For rank and lay on bark *Pioneer* of New Bedford, 1834–1837, and ship *Abigail* of New Bedford, 1839–1843, see "Ship outfits, cargos, and crew list book; 1836–1843," p. 23, 220, Charles W. Morgan Collection, MSM. For voyage on bark *Cherokee* of New Bedford, 1837–1838, see DPT. The "Ship outfits" volume gives DeGrass's *Abigail* earnings before deductions as $318.16 (p. 220). The equivalent figure for the *Pioneer* was $423.76 (p. 23). He or Christiantown guardian Leavitt Thaxter authorized W. A. Mayhew to "settle" his *Abigail* voyage, perhaps for store debts, and DeGrass's wife also received installments on his earnings while he was on the *Abigail* (pp. 74–75), so his deductions apparently surpassed his earnings, leaving him with no final payment. For rank and lay for bark *Draco* of New Bedford, 1843–1847 and 1847–1850, see SHP.

hew $50 on DeGrass's account.[59] Abram F. Cooper of Gay Head made an unusual arrangement with the agent of the *Atlantic* in 1877 to send tuition for Cooper's sister Susannah to train at a "Telegraph Instituttion" in Lynn, Massachusetts.[60] In *Captain Ahab Had a Wife*, Lisa Norling describes this industry practice as a tradition of employer-worker paternalism that faded over the nineteenth century. Although captains' and officers' wives could still retrieve earnings from a voyage in progress, it took a lot of begging.[61] While her husband Amos Haskins was in the Pacific as first mate of the *Oscar* in 1859, Elizabeth P. Haskins corresponded with agent Josiah Holmes Jr., asking to "Settle with you of Mr Haskins Oil And Bone Whitch Has Come Home So What Ever theire is Coming i Would Like to Have it for i Have no money And Would Like to Have What Ever theire is do now Will you Be So Kind as to Call to the House the first time you are to Bedford?" Other women, probably the wives of white captains and officers, had the same difficulty obtaining their husbands' earnings from Holmes, and all must have felt frustrated to be so much at the mercy of high-risk enterprises.[62] Listed in the 1860 federal census with real estate valued at $2,000, Haskins's family had some resources, but his income was neither steady nor secure.[63]

One voyage could be profitable. The next could be disastrous. Theodate Goodridge of Chappaquiddick received $1,765 in whaling money in 1850 but at a price, her husband Simeon having succumbed to yellow fever while third mate on the whaleship *Erie*, one of many native men to lose his life at sea.[64] Whalemen died by falling from aloft, in drowning accidents, from scurvy, in attacks by whales and sharks, and from other ailments and injuries.[65] John S. Keeter of Mashpee was fortunate to survive the wreck of the *Benjamin Cummings* at the Cape Verde Islands in 1876 but three years later must have been one of the frozen corpses seen lying about the *Vigilant* after it became trapped by ice in the Arctic Ocean.[66] Mashpee men, purely from chance, seemed especially prone to having a voyage disrupted by disaster (see map 2). They survived other shipwrecks in the Gulf Stream on the homeward passage, at Table Bay off the Cape of Good Hope, at Fayal in the Azores, off the Kamchatka Peninsula, and in the Bering Strait.[67]

If lucky enough to survive a catastrophe, they were most often penniless, stripped of their possessions, and dependent on other ships to take them aboard or on U.S. consuls to arrange passage to the United States. William S. Webquish returned to New Bedford in 1855 having been promoted from fourth to third mate during the *George Washington*'s four-year voyage. The trade newspaper enthused about the ship's cargo of over 7,000 barrels of whale oil, "the largest quantity ever taken by any whaler during a single cruise."[68] Within a few months, Webquish set out again on the *George Washington* as second mate under the same captain and brought two more Mashpee men along as boatsteerers, Elijah W. Pocknett and James H. Pells.[69] The *George Washington* rounded Cape Horn and pulled into Talcahuano, Chile, for provisions only to have discontented crew members set fire to the vessel. All that could be saved were its sails.[70] The three from Mashpee returned home. Pocknett signed up for another whaling voyage right away. Webquish and Pells may have decided they had had enough of whaling, as I have not come across any records of later voyages for them, although they did continue to work as mariners.[71] Other Mashpee men found themselves adrift at Tahiti; Valparaiso, Chile; and Port Louis, Mauritius, after their vessels were condemned.[72]

Most stranded whalemen managed to return home, but a few disappear from the records. In 1821, in the midst of South American wars for independence, the ship *Hero* of Nantucket was coopering oil at an island whalers

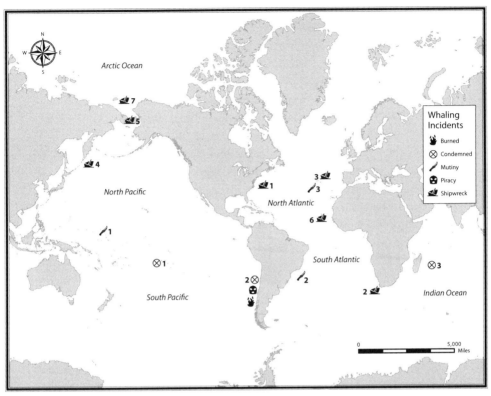

Map 2. *Mashpee Wampanoag whaling voyages ended by disaster. Burned by crew: at Talcahuano, Chile, ship* George Washington *of New Bedford, 1856. Condemned: (1) at Tahiti, ship* Factor *of New Bedford, 1847; (2) at Valparaiso, Chile, bark* Congaree *of New Bedford, 1863; (3) at Mauritius, bark* Laetitia *of New Bedford, 1879. Mutiny: (1) sometime before mutineers reached Mili Atoll, Marshall Islands, ship* Globe *of Nantucket, 1824; (2) at Rio de Janeiro, Brazil, ship* Ann Alexander *of New Bedford, 1824; (3) at Azores, bark* Almira *of Edgartown, 1869. Piracy: at St. Mary's Island, Chilean coast, ship* Hero *of Nantucket, 1821. Shipwreck: (1) Gulf Stream, ship* Henry *of Nantucket, 1813; (2) off Cape of Good Hope, ship* Israel *of New Bedford, 1847; (3) Azores, brig* Helen *of Mattapoisett, 1848; (4) on Kamchatka Whaling Grounds, ship* Huntress *of New Bedford, 1852; (5) Bering Strait, ship* Liverpool II *of New Bedford, 1853; (6) at Cape Verde Islands, bark* Benjamin Cummings *of New Bedford, 1876; (7) off Heard Island, Arctic Ocean, bark* Vigilant *of New Bedford, 1879. All disasters are mentioned with sources cited in this chapter except the mutinies, which are discussed in chapters 3 (Ann Alexander, Almira) and 4 (Globe). Map by Brian Perchal.*

called St. Mary's, near Valparaiso on the Chilean coast, when Lot Cowet of Mashpee, with nearly a dozen others of the *Hero*'s crew, was taken prisoner by the pirate Vicente Benavides.[73] Forced to march with Benavides's army of Araucanian Indians to attack Chilean forces at Santiago, Cowet escaped during the battle. He made his way to safety aboard a Chilean brig of war but does not seem to have found his way home to Mashpee.[74]

Despite its risks, whaling provided income for native whalemen and their families while also offering them occasions to exercise authority and earn respect in ways that small-scale farming and farm labor never could. The journals native whalemen kept show an emotional investment in their work, commitment to the professional standards of the industry, and an ambition to be regarded as good at their jobs. Two journals of William A. Vanderhoop of Gay Head survive, the earlier one recorded while on the *Awashonks* in 1862. On a summary page where Vanderhoop gave credit to those men who had raised (sighted) whales, he listed his own name only once. In pencil but in what looks like his handwriting, he added in the margins, "I wish I was a great man."[75] On his next voyage, on the *Abraham Barker*, the equivalent page shows that, of the thirty-six whales listed, "Wm A. Vanderhoop" had first sight of six of them, worth a $5 reward each, a much better showing, boosting his self-esteem as much as his purse.[76] Both his journals epitomize whaling professionalism in their meticulous attention to detail. A boatsteerer on the *Awashonks*, Vanderhoop minutely described readying his whaleboat for the chase.[77] He precisely noted every barrel of oil and bundle of baleen discharged at ports and sent home on other vessels. At the end of each journal, he identified which of the four whaleboats—starboard, larboard, waste, or bow—caught each sperm or right whale and how many barrels of oil each whale produced (figure 4). These journals testify to Vanderhoop's desire to demonstrate his intellectual command of the industry's fiscal and managerial aspects.

In his two-volume journal of four whaling voyages, Joseph Ammons (Narragansett) similarly conveyed pride in his accomplishments in a style exuding dignified reserve. His daily entries kept on the *James Maury* from 1851 to 1854 better conform to logbook standards than the official volume ineptly maintained by the first mate. Jesse Webquish Jr. of Mashpee replaced this mate at Magdalena Bay off Baja California in January 1854, and his logbook also surpassed his predecessor's feeble efforts.[78] Unlike Ammons, however, Webquish did allow himself an occasional personal remark. A fish caught on the voyage home was "the first good meals of vitels I have eat since leaving Talcahuano." Webquish was also unusually forthcoming about his relations with others. He criticized the second mate, Ammons's replacement,

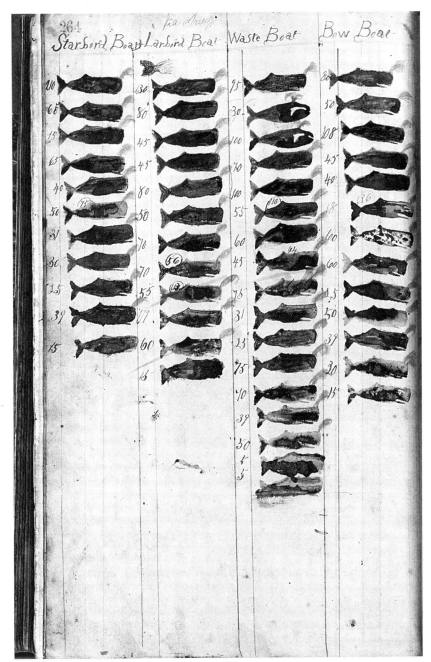

Figure 4. *This page from William A. Vanderhoop's journal shows how many whales the bark* Abraham Barker *of New Bedford caught on its 1866–1870 voyage. The men on the voyage were sperm whaling mostly, but early on the waist boat brought in two right whales. Vanderhoop used red ink for the gush of blood exuding from the whales' spout holes during their death throes. Notice how his anatomical precision captures the different spouts of sperm and right whales. Reproduced by permission from the Nicholson Whaling Collection, Providence Public Library Special Collections, Providence, R.I.*

who was "not what I took him for he is a underminding every man in the ship even to the Mate" (meaning Webquish himself) and was responsible, Webquish believed, for having damaged fourteen bundles of whalebone when stowing it below decks. By September 1855, as the *James Maury* neared New Bedford, Webquish's frustrations grew. Feeling slighted by how the captain and his fellow officers disregarded the authority he held as chief mate, he exclaimed in one logbook entry, "I shall thank god freley unless I git home for I am not Cheaf mate the Capten is Cheaf mate and all hands to been since the 25 of October 1854 Comeng from the Ochkotsck Sea he dose not give me any orders for nothing he gives them to the Second Mate." At the end of the voyage, Webquish transmitted the logbook to the ship's agent, Charles R. Tucker, apologizing in its final pages, "Sir please to Excuse my Remarks in the Book for I am not so good a Scholar as Some But what you Canot find out send for me aney time and I will Come." He also used the opportunity to promote his abilities, asking Tucker to note the number of whales caught by the various boat crews, adding "I don't set this down to Brage of my whaling" but only to show that "I have done my share of it."[79] Webquish earned a hefty $1,237 for his year and a half on the *James Maury*, but his ad hominem comments indicate that he valued more than money. He wanted others to acknowledge his capabilities and treat him with respect.[80]

: : :

White Americans explained Indian whalemen's motivations differently, not as tradition, economics, or a means to earn respect, but as a function of their race. Reuben Tinker, accompanying Dwight Baldwin as missionary on the *New England* in 1831, marveled at how the sight of the first sperm whale "produced a great stir on deck," especially among the Indians aboard—Silas DeGrass, Alexander Cuff, and Lewis Cook—who were "capering in the superabundance of their joy." Tinker added, "Indians are first rate whale catchers, for it is their nature to pursue the game, whether it be a deer in the western forest or a fish in the western ocean."[81] Even though all knew that the industry itself had economic profit as its objective, Indians were said to whale from instinct.

Thus race weighed heavily on popular depictions of Indian whalemen. They were "fearless in the extreme."[82] They threw harpoons with savage precision. If Pacific or Arctic natives attacked, Indian whalemen would defend the ship with inbred ferocity, as a Narragansett reputedly did in the Arctic in the 1850s, when "true to the instincts of his race, [he] seized a hatchet at the commencement of the fight, and in the course of it killed five of the assailants."[83] Keen eyesight supposedly made Indians excellent lookouts for whales at the mastheads. The widely read, fictionalized, and derivative *The Whale and His Captors*, published in 1850 by Henry Cheever, another missionary passenger aboard a whaleship, repeated or invented a story about "Webquish" on the *Cremona*, "a smart, active Gay Head Indian, who was a faithful sentinel on such occasions, with a restless eye, and a keenness of vision seldom surpassed by any of his race."[84] There was no whaleship *Cremona*, and the Webquishes came not from Gay Head but from Chappaquiddick and Mashpee. Cheever probably chose "Webquish" for his Indian lookout because the name sounded aboriginal. However, as was the case with nearly all other nineteenth-century native whalemen, the Webquishes signed shipping articles with their full names: Jesse Webquish Jr. (he spelled it "Wepquish"), Levi L. Webquish, William S. Webquish, and Nathan S. Webquish. Gay Head added extra romantic appeal as southern New England's most isolated Indian place, famous for its landmark cliffs of fantastically colored clays.

Tashtego, the token New England Indian in Herman Melville's 1851 novel *Moby-Dick*, came out of this same mold: "an unmixed Indian from Gay Head . . . an inheritor of the unvitiated blood of those proud warrior hunters, who, in quest of the great New England moose, had scoured, bow in hand, the aboriginal forests of the main." Likening wielding a harpoon to Stone Age spear throwing, Melville cast Tashtego as one of the *Pequod*'s three "harpooneers" along with the South Seas islander and "wild cannibal" Queequeg and the African Daggoo, a "coal-black negro-savage, with a lion-like tread."[85] Having served on whaleships, Melville knew that "harpooneer" was not an official rank. Boatsteerers, petty officers, did the harpooning.

Even though native whalemen more often than not advanced into officer positions in the 1830s and later, popular belief dominated perceptions of their capabilities, so that many in the industry still thought native men worked mainly as boatsteerers. In John Milton Earle's 1861 description of Christiantown, part of an exhaustive report on Massachusetts Indians, he noted that Indians could, "if smart, have the situation of boat-steerer—an important position, and one which draws an extra share in the proceeds of the voyage." Some in the industry had told him that an Indian was often given a better lay than others at the same rank because he could "see a whale further than any other person, and, as a boat-steerer he was more sure to capture it."[86] In keeping with his paternalistic intent to make Indians seem *almost* ready for civilization and independence, Earle was blind to how commonly Indians surpassed boatsteerer to become officers. Of the eight Christiantown men listed in Earle's report whom I have identified as having served on more than one whaling voyage by the time of Earle's investigation, only Asa Peters was still a boatsteerer at the end of a long whaling career.[87] Francis Spencer and his brother John H. Spencer were then at sea as boatsteerers. Only twenty-three and nineteen years old, respectively, they had plenty of time to reach a higher rank.[88] The remaining five whalemen had been officers. James W. DeGrass and Joseph Q. Mingo, whom Earle listed as farmers, retired from whaling in the early 1850s as second mates, and two "mariners," George DeGrass and William S. James, were on or had just completed voyages as third mates.[89] Before that, James had been second mate on the *Osceola*.[90] William James's brother George did not progress neatly up the ranks either but at some point reached second mate.[91] Like many of his contemporaries, Earle failed to realize what shipping records reveal unequivocally: with the whaling industry's expansion, most native men who persisted in the industry could expect to become officers by the third or fourth voyage. So riddled is the documentary record with the assumption that Indian whalemen worked mainly as boatsteerers, the standard paragraph on nineteenth-century Indian whaling in the classic texts of American maritime history typically refer to the superior skills of the Gay Head harpooner, their authors accepting it without question.[92]

The Indian harpooner stereotype simultaneously restricted and enhanced native men's position in the industry. By attributing Indian whalemen's successes to racial characteristics (hunting instinct, naturally keen eyesight, and an innate aptitude for killing), this characterization hid from view what made them valuable as officers: the intellectual abilities they demonstrated through logbook keeping and the mathematical calculations navigation required, their commitment to a voyage's success, and their sense of responsibility when it came to protecting the interests of owners and the crew. And yet at the same time, being imagined as the ideal boatsteerer put them in the right place for promotion. White men worked their way up from foremast hand to boatsteerer to mates to captain.

White, New England-born men had the racial advantage, but there were not enough of them willing to compromise their expectations that they were due a better life than what a whaleship offered. For some, it was "too much like lottery business."[93] For others, the "incessant labor, accompanied with loss of sleep, and indifferent food . . . the constant hurrying shouts, threats and curses of the officers; the grease, filth, storms, upsetting and stoving of boats, as well as other daily casualties and disasters" made the work "intolerable."[94] Many responded the way Charles Nordhoff did. After enjoyable stints in the navy and on merchant vessels, he approached whaling with optimism, but after becoming "entirely disgusted" with "the constant dullness of our monotonous lives," he deserted.[95] If white men could not be had for officers, native men could.

For ship owners, whose primary objective was to make a profit, favoring familiar racial hierarchies that would have kept native whalemen in the forecastle because of their color made less sense than promoting native whalemen into positions of authority. The next chapter will further explore how the policies and customs regulating life on the ship were racially strategic and selective. The social landscape of the whaleship was complicated in its makeup. Native whalemen constituted just one small part of this diverse workforce.

2 : Race, Nationality, and Gender

Native Americans were one small constituency in a diverse whaling workforce brought together by ship owners for one purpose only—to cooperate
in gathering whale products from the world's oceans.[1] The merchant investors, who did the initial hiring, sought trustworthy, skilled officers and cheap,
hardy, and obedient laborers. With profit as their objective, they were open
to hiring any man who could do the job but not if the crew's social composition threatened orderly collaboration. From the top down, federal laws and
industry standards applied measures to enhance productivity by dampen-
ing the volatility such diversity produced: they privileged rank over race and
regulated the number of foreigners serving on American ships. From the
bottom up, seamen brought prejudices on board with them. The color of one's
skin, the land of one's birth, and the language one spoke inflected how shipmates interacted with each other and at any time could combust in conflict. Even though race had no formal role in how the ship operated, it loi-
tered beneath the surface to bear on who was hired to do what job and
shadowed shipboard relations with unspoken assumptions. Cultural differences rooted in national origins, though more institutionalized in industry
policies than race, created another kind of divisive social hierarchy inform-
ing shipboard relations. Gender had the capacity to ease tensions rooted in
race and ethnicity by giving whalemen a means to construct a more uni-
fied shipboard culture around a common identity as men.

Race generalized to create distance between white men and men of color
but also particularized to produce myriad, divergent experiences. That
Native American and African American men were both racial minorities
within the United States or that Native Americans and Pacific Islanders
were both indigenous peoples confronting colonization suggests that bonds
might have formed along these lines, but if any one ethnic group felt a special allegiance to another aboard ship, it is not apparent in whaling records.
Even New England natives showed the strongest attachment to their own
local communities, and Mashpee Wampanoags, Gay Head Wampanoags,
and Shinnecocks often shipped in groups but did not usually intermingle.

Five or six Shinnecocks on the same voyage was especially common. But the rare instances of Long Island natives and Wampanoags or Wampanoags from Mashpee and Martha's Vineyard working on the same vessel appear to have happened only by chance.[2] All whalemen recognized a connection as occupants of a small, floating social community, but their heterogeneity could often pull them apart.

Race was one of the most divisive elements even though it had no official function in how the whaling industry operated. Beginning with the first nationwide census in 1790, the U.S. Census Bureau highlighted race as a vital social characteristic for understanding the makeup of the American populace, but federal maritime law downplayed race. The U.S. Customs Bureau's paperwork for overseas voyages—seamen's certificates of protection, crew lists, and shipping articles—had no category for race. The certificate of protection acted like a passport. Issued by a port authority, it gave a seaman's name, birthplace, place of residence, age, and height and described his complexion and hair for purposes of personal identification. As the early American republic's response to Barbary pirates, French and British privateers, and British impressment of American sailors, the protection vaguely hinted at diplomatic relief for sailors captured by pirates or foreign governments.[3] Inside the United States, federal and state laws left ambiguous the citizenship status of free blacks and did not consider Indians U.S. citizens, but as American-born seamen of color on overseas voyages, they were entitled to the same protection afforded white native-born and naturalized Americans.[4]

Information from protections was transferred to crew lists, which therefore had columns for height, complexion, and hair but still no category for race. One port authority in New London in the 1840s must have thought race important because, after filling in the complexion column with "black" or "Col'd," the official added in the margins "A Negro," "An Indian," or "Mulatto," but the form itself did not ask for racial designations.[5] The absence of a racial category on crew lists has confounded historians investigating race in maritime history. Some have attempted to treat complexion and hair as a proxy for race.[6] However, the plethora of complexion labels defies easy synthesis. Men who probably thought of themselves as white appear on crew lists with fair, light, dark, brown, sandy, ruddy, freckled, and occasionally swarthy complexions. Men of color were all over the map, too—rarely brown or dark, but instead black, African, negro, Indian, native, Kanaka (from the Hawaiian word for "man" and referring to a Pacific Islander), mulatto, colored, yellow, copper, and occasionally swarthy. Hair color, or "quality" as on some printed forms, added racial content. "Wooly" on a man with a yellow or colored complexion implied African descent, whereas a man with a yellow or colored complexion but "black strait" hair suggested Indian ancestry. That "brown" and "dark" rarely described the complexions of men known to be of Indian or African descent in a time when dark and brown had racial inferences, in phrases such as "darkies" or "brown people," is one of crew lists' peculiarities.

Another is how a man's complexion might change over several voyages. On crew lists for vessels out of his home town of Mattapoisett from the 1830s to 1850s, Amos Haskins had a "copper" complexion and "black" hair but was listed as having "marly" hair in 1849 and, in 1851, on his first voyage as captain, a "mulatto" complexion. The complexion of his younger brother Samuel, who resided at Gay Head for most of his adult life, was "dark" in 1844, "mulatto" in 1852, "black" in 1856, "Indian" in 1858, and "black" in 1865.[7] Samuel Haskins's own identity was probably not this quixotic. Rather, he must have acquired multiple protections, and the process of recording his complexion varied each time. Who determined a man's complexion? Did the whaleman himself have a say? Did all three men involved in the process—the seaman, his witness, and the port official—debate the issue, or did the port authority simply decide by looking at the applicant? Because seamen's protections also could be obtained from a distance, more idiosyncrasies entered in. A Cape Cod middleman who bought a share in Jesse Cowet's voyage in 1815 told the ship's agent that Cowet "wants a few things—he wants a Protection he measures 5 feet 5 Inches—not much hare on the top of his head—a yellow skin he is 25 years old." Cowet must have lost his previous protection, which listed him as "mulatto."[8] What one observer judged mulatto, another thought better summed up as yellow. In any case, descriptions of complexions skirted around race without assigning men to racial categories.

Race did not regulate the use of space on whaleships either, since rank dictated where one ate and slept. In the early nineteenth century, during the period crew lists sometimes demarcated a group of men at the bottom as "Black Hands," some ship owners and captains may have extended the same racial segregation to living quarters. Addison Pratt, a white foremast hand on the *Rambler* in 1822, described how the forecastle, where foremast hands usually slept, was "filled with darkies" and separate from where "the white portion of the hands lived." He believed this a deliberate policy intended to prevent foremast hands from plotting mutinous alliances.[9] But the ill-fated Nantucket ship *Essex*, sunk by a sperm whale in 1820, was not racially segregated. Two-thirds of the twenty men making up the ship's complement, including the company's six blacks, resided in the forecastle. The boy Thomas Nickerson lived in steerage, where he felt himself "fortunate indeed to escape being so closely pent up with so large a number of blacks." Rank prevailed over racial antipathies. Race may have factored in more subtly since blacks were among the first to die and be eaten as the *Essex*'s survivors fended off death by starvation.[10] And on some vessels, forecastles may have appeared as though segregated because foremast hands aligned themselves by race when choosing their bunks. But segregation by rank, not race, was the industry mandate.[11]

Racial preferences in hiring were also not codified, but shipping agents made decisions within racial frameworks, perhaps to appease white crew members' fears of associating closely with blacks. Whereas perceptions of blacks and Indians in New England culture often collapsed them into a single racial category as colored people (see chapter 9), on the ship, racial assumptions contrasting each race's abilities expanded Indians' opportunities while limiting those for black seamen. If Indians were the ideal harpooners, African Americans were the ideal servants, and most easily found work on whaleships as cooks and stewards, service positions that offered a better lay than that of foremast hands (1/110 versus 1/170, for example) but led nowhere. After one voyage as steward, Amos Smalley of Gay Head pleaded with the captain on his next voyage to make him a boatsteerer: "I want to get up a little, Captain. I don't want to ship again as a steward. I want to steer a boat." Smalley's father, Samuel, born in New York and identified in vital records as African and mulatto, had served as a steward on whaleships for years, but it was his boatsteerer brother Frankie whom Amos emulated.[12] Some black whalemen were boatsteerers and officers in defiance of typecasting, just as some Indian and white men took the jobs of cook and steward, but everyone in the industry knew that cooks and stewards were typically black.[13]

Occasionally, there was a blurring of racial categories. On the *Draco* in 1850, Captain James Cox found James W. DeGrass in steerage "playing cards with the cook and some of the crew." On his third voyage with Cox as captain, DeGrass had worked his way up to second mate but was now off duty for illness. Or, "he says he is sick days but nights he appears well enough," Cox wrote in his journal, lamenting further that "he has been with me nearly eleven years and this voyage he shows the negro." With a Cape Verdean grandfather, DeGrass had some African ancestry. (Frederick Baylies's 1823 parsing of Martha's Vineyard Indians into fractions recorded six-year-old James DeGrass as five-eighths "Ind" and three-eighths "Neg.") But in the incident aboard the *Draco*, DeGrass's behavior—Cox's belief that he was feigning sickness out of laziness while socializing with the cook—made Cox see him as black at that moment.[14]

Variant notions about blacks and Indians made blacks more vulnerable to expressions of contempt and abuse. Native men fulfilling expectations could spark admiration for their whaling abilities. But black seamen were expected to convey subservience. To survive on whaleships, they may have felt they had to act the part of jovial buffoons who could play the fiddle and dance. Francis Allyn Olmsted, passenger on the *North America* of New London in 1839, praised John Uncas, one of three Indians aboard and a descendant of "the celebrated Sachem of the Mohegans," as a "very active intelligent boy" bound to "become a first rate seaman." The "ebony" cook, in contrast, delighted Olmstead with his comedic and musical talents. Known to the crew as Mr. Freeman, Spot, Jumbo, Congo, Skillet, and Kidney Foot, he had "all the negro accomplishments in full perfection." He danced jigs and fiddled in company with the tambourine-playing, "sable fellow-minstrel" steward, was extraordinarily polite and bowed at every opportunity, spoke quaintly and outlandishly, could "roll up the white of his eye . . . in the genuine negro style," and received "a serio-comic punishment from the captain and officers every day, when his grimaces and exclamations" made Olmsted "almost faint with laughing."[15] Popular entertainments aboard ship similarly drew from a domestic politics of race as American whalemen as far away as Hobart, Australia, watched Jim Crow theatricals, in which white men performed in minstrel blackface.[16] In the Arctic, to endure the long, dark winters, seamen would dress up "*à la negro*" and sing and dance comically for shipmates, captains' wives, and local Inuit.[17]

Meanwhile, blacks suffered disproportionately from punishments and abuses that had none of the "serio-comic" about them, as during the notorious voyage on the *Sharon*, when the captain's persecution of a black crew member culminated in his slow and painful death.[18] A similar scenario unfolded on the *Henry* of New Haven from 1820 to 1823. Greenhand George Attwater wished for the day when "the black rascall" in the galley would get his comeuppance. Early in the voyage, the first mate "pounded the Cook till he bled at the nose & face." The captain then turned against the cook and "gave him a sevier pounding about the face & eyes with his fist, which made the old fellows face & lips swell up like a puff ball." Attwater was now ambivalent. He thought the "old nigrow" deserved to be flogged but questioned whether he "deserved such a pounding." More beatings followed, and the cook's health declined "since our Capt has been in the habit of banging him about." One day, the mate and captain hit the cook repeatedly with fists and then with a rope fifteen to twenty times about the face. The cook begged the captain to stop, but he kept on, "beating him most unmurcifully over his head, sholders, & the back of his neck." Attwater's sympathies turned but not enough to act on the cook's behalf: "I have often seen people flogged at sea but never before seen a man Black or white struck in the face, mouth, & eyes like a dumb brute," all while the "Boat steerers & the ship's company stood by." Finally, the captain's abuses went too far. He tied the cook to the rigging, naked despite the cold, and "all hands went aft & requested the Capt to relice the poor old Blackman," refusing to retreat and hinting at legal redress upon the ship's return. They succeeded at freeing him. Beaten twice himself, Attwater was remarkably resilient in avoiding feelings of kinship with the cook, and even when his sympathies emerged, they took shape as pity for "the poor old Blackman."[19]

Although African Americans were often targets of abuse, they found some protection in shipboard protocols that emphasized rank over other social hierarchies. Anecdotes, jokes, and idle observations in the memoirs of white whalemen reveal a racist culture but one that foremast hands did not always feel free to act on. The standard reference for racism on American whaleships is J. Ross Browne's *Etchings of a Whaling Cruise*, an 1846 exposé shallowly modeled after Richard Henry Dana's *Two Years before the Mast* and one of the most well-reviewed maritime memoirs of the nineteenth century. Browne's disgust at being "compelled to live in the forecastle with a brutal negro, who, conscious that he was upon an equality with the sailors, presumed upon his equality to a degree that was insufferable" is so widely cited, I hesitate to mention it.[20] But it does speak to the ambiguous racial environment whaleships presented. The industry standard allowed for racial equality, but Browne assumed that his readers would recognize the illegitimacy of this affront and sympathize with him. At the height of the whaling industry, antiblack racism flourished in white workingmen's political culture as a salve against fears of declining status in a wage economy.[21] Conditions on whaleships in particular struck many white seamen as too much like black slavery in the South. Whalemen signed contracts that committed them to labor continuously for three to four years, and disobedience was punished by putting men in irons or seizing them up in the rigging to be flogged. Browne hyperbolically proclaimed that rather than "drag out another such year of misery, I would gladly have exchanged my place with that of the most abject slave in Mississippi."[22] Whaleship agents may have confined blacks to service positions to ease white American seamen's anxieties about what a working equality with black men said about their own status.

Despite the prejudices they encountered, black cooks and stewards regarded the whaleship as a symbol of freedom and not at all like slavery in the South. In his 1856 memoir, escaped slave John Thompson portrayed his time as steward on the *Milwood* of New Bedford as liberating. His narrative turned on the captain's and first mate's growing respect for him and how, after the mate beat him early on for no reason, he later "became my friend, and during the remainder of the voyage treated me like a man."[23] Smalley's memoir also highlighted captains' and officers' high regard for his abilities, but he passed quickly over his time as steward to play up his harpooning successes while a boatsteerer.

: : :

Native American men had no special affinity with the whale fishery's large number of foreigners either. Most foreign seamen on American whaleships were Portuguese from the Azores and Cape Verde Islands or Pacific Islanders, called Kanakas in whaling records. Native American whalemen's writings do not convey any of the resentment or patronization of foreigners found in many white-authored accounts, but neither do they suggest any sense of fellowship beyond that expressed for all their shipmates. Moreover, as literate, English-speaking, Protestant Americans, Native American whalemen had more in common with the white coastal New Englanders hired most often as captains and officers and would have seemed more familiar to other American whalemen than the "jabbering," "chattering" Portuguese and Kanakas speaking "gibberings" in the forecastle.[24] Foreign workers' inscrutability evoked wonder and fear. They appear in American whalemen's journals and memoirs as cyphers, whose curious musical entertainments enlivened the dogwatch hours and who sometimes ran amok in a fit of insanity (if Kanaka) or pulled a knife in a fit of passion (if Portuguese).[25]

Ship owners appreciated how willingly the Portuguese and Kanakas accepted low rates of pay and hired them in the thousands but not without concern that too many foreigners could endanger the security of their investment.[26] The U.S. government preferred American seamen manning American vessels for the same reason, making the most important column on crew lists the nationality question: "To what Nation subject" or "Of What Country Citizen or Subject."[27] Because only Americans could obtain seamen's protections, foreigners usually appear on crew lists without personal information beyond their name and nationality, such as Portugal, France, or Sandwich/Hawaiian Islands. When the United States first implemented protections and crew lists, most seamen working American vessels were

American-born and faced the real prospect of capture at sea by foreign powers. They valued their protections and, when in distress, sought national assistance but were often thwarted by the weakness of the early American state.[28] After the War of 1812, the nationality question on crew lists evolved to become less about protecting American seamen from foreign atrocities and more about protecting the American nation from foreign invasion as native-born Americans risked becoming a minority on American-owned vessels, especially whaleships. To ensure that American ships retained American dominance, the U.S. Congress first passed a series of laws that outlawed foreign seamen on American vessels but quickly shifted to make it merely financially burdensome if a crew fell short of an American majority. In 1864, wartime labor shortages further modified these provisions, requiring only that officers be American.[29]

As Americans, native whalemen had an advantage over the foreign-born even though they were not U.S. citizens according to law, not until some measure such as the 1869 Massachusetts Enfranchisement Act or Rhode Island's 1880 dissolution of the Narragansett tribe decreed it.[30] The 1813 "Act for the Regulation of Seamen" limited American citizenship to whites but still acknowledged the Americanness of people of color by making it illegal to employ any "except citizens of the United States, or persons of colour, natives of the United States."[31] Because Native American seamen obtained certificates of protection, they had the same status in maritime law as U.S. citizens. That native men's American nativity helped whaling agents meet their American quota on crew lists must have supported their rapid succession into officer positions, especially after 1864, when American whaling crews became predominantly Portuguese with a sprinkling of British and German immigrants.

Despite U.S. laws intended to curtail foreign seamen, whaling crews became increasingly international. American-born whalemen sometimes interpreted this diversity as a cunning strategy to disempower foremast hands and deliver absolute power to tyrannical captains. White memoirist Cyrene Clarke believed that the "prosperity and aggrandizement of the whaling companies in the United States, has been secured by filching from the foremast hand that which rightfully belonged to him" and that as "Persons unacquainted with their own 'inalienable rights' . . . Portuguese from the Western Islands [Azores]; so many natives of the islands of the Pacific, are crowded in among our American crews, for these men can be brow-beaten and made to succumb, and never dream that they have any means of redress, or any rights to protest."[32] Even though foreign seamen were not eligible to register for a protection, U.S. law, consuls, and federal courts did grant them legal protection if registered on the shipping articles in conformity with customs regulations.[33]

Still, Clarke's assessment that captains felt that they could get away with disregarding the rights of foreign seamen had some truth to it. A few weeks into his voyage on the *Henry Kneeland* in 1851, a young greenhand named Enoch Carter Cloud captured the irony of an American whaleship dependent on foreign labor: "Particular inquiries were made by the Shipping Officer in Philadelphia (when I enlisted), concerning my birthplace. This was done, they said, to prevent foreigners from enlisting in the service. Now, let's have a look at our crew! It is composed of American, English, Irish, French, Dutch, Portuguese & Spaniards! No foreigners, sh!!" Several months into the voyage, while at Wanganui, New Zealand, national prejudices tore apart this crew: "One of our harpooners (a large Portuguese) with some 30 others, fell upon & beat most shamefully one of his shipmates, (an American) while on shore this morning." The "melee" spilled over to other ships then in port, and "a large number of Americans & Portuguese met on shore for the avowed intention of fighting." Whatever the cause, the captain blamed the Portuguese and "seized the harpooneer & 2 sailors (Portuguese) in the mizzens rigging & gave them 2 dozen apiece for assaulting, and beating a shipmate!"[34]

A white memoirist, describing the racial geography of an 1870s forecastle, noted that "whites" from New England, Germany, Hungary, French Canada, and Italy congregated together on the starboard side while the Portuguese, "blacks," kept to themselves on the port side.[35] As many of the foreign sailors on American whaleships belonged to darker races, it is difficult to know which was the most divisive, racism or xenophobia. Although lighter-skinned Azoreans seem to have advanced more easily into officer positions and captaincies than Cape Verdeans, whom one white memoirist called "nigger Portuguese," whaling records usually refer more generically to "Portuguese" without distinction.[36]

Even those white whalemen who enjoyed the novelty of new cultures had difficulty overcoming their discomfort with racial mixing and their sense of racial distance. In his memoir *Nimrod of the Sea*, William M. Davis recalled how when the *Chelsea* of New London arrived in Hawai'i in the mid-1830s, the captain dumped his laggards and malcontents in a Hawaiian jail and shipped ten Kanakas to replace them. Davis reported that those few remaining who had shipped from the United States, who were already angry at the captain, erupted at "the thought of going to sea with such a heathenish crew as now darkened our forecastle." As the crew settled down and the

Kanakas settled in, Davis came to enjoy getting to know them: "They appear to be a cheerful, inoffensive people, and they regard with amazement the angry, quarrelsome race they have come among." He tried to "pick up the lingo of our brown mates," appreciating the sound of it, "low and pleasant, full of vowels and soft sounds." The Kanakas sang familiar hymns but also exotic chants, and Davis learned bits and pieces of Hawaiian lore. Still, their presence meant fewer people he could talk with now that only three English-speaking foremast hands in his watch remained.[37]

Other white memoirists who expressed affection for foreign shipmates often praised them for their childlike innocence, loyalty, and willingness to serve. A memoir of a voyage on the *Emily Morgan* around 1850 described two touching farewell scenes as Kanaka whalemen left the vessel. The first was Friday, "one of our *best* men, though a Kanaka." Friday was "overjoyed" at the prospect of returning home, but "tears gushed from his eyes" when "parting with his shipmates. This was hard for poor Friday, for all loved him, though he had a dark skin. He had been so kind to all on board—so ever ready and willing to do all in his power to serve others' interests—so quick to learn, and so grateful for any kindness shown." Later in the voyage, "a Kanaka from Simpson's Island, whom we called 'Dick Simpson,'" left under similar conditions, prompting the comment that despite his "dingy hue," "we all loved good-natured, obliging Dick Simpson."[38] One British memoirist on an American whaleship in the mid-1870s admitted to having "always had a strong liking for natives of tropical countries" and speculated that the reason "white men do not get on with darkies well, as a rule, is, that [whites] seldom make an appeal to the *man* in them." And yet, he went on to infantilize the Kanakas they shipped at Futuna as "docile, useful, and cheerful. . . . They wept like little children when the time arrived for them to leave us."[39] Expressions of affection for Kanakas, despite their dark skin, were no doubt sincere but still premised on a belief in the racial superiority of white men.

Foreigners of color eased white whalemen's peace of mind if cast as inferiors but could fuel anger if in command. Greenhand Walter Noble Burns, on the San Francisco whaling brig *Alexander* around 1890, recalled his first glimpse of the Cape Verdean third mate: "I saw Mendez, like an ebony statue, standing in the waist of the ship, an arm resting easily on the bulwarks, singing out orders in a clear, incisive voice that had in it the ring of steel. When I shipped, it had not entered my mind that any but white men would be of the ship's company. It was with a shock like a blow in the face that I saw this little colored man singing out orders."[40] Burns framed his humiliation in racial terms, but that Mendez was "little" and Portuguese also counted against him. Strangely, Burns does not mention that Captain

William T. Shorey, of whom he speaks in tones of awe and deference, was also a man of color from outside the United States, having been born in Barbados.[41] Shorey's status as captain, and perhaps personal qualities in how he carried himself, relieved him of the virulent racism mixed with xenophobia that Burns felt free to lodge against the third mate.

Foreigners appear most marginalized in their lack of individuality in whaling accounts, a pattern found in native-authored writings as well. In shipping foreign laborers, captains added to foreigners' genericness and anonymity by christening them with a nickname that Americans could more easily pronounce. Some of these were jokes with racial connotations: Snowball or Jim Crow. Other names paid homage to the ship, ship owner, captain, or an American president. Most often, the newly hired became known more simply as Joe Kanaka or Joe Portuguese, John Kanaka or John Portuguese. In his journal on the *Awashonks* voyage of 1862 to 1865, William A. Vanderhoop of Gay Head scrupulously maintained a crew list showing the comings and goings of the many who deserted, received a discharge, or shipped for only a season. Among the forty-one foremast hands listed, eight men had the surname "Kanaka": two Bobs, three Johns, Friday, Jim, and Harry. Twelve men had the surname "Portugee": two Manuels, Joseph, John, Jacking, Frank, Samuel, Pike, Lucas, Antone, William, and Victorine. There were even three men with an unusual surname for the whaling industry, "Italian": John, Frank, and James. A Kanaka not on the crew list (or if so, not under the same name) was the first death of the voyage. "At 12 Midnight George James a Kanaka died commited him to the deep at 8 A.M." Nine months later, another death inspired more emotion, Vanderhoop writing, "early in the morning one of our Ship mates died a Kanaka from hape island been Sick Some time & now is dead with the Stars & Stripes over him 6 P.M. bairied him."[42] Vanderhoop's sparse entries were typical of logbooks, though more voluble than those that simply reported the death of a "Kanaka" or a "Portugee" without giving a name or other distinguishing information. Although Vanderhoop's comments about his Kanaka shipmates resemble what readers might come across in logbooks and journals kept by whites, he undoubtedly stopped short of resenting them for their dark skin.

Surrounded by so much human diversity, whalemen with racial or nationalistic prejudices had many options as to whom they might most despise or fear, with Native Americans one of the least likely targets. When Asa Wainer served as first mate on the bark *Mercator* from 1850 to 1852 (probably also as logbook keeper), forecastle relations became heated a few months into the voyage, instigated by the noisy dissatisfactions of a white greenhand from Worcester, Massachusetts, Lewis Bremer. A long account in the logbook justifies why Bremer had to be flogged: for "telling the crew that mr. brown Was an irish man & casting slurs on the other officers & telling the crew that He would pitch in to mr brown & fite him"; for picking quarrels with the "inocent portugues" in the forecastle; and for saying he "did not care for portugues nor the Capt." Perhaps Wainer was one of the officers Bremer cast slurs upon, but clearly Bremer had others among the crew to obsess over.[43]

Many voyages sailed more happily along with such tensions held in check. Even though many white American whalemen grumbled over how their race and nationality did not favor them with the rewards and status they expected, there were occasions when men of different races and nationalities intermingled pleasantly and in surprisingly intimate ways. Harvard law student William A. Abbe, who probably went whaling under the influence of Dana's *Two Years before the Mast*, recounted a magical gam involving three ships at sea in 1859—the *Atkins Adams, Chili,* and *Sea Queen.* "Kicking off our shoes as we formed two cotillion parties & kept the decks alive, crowded as they were, with our shouts & laughter & music. I was lady to a stout negro, who laughed till he was hoarse."[44] A metaphor for the transitory nature of whaling society, the gam brought men of varying backgrounds together. The barriers imposed by race and nationality could be set aside but not by all and not with any permanency.

: : :

Gender lessened tensions arising from racial expectations and cultural differences by affording crew members opportunities to coalesce around a common identity as men, defined by the absence or near absence of women, not necessarily by the same gender perspectives. Varied masculine ideals informed shipboard culture, and like race, gender had the flexibility to adapt to meet each situation. Manliness through athleticism, physical strength, and fearlessness found plenty of opportunities for expression in the whale hunt. Men also became sentimental and familial while crying over distant loved ones, without feeling that their manhood had been compromised. Other manly ideals—self-control, personal responsibility, economic independence, and occupational competence—pervade whalemen's writings.[45] Whalemen of color do not seem all that different in their understandings of gender from the white American whalemen whose views have been studied the most. William A. Vanderhoop writing "I wish I was a great man" next to his tally of whales raised, James F. Pells's worries about the price of whale oil with "a wife And child at home now," and the escaped slave John Thompson's pride in his work as steward all reflect a whaleman trying to live up to what he thought a man should be.[46]

Whatever attitudes about gender each man brought aboard, they all had to adapt to ships' unnatural, usually all-male environment. American whaleships did not employ women in any capacity. A few women cross-dressers fooled their way into the forecastle, but if caught, they were re-dressed in women's clothes and immediately handed over to a U.S. consul to be sent home.[47] The few women living on a whaleship for the duration of a voyage were captains' wives, who by the 1840s began in increasing numbers to accompany husbands to sea. A captain's wife gave all but the captain something to talk, or complain, about. She reminded the captain's subordinates of the domestic life denied them, made men feel that they could not act themselves within her gaze or earshot, took up space on cramped vessels by installing pianos and curtains on decks and in the cabin, turned a gam into a painful chore if the crew had to transport her to and from another ship, and distracted the captain from his whaling mission, or so some of the crew thought.[48] There is no evidence to suggest that Native Americans viewed the presence of a captain's wife any differently. We do not know what went on in Gay Head Wampanoag Joseph G. Belain's mind in the days after the steam bark *Navarch* became trapped in Arctic ice in 1897, but we can guess. Charles Brower, a Point Barrow whaling station resident aboard the *Navarch* at the time of the wreck, reported how, when the vessel looked as though it was about to be crushed by ice, Captain Joseph A. Whiteside began "running around excitedly and issuing needless orders," crying, drinking, all while his wife "never made the slightest fuss over what was happening." When Whiteside called out "'Every man for himself!'" it was first mate Belain who stayed with the captain's wife in an arduous march across the ice.[49] As courageous as Whiteside's wife was in the crisis, Belain must have wished the captain had left her at home to free him from assuming the responsibility of helping her to safety.

Other women were featured in shipboard life through stories and songs. The homesick and lovelorn shared with each other cherished photographs, letters, and dreams about mothers, sisters, wives, and sweethearts. William H. Chappell, a white cooper, found consolation in a conversation with the "Indian boatsteerer" Samuel Thompson, who joined the *Saratoga* at Oahu in 1855 and lived with Chappell in steerage. Chappell addressed his journal to his wife and reflected often on how much he missed her, one day telling her, "Thompson said he never was so homesick in his life he said it seems so queer to sleep without a wife and he often wakes himself in the night feeling round for her."[50] Chappell identified with what Thompson was feeling as he said this. Whalemen from diverse backgrounds also found common ground during the dogwatch hours when foremast hands gathered on deck to "eat supper, spin yarns and have fun with games and tricks of all kinds, and talk about the girls we left behind us."[51]

Whalemen's songs borrowed from sailor songs more generally, and many of them narrated stories about courtship or encounters with exotic temptresses in foreign ports of call. Wampanoag Samuel G. Mingo recorded several standard songs in his journal kept on the *Andrew Hicks* from 1879 to 1881. In "The Pretty Maid of Mohe" or "The Lass of Mowee," one of the most popular whaling songs, a sailor meets an "Indian lass" of Maui who invites him to "her hut in a coconut grove" to stay until his ship takes him back home, "For I have a sweetheart in my own country." In "The Girls around Cape Horn," another song in Mingo's journal, "Chile girls" carouse with Yankee sailors until their "money is all gone [when . . .] they rob him of his clothes."[52] Whispered confidences about missing one's wife or raucous gams with an exchange of songs contributed to a gendered culture aboard ship, in which familial ties to women achieved a kind of sanctity and co-existed with fantasies of transient, carefree sexuality with other women encountered during the voyage. Both representations of women reinforced the self-consciously male nature of the whaling enterprise.

Fleeting liaisons with women who sold or traded sexual favors often had a communal dimension, too, though not all among the crew partook or approved. An especially revelatory account on the range of whalemen's relations with women comes from a Japanese investigation into the travels of five fishermen shipwrecked and rescued by the American whaler *John Howland* in 1841. Their ethnographic observations have a fresh quality counter to how American participants described life on a whaleship. They were struck by how "the captain and crew kept pictures of their wives at hand or hung them nearby. They enjoyed seeing them when they went to bed or woke up." One of the rescued fishermen, John Manjiro, lived for a while with the *John Howland*'s captain in Fairhaven, Massachusetts, where he noted of the women, "Their nature was obedient, and it had become the custom of the country for women to be highly virtuous." Two others shipped on the whaler *Florida* and described how, when the vessel stopped at an island in the western Pacific, "the ship's crew took naked women to the bunks in return for tobacco and rings. Some shameless, vigorous men had sexual intercourse openly. Naked men stood by and watched, smoking. Penises were erect and glandes were jumping. Though some pointed to others and laughed, the crew paid no attention."[53] American whaling writers were more tight-lipped about their own or their shipmates' sexual encounters, leaving their readers to imagine the "floating scene of abominations" when "fathers and brothers would bring their daughters and sisters on board, and sell all the virtue they possessed for a fathom or two of calico, or a piece of iron hoop."[54]

Even more cloaked in the documentary record by the mores of the nineteenth century was same-sex sexuality. There are only about a dozen known instances when a sexual act between men on a whaleship was recorded in a logbook, journal, or consular dispatch.[55] In such cases, a collective outrage usually bubbled up among the crew to demand that the captain—or, if the captain was seen as perpetrator, the ship's officers—punish and remove from the vessel anyone who attempted to have sexual relations with other men. In one incident, Hosea Pocknett of Mashpee was serving on the *Joseph Starbuck* of Nantucket in 1839 when the cabin boy complained to the captain of the third mate's "trying to kiss him & caress him" during his watch on deck. After a turbulent night of accusations, threats, and the third mate's drawing a knife, the "Officers and Cabin Company" entered a formal "Protest of the conduct of the third mate" into the official logbook to add moral weight to the captain's putting the third mate in irons and expeditiously heading toward Tumbes, Peru, to rid the ship of him. As the sixth person to sign this protest, Pocknett probably held the rank of boatsteerer and thus ate his meals in the cabin, making him a distant but still eligible authority to help attest with the captains and officers to how "We . . . Consider our Persons and Ship In Danger whilest the said Mr. Fisher is on Board."[56] In the same vein, the sexually inviting woman someone carved or drew onto the central column of the *Sunbeam*'s forecastle (figure 5) told all who entered this space that, even though they were a community of men living intimately together, they should focus their desires on women.

Race and national origins made little difference in gendered situations. Thompson missing his wife was not a trait peculiar to Indians but an emotion he and Chappell shared. The Japanese fishermen remarked on the presence of black men on American whaleships in other contexts but not in their comments about women and sexuality: no one race was more or less prone to possess a picture of a wife as keepsake, nor did the Japanese observers say exactly who were these "vigorous men [who] had sexual intercourse openly."

Race and gender did intersect occasionally in the Old Neptune ritual, a hazing initiation that turned landsmen into seamen through a series of humiliating debasements when a vessel made its first pass through the equator. When the *Charles W. Morgan* neared the equator in 1849, the fourth

Figure 5. *New Bedford artist Clifford W. Ashley drew this picture of the* Sunbeam's *forecastle, which is where the majority of the crew, the foremast hands, lived and slept. Ashley accompanied the* Sunbeam *as far as Brava, Cape Verde, on its 1904 voyage, which had famed Gay Head whaleman Amos Smalley aboard as one of the boatsteerers. Ashley,* Yankee Whaler *(1926), 111. Reproduced by permission of Phoebe Ashley Chardon and Marc Chardon.*

mate dressed up as Old Neptune in a costume of old rope and canvas while others filled blubber tubs with salt water. Calling out one greenhand at a time to come up from the forecastle, the seasoned whalemen blindfolded him and took him to a seat above the blubber tub, where Old Neptune promised to "'make you a good sailor, and learn you how to be a man.'" After asking a few questions, Old Neptune endowed the greenhand with a nickname ("The Lady Killer" in this story) and advised him "'never to eat brown bread when you can get white, unless you like it best. Never kiss the servant maid if you can the mistress, unless the mistress is not so pretty.'" Then he asked the greenhand, "'Did you ever kiss a Negro girl? Answer loud!'" As the greenhand shouted "No," Old Neptune shoved tar down his throat, shaved him with an iron hoop, and sent him backward into the water.[57] A few years later, on the *New England* out of New London, Old Neptune told the greenhands, "Never eat brown bread when you can get white—Never—a black woman when you can get a white one."[58] Presumably, the wording changed when Old Neptune tested men of color with questions. But in these two anecdotes recalled by white whalemen, Old Neptune normalized heterosexuality as manly and made racial crossing transgressive and white superiority the ideal. Gender may have allowed whalemen from different backgrounds to see each other as fellow men, but it did not obliterate the potential of race to divide them.

More than gender, what brought men together in a sense of their common humanity was death. Wampanoag Timothy Belain, while second mate on the *John Dawson*, wrote in his journal on 17 October 1879, "died Ben Butler, a Kanaka, after a sickness of two or three weeks. We buried him the 17 inst,—Oh what a sad & Solemn thing it is, to bury a shipmate at sea But we done all we could for him."[59] Promoted to first mate during the voyage, Belain saw his own health decline over the next two years. His death inspired a less effusive memorial in the logbook—"The Mate died at 2 in the morning Buried at 2 this afternoon"—but his shipmates probably also thought his death a "sad & Solemn thing."[60] White memoirist William B. Whitecar mused after a man fell overboard how they were "all depending on the same fabric for shelter against the storm and wave, it came with a ten-fold force—as none knew whose turn it next might be."[61] When a ship became caught in a typhoon or pinioned on a reef, when a whale crushed a whaleboat in its jaws or shredded it with the power of its flukes, the seafaring skills of one's comrades could be all that mattered.

Technically, under U.S. law, American whaleships were adjunct spaces of the nation, lying within federal jurisdiction and under American ownership and control. The workforce was so diverse, however, and the working conditions so isolated, mobile, and attuned to the single-minded pursuit of the whaling trade, whalemen occupied a unique social world. Race entered into this world in particular ways. Many white, American whalemen clung to a belief in their racial superiority and saw their shipmates through a racial lens. African Americans in white whalemen's journals and memoirs appear most often as cooks and stewards, a true reflection of the jobs they most often held aboard ship. Their comedic and musical talents were greatly appreciated, but violent abuses perpetrated on them rarely stirred white empathy. In white whalemen's writings, the Portuguese and Pacific Islanders also entertained shipmates with culturally singular musical performances. They jabbered unintelligibly and received the most praise for behavior that was innocent, loyal, obedient, and childlike. Native American whalemen had an advantage over other men of color. The particular stereotype applied to them presumed superior ability in fulfilling the purpose of the voyage. In striking contrast to how white whalemen wrote about

African American and foreign shipmates, Indians were never called on to entertain the crew with music and dance.

Despite being stereotyped, many whalemen of color liked the work, probably because they came to it with fewer expectations. White whalemen presumed they had rights to certain working conditions and high status. But as greenhands they quickly discovered that entitlements they took for granted were not guaranteed on the ship, where they could find themselves in equality with or even subordinate to men of color. Race was thus part of whaling life but not nearly as important as occupational rank, which by industry standards was considered fundamental and necessary for the success of a voyage.

3 : The Primacy of Rank

Racial tensions could distract a crew from its main objective, and racial prejudices acted as a gatekeeper in hiring by suggesting what kinds of work individuals of particular races were best suited for. But ship rules mandated foremost that a whaleman's duties and status followed from his rank. Considered fundamental to the safe operation of the vessel and the success of the venture, the social hierarchy of rank rigidly controlled shipboard relations. A high rank brought to an individual whaleman a greater share of the profits, more authority, and better treatment. Moreover, when men of color served as officers, the racial hierarchy of nineteenth-century New England turned around, for it became their job to order white men around the decks.

One sign that rank trumped race in the day-to-day relations aboard ship is in the rarity of references to race in whaling logbooks and journals. Greenhand Ellinwood B. Coleman, for example, makes no reference to race in the daily entries of his journal recorded while on the *Niger* from 1878 to 1882. Coleman took pride in his descent from Nantucket's founding white families, at one point scribbling a familiar ditty playing off the legacy surnames of the island (the Coffins were "noisy, fractous, loud" while "A living Coleman verry rare"). Yet, unlike his Nantucket forebears of the early nineteenth century, he did not distinguish his shipmates of color as "Black Hands." Instead, he acknowledged the superior rank and ability of the ship's officers without commenting on their race in such statements as "Mr. Peters & Mr. Morse have been at work on their new boat sails"; "Captain came aboard and he and Mr. Walker had some words"; "Mr. Walker took two sights finding the error of Chro[no]meter to be 25 minutes and 53 second fast"; "Mr. Peters struck a bull, fired two bombs into him."[1] This formalized deference shown to superiors explains why historians have not recognized the frequency of native officers on whaleships. Coleman no doubt knew that first mate Moses S. Walker was a Long Island Indian and second mate Samuel Peters Jr. a Gay Head Indian.[2] But eager to show his own whaling competence, Coleman accepted—in his whaling writings, at least—that race was not relevant in this context.

All whalemen, even to some extent captains, belonged to a laboring class employed by the merchant capitalists who did not go to sea themselves but resided safely and comfortably in port cities. Thus, while at sea, social relations did not fit the two-tiered class system of capital and proletarian labor that historian Marcus Rediker has argued existed in the early modern, maritime Atlantic.[3] The boldest distinction divided officers and foremast hands, but finer gradations in rank distributed the crew into a long hierarchical line from the captain to first, second, third, and fourth mates to the boatsteerers, who had some responsibilities as junior officers, to the foremast hands. Even the foremast hands fell into degrees as able, ordinary, and green seamen based on experience. Inequalities instituted by rank achieved a clear chain of command but also promised equality to those at the same rank. Because rank was not premised on assumed natural endowments such as those thought to inhere in different races, the emphasis on skill and experience made possible some upward mobility to nearly all. Those who had no aspirations to advance deserted as soon as they could or chose to take up some other line of work. Those who stayed with it—native whalemen almost always—learned to live by rank's rules and appreciated what rank afforded them: pay equity for those at the same rank and, for officers, a high status and better living conditions.

Whalemen negotiated their ranks and lays before signing shipping articles. Therefore, lays varied some within ranks but still within a predictable range—captains between 1/12 and 1/16, boatsteerers between 1/70, and 1/90, greenhands between 1/150 and 1/180, and so on. Because lays resulted from negotiation, race could have informed agents' calculations about what they were willing to pay, but there is no evidence of American men of color being paid at rates lower than those for white men. Even "Black Hands" in the early nineteenth century held lays equivalent to those of white boatsteerers and foremast hands.[4] In the 1840s, as more native men served as officers, they could continue to expect the same lays as white men at the same rank (see Table 2). The average lay of native third mates, falling somewhere between 1/56 and 1/59, was close to and even a little above the industry average of 1/59 to 1/66 for that rank. Given their reputation as superior whalemen, native men may have had a bargaining advantage if ship agents believed that they needed to pay them an above-average lay to retain their services. Over the nineteenth century, in the industry generally, officer lays improved while those of foremast hands degenerated. Ship owners needed reliable and highly skilled officers to train and oversee the larger proportion of novice and foreign whalemen hired as common laborers.[5] In accord with this trend, by the 1870s, native third mates' lays

Table 2

Sampling of Lays of Native Third Mates in the 1840s

Name	Ship	Lay
Gideon Ammons	Ship *Adeline* of New Bedford, 1843–1846 (on at Hawai'i)	1/60
Gideon Ammons	Ship *Emma C. Jones* of New Bedford, 1849–1852	1/50
Joseph Ammons	Ship *Roman* of New Bedford, 1843–1845	1/65
Asa Belain	Ship *Benjamin Tucker* of New Bedford, 1843–1846	1/64
Thomas Cook	Ship *John Coggeshall* of New Bedford, 1847–1850	1/70
Jonathan Cuff	Ship *Adeline* of New Bedford, 1843–1846	1/57
Paul Cuff	Ship *Amethyst* of New Bedford, 1844–1844	1/70
James W. DeGrass	Bark *Draco* of New Bedford, 1843–1847	1/57
James Francis	Ship *Hydaspe* of New Bedford, 1841–1845	1/60
Philip Goodridge	Ship *America* of New Bedford, 1845–1848	1/50
Simeon Goodridge	Ship *Fabius* of New Bedford, 1844–1846	1/50
Simeon Goodridge	Ship *Erie* of Fairhaven, 1847–1850	1/28
William Jeffers	Ship *John* of New Bedford, 1844–1848	1/40
Abel Manning	Ship *James Maury* of New Bedford, 1845–1848	1/64
John Quippish	Ship *Samuel Robertson* of Fairhaven, 1846–1849	1/65
Johnson Simpson	Ship *America* of New Bedford, 1843–1845	1/55

Mean = 1/56. Median = 1/58.5.

The industry average for third mates from 1840 to 1849 ranged from 1/59.4 to 1/66.1.

Sources: Lance E. Davis, Gallman, and Gleiter, *In Pursuit of Leviathan*, 162; ranks and lays from SHP for all vessels.

"shortened" (improved) along with the general average to fall between 1/40 and 1/50.[6]

Pay equity also applied to captains. Amos Haskins's lay on his first voyage as master, on the *Massasoit* in 1851, was 1/14. Compared with the captains of the six other vessels that left on a whaling voyage from Mattapoisett that year, Haskins had an average lay. Three of the other captains had a generous lay of 1/12, one had the same lay as Haskins, and two had a lay of 1/15. All had more experience as captain than Haskins, with two to eight prior voyages to their credit, except for one of the two men with a lay of 1/15. Like Haskins, his only experience as master had come from replacing the captain on his last voyage.[7] Haskins may have been the only Native American whaling master in the industry at the time, but that did not mean that his labor held less value.

With their ranks and lays settled and as the men came aboard, rank pervaded every conversation and act, making the steeply authoritarian command structure palpable. Foremast hands learned quickly that they had to obey officers and treat them with respect. They acknowledged commands by saying "Ay, Ay, Sir" and had to accept direction without question or complaint.[8] Whalemen at lower ranks often went by nicknames. The first mate on the *Platina* called boatsteerer Amos Smalley "Old Tommyhawk."[9] Boatsteerer William H. Cook was known as "Gayhead" on the *Napoleon*.[10] Native officers, however, had to be addressed as Mr. Cook, Mr. Walker, or Mr. Peters, as Coleman did in his journal. This practice was so ingrained in the industry, native whalemen who rose to become officers were identified as such in the port city newspapers that otherwise distinguished men of color, when they died for instance, by putting "(colored)" after their names. No one who did not already know Amos Haskins would have known the race of the "Mr. Haskins" who was first mate of the bark *Elizabeth* and then captain of the *Massasoit*, as reported in the industry's trade newspaper.[11]

Within a day or two of departure, the crew gathered before the captain to hear a speech about how he would treat them well if they did as they were told. The captain and mates then picked their whaleboat crews, beginning with the captain selecting his boatsteerer, the first mate his boatsteerer, and on down the line until the scrawniest greenhand found his place. The captain and officers acted as boatheaders in the whaleboats, giving each officers his own petty kingdom to reign over. The five men in his whaleboat were subject to his authority while chasing whales and during their watch on deck. Second in command in each whaleboat were the boatsteerers. They kept whaleboats ready for the chase, harpooned the whales when the boatheader told them it was time to dart, and commanded watches when mates were below. The unskilled greenhands were allotted the most tedious and dirty tasks and remained greenhands until officially promoted.

One memoir by white New Englander Reuben Delano gives vivid descriptions of the whaleboat's social dynamics as he, "the Indian" Lilley Page, and four greenhands chased one whale after another on the *Sophia* from 1830 to 1831. A decade or two later, Delano would likely have said Mr. Page, not "the Indian," but this voyage took place before many native men held officer positions. As third mate and boatsteerer, Page was the captain's harpooner if the captain chose to whale that day, and if the captain chose to stay aboard the ship, Page became boatheader in the captain's place.[12] Page then gave the orders, which Delano as his boatsteerer and the greenhands obeyed without question.

The first whale chase occurred while the *Sophia* lay off the island of Tristan D'Acunha, and a whale came up near to the shore. "Our line tubs were soon in," Delano wrote, "and we were after him. He was going before sea and wind. The Indian that headed the Captain's boat, motioned to me to stand up. I rose and grasped my iron and when within a convenient distance, fastened him with both irons in the small." Page shouted out "'stern all,'" but the greenhands at the oars did not know to back the whaleboat away from the whale, so they were too close when the whale "lifted his flukes with a sweep over the bows of the boat, and shot off doing no further damage than tipping about half a barrel of water into my neck." Delano and Page then changed places—as Delano put it, "I then took the steering oar"—and as the whale sounded, "the order was given to hold on line, and hold on I did, with a vengeance, causing the eyes of the green hands to stick out with fright and wonder." While they held onto the whale, the second mate's boat came up, and "the second mate complimented [the whale] with a lance which turned him up, and we brought him along side." The next day, they chased another whale, and "the Indian succeeded in getting a lance into him," after which the first mate came up and tried unsuccessfully to lance the whale as well. When describing his first whaling voyage, six years before, Delano complained that they lost a lot of whales because there was "a quarrel among the officers, who, regardless of the reputation of the voyage, refused to assist each other where they individually, could not have the honor killing the whale."[13] On the *Sophia*, Page deferred to his superiors as they came in for the kill. While Delano's stories highlighted his own bravado and skill as boatsteerer, they incidentally document that Delano and the greenhands followed Page's orders without question and respected his judgment.

The choreography of the hunt integrated work tasks with rituals that bestowed honors according to rank. As Delano described, after harpooning the whale, the boatsteerer changed places with the boatheader in mid-ocean, each man climbing over the four men sitting at their oars. Theoretically this exchange at sea put the most experienced man in position to lance the whale to death, but it also brought glory to he who delivered the death blow, making this display of ability an officer's privilege worth competing for.[14] Not all honors were reserved for officers. To encourage men at the mastheads to look sharp for whales, captains promised incentives, such as the gold watch the captain of the *California* presented to "Mr. Mingo" in 1882 for "having raised whales the most times that we have taken them."[15] Christian-town native Samuel G. Mingo was fourth mate at the time.[16] Tristram A. Weeks of Gay Head, second mate (later promoted to first mate) on the *Bartholomew Gosnold*, also won a watch that year for raising the most whales.[17] Foremast hands could aspire to win bounties, but usually those with more experience had an easier time spotting whales. Such rituals of whaling achievement, performed before the crew as audience, intended to inspire productivity and reinforced the status of those in charge.

: : :

Rank structured men's relationships as they fulfilled their duties but also while they slept, ate, and socialized, all well aware of rank's inequities. Simply put, officers had it easier and better. One greenhand on a whaler out of San Francisco at the turn of the twentieth century claimed that even the reindeer-skin clothing purchased from native women as they passed into the Arctic Ocean was distributed according to rank, that of the officers and boatsteerers being "of finer quality and more pretentious."[18] The most resented distinctions in comfort had to do with basic needs, however—living space and food.[19]

When the men first came aboard in search of bunks and a spot of floor to deposit their sea chests, they headed in opposite directions. The mates resided in staterooms aft, next to the captain's quarters, and took their meals in the cabin with the captain, served at table by the steward. Next in rank were the several boatsteerers, who slept in steerage, near the officers' staterooms and cabin, where they also took their meals after the officers had eaten. Specialty hands, such as the cooper, steward, cabin boy, and cook also could be found in steerage. The largest contingent, the foremast hands, crowded into the forecastle. Above decks, each rank also had defined spaces, with the quarterdeck the captain's domain. Foremast hands ventured into the cabin or onto the quarterdeck only in defiance, when shouting out a complaint or holding up a broom or other makeshift club. Although at the bottom of the shipboard hierarchy, foremast hands did have some possessory rights as a community over the forecastle, which like slave quarters or an estate kitchen became a retreat from the oversight of those in power. The intrusion of officers into the forecastle could be read as an affront, and if a spark of radicalism were to unite foremast hands against officers, they used the forecastle as safe haven, to plot refusals to do duty and voice grievances and insults not dared spoken elsewhere on the ship. To challenge the command structure, all one had to do was walk into someone else's space.[20]

George Lightcraft Colburn's memoir gives an anecdote about a green-hand who wandered into the cabin on his first day. A whaling veteran and one of three boatsteerers on the *Hesper* in 1831, Colburn knew his place, steerage. But the greenhand, a "Dutchman from Albany county" did not: "straying aft, he went down into the cabin, where the chief and second mate were at supper. 'Oh, gosh,[']said greeny, 'you have got a table, cups and saucers and tea-spoons, and sugar tu, I guess I'll live in this eend[']; He was allowed to go on for some time in this way . . . and striding across the cabin, entered the Captain's state-room. 'Well, this beats all creation! If here is'nt a little room, as true as my name's Vanlone, and a bed tu with nice curtains, I vow. Well, this beats all; here's lots of little rooms;' in saying which he opened another state-room 'My gosh, going to sea arter all wont be so bad.'" Then, as "greeny" took a chair to sit at the table, the mate "pulled the chair from under him, and down he went upon the deck. Soon picking himself up, he was sent to the other end of the ship."[21]

Not at table at the time but with every right to sit there and to sleep in one of the staterooms was third mate Henry James, Wampanoag from Christiantown. Colburn took orders from James, whom he described as "the best fisherman in the ship, and as I have every reason to believe a Christian." Because James was "a trustworthy man, the charge of the chief mate's watch was given to him, and it was my good fortune, Indian though he was, to be in his watch, the whole of the voyage."[22] James brought along fourteen-year-old James W. DeGrass, who as a greenhand would have lived in the forecastle. Also in the ship's company was boatsteerer Juan Antonio Espencero, a Cape Verdean who had recently anglicized his name to John A. Spencer. Spencer had sailed with James on the previous voyage of the *Hesper* and at some point in their acquaintance married James's sister Mary and took up residence at Christiantown.[23] Three men whose lives intersected on a small Indian reservation on Martha's Vineyard belonged to different places on the *Hesper*. Their separation by rank dictated paths of interaction on the bark.

Colburn's account does not say how the three men with ties to Christiantown responded when the *Hesper's* social world began to deteriorate in a class struggle between boatsteerers and mates, steerage against the cabin. The falling out began with an incident as one watch retired and the other took over. The second mate told the departing watch to "get the boom alongside," a task they considered unnecessary and not part of their duties. When that watch's two boatsteerers, Colburn and Joseph Grant, paused to think about what to do, the second mate hit Grant with his fist. The captain came on deck and with the mates' help tried to put Grant in the rigging to flog him, but a "general scuffle ensued" as "we, who lived in the steerage . . . engaged in keeping Joe from being flogged." The next day, the boatsteerers refused to go to breakfast "at the table of his majestic highness, the Captain of a blubber hunter." Their pride at the indignity put upon them lasted months and deprived them of "the good things we had been accustomed to having" by reducing them to the poor rations allotted foremast hands.[24] The resentment over who got to eat what still nagged at Colburn nearly fifteen years after the *Hesper* voyage ended, as he recalled the foods that came aboard in Hawai'i that "were not for us, but for the great commander and his cabin clique." The "sullen and morose" crew began ignoring whales from the masthead, choosing "to sacrifice their own interest pecuniarily, as a sort of revenge upon the cause of their miserable living."[25] In the forecastle, men huddled over a common bucket, the kid, spearing salted meat with their knives, while in the cabin, the captain, officers, and boatsteerers ate civilly, seated at a table and equipped with forks and spoons. And the cabin ate conspicuously better, with plenty of fresh meat, fresh bread, butter, sugar, raisins, puddings, and pies. The chickens and hogs that cluttered the deck awaiting slaughter and bound for the captain's table constantly reminded the rest of the crew of how well the cabin ate.[26]

While the distinctions in food were starkest as a two-tiered divide between cabin and forecastle, elaborate food rituals also signaled slighter gradations of power. Greenhand William Morris Davis gave an amusing account of dinner as a ritualized display of rank in his memoir *Nimrod of the Sea*. The steward would come onto the deck and tell the captain that "'dinner is on.'" The captain would leisurely pass by the compass to check on the course, then look up to study the sails, and just before heading down to dinner would inform the first mate that "'dinner is on.'" The first mate would then look at the compass, look up the sails, and descend.

> The two other mates go through precisely the same performance, only according to their respective ranks they take yet shorter peeps at the compass and glance heavenward. They then arrive simultaneously at the table, to find the captain and [mate] leisurely in their second plateful. Now, the misery of the arrangement is in this: the officers must come up in reversed order—third, second, first mate, and lastly the captain. A third mate has thus only about seven and a half moments to dispose of his grub. The old man last of all appears on deck, picking his satisfied teeth in the most tantalizing manner, and the four boat-steerers next make a dash for the table, and make clean sweep of the remnants.[27]

As in the whale hunt, these public performances broadcasted the privileges held by those at the highest ranks. That a man of color, as an officer, had special privileges could have fueled white foremast hands' resentment, but ship rules protected and legitimated the privileges of those in command, no matter their race.

: : :

The greatest privilege captains and officers held was their power over each crew member's most prized possession, his own body. In the name of just and necessary punishment, they hit men for disobeying orders, moving too slowly, sleeping during one's watch, talking back, and not talking back—that is, not acknowledging an order. To punish disobedience, they tied men to the rigging and flogged them, restrained men's feet and wrists "in irons," and confined them to the run (a small, dark storage room). Such inflictions on their persons led many foremast hands to suspect that whaling "masters" were akin to slave masters, but "master mariner" referred to mastery of a skill and the competency to train others in that skill. In the artisanal tradition, masters controlled the labor of journeymen and apprentices in return for feeding them sufficiently and paying them their due when their terms ended.[28] Some whaling captains took this to heart and ruled with beneficent paternalism. Others applied discipline so harsh it could cripple or kill. Their power could be checked only feebly and belatedly by U.S. consuls at foreign ports or by federal courts in Boston, New York, and, later in the century, San Francisco. To protect owners' property in distant locales, American law allowed captains extraordinary disciplinary leeway. When convicted for excessive discipline in courts of law, abusers usually paid a trifling fine and left again on another whaling voyage.[29] Over the nineteenth century, an accumulating moral outrage against corporal punishment of seamen led to some protective legislation but still allowed flogging on whaleships, so long as the rope was small and the flogger acted with reason, not passion.[30]

A systematic comparison of violent incidents by race is impossible because crews had such high turnover and information on new recruits, even their names, often went unrecorded. My sense from having read several hundred whaling logbooks and journals is that Native American whalemen stayed away from violence as much as they could. They only occasionally appear as victims or perpetrators. They rarely deserted. They hardly ever complained. However, as officers, they did have to enforce ship discipline, and even if any among them opposed corporal punishment, they had to exert it to survive in the industry.

Native whalemen did occasionally suffer abuse from tyrannical captains and in at least one instance—John P. Jourdain's 1862 assault charge brought against Captain Henry Pease—found vindication in the captain's conviction, brief jail sentence, and $500 fine.[31] Other brutalities fell within the law. Joseph Q. Mingo of Christiantown, while a sixteen-year-old greenhand on the *Lafayette*, received a dozen lashes for not obeying orders in 1841.[32] He embarked on several more voyages and retired at age twenty-eight, after a term as second mate on the *Osceola*.[33] A few other native whalemen were left behind in foreign ports for causing trouble. On the *Ann Alexander* in 1824, five of the crew protested a flogging. In the melee on deck, Charles DeGrass of Mashpee went after one of the officers with a scrub broom. Put in jail in Rio de Janeiro, DeGrass was probably released once the ship left port.[34] In a similar situation, Benjamin Uncas, Mohegan, and ten others were set ashore at Montevideo, Uruguay, for "mutinous conduct" sometime during the 1842–1844 voyage of the brig *Columbus* of New London.[35] On the *Rousseau* in 1839, Gay Head native Daniel Nevers drew a knife on a shipmate and, after scuffling with the mate to keep from being flogged, was put in irons for three weeks until discharged at Paita "for the benefit of all concerned as he is very saucy and quarrelsome."[36] His brother Absalom Nevers's "bad conduct" led to his discharge at Guam in 1851.[37] Logbooks rarely recorded the cause of a dispute. John A. Cole may have been naturally troublesome. On the *Cape Horn Pigeon* with several men from Gay Head in the crew, Cole was the only one fighting with officers and shipmates.[38] Violent flare-ups were par for the course on a whaling voyage, and incidents involving native whalemen read no differently, being distinguished only by their rarity and by my recognizing one of the parties as a native New Englander.

If natives did desert, seek out a discharge, or rise up in a revolt, they usually had just cause. The only major incident at sea in which Native Americans played a leading role as aggressors took place on the *Almira* of Edgartown in August 1869. Five Mashpee men were on board as boatsteerers and foremast hands: James F. Cowet, Frank Hicks, Frederick Jonas, Edmund A. Keeter, and James A. Oakley.[39] After stopping at the island of Flores to trade for provisions, the bark unsuccessfully cruised for sperm whales around the Azores until mid-October, when the captain demoted a boatsteerer for failing to harpoon a whale and sent him to live in the forecastle. The boatsteerer was apparently Cowet, called "James Ketle" in the logbook's scrawl. That night, foremast hands on deck during their watch armed themselves with pistols, tied and gagged the third mate and boatsteerer, stole one of the whaleboats, and deserted the ship. Four Mashpee men (all but Cowet), three Azoreans, three white Americans, and three black

Americans composed the party of mutineers, though "mutineer" may be too strong a word, since they used force only to desert the bark as quietly and quickly as possible.[40]

A day and a half later, the thirteen men arrived safely at the Island of Graciosa and reported their desertion to an Azorean serving as assistant to the U.S. consul at Fayal. One of the Azorean deserters, acting as interpreter, justified their actions as caused by "bad treatment received from said master and mate, not only by word and corporal punishment, but also by threats," and further complained that the bark was "a very old and unseaworthy vessel." The U.S. consul put them in Fayal's jail, which the consul described as "so frail that it won't hold American seamen—unless with their own consent." Two of the prisoners did escape with ease, and the Azorean authorities soon released all the Azorean seamen. The remaining eight, including the four Wampanoag men, were finally sent home in April to face charges in the U.S. federal courts in Boston.[41]

Two of the Mashpee seamen, Jonas and Hicks, served as witnesses at the hearing. Jonas testified that the captain "knocked and kicked the men and half starved them," the ship was "rotten and leaking," and the captain threatened him when he asked to go ashore at Flores. Hicks told of "personal abuse by Captain Marchant" and of how he had been "knocked down for some trivial cause by the first mate who threw a piece of wood at him." Their stories convinced those at the trade newspaper, *The Whalemen's Shipping List and Merchants' Transcript*, that "the men had some reason to leave the ship." In an unusual shift of loyalties away from owners and captains to sympathize with ordinary seamen, the newspaper called it an "Alleged Mutiny," which "showed that life on a whale ship was anything but pleasant." The testimonial coup de grâce was the claim that the third mate had consented to being gagged to help the men to desert.[42]

The third mate was halfway around the world at the time of the hearing, with the *Almira*. Captain Marchant had stopped at Fayal six months after the "Alleged Mutiny" and learned that his deserters were in jail, but he did not want them back. Anxious to resume his voyage, he refused even to leave witnesses behind.[43] Marchant must have known that his reputation could be slandered in his absence, however, for he continued to send back optimistic reports. One of his letters went so far as to praise the *Almira* as "a splendid ship in heavy weather. I like her very much. She will do everything but talk. The best working ship I was ever in."[44] But the deserters had it right, and while whaling in the Arctic that summer, the crew had to abandon the badly leaking bark.[45] Thus, the voyage ended abruptly for all involved, but with the thirteen deserters occupying the higher moral ground as sympathetic seamen who resorted to a modicum of violence after uncon-scionable treatment. The voyage's poorly maintained records obscure what happened to the lone Mashpee determined to ride out the voyage. Among the Mashpees who deserted, except for Frank Hicks, all appear to have for-saken whaling. Hicks went on one more voyage, though not until eight years later when, again with a large cohort of Mashpee men, he sailed on the *Perry* of Edgartown, owned and managed, like the *Almira*, by Samuel Osborn Jr., who must have been very forgetful, forgiving, or desperate for labor. Pro-moted during the voyage from a foremast hand with a lay of 1/150 to boat-steerer at 1/75, Hicks endured what was nearly as unpleasant a voyage as that on the *Almira* until discharged in Bermuda in August 1880, shortly before the *Perry* was shipwrecked in a hurricane.[46]

Coincidentally, the *Almira*'s captain, Cornelius Marchant, was the son of Barnard Marchant, who since 1853 had served as Indian guardian for Christiantown and Chappaquiddick. Cornelius grew up in a household that tribal members must have visited often to pick up their whaling earnings, lodge grievances against white neighbors, and ask for aid for the elderly and impoverished, reservation schools, and other needs. And he probably heard his father complain about Indians in the same way he wrote about them to state commissioner John Milton Earle, calling them "licentious," "ignorant & inconsiderate," and "selfish in the extreme, & this causes a great deal of trouble for their Guardian."[47] However, except for the *Almira* not having on board any native whalemen from the Vineyard, who may have known bet-ter than to sail under Marchant, race apparently had no role in the dispute. Court testimony and depositions make no mention of racial epithets or pre-judices, and the deserters united despite racial and cultural differences.

Because so many native men ranked as officers, they more often appear maintaining discipline in shipboard conflicts. Several voyages after Daniel Nevers was discharged for being "saucy and quarrelsome," he assisted third mate Thomas Cook, also from Gay Head, in preventing six men from de-serting the *John Coggeshall* in 1848.[48] John P. Vanderhoop, or "Mr. Vander-hoop" as the captain's wife referred to him throughout her journal, was third mate on the *A.R. Tucker* in the early 1870s when he and the other officers put in irons five foremast hands who complained of insufficient food and refused duty. A few months later, Vanderhoop called Captain Ricketson up on deck in the middle of the night because of "trouble with the men," one of whom threatened another with a cutting spade and acted "very saucy to the third mate."[49] Joseph G. Belain found himself in an even more difficult situ-ation as second mate on the *Palmetto* while at anchor off Jamestown, St. Helena, in 1873. Seven of the crew refused duty unless allowed liberty on shore. They then locked themselves in the forecastle. Over the next several days, the captain and officers tried smoking them out by setting a pot of peppercorns on fire. The men eventually came on deck, where they were put in irons, tied to a railing, and fed only bread and water. A compromise was reached, and the men went on liberty. But the next year, while again at St. Helena, all the foremast hands refused duty. This time, the U.S. Consul came aboard and punished the recalcitrant crew by again chaining them to the railing and allowing each "1 cake of Bread and one quart of Water" a day. Neither side gave up until after more than a week went by, when the men, angrier and more threatening than when the debacle began, were sent on shore and officially discharged. Shorthanded, the *Palmetto* sailed immediately to the Azores. With twelve new recruits, the *Palmetto* completed a trouble-free voyage.[50]

Native whalemen used customary measures to enforce discipline but were not zealots in meting out punishments. On the *Amazon* in 1857, Shinnecock first mate Milton Lee helped punish shipmates several times. The first incident was unusual in that it involved charging a third mate with disobeying the captain's orders and using "insolent language." One of officers' many privileges was immunity from corporal punishment, so the captain put the third mate off duty and wrote a long explanation of his misbehavior in the logbook, which Milton Lee obediently signed as witness. A few months later, Lee recorded in the logbook that they "seized Richard Holywood and James Walker up in rigging and gave them first 12 lashes and last 8 lashes as punishment for desertion and disobedieance of orders." Another deserter, seaman Robert Clensy, was put "in irons in the forehole" and later "seized up" and flogged as well. Perhaps it was these incidents or some other cause that made Lee discontented, for he took his discharge at the Marquesas in March 1858.[51] Milton's brother Ferdinand, while captain of the *Callao*, also relied on force to discipline but not to excess. Two years into the voyage, in 1873, the cook was put in irons for two hours "for disrespect to the capt." But as the voyage proceeded, all the violence aboard ship emanated from a first mate who shoved, hit, insulted, and threatened the foremast hands until, the day after one of these snarls, Lee discharged the mate "by mutual consent" because he "could not get along in the ship."[52] Lee did not oppose whaleship discipline in principle. On his previous voyage as first mate of the *Eliza Adams*, he recorded in the log one day, "Thomas Coring put in irons and hands tied above his head for using mutinous language and disobeying of orders," but the first mate under his own captaincy exacerbated Lee's problems with the crew.[53]

As officers, native whalemen do not seem to have been among those despised by shipmates for excess aggression, nor did foremast hands steeped in white supremacy from birth seem to balk at taking orders from an Indian. I have run across only one occasion when natives exercising shipboard discipline raised someone's ire because they were Indian. The account comes not from records produced from within the industry but from an editorial in a Barnstable, Massachusetts, newspaper. In 1832, a seaman named Matthias Smith sued Uriah Clark, first mate on the *Uncas*, for various abuses, one of which was Clark's having "ordered *a young Indian* to go and show Smith which the bunt-line was, and to give him the end of it; the Indian obeyed and struck him from 5 to 7 times with it." The *Barnstable Patriot*'s commentary on the court proceedings acknowledged that the $176 awarded Smith in damages was large but justifiable for "to order *an Indian* to apply the end of a rope, as Clark did at that time, is beyond endurance."[54]

Like the young, unnamed Indian on this voyage out of Falmouth, Massachusetts, other native whalemen heeded the command structure imposed by industry standards. When at the bottom of the hierarchy, they tolerated its steep authoritarianism perhaps because centuries of colonial disempowerment had lowered their expectations about just treatment. As officers, besides the better rates of pay, respect, and greater material comfort, they may also have derived self-esteem from this opportunity to exercise authority over other men. However, they refrained from exerting the full brute force government allowed them, perhaps because they lacked the arrogance of certitude that white men more accustomed to power could bring to a command position or because they may have sensed that men of color had to guard carefully the authority granted them by their rank just in case, at any moment, race usurped rank.

: : :

Ship agents who hired native men as officers and the white foremast hands who followed native officers' orders were not color blind. Instead, their racial practices were shaped by the industry's peculiar conditions: the need for skilled labor and the primacy of rank in regulating shipboard relations. What agents and white whalemen thought about Indians and what they thought about whalemen intersected at the Gay Head harpooner stereotype to allow the image of the Indian whale hunter to flourish, but other racial expectations about Indians rarely applied in the setting of the ship.

Tensions between the shipboard hierarchy of rank and American hierarchies of race must have generated volatile moments when racism challenged rank, but the few white men who remarked on what it was like to serve under Native American officers had only good things to say about them. Colburn's praise of Henry James on the *Hesper*—that "it was my good fortune, Indian though he was, to be in his watch"—matches how white Connecticut whaleman Mortimer Camp felt, recalling in his memoir of a voyage on the *Flora* from 1843 to 1845 that "our third mate was a Mohegan from near New London, Ct., and a good fellow." This third mate rescued him from being shanghaied by an American merchant captain at Hawai'i, who drugged him and stowed him away. Suspecting something was amiss, the third mate searched the vessel, found the dazed foremast hand hidden in a chest, and brought him back to the *Flora*.[55] In another white-authored memoir of a voyage later in the century, Ellsworth Luce West of Martha's Vineyard said of first mate William H. Cook, whom he served under on the *William Lewis* in 1888, "He was a Gay Head Indian, and I never saw any man who knew how to handle a crew as well as he did. He was quiet and never shouted when issuing orders and the men were all devoted to him and jumped when spoken to."[56] Racial prejudice may have been Amos Haskins's undoing, however. The *Massasoit*'s crew in 1851 was almost entirely white. They deserted at every opportunity. Did he think race was behind his crew troubles? The only clue to that possibility is that, when he next took the *Massasoit* to sea, men of color had more than doubled to become a majority, and he had as first and second mates George and William Belain, Wampanoags from Martha's Vineyard.[57] Because illness cut this voyage short, we cannot know whether the change in composition secured him a more loyal crew. Ferdinand Lee also lost most of his men to desertion and discharge in the four years the *Callao* was at sea, but whether this had anything to do with racial tensions over his command is indiscernible in the logbook.[58]

Other sources for assessing how Indian officers were perceived are evaluations whaling companies maintained as a reference for future hiring. Based on feedback from captains, ship agents gave officers two grades, one for whaling abilities and the other for "officership." An "A1" whaleman excelled at raising and killing whales. An "A1" officer was able to lead the crew. Some were commended for both skills equally. Shinnecock David W. Bunn, returning to New Bedford on the *Lagoda* in 1864, was a "Good" whaleman and a "Good" officer. More commonly, however, native officers received more praise as whalemen. Arriving back to New Bedford in 1860 on the *Christopher Mitchell*, first mate Milton Lee was considered a "Good A1" whaleman and a "Good" officer. Shinnecock Orlando Eleazer, boatsteerer on the *Young Phenix*, 1860–1863, was recommended for third mate because he was a

"Good" whaleman and a "Fair" officer. The tendency to view native officers as better at pursuing whales than managing men may have been a bias-free determination or more likely an example of how captains' and agents' expectations of native men's capacities informed their opinions. A few of these evaluations added a notation identifying individuals by race. Joel G. Jared, second mate on the *Anaconda* from 1856 to 1860, may have been regarded by Massachusetts as an Indian of Gay Head, but someone had written "Nigger" under officership in his case. He was a "Good" whaleman and a "Fair" officer, but they did not recommend him for a position beyond second mate.[59]

Given the range of negative ideas about Indians prevailing in nineteenth-century New England culture (see chapter 10), native whalemen faced surprisingly few stereotypes on whaleships beyond their alleged superior whalemanship. One whaling captain came close to adding more content to what he thought "Indians" were in a comment about Levi Webquish of Mashpee, but what stands out in this episode is Webquish's shared ambition with the ship's officers to realize a successful voyage. In late 1863, the captain of the *Mount Wollaston* and all its officers except Webquish, who was third mate, wrote letters to the ship's agents, Wood & Nye of New Bedford. They had just returned to Honolulu with no oil after a season on the Okhotsk Sea, and in an unusual sweep of the cabin, all the officers asked for and received their discharges. The captain had been too cautious, first mate Charles Bailey complained, and refused to lower whaleboats in the fog. The only time they did lower, it was third mate Webquish's boat that came closest to a whale. Webquish "told his Boatsteerer to dart but the scamp could not which made Mr Webquish rather mad & he wanted the capt to take him out of the Boat but the capt would not the consequence was it made disagreeable feelings all around." That the captain did not heed Webquish's request to remove his boatsteerer was, in Bailey's mind, one of many mistakes the captain made. In his letter, the captain tried to put the blame on his officers, who were all "a set of villains." One acted spiritless, "like a dead man," and another had shipped only to get away from his wife, whom he had deserted and left "destitute." The worst he could come up with to say about Webquish was that he was "an Indian with an Indian disposition, [and] never was in a ship that made a good voyage."[60] What exactly characterized an "Indian disposition" the captain did not say.

Especially surprising for its absence on the ship was the drunken Indian stereotype, so pervasive in depictions of Indians in New England culture. Mortimer Camp's affection and respect for the Mohegan third mate on the *Flora* contrasts with his childhood memories of "old Jim So Buck, an old chief of the Mohegian Indians that used to roam about the country begging cider" and who became "ugly" when drunk. Parents used to scare children into good behavior by telling them that "Jim So Buck will be after you."[61] In contrast, Indians on whaleships did not seem to drink much, or for those who did drink to excess at times, their reputations as fine whalemen survived unscathed.

In antebellum American culture, reform literature presented drinking as a universal weakness of sailors as a class, but stories about the dangers that drinking presented to competence and self-control tended to feature white protagonists as the sailors at risk.[62] It is as though whites had priority, or ownership, over sailor imagery. Both Colburn's and Delano's whaling memoirs were confessional temperance tracts written by as yet unredeemed alcoholics. Their narratives have the same plot. As naive youths from moral families, they were driven to dissipation by uncontrollable urges, the bad company of other sailors, and the temptations posed by a life at sea. Colburn was not the only white man with a drinking problem on the *Hesper*. While the Indian third mate Henry James was the best whaleman on the ship and a Christian, the *Hesper*'s captain was "moderately fond of his glass, and the second in command was a consummate drunkard."[63] One of Delano's stories, intended to expose the evils of drink, tells how, when the voyage on the *Sophia* ended and as the crew were all waiting for the final settlement from the owners, he learned of the death of the ship's third mate. Delano went to a "boarding house to witness his remains, and there stretched in death in the prime of life, I beheld the ghastly features of our third officer." According to the landlady, the deceased had eaten little but drunk two quarts of liquor a day since the *Sophia*'s return. This man was Lilley Page. In telling of Page's death from drink, Delano did not give the third mate's name nor did he call Page "the Indian" as he did when they were chasing whales. Delano obscured Page's race so that he could claim kinship with "our third officer" and "our third mate," who Delano implied should have been capable of a better fate.[64] Narratives about drunken Indians aimed to support a domestic racial hierarchy of white superiority. To cast an Indian as the dissipated sailor in need of reformation would have muddled the two genres, lessening the impact of the morality tale on its target audience, white sailors.

Native whalemen's drinking occasionally comes up in whaling agents' evaluative comments but is not represented as a trait peculiar to Indians, nor was it viewed as a problem. In the late nineteenth century, the New Bedford firm Aiken & Swift recorded only one native who drank among the two dozen or so who received evaluations in this volume: Abram F. Cooper of Gay Head. When the *Hercules* returned to New Bedford in 1882, the captain told the ship's agent that Cooper was a "good man—good officer good whaleman—drinks in port—fair Masthead would make a good mate would take him." After a voyage on the *Swallow* in 1883–1887, Cooper was reported to be a "good whaleman drinks too much rum." And in 1889, upon his return from a voyage on the *Jacob A. Howland* with the same captain and at a higher rank, that of second mate, Cooper was a "Good man—Drinks—Make mate—A.1 second mate."[65] Cooper merited favorable ratings and promotions despite his drinking.

William H. Cook also drank to excess. Although highly respected by the men under his command, Cook did have one problem according to second mate West: "he always came on board drunk." Cook asked West to keep his bottle, giving out "just enough to help him taper off. Within a week he was fine and never touched a drop the rest of the voyage."[66] Aiken & Swift's evaluations of Cook as first mate never mention his drinking, at least not explicitly. After the 1877–1880 voyage of the *Reindeer*, they described him as an "A1 whaleman, as good as can be, can catch a sp[erm] whale with any man living—no officer—not a reliable man in port—very good eye—raised whales 6 times." In another instance, Cook was an "A2 mate A1 whaleman good officer and trusty at sea"—thus by implication not so trusty on land.[67] Drinking to excess in port did not prevent Cook from finding work as first mate, nor did the agent think it necessary to cite his drinking as hazardous. Whatever drinking native men did, agents and shipmates did not cast it as so excessive to hinder the success of the voyage.

Emphasizing rank over race as the preeminent social hierarchy aboard ship was an economic strategy to further the business of whaling—to produce wealth for a small mercantile class and a modest living for those who went to sea. Native whalemen committed themselves to succeed, and their skills, diligence, and endurance of even the harshest conditions made them valuable employees. The racial typecasting of Indian whalemen as harpooning hunters with superhuman eyesight misled peers to think that was the sole value they brought to the whaling enterprise. By attributing native whalemen's achievements to natural abilities (keen eyesight, athletic agility, ruthless instincts, and an intuitive understanding of the movements and intentions of their prey), the stereotype reinforced the suspicion that native men lacked intellectual acumen in navigation, ship and crew management, financial accounting, and the diplomacy necessary to maneuver in foreign ports, skills one needed to demonstrate to advance into captaincies. However, the stereotype helped native men by positioning them in line to become officers. And once they attained officer positions, social codes aboard ship dictated that they be treated with respect. Rank was so crucial, there was no room for race to operate simultaneously as an alternative, competing social hierarchy.

Treated with patronizing condescension as incompetents at home in New England, native men held positions of authority and respect at sea as officers entrusted with property worth many thousands of dollars and the safety of the crew. Whaling investors needed their expertise and commitment to make profitable voyages, but the value placed on their whaling capabilities in this niche economy made no dent on the perception of what an Indian was supposed to be like outside of the context of the ship.

PART II : THE BEACH

4 : Cultural Encounters

Standing on the decks of their whaleships, gazing on the verdant volcanic peaks, coral reefs, and sandy bays of a Pacific island, many Americans had in their heads a narrative that borrowed its content from the distant past, when Christopher Columbus, Samuel de Champlain, and John Smith encountered "Indians" on a beach and opened up the Americas to European settlement. This cultural encounter narrative gave white American seafarers a way to interpret their experiences with other peoples around the world. (Native American whalemen's perspectives on their travels appear in chapter 6.) They saw themselves, the ship, and whaling enterprises generally as manifestations of European and Euro-American intellectual and technological superiority: they were clothed, civilized, Christian, and white. They depicted the people they encountered on the beach—called variously Indians, natives, and Kanakas—as primitive, exotic, naked, heathen (or newly missionized naive Christians), savage, and dark skinned. The cultural encounter narrative as a way of seeing had an ideological utility, which gave it an endurance despite its inherent illogic arising from the simultaneous presence of "Indians" on both sides of the beach. Although the obvious diversity of whaling crews should have been enough to expose the cracks in tales of white exploration and conquest, nineteenth-century whaling literature did not confront the ambiguity of the category "Indian" head-on. One consequence is that such representations made invisible the labor of colonized people in imperial expansion. That Indians were both on shore and on the ship confounded the racial category "Indian" with unacknowledged complexity and unresolved contradictions.

For example, the ship *Globe* of Nantucket had "Indians" on the ship and a cultural encounter with "Indians" on shore, after the notorious mutiny led by boatsteerer Samuel Comstock in 1824. One of these Indians was Mashpee Wampanoag Anthony Hinson (sometimes spelled "Hanson" or "Henson"). Ironically, Mashpee Indians had been called "South Sea Indians" during the first century of European contact because of their proximity to the stretch of water known today as Nantucket Sound. No longer in use as a name for the Mashpee in Hinson's time, "South Sea Indian" in nineteenth-century New England meant a Pacific Islander.[1]

Hinson joined the *Globe* in Honolulu. He had arrived at the Hawaiian Islands on the Nantucket whaleship *Sally*, whose captain reported that Hinson deserted there in October 1822.[2] More than a year later, in December 1823, the *Globe* engaged Hinson and six other men to take the place of its deserters. Hinson shipped as cook.[3] Within a month, most of these new recruits helped Comstock slaughter the captain and the ship's three officers, after which Comstock assumed command and steered the ship to an island in the Mulgraves (Mili Atoll, Marshall Islands), where he planned to ditch the ship and take up residence. There, the mutineers turned against each other, and then the native residents turned against the mutineers and others of the crew, killing all but two, William Lay and Cyrus Hussey. Before the massacre of the crew occurred, another boatsteerer, Gilbert Smith, stole the *Globe* away one night, with only five other men aboard, one of whom was Hinson. On a journey that took nearly four months, these six men sailed the ship across the breadth of the Pacific Ocean hoping that, if they just kept heading east, they would eventually come to the coast of South America, which they did. Landing at the port of Valparaiso, Chile, in June 1824, they presented themselves to U.S. consul Michael Hogan and told their story. Hogan collected statements from each man. Hinson's short testimony sufficiently convinced Hogan that Hinson had not aided the mutineers except, like others of the crew, in following orders after they took over the ship.

Meanwhile, back at the Mulgraves, the U.S. schooner *Dolphin* made a long and thorough search for the rest of the *Globe*'s crew, eventually finding Lay, "dressed and looking like a native," behind whom several hundred natives had gathered on the beach. As Navy lieutenant Hiram Paulding tried to pull him away, Lay panicked. Babbling in a mix of languages, he finally said something Paulding understood: "'The Indians are going to kill you; don't come on shore unless you are prepared to fight.'"[4] Paulding grabbed Lay and retreated. They made their way to another island to retrieve Hussey. Advertising themselves truthfully as "The only Survivors from the Massacre of the Ship's Company by the Natives," Lay and Hussey published an account of the mutiny and their "Residence of Two Years on the Mulgrave Islands; with Observations on the Manners and Customs of the Inhabitants." In the tradition of captivity narratives such as that of Mary Rowlandson, taken captive by New England Indians during King Philip's War 150 years earlier, Lay and Hussey recounted the anxieties and physical strains they endured as servants to "savage masters" and interspersed their account with an ethnography of the exotic. Forced to wear native "dress, if it may be so called," their white skin, which they claimed greatly fascinated the natives, became painfully sunburned. Their hair grew long. They subsisted on coconuts and fish. They learned the native language. Acknowledging that the mutineers had been "more savage" than the islanders, they understood their situation as a contest between civilization and savagery. Using "savages," "natives," and "Indians" interchangeably and without distinction in meaning or context, they described to the American reading public what it was like to live among "untutored children of nature," "strangers to the endearing ties which bind the hearts of civilized men."[5]

These images of the savage Indians of the Pacific promulgated in the published account of Lay and Hussey, and a few years later in Paulding's memoir, contrast with the picture we can recreate of Wampanoag Anthony Hinson, sitting before U.S. consul Hogan at Valparaiso, English-speaking, literate (he signed his deposition), and presumably dressed much like other American sailors in a cotton shirt, duck trousers, and shoes. Hinson was not exactly a child of nature but competent and worldly. He and five other men had just traversed an ocean studded with perilous coral reefs in a vessel normally equipped with four times as many men aboard.

On its surface, the Lay and Hussey narrative of cultural encounter and captivity assumed a clean dichotomy separating Indians on the beach from whites on the ship, but putting side by side their account with the rest of the extensive documentation on the *Globe*'s ordeal suggests a much messier collision of racial suppositions. Three kinds of Indians met at Mili Atoll: the New England native Anthony Hinson; a Hawaiian native shipped as a whaling laborer at Oahu along with Hinson; and the Mulgraves Islanders who killed most of the crew and held Lay and Hussey captive. At the time of the mutiny, the crew also included African American William Humphries, who joined the *Globe* at Oahu and with the other new recruits—Silas Payne, John Oliver, Thomas Lilliston, and possibly Joseph Thomas—helped Comstock, an original member of the crew, take over the ship.

Because so many of the seven "abandoned wretches" shipped at Oahu became mutineers, witnesses to the mutiny often felt compelled to list all those who joined the vessel at that time. For no apparent reason, those naming the men shipped at Oahu often forgot to mention Joseph Thomas, who was later suspected as an accessory to the mutiny, and so the lists vary by giving either six or seven names, but here they are:

Lay and Hussey memoir: "Silas Payne, John Oliver, Anthony Hanson, a native of Oahu, Wm. Humphries, a black man, and steward, and Thomas Liliston."[6]

Gilbert Smith deposition: "John Oliver of Sheilds, England, Silas
   Payne of Rhode Island, Thomas Lilliston Virginia, William
   Humphreys Stewart a Black of Philadelphia, Joseph Thomas
   connecticut, Anthony Hanson of Barnstable Massachusetts &
   the Native."[7]
George Comstock memoir: "Silas Paine, John Oliver, Thomas
   Linneston, Anthony Hanson an indian, and a Woahoo Indian,
   William Humphrey a bla[ck] stewart."[8]

All three identified Humphries as black and the steward. Given these
white crew members' fixation on Humphries's race and rank, it comes as a
bit of a surprise to find him among the mutineers—that, in this instance,
black and white joined in the conspiracy to take the ship. Racial distinctions may have been reasserted later as an explanation for why Humphries
was the first mutineer to die. When he was caught loading pistols—he said
because he feared that Smith and others planned to retake the ship—Samuel
Comstock, in what seems a fit of paranoia, ordered Humphries tried and,
once convicted, hung by the neck until dead. An 1840 biography of Samuel
Comstock by his brother William attributed "the Execution of Humphries"
to Samuel Comstock's "strong dislike to colored persons" and depicted a racialized caricature of Humphries with black skin, wooly hair, white eyes,
and thick lips, with a noose around his neck, his arms raised up as if
begging for his life (figure 6).[9]

Even though Hinson was cook, a position like steward often held by
blacks, no one in listing thought it necessary to say what position Hinson
had held aboard ship. And only one of the three accounts assigned Hinson
to a racial category. George Comstock, who had watched in horror as his
older brother Samuel headed below to commit these cruel murders and who
later escaped to Valparaiso on the *Globe*, called Hinson "an Indian." Consul Hogan also made no mention of Hinson's race, the deposition referring
to him only as "Anthony Hanson of Falmouth, Massachusetts." That only
George Comstock identified Hinson as Indian suggests that he was not making a snap judgment based on quick acquaintance as he must have done with
the "Woahoo Indian." He recognized Hinson as an Indian after months of
close association on the *Globe*. He had known Hinson for the month before
the mutiny occurred followed by an additional four months in the miracu-
lous feat of sailing the *Globe* eastward with only six men aboard. Surely it
was Hinson whom George Comstock meant when he said, "the part of the
crew shipped in Woahoo were *except one* a rough set of cruel beings which
were neither fit to die or live" (my italics).[10]

THE EXECUTION OF HUMPHRIES.

Figure 6. *The execution of William Humphries aboard the* Globe *in 1824, as depicted in William Comstock's 1840 biography of his mutineer brother Samuel. Not on the* Globe *during the mutiny, William (or his publisher) did not strive for historical accuracy since Lay and Hussey* (A Narrative of the Mutiny, *p. 36) remembered that Humphries had a "cap drawn over his face" before Samuel Comstock ordered all among the crew to put their hands to the rope and hang him. William Comstock,* The Life of Samuel Comstock, The Terrible Whaleman *(1840), opposite p. 91. Courtesy of American Antiquarian Society.*

As is typical in whaling accounts, all three lists slighted the Hawaiian foremast hand who was among those killed by Mulgraves Islanders in the massacre of the crew. They did not name him and referred to him thus not as an individual but as a type: the "native of Oahu," "the Native," and "a Woahoo Indian." Smith later gave Hogan a fuller account of him as "the Sandwich Island Native called Joseph Brown," a name clearly not his own but a more easily pronounced name for English speakers, likely given to him by the *Globe*'s captain when he shipped at Honolulu.[11]

Race was an integral aspect of the mutiny, starkly visible in the case of black and white but murkier when it came to identifying Indians, constituting all at once the Mulgrave Islanders, a native Hawaiian foremast hand aboard the ship, and an experienced seaman native to Cape Cod. None of the *Globe*'s crew who left accounts of the voyage, or whaling records more generally, explained or wondered at why three men from such different parts of the world all deserved to be called Indians or natives. Nor do we know what Hinson, "Joseph Brown," and the residents of Mili Atoll thought about these designations or whether they puzzled over how and why they all qualified as "Indians" and "natives" without any apparent historic or cultural affinity linking them as related peoples. Indeed, of the three, Hinson seemed least recognizable to his American shipmates as an "Indian," presumably because he least met their expectations about what an Indian was.

: : :

History did tie these three men together but not their own histories. Long before the *Globe* landed at Mili Atoll, European explorers, cartographers, naturalists, and philosophes had imagined vast stretches of the world inhabited by savage Indians. The distinction between landmasses and oceans that divides historians today into regional specializations should not be imposed retrospectively on earlier centuries, for the Wampanoag and Narragansett people of New England before the twentieth century had no more in common with the Hopi and Navajo of the American Southwest than with Hawaiians, Fijians, or Gilbert Islanders. What made all these people Indians and natives was European and Euro-American perceptions of them as the culturally backward inhabitants of new "discoveries" made in the name of commerce and science.

When Samuel Wallis landed at Tahiti in 1767, followed by Louis-Antoine de Bougainville a year later and James Cook the year after that, they all saw Indians—or in the case of the French, *sauvages*—on the beach.[12] Wallis's Indians caused him innumerable problems, swarming around his ship in their canoes brandishing "clubs and paddles," the women tempting the crew with "wanton gestures."[13] Violence, fear, and desire intermingled as the stuff of epic poetry for the barber on Wallis's expedition who on the journey home composed a saga of their adventures, which Wallis recorded in his log. A stanza recounting their time at Tahiti reads,

> The Swarthy Indians round us flock
> With each a pittance from their Stock
> Which they for various trifles truck
> Content with what we spare
> Oft on our Ship they fix their Eyes
> As oft on us with Deep Surprize
> And deem our Floating world a prize
> For them next Morn to share.[14]

In the prose version of Wallis's voyage, transposed into print by John Hawkesworth, Tahitians are sometimes "Indians," sometimes "natives." In his voyage writings, James Cook used "native" most of the time but occasionally picked "Indian": "a naked Indian frighten'd of f[i]rearms as they are," "our Indian guides," and "a wonderfull peice [*sic*] of Indian Architecture."[15] "Indian" is incidental, adding variety to the text with little impact on meaning; he could just as easily have written "native" in these instances.

Experience made no difference in perception. Bougainville had credentials in both the Pacific and the North American continent. In 1756, at the start of the Seven Years' War, he had watched *sauvages* in Canada dance like Greeks, a "strange spectacle," he wrote, "interesting to a philosophe desirous of studying human nature, especially in its most primitive state."[16] Eleven years later, at Tahiti, "A crowd of Indians welcomed us on the shore with the most emphatic demonstrations of happiness. Not one carried any arms, not even sticks. The chief of this settlement led us to his home where we all sat down on the ground, they brought fruit, water and dried fish and we had a golden age meal with people who are still living in that happy time."[17] Whether in Canada or in Tahiti, Bougainville saw what he wanted, or expected, to see.

John Ledyard, an American member of the crew on Cook's third and final voyage into the Pacific, had even closer connections to Native Americans. Born in Groton, Connecticut, home to the native survivors of the 1637 Pequot War, Ledyard's family had had New England natives as near neighbors for over a century. Pequot lands even fell within the part of Groton that would later become the town of Ledyard.[18] As a child, Ledyard may not have known many native people personally since his parents moved to Hartford, Connecticut, where he grew up. However, when he came of age, Ledyard attended college at an institution with Indian associations, Dartmouth, which had been recently established by Eleazar Wheelock under the pretense that it would be an Indian school and serve Indian students. Wheelock had educated many New England natives, most famously the Mohegan minister Samson Occom. Occom helped Wheelock raise funds to establish Dartmouth only to be disappointed when Wheelock redesigned Dartmouth as a college for white students.[19] Ledyard probably knew natives within Wheelock's circle of acquaintances, and certainly he would have had at least heard of Samson Occom.

However, Ledyard was a romantic, and the literate, Christian natives close to home lacked the allure of more distant Indians. Modeling his earliest adventures on primitivist fantasies, Ledyard left Dartmouth at one point to seek out Indians further to the west and north, the Mohawks or the Abenakis, and later he left Dartmouth again, this time mimicking Indians by making a dramatic departure in a dugout canoe.[20] Ledyard found more Indians later in life, in the Pacific, and recorded in his journal his secondhand version of Captain Cook's death as heard from others of the crew who had witnessed it—how a crowd of "Indians" at Kealakekua Bay, Hawai'i, knocked Cook down with stones, stabbed him to death, cut his body into pieces, and ate him.[21] By treating "native" and "Indian" as synonyms, Ledyard and others among his contemporaries who came to the Pacific by ship revealed that they thought of themselves as simply carrying on the journey that had taken their predecessors across the Atlantic Ocean and into the North American interior.

Those who had lived through the cultural encounter as explorers, missionaries, beachcombers, traders, and ordinary seamen acquired a unique and essential authority as sources of information on native bodily adornment, religious practices, governance, technology, and material culture upon which larger claims about human difference rested. However, much of the knowledge these Pacific travelers produced was difficult to synthesize. Sometimes Pacific natives had complexions like "Negroes" but hair like American Indians. Others were copper-colored like Indians but had the curly hair of mulattoes. Some were born white and turned tawny by the sun. The novelty of new peoples led to tangled thickets of description and rampant speculation about origins, migrations, and the relationship between nature and culture.[22] Despite physical and cultural variety, the peoples encountered in these new worlds seemed to share certain characteristics. They ornamented their nudity with tattoos or paint, lived in huts, flocked to ships eager to trade all they had for a scrap of metal, and acted in bizarre, unreadable, and usually sexually promiscuous ways. They were childlike, innocent, naive, and generous but in the blink of an eye could turn into horrifically savage, bloodthirsty cannibals. Both Native Americans and Pacific natives provided the raw data from which European enlightenment thinkers and their Euro-American descendants devised their noble and brutal savage prototypes.[23]

Melding American and Pacific Indians into a single category distinct from peoples of European descent linked a dichotomy between primitive and civilized to another dichotomy, native and foreign. Granting to the world's supposed primitives the word "native" would ultimately create an awkward situation for the native-born white settlers in the Americas or the Pacific, who could not then comfortably claim "native" for themselves. However, the earliest waves of Europeans in the Pacific depended on this association between native and primitive to subordinate their status as foreign invaders of native space to a more pressing and, to their eyes, obvious hierarchy that would allow civilization precedence over savagery.

Eventually, the racial discourses of European–Pacific encounters concluded that Indians belonged to the Americas—and to India, of course—

but nowhere else, while two distinct categorizing schemes designed especially for the Pacific gradually developed: a scientific language and a popular vernacular used by seamen. Europeans who dabbled in scientific enlightenment and advocated Pacific colonization would come to divide the region into three areas—Polynesia, Micronesia, and Melanesia—with bodily difference the crucial distinction. "Polynesia" emerged first, when in 1756 the Frenchman Charles de Brosses invented *Polynésie*, from the Greek for "many islands." "Polynesia" then spread throughout the English-speaking world, propelled into wider scientific usage with English missionary William Ellis's popular ethnography, published in a series of enlarged editions and for the first time under the title *Polynesian Researches* in 1829.[24] In 1832, French explorer Jules-Sébastien-César Dumont D'Urville's essay "Sur les îles du Grand Océan" further specified "Polynesia" by refining the mishmash of travel commentary to distinguish three Pacific regions, inhabited by those who were light skinned and lovable (Polynesia), the dark-skinned cannibals of Fiji and the western Pacific (Melanesia), and the ambiguous people to the north and in between (Micronesia). His was an elegant, simple, and effective deployment of a categorizing scheme that positioned the light-skinned peoples of the world at civilization's apex.[25] Embarrassed by the racist origins of the tripartite Pacific model and annoyed with its assertion of pronounced differences, scholars are now retreating from it to embrace a more expansive and inclusive "Oceania."[26]

The scientific racism behind the invention of Polynesia, Melanesia, and Micronesia did not trickle down to ordinary sailors, such as American whalemen, who most often categorized all Pacific Islanders using the Hawaiian words for man and woman, *kanaka* and *wahine*. Missionary Lorrin Andrews, author of the first Hawaiian–English dictionary, translated "ka-na-ka" as "To be or dwell as men," "To act the man," "to act courageously or firmly," "To observe rectitude of conduct," to be "not a fool," "not silly." He defined "wa-hi-ne" as "A female in distinction from kane, male."[27] American whalemen probably did not understand the premise of respect lying behind the word "kanaka" but used it indiscriminately when referring to newly recruited foremast hands sharing quarters in the ship's forecastle and natives observed alongshore and throughout the Pacific, not just for those who spoke Polynesian languages.

These categorizing terminologies that eventually distinguished Pacific Islanders from Native Americans—the scientific terms used by elites and the pidgin Hawaiian terms used by whalemen—became popularized slowly. At the start of the nineteenth century, it was easy for Europeans and Euro-Americans to lump Pacific Islanders and North American Indians together as primitive peoples "discovered" in the course of European expansion because they rarely interacted on the same stage. However, Europeans' figurative linking of peoples from around the globe into fellowship occasionally did bring individual Native Americans and Pacific Islanders into the same orbit.

One such meeting place was the royal court and salon circuit afforded Indians who visited Europe, where they served as cultural informants, designated or presumptive ambassadors for their people, and public curiosities. The most infamous of these distant visitors to England in the eighteenth century were the "Four Iroquois Kings" of 1710; several Cherokee delegations; Samson Occom, who came to Britain in 1766 to help raise funds for Wheelock's Indian school; and a party of Inuit who left England for home in 1773, missing by a year the return of Captain James Cook's second Pacific expedition and the arrival of Britain's most celebrated Noble Savage, Omai, who hailed from Raiatea in the Society Islands. From different parts of the world, speaking different languages and inhabiting wholly different cultures, all found themselves positioned as objects of European fascination and fantasy.[28]

A more coordinated and ambitious project that created similitude where there was none to begin with was the Foreign Mission School at Cornwall, Connecticut, founded in 1817 by the recently established American Board of Commissioners for Foreign Missions (ABCFM). Inspired by their acquaintance with Henry Opūkahaʻia and other Hawaiians whom China traders and whalers had brought to New England as cabin boys and sailors, the American Board collected these young men at a school in rural western Connecticut. Shortly after the Foreign Mission School at Cornwall opened, Opūkahaʻia succumbed to typhus fever, departing with an *"Alloah oʻe'—*My love be with you" to the other Hawaiian students crying at his bedside.[29] Thomas Patoo arrived at the school in nearly the same way and met with a similar fate. He had left the Marquesas in 1818 at age fourteen on a foreign ship and, while employed on whalers, sealers, and China traders, traveled to Hawaiʻi, Canton, the South Shetlands, and Boston, where aspiring missionaries made a church project of him. Three months after Patoo's arrival at the Foreign Mission School in March 1823, he fell ill and died.[30] In the Cornwall school's first decade, its twenty to thirty students in residence at a time comprised Pacific Islanders from Hawaiʻi, the Marquesas, Tahiti, and New Zealand; a few young men from India, China, and Greece; Native Americans from the greater Northeast and Canada, including one Narragansett from New England but mostly Cherokee and Choctaw natives from the American Southeast; and white New Englanders preparing to enter foreign mission work. Particularly active ABCFM missions in Hawaiʻi and the Cherokee Nation helped make these two peoples the largest constituencies represented among the students attending the Cornwall school.[31]

The school closed soon after two Cherokees, John Ridge and Elias Boudinot, married local white women, sparking a riot and raising the specter of hypocrisy in the ABCFM's premise of a race-blind equality made possible through civilization and Christianity.[32] A commemorative history of the American Board gave other reasons for the school's 1827 closure: "enthusiasm had begun to lag, and serious difficulties appeared in managing a company so mixed as to race, so unlike in training and capacity."[33] Indeed, the students do seem to have retained loyalties foremost to their own ethnic groups, so that while in New England, Hawaiians formed friendships with Hawaiians, Chinese with Chinese, and Cherokees with Cherokees.[34] The ABCFM's interest in foreign missions continued, each designed specifically for the Cherokees or the Dakotas, Hawaiʻi, or, later in the century, the Caroline Islands. The ABCFM did not create missions for New England Indians, even though that is where its headquarters and original members were located. The sites of ABCFM missions indicate that the American Board located the "foreign" on the edges of U.S. territorial expansion and, like Ledyard, had little interest in New England's native peoples.

When brought into the same circles of acquaintance through diplomacy or missionary activity, the indigenous peoples of the Americas and Pacific did not recognize commonality, nor did they fall into the same category in the place where they saw each other most often and most intimately, as shipmates and in cultural encounters on a beach. Despite the entrenched predisposition in American culture to imagine a clear divide between civilized whites and savage natives, both sides of the beach—Pacific islands and foreign ships—were much more ethnically complicated settings than the standard cultural encounter narrative could accommodate.

: : :

White American seamen on the hunt for whales were steeped in the romance of the cultural encounter narrative and knew their role. Like Columbus and his successors, they casually drew on a familiar vocabulary to label the people they saw as "Indians," layering on another few centuries of contact experiences to describe a world in which these Pacific Ocean Indians paddled "canoes," lived in "wigwams," wielded "tomahawks," and had "squaws" for wives.[35] As his vessel came to anchor at Tahiti in 1842, white greenhand William Allen White mused in his journal, "What a curious sight was it for an American! The ship surrounded by canoes filled with half naked indians."[36] "Canoe" was a Native American word picked up by European explorers and conquerors in the sixteenth-century Caribbean, while "wigwam," "tomahawk," and "squaw" all had origins in the Algonquian languages the English had heard on the beaches of seventeenth-century New England and Virginia.[37] American English incorporated these words, with their North American Indian associations, and carried them westward into the Great Lakes and across the Great Plains, around Cape Horn and the Cape of Good Hope into the Pacific, Indian, and Arctic Oceans.

Reenacting cultural encounters in different parts of the world was a stock feature of the profuse literature that formed a by-product of the American whaling industry. Written largely by ordinary seamen, sometimes with the help of an amanuensis, whaling Americana flourished in the antebellum period, as did maritime travel literature more generally. Exemplified by Herman Melville's *Typee* of 1846, hundreds of published memoirs recalled a life at sea or a single voyage, the most aspirational of which went beyond replicating the sparse style of the logbook to meditate on sublime scenery and engage in ethnographic observation. In most of these texts, the authors positioned themselves as white Americans encountering darker, exotic, and savage people met far from home.

To make sense of Pacific peoples, this seafaring literature employed a scant and erroneous knowledge of North American Indians to draw comparisons. Sometimes analogies compared physiology: Fijians were "very near to the Negroes" in complexion, one seaman wrote, but "like other Indians are very straight and well built"; another described a woman on an island near Bali as having a complexion "about as dark as that of our Indian squaws"; while another observed at Palau that the natives' hair, "naturally coarse and black, like that of the Indians of America, was very long, and hung loosely over their shoulders, giving them a singular and frightful appearance."[38]

More commonly, Pacific peoples seemed to be like Native Americans in their cultural practices. There was the innocent and childlike native, whose "gestures, songs, and dances very much resemble those of the North American Indians."[39] There were "the Polynesian savages" for whom sperm whale teeth were "as important a treaty article as wampum among our Indians."[40] There was the degraded native, such as the Australian Aborigines, who like "our aborigenes (the North American Indians)" had "the same love of rum and tobacco, and a mean habit of pilfering," or the Maori of New Zealand, who were "a lazy drunken race resembling much in that respect the North American Indians."[41] Finally, there were the fearsome, ruthless natives, several of whom even took a whaling captain hostage and "in imitation of our

North American Indians, they put his head on a block and held a war club over his head until the chief's son, 'Pocahontas-like' intervened, pleading 'they must not murder the white men; if they do, plenty America Fire Kiabuka com[e], kill all Kanaka.'"[42] Most tellingly, Pacific natives, like "our North American Indians," were vanishing. They were destined "to become annihilated" by civilization's progress, to "shrink away before the irresistible march of foreign enterprise."[43] The possessive "our North American Indians" expressed writers' attachment to the North American continent, positioned them as authorities on the behavior and characteristics of Indians, acknowledged North American Indians as central to their own identity, and consigned America's original natives to a savage and distant past or to a savage and distant western frontier.

Even when they made finer distinctions, white American whalemen helped to create a generic Indian. One whaling memoirist, for example, described the Maori as having "had more the look and manner of the Sioux, Winnebagoes, or Crow Indians, than they did any Kanakas of the South Sea Islands."[44] He had probably never seen a Sioux, Winnebago, or Crow but knew enough to associate the Maoris with the wildest Indians featured in American newspaper accounts of the western frontier. Although generalized, "Indian" as a category still allowed for a plethora of cultural practices. Some Pacific peoples blackened their teeth with betel nut juice, ate poi with two fingers, drank kava after it had been chewed into a pulp by virginal youth, wrapped hogs and fish in banana leaves to roast in underground pits, went about naked with just a string around the waist, or appeared at a ceremony wrapped in swaths of tapa (bark) cloth.[45] Such ethnographic minutiae fit within a formula for describing primitive peoples, so that even such cultural specificity helped make Pacific peoples seem just another kind of Indian. Identifying commonalities among people who lived oceans apart reduced the meaning of "Indian" to a few essentials denoting stark differences between themselves and others while pushing the boundaries of the category outward to encompass native peoples from around the world.

The popular imagery of cultural encounters circulating in American culture gave ordinary white American seafarers the opportunity to reproduce tales of discovery and expansion in which they could claim roles as victims of Indian captivity or as civilized observers of new, curious, and savage customs. In their memoirs and journals, these observers did not seem aware of any tension in how race functioned in different ways in different contexts, though in each instance supporting notions of white supremacy. "Indian" was flexible enough in their minds to encapsulate the Gay Head harpooner on the ship whose savage hunting instincts furthered their whaling mission, the anonymous Kanaka shipmates in the forecastle, and the dangerous or titillating hordes of savages encountered in canoes or alongshore islands. If any stepped outside those expectations—Anthony Hinson, for instance, while cook on the *Globe*—they were not always visible as Indians.

5 : Cycles of Conquest

The "Indians" whose paths crossed by way of the *Globe*—the Mashpee Wampanoag whaleman, the Native Hawaiian laborer, and the natives of Mili Atoll—fell subject to similar historical processes but at different stages. Anthony Hinson's people had first seen European ships off of Cape Cod sometime in the late 1500s or early 1600s. He spoke English and lived in a state-regulated Indian community surrounded by white settlement. The Hawaiian Islands had witnessed considerable foreign ship traffic since the 1779 death of Captain Cook and by the 1820s had fully entered the world economy to become a major trading depot and recruitment center for seafaring laborers. The islands remained under Hawaiian political control for several more decades, but the kinds of changes that had already so altered the lives of the Mashpee Wampanoag were well under way. Three years before Hinson boarded the *Globe* in 1823, for example, the first contingent of New England missionaries had disembarked from the Boston China trader *Thaddeus* and established the Sandwich Islands Mission at Honolulu.[1] At Mili Atoll in 1824, the islanders had had little to no prior contact with foreign ships and sailors, but many of them would soon leave on whalers, too. "Cycles of conquest"—a phrase the anthropologist Edward Spicer coined for comparing the impact of Spain, Mexico, and then the United States on native peoples in the American Southwest—seems to me useful for encapsulating how the same colonizing practices have repeated themselves around the world.[2] Just as the whaling industry exhausted one whaling ground and then moved on, it incorporated natives from one part of the globe and then another. The wealth and human resources expropriated from one place became a building block to colonization in another place, with enlistment of a workforce a key component to the success of future ventures.

Nineteenth-century North American native whalemen personified this entire process of colonization from cultural encounters to deeper engagement through trade to life under colonialism. They had seen it all. Long since dispossessed and marginalized by European conquest, they now went far afield themselves to engage in cultural encounters and trade with other native peoples. At the same time, their own history of the colonizing trajectory from encounter to conquest animated the ideological narrative underlying American expansion. The historical memory of seventeenth-century Indian defeat in New England, a celebration of white superiority and civilization's conquest over savagery, flourished in antebellum New England concurrent with the rise of the whaling industry and modeled white American understandings of what it meant to explore, discover, and barter with "Indians" in distant seas.[3] In situ, colonization may have appeared as a singular occurrence, but Native American whalemen experienced colonization as three simultaneous developments: as part of colonization's workforce, they witnessed the often violent expansion of the United States into the Pacific and Arctic; at home in antebellum New England, they knew firsthand a less overtly violent colonialism that threatened their remaining lands and sovereignty; and the Euro-American memories of New England Indians' subjugation provided content to stories legitimating American expansion elsewhere around the world.

This chapter weaves together these three simultaneous occurrences in different parts of the world, with ships as the connecting thread. Naming a whaleship—the *Globe*, for instance—was not an idle activity but an opportunity for self-expression. Ship owners most often named their ships after themselves or members of their families, as in the many ships named *Sarah, Mary, George,* and *Henry*; or the *Two Brothers*, the *Abraham Barker*, and the *Charles W. Morgan*. They also named vessels after the whaling experience (the *Balaena, Spermo, Arctic,* and *Cape Horn Pigeon*), presidents and other political figures (the *George Washington, John Adams, John Jay,* and *Daniel Webster*), and exotic places and romantic heroes of classical literature (the *Lalla Rookh, Walter Scott, Hercules,* and *Cicero*). American place names constituted another common theme (*Nantucket, New Bedford, New England*), and because many New England place names derived from Algonquian precedents, vessels such as the *Acushnet*, famous for having Herman Melville aboard in 1841–1842, indirectly alluded to America's Indian forebears.[4] A host of whaler names more blatantly made European colonization of North America their reference point (*Mayflower, Pilgrim, Columbus, Columbia, Tobacco Plant,* and *Roanoke*). Soaking up nationalist imagery through Fourth of July commemorations, presentations at learned societies, and print culture, whaling investors contributed in their own way to memorializing conquest as righteous and benign by branding their whaleships with historical names and figureheads.

Some of these paid homage to Indians generically, like sports mascots in the twentieth century, with names such as the *Indian Chief, Narragansett,* and *Cherokee*. Melville worked within this tradition when he invented the "Pequod" as the setting of *Moby-Dick*. More frequently, Indian-themed whaleships adopted a historical figure from the seventeenth century, foe and friend alike. The *Metacom* originated in the Indian name of the instigator of New England's last and deadliest Indian war, King Philip's War of 1675. The *Annawan*'s namesake was Metacom's head warrior, said to have surrendered various Indian tokens of possession to the English victors upon Metacom's death, thereby acknowledging the Wampanoags' complete defeat.[5] Other New England sachems inspired the *Miantonomi* and *Sassacus*. Although most of such ship names drew on the seventeenth-century settlement of New England, the United States' victory over the Seminole Nation in 1842 made *Osceola* a name so appealing to whaleship owners that New Bedford had three *Osceola*s at sea in the early 1850s.[6] Ship owners considering what to name their vessels could draw from a voluminous antebellum print culture fascinated with the New England region and its early history. The multiple editions of Samuel G. Drake's *The Book of the Indians* put in circulation hundreds of stories that amounted to an American mythology equivalent to that for Mount Olympus. Devoted to the rivalries, passions, and ultimate subjection of fallen sachems, these stories helped whaling merchants give their ships a melodious and unique sobriquet conveying as well a New England–centered nationalism.[7]

Native New Englanders often worked on whalers whose names resounded with the history of conquest. The *Bartholomew Gosnold*, for instance, departed New Bedford on a three-year whaling voyage in 1844 with two native whalemen from Chappaquiddick aboard, Nathan Webquish, second mate, and his nephew Henry Jonas.[8] Built at Falmouth, Massachusetts, in 1832, the *Gosnold* had just been acquired by one of New Bedford's largest whaling firms, Isaac Howland, Jr., & Company. A fairly new ship, larger than average, the *Gosnold* would have seemed a good prospect for a whaleman looking for a voyage.[9] But did Webquish and Jonas pause before signing the shipping articles to think about the name of the ship and its figurehead of a young white man lushly clothed in a jacket and cravat? They must have known who Gosnold was, for in the publications, oratory, and art of southeastern Massachusetts, Gosnold had the status of a founding father. As early as 1736, Thomas Prince had published a history of New England that began with the English explorer's 1602 expedition.[10] In 1797, a few years after having gathered a circle of antiquarians to form the Massachusetts Historical Society in Boston, the historian Jeremy Belknap led an expedition out to the smaller islands off of Martha's Vineyard to search for traces of Gosnold's landing. He found a cellar hole on Cuttyhunk Island and proclaimed it built by Gosnold's men, a contention heatedly debated, sometimes even ridiculed,

Figure 7. *William Allen Wall,* Gosnold at the Smoking Rocks *(1842).*
Courtesy of the New Bedford Whaling Museum.

but cause enough to provoke still further investigation into the precise places in New England that Gosnold saw, named, and claimed.[11] Just a year before Webquish and Jonas left for the Pacific on the ship *Bartholomew Gosnold,* the explorer's feats again became the talk of the day in the streets of New Bedford when landscape artist William Allen Wall opened up to public exhibition his recent painting, *Gosnold at the Smoking Rocks,* a reenvisioning of Benjamin West's *Penn's Treaty with the Indians* but situated at a landmark pile of rocks on the New Bedford shoreline (figure 7).[12]

If Webquish and Jonas knew much about the history of Gosnold's "discovery," their interpretation of its consequences would have differed dramatically from those memorializing it for the wider public. The contemporary chroniclers of Gosnold's voyage, Gabriel Archer and John Brereton, reported that Gosnold's ship traveled south along the New England coast, stopping to explore bays and islands, searching for a site to build a fort. They took soundings of the depths, tallied up the region's commodities, named the places they passed "Cape Cod" and "Martha's Vineyard," and had a series of encounters with the region's native peoples. Webquish and Jonas's forebears were probably among the thirteen "Savages" Gosnold's party met on Cape Poge, a small island near Chappaquiddick, or among the "fiftie Savages, stout and lustie men with their Bowes and Arrowes" who came in a fleet of canoes to the place Gosnold had named "Elizabeth Island" and where he built his fort. At first, Gosnold's party met only amicable Indians eager to trade. The natives brought furs, deerskins, tobacco, and fish. Gosnold and his men gave them in return a straw hat, some knives, and beer. The knives met "with great marvelling, being very bright and sharpe, this our courtesie made them all in love with us," and in their eagerness to obtain "a knife or such like trifle," the Indians offered up their most valuable possessions. However, a group of natives then attacked some of Gosnold's men with arrows, and Gosnold abandoned the encampment to return to England.[13]

But for the bows and arrows, the beaver furs, deerskins, and wampum shell beads indigenous to New England, these encounters sound remarkably like those that would occur two centuries later in the Pacific, in the space between ships and canoes, ships and islands, as natives exchanged their "commodities" for "trifles." Even European descriptions of the native people read much the same, with Europeans expressing pleasure at the strength and healthful form of native bodies and the natives' welcoming response. To Archer and Brereton, the Indians with whom the English traded seemed "exceeding courteous, gentle of disposition, and well conditioned" and "of a perfect constitution of body, active, strong, healthfull, and very wittie." Two women Gosnold's party came across appeared "cleane and straite bodied, with countenance sweet and pleasant." Although they "would not admit of any immodest touch," they showed "much familiaritie with our men," and all the women in New England, it seemed, were "much delighted in our company." The natives' only failing was "some of the meaner sort [were] given to filching, which the very name of Salvages (not weighing their ignorance in good or evill) may easily excuse."[14]

Webquish and Jonas probably realized the irony of their situation and would have already come to terms with the knowledge that Gosnold's voyage precipitated an overwhelming, disempowering English settlement of coastal New England. And they likely thought of colonization as an ongoing process, visible every day of their lives. Relegated to an infertile patch of ground on the northern end of Chappaquiddick Island, their small community of Wampanoag Indians nursed a long-standing grievance against "the white Inhabitants of said Island who have suffer'd their creatures to eat up our grass & grain." From the late eighteenth century well into the 1860s, when Massachusetts dissolved its tribal status, the native community at Chappaquiddick struggled to protect the integrity of their remaining acreage through numerous petitions to the state and appeals to reluctant, state-appointed Indian guardians to enforce the law calling for the erection and maintenance of a "divisional fence" to keep the "Indian Lands" at Chappaquiddick secure from encroachment.[15]

History may have factored in Webquish's search for employment, but so also must have the whaling agent's offer that he ship as second mate, a high rank with a lay that promised some return on his labor after three years at sea. Like other whalemen deciding on their next voyage, both Webquish and Jonas likely also considered which whalers were imminent for departure, the condition and age of the vessel, the success of its prior voyages, and the reputations particular owners and captains had for looking after the well-being of their crews. Webquish and Jonas probably even developed an affection for the *Gosnold*, since it was their home for three years and keeping the *Gosnold* fit and clean would have occupied most of their days.[16]

What native whalemen thought about the many vessels named after Indians is similarly open to multiple possibilities. The whaler *Gay Head*, launched from Mattapoisett in 1852 and distinguished by a "finely carved full-length figure head, representing an Indian Warrior, holding a spear in his hands," appears to have had no native whalemen on any of its five voyages.[17] However, many of New England's native whalemen may have enjoyed leaving home on the *Indian Chief* or the *Metacom*, taking pride in the vessel's Indian associations. This must particularly have been the case for Amos Haskins, twice master of the *Massasoit*, a ship named after the powerful Wampanoag sachem who befriended the Plymouth Separatists as they struggled to survive their first New England winters. A generation later, it was Massasoit's son Metacom, his patience with the fragile alliance between his people and the English exhausted, who embarked on the war that led to his death and the subjection of the Wampanoags to English control. Nineteenth-century histories of the seventeenth century made little distinction between Massasoit, intent on making peace, and the son Metacom, who saw no choice but war. Both held a featured place in American memory.

Native New Englanders cherished the memory of both men, too, and proudly traced their descent to one or the other, based on stories passed down in families but also on temperament and political positioning. Pequot minister William Apess, angry about the slew of racial insults faced by people of color in antebellum New England, claimed descent from "the royal family of Philip," whom he mistakenly called "king of the Pequot tribe of Indians."[18] Frustrated with her unresolved land claims against the Commonwealth of Massachusetts, Zerviah Gould Mitchell, matriarch of a small community of natives still holding onto Betty's Neck in Middleborough, Massachusetts, identified herself as "a lineal descendant, in the seventh generation, from the great and good Massasoit, whom both the red and white man now venerate and honor." She raised the funds to publish local historian Ebenezer W. Peirce's 1878 chronicle of New England's Indian wars, which included a genealogical chart documenting her family's connections to Massasoit's daughter Amie, wife of Tuspaquin, known to the English as the "Black Sachem," who, with Metacom, had fought against the English in King Philip's War.[19] Laying claim to the heritage of their ancestors emphasized their indigenous belonging and held up as role models those natives of the past renowned for their intelligence, dignity, and wise leadership. If Haskins felt the same as Apess and Mitchell about these sachems of the past, he may have understood his command of the *Massasoit* not as conquest and subordination but as endurance, survival, adaptability, and achievement, a great achievement indeed as he was one of the few native men to rise to the position of whaling master in the entire history of the American whale fishery.

: : :

The largest cluster of vessels named after Indians sailed from Falmouth, Massachusetts, and originated with the town's most prominent citizen, Elijah Swift. Swift built ships; traded in live oak lumber from the southern states, most of which he contracted to sell to the U.S. Navy; invested in the local candleworks, saltworks, and bank; and served as managing agent for a half-dozen whaleships in which he owned the majority share. In the mid-1830s, at the peak of his whaling ventures, his fleet included the *Awashonks*, *Hobomok*, *Pocahontas*, *Popmunnet*, and *Uncas*. Most of these he had built himself or had had built by Falmouth shipbuilder Solomon Lawrence out of imported live oak timbers.[20] Falmouth was also home to the newly built whaler *William Penn*. Swift did not serve as the managing agent for the *William Penn* on its maiden voyage in 1833, but he probably supplied the lumber and held shares in it.[21] Invoking foremost Penn's Quakerism, a religion that had been as vehemently supported on Cape Cod as in Pennsylvania, the *William Penn* would have blended in well with the Indian-themed ships lining Swift's wharf in Woods Hole, for it invoked a peaceable kingdom of English and Indians living in harmony. Ever since Benjamin West had painted *Penn's Treaty with the Indians* (1771–1772), the popular imagination had sustained Penn's reputation for fair dealing with Indians when settling Pennsylvania. These iconic images of a mutually beneficial cultural encounter occurring on a beach were both still lifes and moving pictures, casting the meeting between Europeans and Indians as moments of transition and growth and telling the story of how Europeans arrived in the Americas, where they bought land from Indians with bolts of cloth and other trade goods, and a nation was born. The Indians, satisfied with their purchases, would then vanish from the landscape.[22]

This memory of a benign and uncomplicated past in which Indians welcomed and assisted English colonization must have inspired Swift to adopt famous Indians as his signature motif when naming whaleships—not just famous Indians but more particularly English helpmates. Pocahontas, of course, aided English settlement of Virginia. Uncas was the Mohegan sachem who allied with colonists in Connecticut to defeat the Pequots in the 1637 Pequot War. Hobomok was Squanto's lesser-known counterpart. He helped the Plymouth Separatists settle in to the New England region in the 1620s. Awashonks was the *sunksquaw*, or squaw sachem, who early on in King Philip's War faced no choice but to submit her people to English subjection (figure 8).

Popmonet was of the most local interest to Falmouth. He had been a prominent and respected sachem over territory that would become part of the colonial town of Falmouth, founded in the early 1660s. His name, spelled a hundred different ways (Paupmunnucke, Paumpmunet, Popmunnet), appeared on some of Cape Cod's earliest Indian land deeds. An advocate of Christianity, Popmonet also helped sponsor Mashpee, the Christian Indian praying town surrounded by the English towns of Falmouth, Sandwich, and Barnstable. The surname evolved in the nineteenth century into Pocknett.[23] That Swift chose *Popmunnet* as the name of his whaleship, when he had so many spellings to choose from, suggests that he may have been influenced by antiquarian interest in an old gravestone in the cemetery next to the Mashpee meetinghouse, the epitaph for which read, "In memory of deacon Zacheus Popmunnet died 22d Octr. 1770 aged 51 years. The Righteous is more excellent than his neighbor."[24]

The stone's inscription left open who these less-excellent neighbors were— were they the less Christian among the Mashpee or, more likely, Mashpee's white neighbors, such as those residing in the town of Falmouth, who seemed so often to spill over the town's boundaries to help themselves to Mashpee's wood? In 1833, at the same time that Elijah Swift's whaling enterprises reached their peak, so did Mashpee's grievances, in an event known as the Mashpee Revolt. Pequot minister William Apess instigated the rebellion with a visit in May of that year. Surprised by the absence of Indians in the congregation at the Mashpee Meetinghouse, Apess sought them out and then participated in submitting a flurry of petitions to the Commonwealth of Massachusetts articulating Mashpee's problems with the minister Phineas Fish, whites from neighboring towns who trespassed on the reservation, and the state-appointed Indian overseers who did little to stop whites from

Figure 8.
*Figurehead of
the* Awashonks,
*built in 1830 at
Falmouth,
Massachusetts,
on Cape Cod.
Courtesy of the
New Bedford
Whaling Museum.*

carting away Mashpee's wood. Apess and several Mashpee men confronted some outsiders from Cotuit who were doing just that and soon found themselves before the County of Barnstable's Court of Common Pleas, which convicted Apess, Jacob Pocknett, and Charles DeGrass for causing "a great noise, riot, tumult and disturbance" and taking a cord of wood worth five dollars away from William Sampson, "to the great terror of the people of the said Commonwealth."[25] Incidentally, DeGrass was the same man who eight years earlier had been left behind in Rio de Janeiro for a revolt of a different sort, protesting with other seaman a flogging on the ship *Ann Alexander* (see chapter 3).

The Mashpee Revolt caused a stir throughout New England and further afield. Its simultaneity with an upswelling of humanitarian protest against the prospect of Cherokee removal made some white New Englanders eager to defend the Mashpees' desire for self-government while others became anxious at the threat of Indian unrest occurring so close to their own towns and among Indians long thought pacified. The amount of fear the Mashpee Wampanoag were able to leverage is especially impressive given that the squabble over wood, the "pretended riot" as Apess called it, constituted the only hint of violence during the yearlong conflict.[26] The governor of Massachusetts commissioned Josiah Fiske to visit Mashpee and investigate their complaints. When Fiske returned to the statehouse, his colleagues congratulated him on "allaying a deep rooted and violent hostility to the Laws" and foresaw that his visit to Mashpee would have "an effect highly beneficial to these aboriginals" by showing them that "interlopers," meaning William Apess, "who disturb the peace, excite the fears and interrupt the harmony of that community" would not be tolerated.[27] The revolt ended in March 1834 as peaceably as it had started, with the Mashpee complainants pursuing reform through well-established, lawful procedures. Mashpee spokesman Daniel B. Amos appeared before the state legislature in Boston to present an impassioned, scroll-like "Bill of Complaints," after which Massachusetts granted Mashpee more self-government in the form of elected town selectmen who would report not to a "Board of Overseers" as before but to just "one able and discreet person" from a neighboring town to act as "commissioner" and "treasurer."[28]

Elijah Swift was supremely placed to observe the Mashpee Revolt firsthand, for not only did he live in one of the towns next to Mashpee; he was also serving on the Governor's Council. He was absent on the days the council discussed the Mashpee grievances, perhaps on purpose, for he had an interest in the situation.[29] Apess listed him among the leading men—along with Nathan Pocknett of Mashpee—who tried to prevent the Bill of Complaints from being read and resolved. Nathan Pocknett allied with Swift against the majority of the tribe, but the Pocknett name was so common at Mashpee, Pocknetts stood on both sides of the issue, many having signed the Bill of Complaints. Swift may have tried to quiet the rebellion because, as the region's most prosperous and active shipping entrepreneur, he must have been implicated in one of the petition's grievances: "Their is several tonns of our most exclent ship timber that is cut and carried of yearly."[30] That Swift chose the losing side in the debate over Mashpee rights had little effect on his own fortune, and Falmouth seems to have carried on its tradition of honoring Indians in its whaling fleet, with the launch of the *Popmunnet* two years later, in April 1836.[31]

A colonized enclave within New England, the Mashpee Wampanoag had long resigned themselves to being outnumbered and disempowered in state politics. Like the Chappaquiddick Wampanoag and other New England Indians, they acknowledged the power of the state not by testing its capacity for violence but through petitions that stated their grievances and begged for relief, thereby acting from within the American legal system.

: : :

The procedural course the Mashpee Revolt took contrasted with the unpredictable and fatal violence American whaling incurred in the Pacific. Elijah Swift was one of several hundred American whaling investors riding the sperm whale boom of the 1830s, building ship after ship and sending them off around Cape Horn, where the usually peaceful trading with native peoples for food and water sometimes turned deadly. Two such incidents in the mid-1830s, occurring on the Falmouth whalers *William Penn* and the *Awashonks*, became headline news stories and precipitated a more visible U.S. presence in the Pacific region.[32]

The *William Penn* departed Falmouth in January 1833. The captain soon fell ill and returned to New England, leaving the vessel under the command of first mate Peleg Swain. Under Captain Swain, the officers and crew roiled with dissatisfaction—frequently deserting, demanding discharges, and refusing to do duty. The only constant in the logbook as they cruised the Pacific for sperm whales with little success was the periodic trade with natives for fish, pigs, fruit, and coconuts. Even these simple acts could be dangerous. Early on in the voyage, as they approached one island, Captain Swain decided not to land for they saw "Saviges . . . on the Shore armed with spears," and in January 1834, they spoke with an English whaler that three weeks earlier had "lost" its captain and another man to "the natives at Strongs Island."[33]

A year and a half into the voyage, in September 1834, the *William Penn* had its own fatal encounter with natives at Otweewhy, Navigators Islands (Savai'i, Samoa). The ship's log recorded that the first and second mates went ashore with two boats crews intending to trade for coconuts and pigs. The islanders seized them and sent canoes out to take the ship, but the *William Penn* evaded their reach. For three days, Captain Swain perused the shore for signs of his missing men and boats until, concluding that they had been killed, he steered for Oahu, where he shipped replacements and continued with his whaling voyage.[34] When Swain told of the "massacre" of half his crew at Honolulu, Captain William Worth of the Nantucket whaleship *Howard* had trouble believing it. Just five months before he had stopped at Savai'i for water and fresh supplies and had "met with very civil treatment." As Worth was heading back that way for a sperm whaling cruise, he resolved to discover the fate of the two boats' crews. On arriving at Savai'i, two English beachcombers came aboard with new information on what had happened. They reported that Swain had visited a part of the island where ships rarely traded and "where a misunderstanding occurred between the chief and Capt. S. relative to a musket." More trouble had ensued the following day when Swain sent his boats crews ashore to collect firewood, and they "made themselves too free with property placed by the chiefs under a strict taboo." The islanders' appeals to the crew to stop went unheeded, and so the natives attacked, wounding the first mate, who later died from his wounds, killing a Hawaiian crew member, and taking the remaining men hostage. The two Englishmen disagreed as to whether the second mate had also died. By the time Worth arrived at Savai'i, another American whaleship had already come by and retrieved the "white men belonging to the Wm. Penn (leaving 2 or 3 Sandwich Islanders)," also paying a ransom in muskets for the two whaleboats.[35]

This unnamed American whaleship took the two boats' crews of the *William Penn* to Vava'u, Tonga, where the U.S. sloop-of-war *Vincennes* happened to be at anchor. Then on a solitary cruise of Pacific island groups frequented by American ships, the *Vincennes* had no particular mission beyond "the protection of our citizens, & their interests."[36] When the *Vincennes* commander, John H. Aulick, heard that the first and second mates of the *William Penn* had died from wounds received when taken prisoner, he left immediately for Savai'i to punish the murderers. Because a few years earlier, in 1832, the U.S. frigate *Potomac* had set an example by bombarding and burning the town of Quallah Battoo, Sumatra, in retaliation for an attack on the Salem pepper trader *Friendship*, Aulick had no doubts that his chosen course of action would be considered just, necessary, and in keeping with the *Vincennes*'s Pacific objective.[37] Arriving in the vicinity of Savai'i just a month after the *William Penn*'s two boat crews had been taken hostage, Aulick learned from two foreign residents, one English and one Portuguese, that the instigator was named Papatoono. Aulick sent "an expedition against him, to secure him, dead or alive, and to burn his villages." Marching to each of Papatoono's three villages, the expeditionary force set fire to his houses and other property but never found Papatoono himself. Along the way, they attracted a crowd of Samoan natives, who reached threatening proportions but were too intimidated to fight back, one naval officer explained, because "our muskets and bayonets, as few as they were, looked too formidable." A "sub-chief," Tongalore, promised friendship and begged for peace, threw the members of the expedition a feast, and accompanied them back to the *Vincennes*, where the ship eventually "took leave of Tongalore with presents, and bore away to the westward."[38] The *Vincennes* then continued on its Pacific tour.

The *Awashonks* suffered greater losses. It had left Falmouth in 1833 as well and in October 1835 came to Namorik Atoll in what is now the Marshall Islands, where the captain hoped to trade for fresh fruit. Natives boarded the ship, making signs that they coveted the ship's iron. Third mate Silas Jones later wrote in that day's logbook entry, "we soon discovered barbarous intentions," and a "Bloudy contest" ensued as islanders and crew armed themselves with whale cutting spades. In the slaughter, an unknown number of islanders and five of the crew died: the captain, first mate, second mate, and two seamen, one of whom expired later from wounds received in the battle. While the bloody affray held sway on deck, Jones managed to reach the cabin and its stock of firearms. The crew gained control of the ship, threw the dead bodies overboard, buried their officers (which presumably entailed throwing their bodies overboard, too), and sailed to Hawai'i.[39]

The *William Penn* and *Awashonks* incidents joined a growing list of "outrages" and "massacres" in which Pacific natives attacked American ships or took seamen hostage to elicit ransoms. Adding to the clamor, American sea captains and merchants begged for more U.S. warships to navigate Pacific waters, show the flag, and offer protection to American commerce. Jeremiah Reynolds cited the *William Penn* incident in 1836 when urging the United States to commission the navy to conduct a "voyage of discovery" to the Pacific to chart the waters, conduct scientific research, and establish a U.S. presence. The United States Exploring Expedition, under the command of Charles Wilkes, left for the Pacific two years later.[40] The U.S. Ex Ex, as it is popularly known, reached Samoa at the end of 1839. Failing in its efforts to capture the elusive Papatoono, Wilkes met with other Samoan leaders who agreed to a standard set of "regulations" about treatment of American seamen and a judicial process to punish anyone who murdered or committed acts of violence against Americans. Arriving in Fiji a year later, the Expedition immediately set out to punish those responsible for an 1833 attack on the Salem bêche-de-mer trader *Charles Doggett*. Identifying Veidovi as the perpetrator, Wilkes took him prisoner, carrying him back to the United States with the intention of teaching him and other Fijians a lesson and to show him firsthand the vast power of the

United States. However, Veidovi died shortly after the expedition's flagship, the U.S.S. *Vincennes*, arrived in New York City harbor in 1842.[41]

The U.S. Ex Ex's survey of Fiji provoked new hostilities that led to more punitive raids on Pacific villages. In July 1840, Wilkes's forces burned one town for theft of a boat, and a few days later, when trading negotiations went awry and Fijians murdered two of the expedition, Wilkes ordered a retaliatory raid on the island of Malolo, slaughtering a hundred Fijian men, women, and children.[42] The mood of the U.S. Ex Ex darkened, and when a contingent sent to Samoa for one more try at capturing Papatoono heard of the murder of an American seaman at the town of Salufato, Passed Midshipman William Reynolds recorded in his journal how he readied himself in "expectation of a tremendous conflagration and of great deeds to be done." Assigned instead to lead a smaller party in search of Papatoono, Reynolds did not participate in the expedition's devastation of Salufato, but word of it spread to other villages, sending residents into a panic and Papatoono into hiding, frustrating once again the expedition's plans to take him prisoner as punishment for the attack on the *William Penn*'s two boats crews. Leaving Samoa to conduct surveys in the Gilbert Islands, the U.S. Ex Ex sacked yet another village in retaliation for the death of one of the expedition at the hands of natives. Sailing to Oahu in anticipation of there receiving letters from home and "mingling again with white people, who wear clothes," Reynolds expressed his relief: "D—n these cannibal Islands—I am fairly sick of them."[43]

Like many other Americans writing about their experiences in the Pacific, Reynolds saw only two sides. Although his journal mentions Pacific natives and American blacks as seamen working on behalf of the U.S. Ex Ex—the native New Zealander John Sac; "our smart little *Kanaka* 'George Wash'"; Whahoo [Oahu] Jack; and "this black Townsend," "a negro who sailed in the *Potomac* with me"—Reynolds reduced the conflicts at Fiji and Samoa to a racial contest between civilized "whites" and savage "natives."[44]

But in both the *William Penn* and *Awashonks* episodes, Pacific Islanders among the crew fell victim to attacks on the ship by Pacific Islanders. In the attack on the *William Penn* boats, a Hawaiian crew member was among those who died for following the captain's orders to collect firewood and thereby violating the islanders' taboo. Others stayed on the island, either voluntarily or because the American whaleship that rescued the others did not invest in bargaining for their release as well. The *Awashonks* had aboard several Tahitian crew members, who when the bloodshed started were seen swimming away from the ship, their fate unknown. There may have been New England natives aboard the *Awashonks* as well. Two young

Mashpee greenhands, Joshua Pocknett and John Mye, did serve on the *William Penn*. Apparently not among those taken captive at Samoa, they were listed in the final settlement as having completed the voyage. For their three years on the *William Penn*, Pocknett owed the ship $46.38 while Mye earned a final payment of $24.98.[45] At least they had survived the voyage.

During Pocknett's and Mye's absence, the complainants at Mashpee who in 1834 presented to the Massachusetts legislature their many grievances about white trespassers stealing their resources and monopolizing church services at their meetinghouse added their names and those of seventy-seven other "Males who are absent at sea" to the petition that brought the Mashpee Revolt to an end. These two young men returned to a new political structure at Mashpee, with the Commonwealth of Massachusetts having conceded a modicum of self-government to the community while still keeping a white "treasurer" in a supervisory position over them. Justifying the inclusion of these absent seamen as signatories, the petitioners asserted that "all of them are opposed to having Masters & say they will not return, many of them, to live with us while in this situation We want our friends to return & live with us for they are near & dear to us, as your honors children & we hope that you will think of this."[46] Couching their demands in conciliatory language, the Mashpee Wampanoags struggled to maneuver for more protection of their lands and resources despite their colonial subjection while other natives halfway around the world were realizing for the first time the military power of the United States and the prospect of a violent subjugation.

: : :

Whalemen more often encountered other peoples through amicable exchange than through violence, but as the American whaling industry expanded onto new whaling grounds, the kinds of conflicts that had inspired the U.S. Ex Ex in the 1830s now erupted occasionally in the North Pacific. In the summer of 1851, the *Armata* of New London foundered in the icy waters of the Anadir Sea. A whaleman on another vessel in the vicinity reported that, after the wreck, "Indians undertook to take the ship the contest was decided by the death of one white man and 13 Indians," all killed with the tools of the whaling trade: hatchets, lances, and harpoons.[47] As the tale spread to other whalers, rumor had it that a Narragansett Indian among the crew had helped save the ship, perhaps referring to the Mohegan William H. Fielding or, more likely, William Gardner of Stonington, Connecticut, both of whom appear on the *Armata*'s crew list with "copper" complexions.[48] Before the *Armata* was lost in the North Pacific, it had spent the winter season replenishing at the Hawaiian Islands, tying all three locations—New England, the Hawaiian Islands, and the Arctic—and different native peoples from around the world into a web of economic and social exchange.

A telltale anecdote illuminating the complexity of these indigenous connections created through global trade, which hints also at cycles of conquest in process, appears in the diary of fifteen-year-old Alexander Liholiho, while a passenger on the schooner *Honolulu* bound for San Francisco in September 1849. A month or two after Liholiho departed from Honolulu, more than a hundred American whalers, such as the *Armata*, would arrive to spend four or five months there, from about late October to early April, repairing their vessels and replenishing their provisions before heading up north. The Hawaiian Islands had been so transformed by contacts with foreigners that Reynolds of the U.S. Ex Ex could regard it as a safe haven from Pacific savagery, a place where he could feel at ease among "white people, who wear clothes." Not only did several thousand whalemen flood Honolulu, Lahaina, and Hilo during the whaling season. ABCFM missionaries, American merchants, American employees of the Hawaiian government, U.S. consuls in residence on three different islands, a seaman's bethel in Honolulu, and a U.S. seaman's hospital at Lahaina all advertised an increasingly pervasive American presence.[49] In addition, land redistribution was well under way. In 1848, King Kamehameha III had put into law the radical changes in land tenure known as the Great Mahele.[50]

With his brother, Liholiho, who within a few years became King Kamehameha IV, left the islands in 1849 to accompany the American-born Gerrit P. Judd to Europe and the United States. A former ABCFM missionary, now Hawai'i's minister of finance and Kamehameha III's emissary, Judd was on a diplomatic mission to England, France, and the United States to gain these imperial powers' consent to respect Hawaiian independence. A week into his journey, Liholiho wrote, "Last night was up pretty late reading the 'Last of the Mohicans,'" James Fenimore Cooper's 1826 novel of Indians vanishing before the expanding American frontier. He did not explain why he found the novel so compelling that he had to stay up late to finish it, nor did he say what made him launch almost immediately into another of Cooper's epic novels in the same series, *The Pathfinder* of 1840. As Liholiho's journey came to an end, he had his own encounter with natives on another American frontier. On a visit to Niagara Falls, he bought "some Indian Curiositys . . . bead work on slippers, some smoking caps, bags &c."[51] While Liholiho toured Niagara Falls, native New England whalemen were in Hawai'i, probably doing much the same, collecting shells or other souvenirs to take home with them, participants in but not in control of the changes taking place around them.

These native histories were entangled, but because native Hawaiians and native North Americans interacted in the same settings that brought white sailors and tourists into contact with native peoples, their relations to each other as natives at different stages of colonization may not have been obvious to them. The American whaleship was not overtly an instrument of U.S. imperialism but an incidental one. The threat of starvation and scurvy necessitated the replenishment of food, water, and wood stores, through trade or through force, from indigenous peoples occupying islands and coasts near whaling grounds. The narrative of global expansion through maritime exploration and enterprise rested on the premise of a civilized, white race of seafarers coming into conflict with dark-hued, savage, culturally inscrutable natives. That narrative obscures the complicated motivations of the multiethnic maritime workforce whose mundane but essential labor made expansion possible. Native men from New England, from Hawai'i and other Pacific islands, and from Arctic regions were incorporated into American economic development abroad as laborers in the maritime trades, at different times and in different ways. More than their labor sustained the industry. Mashpee wood, taken surreptitiously, ended up as ship timber in vessels that purportedly paid homage to their forebears while whalemen from around the world felled trees in the Pacific to burn as fuel and to keep those ships afloat and their cargo holds full.

6 : New Heaven

European expansion generated the idea of the savage Indian, but those people identified in whaling literature as "Indians"—Pacific island residents, Kanaka whalemen, and North American native whalemen—do not seem to have recognized any special bond as colonized, or indigenous, people. As historian David A. Chappell noted in his study of Pacific Islanders on European and American ships in the age of sail, "indigenous voyagers were not necessarily any more sympathetic or adept at interpreting local cultures than Euroamericans were."[1] Historical hindsight tempts us to assume an indigenous fellowship different from the assumptions of early European and Euro-American ethnographies, which portrayed inherent savagery as the basis for an imagined commonality. We can see instead how an initial encounter between ships and natives led eventually to similar assaults on native sovereignty, land, and culture. But when an American whaleship, like the *Globe*, arrived in Honolulu and filled its forecastle with whoever was available, or arrived at the Mulgraves, with its crew in the midst of killing off each other, all the "Indians" involved would have thought these events singular, immediate, and volatile. Anyone on the ship might be taken hostage or have to defend himself in an attack.

Such violence was rare, however, and American whaling had more of an impact on local communities around the world through the slow creep of economic, social, and cultural exchanges. In these interactions, whalemen of all backgrounds still had interests that bound them to the ship and their shipmates. Because all among the crew depended on island and coastal peoples to supply the ship with basic provisions, every laborer living and working on an American whaler, even newly shipped Portuguese and Kanakas, could be considered participants in the gradual spread of American influence into distant places.

The journals and logbooks kept by native New England whalemen, though not given to self-reflection, lend some insight into the nature of their relations with other native people and their perspectives as travelers. The earliest of these date to the 1830s and 1840s. James F. Pells of Mashpee kept a daily record of his 1835–1839 voyage on the *Barclay* of Nantucket, and

Joseph Ammons, a Narragansett from Charlestown, Rhode Island, left behind a remarkable two volumes of private journals covering four consecutive voyages spanning the years 1843–1853.[2] Because both authors kept up with daily entries when their vessels anchored at foreign ports, we can piece together some of their activities ashore.

Neither Pells nor Ammons gave any hint as to why they chose to keep a journal. Ammons kept his tone serious, to the point of speaking of himself in the third person even when boasting ("it may seem strang that the B.B. [bow boat] or J. Ammons kills so meney whales it however is no more strang then true") and when recounting a near-death experience with a whale ("when the other Boat got thare J A was in the state of drounding").[3] The impressive size of Ammons's two volumes, purchased at a whaling outfitters' store in New Bedford and measuring eight to nine inches wide and fourteen inches long, must have made him a conspicuous scribe aboard ship, suggesting he intended his journal less as a private endeavor and more as a public statement of his whaling professionalism. What drove Pells to keep a journal is more mysterious because he gave free rein to a humorous writing style while in every other way meeting the expectations of the logbook genre. Apparently, Pells kept this journal for his own amusement.

Although Pells's and Ammons's perspectives could not have been more different from each other, their particular experiences connected both men to the same larger narrative of American expansion into the Pacific—a narrative of savage encounters, carefree sensuality, sailors' riots, and Christian mission. Their voyages brought them to various Pacific locales, with Hawai'i their most frequent port of call, usually staying weeks at a time to cooper oil, paint the ship, stock up on provisions, and go on liberty. Wherever they traveled, they and their shipmates depended on native peoples to supply the fresh water, fruit, wood, and supplemental labor needed for a three- to four-year sojourn around the world. In their fleeting, yet intense and memorable contacts with native people, Pells and Ammons fell into the position of American seamen meeting cultural others in much the same way as non-native seamen. If they had a unique perspective as native peoples (albeit from distant native lands), it is not evident in their journals.[4]

∶ ∶ ∶

An experienced whaleman in his mid-thirties when he embarked on the *Barclay*, Pells had been on at least three prior voyages to the Pacific: the *Washington* of Nantucket, 1819–1822; the *Triton* of New Bedford, 1825–1827; and the *Ann* of Nantucket, 1827–1830.[5] Because he sailed so often out of Nantucket, which has few surviving crew lists, I suspect that he was on continuous voyages up until the 1835 departure of the *Barclay* but cannot document his entire career. His journal does not mention his rank. His references to the mates show that he was not one of them, but with that much experience, he likely held the rank of boatsteerer. Not only was he a practiced and knowledgeable whaleman; he must have circumnavigated the globe multiple times and spent an accumulated several years in the Pacific Ocean before the *Barclay* brought him there.

From Pells's journal, we can reconstruct the ship's itinerary. The *Barclay* left Nantucket in November 1835, went around Cape Horn to Callao, Peru, and passed through the Juan Fernández Islands to arrive at the Marquesas in August 1836, where the ship stayed for nearly three weeks to stock up on fresh food. They spent the next several months whaling "on the line" (along the equator) and then made landfall briefly at Aitutaki, Cook Islands, where natives climbed aboard from their canoes, presumably to trade. The *Barclay*'s next extended stay was three weeks at Tahiti, then back to the line and on to the Japan Grounds, ending 1837 in Hawai'i, first with a week at Lahaina on Maui and then more than a month at Honolulu, Oahu. In 1838, the ship briefly stopped at Aitutaki again, to load up on wood, which appears to have been arranged when "The kings man came on board." They then headed directly to whaling grounds off of New Zealand. In mid-April, they anchored at Vava'u, Tonga, to trade for hogs, yams, vegetables, and fruit; stowed away water and wood; and "had a row With the black cheaf About things that was Not good."[6] Another whaling cruise on the line and on the coast of Japan ended in November, when they returned to Oahu, again staying more than a month, to prepare for the passage to Nantucket. Homeward-bound, the *Barclay* stopped at Moorea, opposite Tahiti, rounded Cape Horn, anchored briefly at Pernambuco, Brazil, and, after passing the local landmarks of Montauk Light on Long Island and the Gay Head cliffs on Martha's Vineyard, arrived at Nantucket Bar on the 23rd of June 1839. The *Barclay* had been "gone 43 monthes and 10 days," and "she has Ben as fare south and as fare North as fare East and as fare West as eney other ship out of Nantucket," Pells wrote in his last entry.

Of all the places the *Barclay* visited, Pells's favorite was the island of Nukuhiva in the Marquesas. His scrawl looks like "New Heaven," a fitting name for the place given how much he loved Nukuhiva, but he probably intended "New Heaver," a mispronunciation of Nukuhiva found occasionally in other sailors' journals.[7] The largest island in the northern group of the Marquesas, Nukuhiva is famous in American literature as the locale for Herman Melville's *Typee*, a fanciful memoir of leisure and lovable cannibals loosely based on Melville's brief residence with the Taipi on Nukuhiva in 1842, after his desertion from the Fairhaven, Massachusetts, whaler *Acushnet*.

The northern Marquesas had a significance in American history long before the *Barclay* and the *Acushnet* stopped there for provisions. In 1791, Boston sea captain Joseph Ingraham claimed these islands for the United States while on his way to the northwest coast to trade for furs to sell in China. He recorded how as "first discoverers," he and his crew held a "ceremony of taking possession" aboard the *Hope* and that he named Nukuhiva "Federal Island" and named other islands after founding fathers Washington, Adams, and Franklin.[8] Upon his return, Jeremy Belknap of the Massachusetts Historical Society published excerpts from Ingraham's log to celebrate April 19, 1791, as "a day ever memorable to Americans."[9] Belknap also circulated the account of Josiah Roberts, captain of the Boston brig *Jefferson*, who, unaware of Ingraham's precedence, named the uncharted group "Washington Islands."[10] Americans continued to call the northern Marquesas "Washington Islands" for several more decades. During the War of 1812, U.S. naval officer David Porter had a more profound impact on the Marquesas. Making Nukuhiva his headquarters to prey on British ships, he built a fort at Taiohae Bay, or "Massachusetts Bay," asserting that Americans had a "prior right" to these islands. He exacerbated conflicts among the island's three largest political groups—the Tei'i, Hapa'a, and Taipi—by empowering the Tei'i with American trade goods and weaponry, choosing their bay over the others to transform into a service port for American shipping, promoting wars to unify the island under Tei'i authority, and extorting tribute from them all in hogs and fruit.[11]

Porter's unabashed pursuit of American interests in the Marquesas imprinted a pattern of food shortages and hostile trade relations still at play in August 1836 when the *Barclay* stopped there and which continued into the 1850s and 1860s.[12] Coming to Nukuhiva, the *Barclay* entered Taipi Bay first. Unaware of the island's perennial wars, Captain Reuben Barney hoped to trade for food, but the Taipi instead took him and the third mate hostage. The *Barclay* retreated to anchor at Taiohae Bay and sent a boat back to negotiate for the release of its men. Initially welcomed, the *Barclay* could not obtain the hogs and fruit needed to continue the voyage and moved up the island to trade with the Hapa'a. Although eager for trade with foreign ships, the Tei'i and Hapa'a had difficulties maintaining friendly relations with foreigners, who made unreasonable demands and were quick to retaliate with hostage taking or by rampaging through villages to hunt down perpetrators of insults, thefts, and assaults. In his account of a voyage on the U.S. war sloop *Vincennes* in 1829, the ship's chaplain Charles Stewart reported that many Marquesans ran into the hills when foreign ships arrived and how recently a French captain had taken a prominent man hostage until as many hogs as he wanted were delivered to his ship. In 1834, when the *Vincennes* stopped again at Nukuhiva, hundreds fled into the hills to escape a retaliatory raid in search of a man who had killed an American seaman.[13]

The Taipi had evolved hostage taking into a strategy of their own. Ransoming American seamen, either deserters or captives, brought them trade goods, especially muskets essential in their war with the Tei'i and Hapa'a. Perhaps Barney fell victim to the same ruse the Taipi used in 1840, when they lured Captain John Brown of the Nantucket whaleship *Catharine* with a bevy of hogs tethered to the beach. Letting the hogs loose as Brown's party landed, the Taipi captured Brown and demanded more than forty muskets and gunpowder as ransom. With the help of a South American beachcomber, Brown escaped to the friendlier side of the island.[14] Two years after the incident involving the *Catharine*, Melville deserted at Taiohae Bay with shipmate Toby Greene. They ran up into the interior, crossing the mountain ridge dividing the valleys of the Tei'i and Taipi. The idyllic month Melville spent living with a Taipi family, which he stretched into four months in his best-selling *Typee*, was not as exotic an experience as he led his readers to believe, for at Nukuhiva, seamen had become trade currency.[15] The Taipi must have thought themselves especially fortunate whenever deserters such as Melville preferred "cannibals" to sea captains. Not worth as much as a whaleship captain, deserters still had some value. Captain Barney's freedom cost a hefty $500 in trade goods, more precisely "fifteen muskets, some powder, and four red shirts. The savages kept the boat, oars, &c."[16] Melville gave as the ransom offered for him one musket, some gunpowder, and a bolt of cotton cloth.[17]

Although the *Barclay* visited several bays and islands, the crew could not satisfy their provisioning needs. After his release from the Taipi, Captain Barney may have made his own extraordinary demands and taken his own hostages to induce the Marquesans to trade, because some falling-out occurred, first with the Tei'i and then with the Hapa'a. Three other whaleships, one British and two American, visited Nukuhiva at the same time as the *Barclay*, and all left together "on account of threats made by the people on shore," as explained in the logbook of the *Leonidas* of Bristol, Rhode Island.[18]

Hostage taking and food shortages did not dim Pells's fondness for the Marquesas, however. His first journal entry upon arrival at Nukuhiva reads simply, "At ½ past Mr [meridian/noon] found our selves in tipos Bay whare the natives ro[a]st me[n] and Eaght them at 8 A.M. our captin and third mate Went on shore and Thay took them we got under way and went Down to new heaver," meaning Taiohae Bay. Pells made the Taipi out to be cannibals, but cannibals who, as Melville would later represent them in *Typee*, seemed to provoke no horror. Indeed, Pells scems to have been surprisingly disinterested in the fate of the captain and third mate. When the two men returned to the *Barclay* anchored in Taiohae Bay, Pells reported laconically, "At 2 P.M. th[ey] came With the captin And third mate At 8 A.M. one half Went on liberty So ends the day."[19]

Cannibalism, hostage taking, and trading conflicts seemed minor inconveniences in light of what the Marquesas offered whalemen: "girles." In the more than two weeks spent at Taiohae Bay, then with the Hapa'a further up the coast, and in a final trading stop at the island of Ua Huka, Pells devoted nearly every entry of his journal to sexual pleasures.

28 August: "fine times girles With out number"

29 August: "Employed watering And wayghting on The girles"

1 September: "New Heaver is a Fine place for girles And when you heave sayed that you heave sayed all"

2 September: "i shell all ways Remember new heaver And the girles that is thare but dam The men"

5 September: "We are now on Liberty no whare To go nor nothing to Eaght"

6 September: "My girle is dinner Enough for me"

7 September: "Pay one of[f] and Take another that is the tuch"

8 September: "Harpar girles is the danday but give me New heaver yet"

11 September: "Wayed anchor in new heaver And went to sea . . . So fare well girls on shore i nare shell see you more"

13 September: "at 8 A.M. went with 2 boats on shore at Wohego at 5 returned with girles"

14 September: "At 8 A.M. went again Returned with hogs And so ends the day"

15 September: "At [Meridian] got through Treading and hauled our wind to the South"

Pells's experiences can be filled in from other sources. When the *Barclay* came to anchor in Taiohae Bay, a horde of young, startlingly beautiful girls would have swum to the ship and climbed aboard, naked or dressed in a small strip of tapa or trade cloth. If the captain allowed it, which was usually the case, they stayed aboard while the ship lay at anchor, floating from man to man, giving themselves to foreign seamen so cheaply that their sexual favors seemed to be free.[20] Captain Barney would have traded for food, water, and wood with the most valued objects in the Marquesas, muskets and sperm whales' teeth, but Pells and other seamen had nearly as valuable items in the ordinary contents of a sea chest: handkerchiefs, worn-out pieces of clothing, tobacco, knives, buttons, and small broken bits of iron.[21] From the days of first contact in Polynesia, foreigners—who were at that time nearly all men—felt overwhelmed with surprise, delight, or consternation at the vehemence with which native girls and women offered themselves or were offered up to them at the urging of husbands, mothers, and fathers. What had started as a sacred offering, a way to empower through an exchange of *mana* or a sacrificial offering to call on the power of the gods, rapidly devolved to become purely a commercial transaction engaged in by women of the lowest rank. Those who boarded the *Essex* and its prizes in 1813, Porter noted, were "of the most common kind" and so accustomed to visiting ships, they knew "some few English words, which they pronounced too plain to be misunderstood."[22]

They also incorporated new words, according to ABCFM missionary William Patterson Alexander in a reference to venereal disease: "*papae* the name the natives give to *that disease*, is also the term by which they designate a *sailor*."[23] The Marquesas, more than any other Pacific island group in contact with whalemen, were especially beset by the virulent spread of venereal diseases. Whalemen heading in to the Marquesas warned other sailors of the flagrant "vice and immorality" on the beach and told stories such as how recently only seventy of the 700 men on a French frigate had escaped "disorders brought upon them by their familiarity with the women of these islands."[24] The islands' reputation for sexual contagion did not put a dent in the sex trade. Women's sexual liberty was one local custom numerous American seamen in Polynesia did not repudiate as repellent but instead cultivated and enjoyed, interpreting it as a sign of savagery at its most innocent.

Pells's shore experiences in all the Pacific islands the *Barclay* visited seem those of the stereotypical sailor, with women and wine, gin, and rum preoccupying his entries. Those islands with the largest settlements of European and American merchants and drifters involved seamen in a different kind of violence than what the *Barclay* encountered at the Marquesas, a street violence of drunken brawls and sailors' riots, which newly consolidated kingdoms at Tahiti and Hawai'i tried to regulate but with mixed success. Pells thought Tahiti in 1837 "a fine place for cold water people no rum or gin to be sold in this place." But it was sold anyhow, and those among the *Barclay*'s crew caught drinking had to go to the courthouse and pay a steep $18 fine. Pells went on a spree: "Play all day and a Prity girl at night"; "Ashore all day and Ashore all night And what more can a man want"; "Ashore day and night And wine and rum Enough to drink."[25] In Hawai'i, despite laws limiting the sale of alcohol, Pells complained, "there is one bad thing in this place that is rum ther is so much that men gits drunk by the smell of it." Perhaps he condemned the rum out of regret for overindulging, but drunken hands lolling about the decks also made more work for the sober: "No work to be dun untill this rum has its way dam all the Rum i say."[26]

Pells never questioned the ready availability of sex, the other vice besides alcohol let loose on Pacific ports by the demands of foreign seamen. The nineteenth-century Hawaiian historian S. M. Kamakau captured the tragedy of the sex trade: "The sailors used to pay for women with a piece of cloth, a small mirror, or a pair of shears, beads, a small piece of steel, a plug of tobacco, or a small coin; and for these things the women paid in venereal diseases."[27] If Pells was conscious of this most deleterious effect of sailor town sexuality, he never mentioned it in his journal. Instead, he wrote about native women as though sexual pleasure was a game or sport, and one that whalemen were entitled to enjoy. During the *Barclay*'s first extended stay in Hawai'i, in October and November of 1837, the crew could expect to find willing women on shore: "All hands on Board but baker And he is a squaw Hunting no fear saturday morning At 8 A.M. he came on board like a man And the starboard watch Went on shore."[28] (Baker was a Mashpee surname, and so this Baker could have been from Pells's home community.) But by the time the *Barclay* returned to Oahu a year later, Kamehameha III had fallen into a penitent mood, his "Great Awakening," as ABCFM missionary Titus Coan called it.[29] Conceding to the wishes of the missionaries and his half-sister and co-ruler Kina'u, the king reinstated earlier decrees banning prostitution. The 1820s initiatives enacted during Kamehameha III's youth by regent and co-ruler Ka'ahumanu had resulted in violent protests by British and American ship captains, who blamed the new laws on missionary interference. Lieutenant John Percival of the U.S.S. *Dolphin*, stopping at Honolulu on its return from the Mulgraves with *Globe* mutiny survivors Lay and Hussey, threatened military force if his men were not allowed to entertain themselves with women.[30]

These protests tested Hawaiian sovereignty. Percival won his demands, and prostitution serving foreign sailors continued to flourish in the harbor, despite Kamehameha III's reinforcement of the earlier ban. In a study of Honolulu crime data beginning in the years 1838 and 1839, Robert C. Schmitt found that over half of the convictions were for sex crimes, variously categorized as adultery, fornication, prostitution, lewdness, seduction, and pimping, so this was a law the Hawaiian government took seriously.[31] Pells called it a "tarboo," recording the punishment for a man and woman caught together as a $10 fine each. Now, the crew could "go on shore to see the girles But we are not Alowed to touch them no how." A few days later, he wrote, "the law is so now that We can not git no girles for lov nor money." Sad that "Times is not as they Was last year," he seems to have had his fun anyhow, mentioning as they weighed anchor, "Hear is hell to pay And no cash."[32] To leave port, the captain may have had to add one or more $10 charges to Pells's slops account.

: : :

Where Pells reveled in the sybaritic and sacrilegious, Joseph Ammons's demeanor aimed for the devout and respectful. Nearly the same age as Pells when he began his journal, while engaged as third mate on the *Roman* in 1843, Ammons too had made a career of whaling, with seven known voyages from the 1830s to his final voyage as second mate on the *James Maury* in the early 1850s.[33] Ammons's professional tone is nicely captured by his entries for 11–12 November 1852, three days after the *James Maury* had come to anchor in Honolulu harbor: "all hands on board Drying bone so Ends [the day] the men from the ship had A mob burnt About 3 houses broke open stores &c."; and the following day, "with fine hot wether drying bone &c several ships came in Put the port under marshal laws." This was the second riot to visit the Hawaiian Islands while Ammons was there. On 15 March 1844, a mob of drunken whalemen broke into the jail and rescued one of their own who had been imprisoned by native authorities. They controlled the streets of Lahaina for two nights, throwing stones and obscenities, until subdued by armed guards.[34] Ammons spent that day overseeing yams that were being brought aboard as the *Roman* made ready to return to sea. The 1852 sailors' riot had similar origins. Hundreds of angry seamen became riled up over the suspicious death of an American whaleman in prison. The rampage through the streets so threatened public order, the king declared martial law.[35] Yet Ammons did not allow himself to be diverted from the more immediate tasks of his occupation, the drying and bundling of bowhead baleen that the *James Maury* had just brought back from the far north.

Changes in the whale fishery as much as distinct personalities caused differences in Pells's and Ammons' journals. The opening up of officer positions to Native American men by the 1840s gave Ammons greater opportunity than Pells to reach a position of authority and status. And even though

Pells and Ammons visited some of the same places, Ammons chased new prey, bowhead whales, on whaling grounds that Pells had never heard of—Kamchatka, Kodiak, the Bering Sea, and, by the end of Ammons's whaling days, the Arctic. The commercial expansion of the Hawaiian ports of Honolulu, Lahaina, and Hilo accelerated to accommodate the ship traffic. In early November 1837, while the *Barclay* lay at anchor in Honolulu, the harbor held ten other American whaleships, three British whaleships, and four Hawaiian-owned schooners.[36] Fifteen years later, when the *James Maury* anchored at Honolulu with Ammons aboard, the number of vessels in the harbor had more than quadrupled to sixty-two American whalers, two American merchant vessels from Boston, and eight whalers from France, Bremen, Great Britain, and Chile.[37] With about thirty men to a whaleship and the standard rotation of watches each taking a turn ashore, as many as 1,000 foreign seamen could come into Honolulu on a single day, surely one of the factors behind the 1852 sailors' riot.

Another change in the whaling industry reflected in Ammons's journal was the rising interest in the moral reform of sailors. The bethel movement, founded originally in England in the 1810s, provided religious instruction to seamen in ports and on ships carrying the bethel flag. Antebellum New England's upswell of religiosity, Sabbatarianism, and temperance advocacy inspired some whaleship owners and captains to designate their ships bethels. They spent the voyage encouraging prayer meetings, Bible reading, and a moral lifestyle.[38] Swept away by this bethel spirit, the officers on the *Roman* from 1843 to 1845, and with less intensity during its 1845–1847 voyage, met for religious services every Sunday afternoon in the ship's cabin. At these "Gloryous meetings," Ammons wrote, "my soal response, with the Praises of glory to god in the highest" and "the lord voreyfyed [verified] his Promis & Poared out A blessing."[39]

This religious fervor continued while in port at Lahaina, in March 1844, before the *Roman* headed up to the Kamchatka whaling grounds, and in September, when the season on the northwest came to a close. Instead of carousing on shore as Pells would have done, Ammons spent his free time in "Preaching Exhorting & Prayers" led by former ABCFM missionary, now seamen's chaplain, Lorrin Andrews who held services on the *Roman* and on the bethel whaleship *Nantasket* of New London, anchored nearby.[40] Once the *Nantasket* sailed, Ammons attended daily prayer meetings at ABCFM missionary Dwight Baldwin's house on the Lahaina waterfront. On its next voyage, the *Roman* used Hilo as its main port, and again Ammons spent his liberty days attending missionary preachings, including one English-language service at the "Connacco [Kanaka] meeting hous," the church

ABCFM missionaries had built to bring native Hawaiians to the Christian faith.[41] If Ammons met or spoke with native Hawaiians, Christian converts, or otherwise, he makes no mention of it in his journal.

Evangelical Christianity in antebellum America considered natives (of North America and the Pacific) and seamen similarly salvageable constituencies of dissolute innocents capable of redemption. Native American whalemen experienced Christian proselytizing in two settings, as sailors while at sea and as Indians when at home, but not as Indians while at sea. When Baldwin came to Hawai'i in 1831 on the New Bedford whaleship *New England* (on the same voyage with Wampanoags Alexander Cuff, Lewis Cook, and Silas DeGrass, whose excitement at seeing a whale Baldwin's colleague Tinker credited to Indian instinct), the missionary party practiced on the seamen what they would do in Hawai'i with the natives. They gave sermons, taught Sunday school and Bible classes, and distributed religious tracts in hopes that the officers and crew would come to realize "the *one great thing.*" The missionaries became discouraged, however, by how the seamen resisted their efforts. While the missionaries preached sermons and sang hymns, the dogwatch hours became more raucous with "loud singing," dancing, and fife playing. Attendance at missionary events dwindled to a few whom Baldwin suspected came only "to gather matter for ridicule."[42] The missionaries singled out the Gay Head Indians for their whaling enthusiasm but not as distinguishable from other sailors in their religion.

Ammons clearly was a believing Christian, like other Narragansetts probably a Second Adventist, and when not at sea, he would have attended church at the Narragansett meetinghouse. His brother Gideon, whom he sailed with on his early voyages, served as a church deacon and, after he retired from whaling, was one of the stone masons who built the Narragansetts' new meetinghouse in 1859.[43] But on the *Roman* and in Hawai'i, Joseph Ammons encountered Christianity through his occupation as a sailor. His expressions of religious sentiment appear only in the two journals kept while he was on the *Roman*, so either his own religious fervor was quelled over time or the *Roman*'s bethel sympathies gave him an allowance to record religious activity in a journal intended to be as impersonal as the official logbook. For those two voyages on a bethel ship, his commitment to excel as a whaleship officer made expressions of religiosity now part of his job.

Ammons's sense of professionalism informs the journals further in his self-representation as a moral person. He often mentions others' lapses while he stayed on board working. Thus, on the coast of California in 1846, a fellow officer went with a boat's crew to a fandango, and Captain Humphrey

Shockley went to a ball and visited a "Berdago," presumably either a bodega or bordello. This event may explain why Ammons seemed to develop a disdain for Captain Shockley. Two months later, in an unfortunately not fully legible passage in his journal, Ammons took on the persona of a mock explorer engaging in a ceremony of possession while passing a reef northeast of Clipperton Island "to which I giv the name Humphrey S reef &c &c Shocklyes belsuebub S reef." While other whalemen found sensual pleasures ashore, Ammons indulged himself in only one kind of entertainment—hunting deer, ducks, and geese—but even gave up that when he sold his gun to another whaler's second mate.[44]

By listening to missionaries instead of carousing, Ammons chose to spend his time in port in different ways than Pells did, but as American whalemen they both depended on trade with Pacific Islanders for basic sustenance. In February 1846, the *Roman* stopped at Pitcairn Island to purchase sweet potatoes from the part-Tahitian descendants of the *Bounty* mutineers. A year later at Easter Island, "the natives came of[f] with 10 or 12 Canoes and A number of men and wiming [women] swam of got About 12 bl of potatoes with shuger cane bananers yams tara &c for black fish scraps A few stavs, iron, hooks &c with A few fish hooks."[45] And the prospect of trade turning into an attack by "savages" was as much a part of Ammons's world as Pells's. The most dramatic incident he recorded in his journal on 7 October 1844. At Penrhyn Island (Tongareva, Cook Islands), several canoes carrying more than fifty people "came within Hail" of the *Roman*. They "gabered [jabbered] much," so that the two Hawaiians in the crew could "not understand one word." They had no hogs or fruit, causing Captain Shockley to remark, "Poor buisness when thare onley barter was thare wiming [women]." More ominously, when the canoes came within a "Pistol shot" of the ship, the islanders hauled up as though waiting for a signal, so Captain Shockley armed his men with muskets and cutting spades and set the sails to back away from the island. To keep them from pursuing, Shockley threw out a box of tobacco, which several of the natives dove for in the water "As if A Presous tresure had been lost."

This scare led Ammons to write a longer than usual entry, in which he situated himself as an outsider observing people whom he considered different from himself: "the People ware vary larg and muskuler long bodeyed & strait the most Part of them tall men not Copulent the larg Cano had females in it how meney is not none [known] Whyenes [wahines/women] ware seen in Each of the Canoes . . . the Canaccoas ware stark necked and from Every appearenc ware saveag." Other foreigners in the Pacific had an identical experience at Penryhn and, concluding that it was "inhabited by a race of hostile savages," also backed away from the island, scared by the aggressiveness of its people.[46]

Such incidents were rare, however, in the thousands upon thousands of exchanges taking place throughout the nineteenth-century Pacific. As new whaling grounds opened up, whalers usually found amicable trading partners nearby. On the *James Maury* at the end of his whaling career, Ammons came to know and work with Yupik and Inuit peoples. Arriving at St. Lawrence Island, he reported "traiding with the Esqemot indeon" one day and how, on the following day, the captain left with "the Chief of the Bay to the Inden Setelment," returning two days later with "3 rain Deer ready dressed" while "the Chief went Away with 7 Boxes of tobackco." Over the next few days, they met again "with Pittarah and others [and] soalde 2 cags of tobacco and A rifle &c for ivery and Bone."[47] Missionaries had not yet arrived at St. Lawrence Island, and so Ammons had no opportunity to attend church.

: : :

As the whaling industry expanded further into the western Arctic and Hudson Bay in the latter half of the nineteenth century, native New England whalemen continued, like whalemen in general, to depend on other native people for sustenance and a successful voyage. The *Navarch* in the 1890s, which had Joseph G. Belain of Gay Head aboard as first mate, had a long-standing relationship with particular Arctic communities as trading partners and helpmates. As the *Navarch* steamed through Bering Strait toward the overwintering grounds at Herschel Island in April 1894, it stopped at several established trading points where the crew purchased over 600 pairs of native-made boots, fur coats and pants, and dogs for sledding. Along the way, they also picked up Mungi and his wife, with other Inuit families, to work for them. The *Navarch*'s captain, John A. Cook, acknowledged Mungi's importance to the voyage and how his "skill and markmanship" kept the crew alive with fresh meat during the winter. The 200 or so native residents of Herschel Island also hunted for the several overwintering whalers and cared for the hundreds of dogs needed to cart food to the vessels. As the *Navarch* headed back to San Francisco in the fall of 1896, Cook dropped native hunters off at their home communities and "paid them in trade for their work."[48]

Native New England whalemen had similar encounters with Inuit on the eastern side of the continent. The schooner *Abbie Bradford* of New Bedford routinely whaled in Hudson Bay in the 1880s, sometimes overwintering.

William Garrison Lee, Shinnecock, served as first mate on the 1880–1881 voyage. After the captain died early on, Lee had to take charge. As in the western Arctic, the natives who camped near their vessel hunted to supply the crew with meat but interacted socially as well. Lee's young nephew Milton Winfield Lee came along on the voyage as a greenhand. Family members recalled his memories of the voyage: the walrus tusk souvenir that they kept in the family parlor and had to dust as children, how he said he could never seem to get free of the smell of boiled blubber, and fonder memories of how the native women used to come aboard and dance during the long winter while the schooner lay mired in snow and ice.[49]

On the 1886–1888 voyage of the *Abbie Bradford*, first mate William H. Morton of Gay Head did not mention what the crew did for entertainment, but the logbook he kept details the extent of work Inuits performed on behalf of the crew's survival. The schooner entered Hudson Bay in the fall, and the crew built a tryworks station on shore for processing whales, waited for snow so they could bank it up alongside the ship, and traded with the natives for "fresh meat"—240 pounds one day, 782 pounds another day, 1,164 pounds another day.[50] The logbook mentions no trading with the natives in the harshest winter months, but in March trade picked up again, and every few days thereafter, natives brought in loads of meat for the crew. In June, they all began whaling. Morton and one of the boatsteerers each took charge of a whaleboat manned entirely by locals and, to maximize their odds, concentrated their efforts in different locations, with Morton taking his boat's crew to Whale Point. On an "expedition" that lasted about two months, Morton must have come to know his Inuit workers well despite language barriers, but because the logbook stayed with the schooner, we learn little about his experiences except that their efforts earned them a poor return of only a few animal skins.

During the summer, those who remained with the schooner had constant interaction with the native camp on shore. Natives brought deer and seal meat, salmon, skins, seal blubber and white fish blubber to be boiled into oil, and news of whale sightings. The captain even fitted their boats for whaling New Bedford–style, incorporating native men fully in the schooner's whaling enterprise, though not according to the lay system by which New Bedford crew members received their pay. Native laborers must have been paid with the various trade items mentioned in the logbook: rifles, bullets, gunpowder, needles, and whaling equipment. Natives who wanted these items badly enough might resort to violence, but as was the *Abbie Bradford*'s experience, relations between American whalemen and Arctic natives tended to be friendly because each party perceived an advantage in the situation.

Even though whaling journals, logbooks, and memoirs recounting Arctic voyages rarely mention sexual relations, trade in sex continued to be commonplace. Some whaling captains formed long-standing associations with a female relative of the man acting as liaison between the whaling vessel's captain and the Inuit workers. From the native point of view, such relationships generated personal bonds to sustain otherwise impersonal exchanges. The most well-known case of an enduring relationship is that of George Comer and Shoofly, a wife of one of the Inuits who assisted Comer. Comer's journal of a 1903–1905 voyage on the *Era* of New London mentions "our natives" hunting, fishing, whaling, and transporting materials on the *Era's* behalf several times a week. Nearly all are references to Inuit men. The journal never mentions Shoofly, who we know from other sources, especially from Inuit family memories, lived with Comer year after year while he sojourned on the Hudson Bay whaling grounds.[51]

Even whalemen of lesser rank found female companions.[52] Many of the men with William H. Morton on the *Abbie Bradford* were having sexual relations with native women, as is apparent in his reports of crew illnesses in the logbook. Morton's only ailment was a weeklong case of snow blindness recorded on 24 April 1887. However, his shipmates mostly suffered "with venereal." On 3 December 1886, five months after the schooner had left New Bedford, two men came down with it, two more on 29 December, and one more on 2 January 1887. When Morton was away on his whaling expedition in the summer of 1887, the second mate took over the logbook and reported one more case, this time specifically gonorrhea, on 20 June 1887. These particular whalemen must have picked up the disease from native women, but visiting whalemen, along with other foreign visitors to Hudson Bay, such as fur traders, introduced these diseases to the region and contributed greatly to the rapid spread of disease among the native population.[53]

Dorothy Eber's interviews with Inuits about turn-of-the-century industrial whaling in the eastern Arctic put a positive face on this history, as the people she talked to told of the new, exciting experiences and prosperity that cooperation with foreign whalers brought to their parents, grandparents, and the community as a whole.[54] As with Oceania, it is in hindsight that the negative consequences of colonization—demographic effects of introduced diseases, cultural loss and prejudice, environmental unsustainability, and diminishment of sovereignty—loom the largest. However, initially, when trade inspired the coming together of native and foreigner, they could see mutual benefit in that relationship.

Wherever they went around the world, American whalemen gave out guns, knives, and tobacco, but what the native peoples had to offer changed dramatically as they produced items for sale from their distinct environments. Arctic peoples had no pigs or coconuts. They traded in deer and seal meat, whalebone, and blubber from the marine mammals they hunted and cold-weather jackets, boots, and mittens, which they mass-produced to sell to passing whalers. Whalemen needed native help, not just materials of native manufacture but also native survival skills and knowledge of their particular environments. Like Hawaiians, Maoris, Tahitians, and other Pacific peoples, Arctic peoples contributed more than the products of their respective regions, for their labor also became vital to the business of catching whales. Whereas Pacific Islanders usually joined whaling crews for the remaining years of a long voyage and could end up displaced as part of a labor diaspora, Arctic peoples usually contracted with a particular captain for the season, year after year, and rarely returned to New England or San Francisco with the ship.

The American whaling industry's movement outward around the world created "natives" and "Indians" in a multitude of places. The processes of cultural contact and exchange, resource and labor expropriation within a globalizing economy, the spread of Christianity and the English language, and the concomitant migrations and mixing of people connected native New Englanders to Pacific Islanders and to Arctic peoples by giving them elements of a shared past as peoples subject to the forces of foreign imperial expansion. Simultaneously, these "natives" shared a past through actual interactions, but when native New England whalemen encountered Pacific Islanders or Arctic peoples, structural expectations about such encounters made laborers on whaleships less visible as natives and Indians themselves. The dominant culture imagined the situation of the cultural encounter as having only two sides—whites and Indians, civilized and savage, Christians and non-Christians, the familiar and the ethnographically exotic, people who came by ships and people who lived on shore. James F. Pells, Joseph Ammons, William Garrison Lee, and William H. Morton all resided on Indian reservations in the United States, and thus they appear as Indians and natives in records produced about their home communities. But their Indian, or tribal, identities are only barely discernible in whaling records, even in their own writings. Joseph Ammons did sign the front of one volume of his journal, "Charles Town Nareganst Joseph Ammons."[55] Being

Narragansett was a part of his identity, but when he sat down each day to write an entry in his journal, he wrote in his role as third and then second mate on a whaleship. He and other Native American whalemen were not identifying as or claiming to be white, but their status as American sailors took precedence in defining them when they traveled to foreign lands because the situation they were in delegated to others the role of native.

PART III : ISLANDS

7 : Native American Beachcombers in the Pacific

The American whaleship was a world of its own, but whenever vessels made landfall, whalemen found themselves in a local culture where formulations of race had a unique character arising out of the history of that place. These islands of particular racial beliefs and practices sometimes bore similarity to each other, especially in the nineteenth-century Pacific, where the arrival of new peoples as explorers, traders, and settlers generated schemes of racial categorization built on the juxtaposition of native and foreigner. Having been born elsewhere, as speakers of the English language, dressed as American seamen, and often Christian, Native Americans who settled in other places around the world counted among the foreigners. Because the majority of foreigners espoused identities as white Europeans or white Americans, "foreigner," "white," and "European" often operated as synonyms in opposition to "native," and racial distinctions within the category "foreigner," although acknowledged, had little bearing on individual experience. Even while their acquaintances recognized them as American Indians and even though they seem to have carried that as an expression of their own identities throughout their lives, circumstances put Native American beachcombers into the role of foreign settlers and gave them more in common with other Americans than with natives of other lands.

Most Native American whalemen died at sea or from illness or old age in the land of their birth. Only a few never returned because they chose the life of a beachcomber instead. Usually escaped convicts or sailors, who through desertion, shipwreck, or other happenstance found themselves captives or guests of a native community, beachcombers had a bad reputation. One white whaleman derided "beachcomber" as "the worst insult you can offer an able seaman": it "shows how low a white man will get when he sells his birthright and goes to live with savages."[1] Sharing the same connotations as "squaw man" in the American West, "beachcomber" conjured up an image of a man who began life with all the privileges of the white race and civil society but, choosing to live among Pacific Islanders, degenerated into a nude, tattooed, polygamous scoundrel who was not to be trusted. In actuality, few beachcombers acted all that scurrilously. As linguistic and cultural interpreters, they helped ship captains and newly arrived mission-aries find their way and usually remained loyal to other foreigners. Like "squaw men" in the American West, American beachcombers seem in ret-rospect the vanguard of expansion into the Pacific, many serving as the most effective instruments the United States had for furthering its com-mercial interests at the far edges of the American frontier.[2]

Part 3 looks closely at two American beachcombers—John Sparr in Fiji (in this chapter) and Elisha Apes in New Zealand (in chapter 8)—but there must have been more Native Americans who became lifelong Pacific resi-dents than the half-dozen I know of. Maybe information will someday turn up to reveal what happened to Jophanus Salsbury of Gay Head, who "'went to sea and never came back.'"[3] Other native New Englanders spent time as drifters but found their way home eventually. After a long absence, Aaron Cooper returned to Gay Head fluent in French and with a set of navigational instruments.[4] Had he served on French whaleships or lived and worked in French Polynesia? Other native whalemen took their chances in the gold-fields of California and Australia, some leaving forever, others coming home. Sylvanus E. Wainer gave up on the Australia goldfields to return to West-port, Massachusetts, where he lived out his life a farmer.[5]

Another fleeting beachcomber was Wainer's relation Paul Cuffe Jr., whose Pacific adventures an upstate New York hotel keeper published in 1839 as the *Narrative of the Life and Adventures of Paul Cuffe, a Pequot In-dian: During Thirty Years Spent at Sea, and in Travelling in Foreign Lands*. Discharged from a whaler at Paita, Peru, Cuffe wandered through the countryside, picking up odd jobs, first at a distillery and then on a farm. Returning to Paita, he shipped aboard the Newport, Rhode Island, whaler *Mechanic*. The vessel stopped to trade at "Reupore Islands," probably Rapa Nui (Easter Island), since Cuffe said of the place, "they worship idols made of stone." Then, at Raiatea in the Society Islands, Cuffe left the *Mechanic* "and went among the natives, who were a very friendly, hospitable people. Here I stayed five months, and learned much of the customs and manners of the country." When a Martha's Vineyard whaler appeared off Raiatea, the captain urged him to ship. Swayed by the captain's suggestion "that my folks at home would be glad to see me, I finally concluded to go with him." Cuffe's account represents the Raiateans in a manner typical for the time, as "naked," living "promiscuously together," "poor, but happy," "very indo-lent, having every thing necessary for their subsistence growing spontane-ously around them," "peaceable and happy," "happy in their poverty, and contented in their simplicity." However, as this is an as-told-to memoir, the exact wording may not have been Cuffe's own.[6]

Some Native Americans did settle permanently in the Pacific. Besides Sparr and Apes, I know of two Shinnecock men, two men from Gay Head, and even one woman from Chappaquiddick who did so. William Garrison Lee told a visitor to the Shinnecock reservation in 1882 that his brother Notley had "deserted his ship, reached the Kingsmill group of islands in the Pacific, married the chief's daughter, and is now king there."[7] Since their brother Ferdinand, while captain of the *Callao* in 1874, hired Notley from Tongatapu as fourth mate for a season of humpback whaling, Notley probably had formed a connection in Tonga, though he may have later moved to the Kingsmill Group (southern Kiribati).[8] The other Shinnecock who became a permanent resident in the Pacific I learned of from David Bunn Martine, director of the Shinnecock Nation Cultural Center and Museum. An American stationed in the Pacific in World War II told Martine's grandfather that at Penrhyn Island (Tongareva, Cook Islands) he had run into Daniel David Kellis, a local administrator or magistrate who had lived on the island for decades but still recalled many old acquaintances from Shinnecock.[9]

Of the two Gay Head men who settled on the North Island of New Zealand, the most is known about Marcellus Cook because some of his descendants contacted the tribe at Aquinnah and have come to Martha's Vineyard on ancestral pilgrimages. At age eighteen, Cook deserted from the *Swallow* of New Bedford in 1885 when it stopped for extended repairs at Russell, Bay of Islands. He stayed in the area and married a series of Maori women, had many children, and worked most of his life as a fisherman.[10] A contemporary of Cook's, William Wallace James, married Annie Mabel Allen of Norfolk Island in 1890 while "on a run" (on liberty) at Russell, New Zealand, as first mate on the *Niger*.[11] Allen's father was a whaleman from Nantucket, and her mother descended from a prominent Ngapuhi family.[12] James probably arranged for his wife to come back with him on the *Niger*, as a year later she gave birth to a daughter at Gay Head.[13] While James served as second mate on the *Charles W. Morgan* out of San Francisco on several voyages over the next few years, he was one of many in the crew with family connections to Norfolk Island and the Bay of Islands.[14] The couple left the United States in 1896, probably to live with her family at Norfolk Island, and by 1908 they had resettled in Auckland, New Zealand, where James registered as an American citizen with the U.S. consul.[15] In 1935, he became a naturalized citizen of New Zealand but over the years still kept in touch with his Wampanoag kin.[16]

As for the woman from Chappaquiddick, Elizabeth James Perry of the Aquinnah Wampanoag tribe told me that she had run across an 1899 land deed noting that Lucretia Belain had died at Tahiti thirty-five to forty years earlier, leaving a four-year-old daughter "whose present whereabouts is unknown."[17] In an earlier deed signed in February 1861, two days after her marriage to whaleman Elijah Johnson (identified as "col'd"—colored—and from Falmouth, Massachusetts, in the marriage record), Lucretia Johnson and her new husband quitclaimed her rights to the "Indian Lands" at Chappaquiddick to her father Isaiah Belain for $30.[18] They must have already decided to emigrate to Tahiti. Perhaps Elijah had visited Tahiti on an earlier voyage and fantasized about a life in paradise, or maybe whaling kin or acquaintances had landed there as beachcombers and encouraged them to join them. Elijah could have made an off-the-books arrangement with the agent of the *Almira* to take his wife as passenger in exchange for his labor. The *Almira*'s final settlement accounts for the 1864–1868 voyage list him as a boasteerer and indicate that he left the vessel about two years into the voyage.[19] A surviving journal from the voyage documents the *Almira*'s presence in French Polynesia at that time but does not mention Johnson's departure or whether there was a woman aboard.[20]

None of these native North Americans who settled in foreign places as a by-product of the whaling industry seems to deserve the disreputable taint of beachcomber. From what little is known of them, they led lives of respectability, often marrying into a native family in their new home. That did not make them natives, however. In the cases of John Sparr in Fiji and Elisha Apes on the South Island of New Zealand, their status as transplanted foreigners remained an influence on how their adoptive communities regarded them.

: : :

John Sparr received his discharge from an American whaleship at Fiji probably in the mid-1840s, at the end of the beachcombing era, when most of Fiji's several hundred foreign residents still had origins as shipwrecked, deserted, or discharged seamen but well before the Fiji land boom of the 1860s.[21] Fiji's most notorious beachcombers had come to harvest sandalwood at the beginning of the century. Charley Savage and Paddy Connell so accustomed themselves to the ways of Fiji that tales of the high status their muskets earned them, their harems of a hundred wives, and cannibal feasts they may have attended still circulated decades later.[22] Trade in bêche-de-mer (a sea slug valued in Chinese cuisine) and tortoise shell brought a second generation of stranded sailors in the 1820s, among them David Whippy of Nantucket, Fiji's most influential beachcomber and the most famous American beachcomber in Oceania.[23] Although Sparr belonged to an even later generation of beachcombers, he and Whippy overlapped and were involved in many of the same events. If they had stayed in the United States, they never would have met or found a common history. Sparr was a Seminole from Florida. Racial prejudice in American society denied him the advantages that gave the Whippys of the world the promise of social mobility. Moreover, his people were at war with the United States in the first half of the nineteenth century. As residents of Fiji, however, Sparr, Whippy, and their "half-caste" children found themselves in a similar situation. Sparr's status as a native elsewhere did not make him any less an outsider in Fiji. Although Whippy had more prominence and visibility than Sparr, they led parallel lives by belonging to the small, weak community of foreign residents in Fiji who looked to the United States to protect them.

In the more than twenty years in between Whippy's 1824 arrival and when Sparr begins to show up in the records, relations between beachcombers and native Fijians deteriorated. Whippy had come to Fiji indirectly. After deserting from a Nantucket whaleship in South America and sailing on English merchant vessels, Whippy landed at Fiji with instructions from Captain Peter Dillon of the *Calder* to trade for tortoise shell, but Dillon never returned for him or the cargo.[24] Whippy took up residence at Levuka on the island of Ovalau under the protection of Tui Levuka (a title that meant ruler of Levuka), who was then in league with Bau, soon to become Fiji's most powerful province under the leadership of Cakobau (pronounced "Thakombau").[25] Early on, Whippy dressed as a Fijian, fought in Fijian wars, became Tui Levuka's royal messenger to Bau, and married Tui Levuka's sister along with several other women while also gathering other foreigners around him—Yap islanders, sailors from a Manila brig who had mutinied, British, and Americans. By the 1830s, he was reckoned "chief" of Levuka's "white men," as they were called despite their diversity. Because of its concentration of foreigners, Levuka became the first stop for ships seeking interpreters to negotiate trade with Fijian leaders such as Cakobau.[26]

When the U.S. Exploring Expedition came to Fiji in 1840, Whippy and other beachcombers served as pilots and cultural intermediaries, assisting in surveying the islands to enhance charts and make ship traffic through the islands safer. Whippy's support of the U.S. Ex Ex—his condoning of the retaliatory violence that concluded the expedition's three-month sojourn in Fiji, for example—shows how increased American interest in Fiji gave beachcombers such as himself more opportunity to assert an American identity. Years later, Whippy's "half-breed" son David Jr. reassured an American visitor that foreigners at Fiji could now feel safer because of "the prompt and decided punishment awarded by the commander of the Expedition for the murder of two of his officers."[27] On his return to the United States, the

Expedition's commander, Charles Wilkes, recommended Whippy as vice consul to serve under Salem merchant John B. Williams, the first U.S. consular agent in Fiji.[28] Appointed in 1846 under the official title of U.S. commercial agent, Williams set up his trading entrepôt and consular office at Nukulau Island opposite Rewa, where another cluster of beachcombers resided (see map 3).[29]

Preoccupied by war with Rewa and a delicate alliance with King George of Tonga, Cakobau did not anticipate the slumbering powers such paltry foreigners could claim by birthright. Williams wanted the United States to exercise more aggression and begged repeatedly for U.S. ships of war to make Fiji a routine stop. In a scandalous letter to a Sydney newspaper, Williams proclaimed that "Bau ought to be destroyed, and the people swept from the face of the earth. . . . A ship of war could lay off Bau, knock down and destroy that town, while one is smoking a cigar."[30] In March 1851, the U.S. sloop of war *Falmouth* arrived in Fiji at Williams's behest. He had reached back ten years to compile a list of grievances that included plundering of the wrecks of the whalers *Elizabeth* and *Tim Pickering* and losses Williams incurred during an 1849 Fourth of July celebration. (A misfired cannon burned down Williams's house, and in the confusion, some people from Beqa had helped themselves to whales' teeth, muskets, and other trade goods.)[31] Williams proposed to Captain Thomas Petigru of the *Falmouth* that a fine of $17,000 in bêche-de-mer, coconut oil, and tortoise shell be levied against Cakobau, whom Williams now addressed as Tui Viti, "King of the Feejees," a ploy to make the individual with the most resources diplomatically responsible for all incidents of violence between natives and foreigners.[32] Four years later, when the U.S. sloop-of-war *John Adams* came to Fiji to investigate the American claims, Williams found a sympathetic audience in its commander, E. B. Boutwell, and the fine climbed to $45,000. Whippy had joined the list of American claimants. He demanded $1,500 from Cakobau for damages from the burning of Levuka in 1846 and $4,500 from the people of Viwa for the burning and destruction of Levuka in 1853, when the foreign residents became casualties in a war between the Christians of Viwa and Tui Levuka.[33]

In the 1850s, new coalitions emerged as Fiji's foreigners began moving from the periphery toward positions of influence. Cakobau remained the most powerful person in Fiji, but he faced challenges from all sides: ambitious rivals that now included Tui Levuka (son of Whippy's patron), tributary peoples challenging his customary privileges by choosing Christianity, Tongan expansion, and Williams's threats to unleash American ships of war to enforce payment of the American claims. Whippy and other beach-

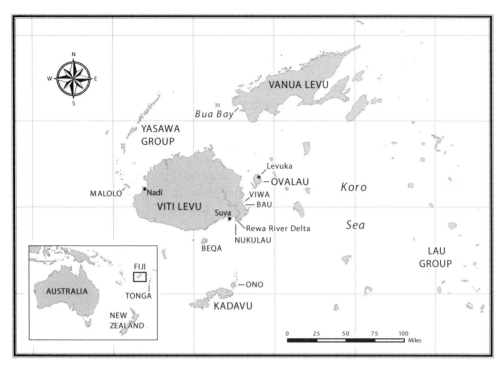

Map 3. *Fiji Islands. John Sparr ended his days at Kenia, on the island of Ono, where he resided with his Fijian wife and children. Before he acquired Kenia in 1855, he probably lived at properties claimed and built by U.S. commercial agent John B. Williams: Nukulau Island and Laucala in the Rewa River Delta area. Map by Brian Perchal.*

combers allied with Williams against Cakobau, even to the point of plotting his assassination.[34] In need of allies, Cakobau resorted to the English missionaries, who then undertook battle with Williams on his own terms, by writing letters to Sydney newspapers and appealing to warship commanders for justice. Although the claims Williams pursued were technically American claims, national origins among Fiji's foreign population had little impact on their allegiances, and any ship of war arriving in Fiji— American, British, and even French—became embroiled in foreign residents' pleas for protection of their lives and property.[35]

: : :

In the storm of protests, reports, and correspondence Williams stirred up with his outlandish demands appear references to John Sparr. Sparr was a claimant, too, and moreover one of the few to see his claim expeditiously satisfied. A few months after the departure of the *John Adams*, Williams noted that Charles Rounds of New Bedford had received the $155 due him from the people of Kadavu, who also paid "John Sparr (An American Indian) in lands for goods pillaged from him."[36] The missionary James Calvert, stationed at Viwa, attributed to Sparr an even deeper role in the pursuit of the claims than mere recipient. Hoping to expose the injustice of Williams's machinations, Calvert wrote the U.S. secretary of state a lengthy letter, which along the way implicated Sparr by stating that Williams, America Shattuck, and "a Florida Indian . . . spent three days to get up a statement designed to prejudice the Commanders of Ships of war against the missionaries."[37] Published as "Doings in the South Sea Islands," the article appeared in the Sydney *Empire* in May 1853 and purported to be a speech Shattuck and others heard at Rewa in which Fijians wondered who the "big chiefs" really were—commanders of ships of war or missionaries.[38]

I have not run across any documents in Sparr's own voice to know whether he supported Williams's pursuit of the American claims out of necessity or obligation, from self-interest so that he could secure a foothold in Fiji through this opportunity the American claims presented, or because he, like Whippy and other beachcombers, found that ultimately his status as a foreigner defined the bounds of his community. The small size of the foreign population made them vulnerable. In 1851, Williams gave the figure as "about 250 white men—that is whites & cold. [colored] Europeans & Americans."[39] While Williams acknowledged Sparr's racial distinctiveness as an "American Indian," he went out of his way to claim Sparr as a fellow American. Sparr's own views on his situation and motivations may be irretrievable, but what is certain is that Americans in Fiji embraced him as one of their own.

Exactly how and when Sparr came to Fiji remains a mystery. Florida was not frequented by American whalers. He may have been a refugee from the dislocations of the Seminole–U.S. wars, perhaps entering the maritime world by way of the vessels that transported defeated Seminoles into the American interior. Or Elijah Swift's live-oak timber operations in north-central Florida could have brought him to Falmouth, Massachusetts, and then out into the ocean again on whalers. Since American whaleships more often stopped at the Bay of Islands than at Fiji, it is possible that Sparr disembarked from a whaleship at the Bay of Islands and came to Fiji with Williams in 1846. Although I know of no other Seminoles employed in the New England whale fishery in Sparr's time, there was a well-known Seminole on the lecture circuit, John Bemo, who told of how, upon the death of his father while they were in St. Augustine, sailors brought him aboard their ship as cabin boy. In his several years spent at sea, he took the name of a mentor and converted to Christianity. When he visited a sailors' bethel in

Philadelphia, the pastor cultivated his religious convictions, which led Bemo eventually to become a missionary and teacher among Seminoles in Indian territory.[40] Sparr was also Christian. When Calvert implicated Sparr as Williams's coconspirator, he disparaged Sparr as someone who styled himself a preacher because he "formerly 'made 'em religion, and 'baptized 'em.'"[41] But mainly Calvert and the other missionaries at Fiji so despised Williams, Sparr became a target of their derision as one of Williams's helpmates.

And Sparr did indeed help Williams. During the two months' stay of the *John Adams* in Fijian waters, Williams moved on board, where he persuaded Boutwell to take his side unflinchingly and make a show of force.[42] In late October 1855, Boutwell launched a series of raids, which resulted in the burning of five towns within a week's time. The first of these was at Vutia. To assist Williams in "quieting the people of Vutia, (his neighbors,) and who are a complete set of robbers and murderers," Boutwell assigned acting master O. C. Badger and a contingent of twelve men. Badger demanded the surrender of two Vutians who Williams claimed had threatened to kill him and take his property once the *John Adams* left. When the people of Vutia did not hand over the two men, "we then opened fire with shrapnell and grape, and, after two discharges, one-half of our force jumped ashore and fired the place, which was soon reduced to ashes." In his report of the mission, Badger singled out for commendation the "North American Seminole Indian" who had acted as "pilot and interpreter." When the natives of Vutia "returned with tokens of submission" and promised not to harm Williams, further agreeing to "plant his yams for him the ensuing year . . . a speech was interpreted to them in a very impressive manner by the Indian, in which they were told that they had now seen what white men can do." Not only did Sparr serve Badger well as interpreter, "he took a forward part in burning the town. He is a very brave man, and in the excitement of a fight, shows very clearly what kind of blood flows in his veins." Both Boutwell and Badger attributed to Sparr a critical role in Boutwell's efforts to secure "the rights of my countrymen, and justice for them."[43]

Along the way, the *John Adams* had acquired a hostage on Sparr's behalf, Koroiravulo. Boutwell wrote in his summary of the events, "On the 1st November, the friends and relatives of the chief I took on board for robbing John Spear, an American Indian, and a citizen of the United States, paid up the amount, and the chief was released." Boutwell "made the natives pay" Sparr $300, about the same amount on average received by four other redressed Americans.[44] Boutwell probably knew that as a Seminole Indian Sparr was not an American citizen according to U.S. law and yet wanted to distinguish him as someone fully on the side of American interests in Fiji.

The $300 ransom paid for Koroiravulo's release took form as a piece of land called Kenia, an abandoned village site of about seventy-five acres on the island of Ono, adjacent to the larger island of Kadavu. The trajectory of events enabling the ransom gives insight into the complicated hierarchies of deference and obligation informing Fijian politics. Cakobau brought about Koroiravulo's release by asking Tui Dreketi to arrange for Sparr to receive some land at Kadavu. Tui Dreketi then sent an emissary to Tui Vabea at Ono asking him to give Sparr Kenia, land Sparr specifically requested.[45]

Sparr would go on to acquire other lands in his own name and in Williams's name. Beginning in the late 1850s, Fiji's foreigners rushed to document land purchases in a paper trail of deeds signed by sellers and witnesses and registered before consuls at Levuka or Sydney. While pursuing his damages claim, Williams went on a shopping spree, speculating on harbors and copper mines amid rumors that either the British or French would take formal possession of Fiji. "Surely," he wrote his brother in Salem, "no one would buy land in this Savage Country . . . unless they believed some nation would take possession and make a colony of it."[46] Williams supplied Sparr with some fill-in-the-blank deeds and made Sparr his agent at Kadavu, near Kenia, where Sparr had established himself soon after the *John Adams's* departure.[47] A newcomer to Fiji, John Smith, lived with Sparr for seven months beginning in December 1856, and he drew up the paperwork for Williams while Sparr, who apparently could not write, handled the negotiations and did the interpreting. Williams wanted Na Cevu in Kadavu, and Sparr arranged for its purchase from Tui Navulivuli for several axes worth $16.00. Sparr received his compensation from Williams in the form of a voucher stating, "In the case the undersigned [Williams] gets a good title to the land the Territory of Na Thabu, the small Island at high Water, or point of land, called and known by the name of Tauer Drome, the grant of which is to be conveyed to John Sparr, an American Indian, at present residing in Feejee."[48]

Correspondence related to this purchase shows that the Fijians Sparr negotiated with approached these land sales from within a Fijian cultural framework at odds with how a land deed was conceptualized in U.S. law. Tui Navulivuli of Kadavu communicated to Williams, presumably through Sparr, that he was willing to sell Na Cevu for "no payment further than you put me in my place as king of the same" and for protection from contenders to his position.[49] As Williams's objective was not to hold the land but speculate on its future sale, there was no urgency to explain what a deed meant within his own culture, and he responded to Tui Navulivuli by consenting to the arrangement but in different language: "should you be molested whilst in charge of the property and looking after the premises I shall request the

Commander of the first US Ship of War arriving in these Islands to Seek redress for you."[50] This exchange angered the occupants of the land, who claimed Tui Navulvuli lacked authority to hand over such a large piece of Kadavu. The English missionary stationed closest to the controversy, James Royce, later called Williams's scheme "a clear swindling case. A rascal by the name of Indian John was employed some 3 years since to induce the chiefs to sign the deed. Some did it through fear; one name we have found is a forgery, the man was dead at the time the paper was professedly signed; and now the noted [Charles] Pickering has been employed [by Williams] to induce Tui navulivuli to receive the property."[51]

Although the legitimacy of Williams's purchase of Na Cevu was questionable, Sparr seems to have immediately taken ownership of Tawadromu. A British government naturalist visiting Kadavu in 1860 remarked with surprise that "Taudromu, another of the islands of Ga loa Bay, scarcely half a mile round, now belongs to an American Indian of real flesh and blood."[52] Sparr's son Viliame (Fijian for "William") later recalled that, when he was very young, the family used to anchor off the island for a week or two at a time to collect breadfruit and bêche-de-mer. In September 1864, Sparr sold the island to a trader at Rewa, F. H. Davis, for $100.[53] A few months earlier, Sparr had purchased for himself another island off Kadavu, Vesa Island, for $28 in trade goods paid to Tui Lawaki. The people of Lawaki, believing the land belonged to them, tried to repurchase it from Sparr with a gift of eight baskets of cotton. However, he refused the cotton, frustrating their efforts to repatriate the island. According to Viliame Sparr, the family used the island as a location for collecting bêche-de-mer, but "There are no cocoanuts on it—it is not much good."[54]

Although clearly Sparr had made these purchases, he and his family did not feel secure in their landholdings. In late 1869, the U.S.S. *Jamestown* came to Fiji to resolve the long-standing monetary claims initiated by Williams twenty years before. As arranged with Cakobau, the Polynesia Company of Melbourne, Australia, would cover the indemnity charges due American claimants in exchange for 200,000 acres of land. While the *Jamestown* was in Fiji, its commander, W. T. Truxton, held courts of arbitration to hear other grievances. One complaint was the "Case of John Esparr, an American Indian, who claims he is not protected in the free and untrammeled occupation of his lands. Complainant recently deceased."[55] Truxtun warned Cakobau in writing "that no further annoyance or interference should be permitted to John Esparr, a U.S. citizen, resident on the Island of Ono, in the possession of his Lands. . . . I have therefore to notify you that the Government of the United States require you to protect the aforesaid John Esparr, or his heirs, in the free and unrestrained exercise of all his rights and privileges." Sparr's heirs were five children by a Fijian wife. Cakobau grudgingly conceded to Truxton's demands but asked that Truxton send along the precise boundaries of Sparr's tract, for he believed Sparr had taken more lands than Boutwell had arranged for in 1855. Once again, a U.S. naval officer went out of his way to protect Sparr's interests—or rather his children's interests, now that Sparr had died.[56]

The issue of the old monetary claims finally reached conclusion, but a new round of American claims—land claims—was about to begin, and what appears to be all of Fiji's foreigners able to trace some connection to the United States, including Sparr's and Whippy's descendants, became involved. Pressured by the American monetary claims and the expansionist ambitions of the Tongan Ma'afu, Cakobau had warmed to the idea of a British protectorate in the 1860s, but Britain vacillated on Fiji's value. Shortfalls in American cotton production during the U.S. Civil War brought a wave of aspiring planters to Fiji, most of them British, raising the prospect of British colonization once again. Finally, the long-rumored cession of Fiji to Britain took place in 1874.[57] Williams had died in 1860. His share of the monetary claims went to his heirs in the United States, who also inherited possession of his land deeds.[58] In 1871, a year after he received final payment of his $6,000 claim for the burnings of Levuka, Whippy died on Vanua Levu, where he had purchased a large block of land, most of which was bequeathed to his children, several of whom had purchased land also.[59] After Fiji's cession to Britain, they all—Williams's heirs, Whippy's children, and Sparr's children—found their landholdings challenged by British colonial land policies.

Fiji's first British governor, Arthur Gordon, wanted the islands to retain native purity. As part of an aboriginal protection plan, Gordon's team of functionaries identified a political and kinship category called the *mataqali* as the repository of indigenous land rights and set about attempting to register the majority of land in Fiji as the communal property of each *mataqali*. This kept most of the land in Fiji in Fijian hands and out of the market. In addition, the colonial administration established a land commission in 1876 to review pre-cession purchases of land, allowing as legitimate only those for which claimants could prove that the seller had the authority to sell, a fair price had been paid, the land was occupied and used by the purchaser, and other considerations.[60]

The "five half caste sons & daughters of John Sparr an Indian of Florida U.S. America"—Viliame, Vilise, Jioji (George), Mere (Mary), and Ana (Anna)—applied to the commission to have their father's purchases declared legitimate. They brought two cases, one for Kenia on Ono, where Viliame, Ana, and Mere were then living, and another for Vesa Island. Sparr's name also came up in other hearings because he had made the original purchase. During the inquiry, Viliame Sparr spoke for his siblings. His and other witnesses' testimonies give insight into how the Sparr family derived their subsistence at Kenia. Sparr put in 100 coconut trees along the beach, a source of food but also of oil, which could be sold to traders. In addition, they planted yams and arrowroot, which like coconuts doubled as a staple food and trade item. They grew taro along a creek and hired specialists from Viti Levu to build them a "stone fish fence" on their beachfront. Viliame further testified that Cakobau often made inquiries into their well-being.[61] The commission "disallowed" the family's claim to Vesa Island in 1882 and F. H. Davis's claim for Tawadromu based on purchase from Sparr but allowed Kenia to stand, largely because his descendants had continuously resided there and lived off its resources. In 1881, Sparr's children received a crown grant for Kenia.[62]

As the commission ruled against most of these early land purchases, pre-cession residents raised a clamor of protest, which eventually reached the United States as an 1887 petition asking for intervention and redress. Many of the petitioners for U.S. assistance were men and women of mixed descent whose fathers had been American beachcombers or bêche-de-mer traders: Sparrs, Whippys, Magouns, Dunns, Drivers, and others. Several petitioners were American beachcombers still living, who brought claims and testified on behalf of others. At least two of these were African American, John Farrell and William Berwick. Berwick had been especially active in making land purchases and serving as an interpreter and witness for others in the 1860s. Born in Virginia, he had arrived in Fiji in 1853, built and then captained a schooner for Cakobau, and lived at Bau for many years.[63] Other frustrated claimants were more recent transplants who came with the planter boom, such as G. Rodney Burt, notorious in Fiji for abuses against the native and imported laborers employed on his plantations.[64] This aspiring planter class often acquired land secondhand or thirdhand from deeds originated by or interpreted and witnessed by the "pioneer settlers of Fiji," and so they had an incentive to join forces with beachcombers and their descendants.[65]

A succession of U.S. commercial agents in Fiji, most of whom held disallowed claims themselves, fronted the appeals to the United States and may have been lead instigators in instilling hope, especially among those who had never even been to the United States. In 1889, documents about each case were forwarded to the U.S. State Department, including oaths of U.S.

citizenship made by several of the descendants of American beachcombers. In a formulaic statement drawn up by the U.S. commercial agent, Viliame and Vilise Sparr each swore to being the son of "John Sparr deceased. An American Indian of Florida U.S.A. And that I have never acknowledged allegiance to any foreign power or Government nor by any act or deed forfeited my rights of or title to American citizenship."[66] Whippy's son Samuel signed a similar statement.[67] The consular agent forwarding on the petition acknowledged that Sparr had never been a U.S. citizen but argued for the rights of his children to U.S. protection because he was an American Indian seaman discharged from an American whaleship.[68] Factionalism among these men who at various times held the post of U.S. commercial agent led one, W. H. Bruce, to accuse another, Isaac Mills Brower, of self-interest in his handling of the American claims: "the half-breed[s] (descendants of old U. States Citizens in Fiji) are his prey and from such quarters he derives a large income."[69] But Brower allowed the Sparr family's inclusion as claimants even though the story of how their father acquired possession of Tawadromu conflicted with Brower's own claim to the island.[70] Like Williams before him, Brower acted as though recompense could be more readily achieved by enlarging the number of aggrieved Americans so as to draw U.S. political interest to their cause.

U.S consular representatives in Fiji interpreted U.S. citizenship law as expansive and inclusive: they could point to precedents establishing the principle that the foreign-born children of American-born U.S. citizens held rights to U.S. citizenship.[71] As demonstrated by an earlier case in Samoa, however, the U.S. State Department was less willing to recognize mixed-race foreigners of American descent as eligible for U.S. citizenship.[72] The State Department sent a special investigator, George H. Scidmore, to Fiji in 1892. With Berwick as his interpreter, Scidmore spent nearly a year interviewing claimants and collecting documents. In his report, Scidmore did not say outright that the beachcombers and their descendants should be excluded from consideration, but he cast an unattractive shadow over the "Half-Caste Claimants" as the product of "nuptial contracts [that] were, as is usual in savage countries, of a very loose and irregular character, and practically amounted to gross concubinage. Polygamy was common among the natives, especially the chiefs, and some of the early white settlers were not guiltless of it."[73] Nonetheless, to the claimants, Scidmore's visit seemed to indicate U.S. interest in their situation, and in 1896 they submitted another petition asking that the U.S. government "not lose sight of these long standing claims and our consequent hardships." Over 100 men and women signed this petition, nearly all descendants of beachcombers, Sparr's five children included. They had Fijified the Sparr surname to "Sipa" but continued to identify themselves as "Merekeni idiani, american Indians."[74]

The claims against Great Britain, brought by the United States on behalf of its citizens in Fiji, went forward in 1902, but only a handful of cases were seen as deserving: three of the planter class (G. Rodney Burt, Benson Robert Henry, and I. M. Brower) and the heirs of the long-deceased U.S. consul John B. Williams.[75] When the claims finally came to an end through arbitration in 1923, only two awards were made: £10,000 for Burt's widow and £150 for Williams's heirs.[76] Race did matter, it turned out, more so in Washington, D.C., than in Fiji and more so for the second generation of Americans in Fiji than for their parents. Whippy, Sparr, Berwick, and others could find common interests as American foreigners in Fiji, but from the perspective of the U.S. government, they and especially their children lacked the racial and class status that made Burt's and Williams's claims more worthy of U.S. protection.

: : :

When Sparr told the people of Vutia in 1855 that "that they had now seen what white men can do," he did not literally translate "white men" into the Fijian language but would have said *papalagi* (or *vavalagi*). A word common in the Pacific but of uncertain origins, *papalagi* dates to at least the eighteenth century and derived either from distinguishing certain foreigners by their manufactured goods (cloth, beads, and iron) or from a reference to the sky, as in people who came from the sky or burst through the sky. Translated as "foreigner," "European," or most frequently "white," the word did not have anything to do with race originally.[77] One American seaman in Fiji even translated the term to mean "a civilized man."[78] In English translation, *papalagi* could confuse by making, for example, the American-born Whippy "European" and the American native Sparr categorically "white." An American sea captain's wife, at Wallis Island after having collected a cargo of bêche-de-mer in Fiji, recorded with amusement a conversation she overheard. A ship's officer approached an American beachcomber, "An African negro, as black as Africans ever are," and "asked if there were any white men on the island." The black man responded, "'Oh, yes, sir, there be *three* besides myself.'"[79] In the Pacific, "foreigner" acted as a synonym for "white."

The familiar racial categories found in nineteenth-century American society could not be transplanted to small communities of Americans residing in the Pacific because more pressing for Americans of all races was their status as foreigners in Oceania. For African American beachcombers such as Bill Berwick in Fiji or Anthony Allen at Hawai'i, the differences this meant in status were the most dramatic.[80] Given the physical abuse and expectations of servitude that many African American seamen faced on whaleships, resettling in the tropics gave African American sailors an equivalence with other American beachcombers. In pursuing his land claims, Berwick accused a British colonial official of trying to "poison Cakobau's mind against me by telling him he must dismiss me as I was only considered a slave in my own country and that if he persisted in employing me he would be looked down upon by all English gentlemen arriving in this country."[81] The colonial administrator's ploy to marginalize Berwick and reduce the legitimacy of his claim by invoking American racial categories had not been part of Berwick's experience in Fiji up to this point. As with Sparr, consuls, naval officers, and other beachcombers acted as though Berwick's American origins took precedence over his race.

Sparr's acquaintances in Fiji—Williams, Boutwell, the English missionaries, his children before the Land Commission—all identified him as an American Indian and knew also that he was from Florida, a detail about Sparr's past that he must have commonly mentioned himself for it to be so widely known. However, in his actions and relationships, Sparr allied himself with other foreigners and, more particularly, with Williams, the official U.S. representative in Fiji. Sparr chose an American identity by aligning his economic interests with those of foreign trading vessels, by benefiting from the violent and threatening postures that periodic visits from U.S. ships of war afforded beachcombers, and by appealing to the United States for diplomatic intervention and protection. Ironically, he may have more stridently identified as American the farther he moved away from North America. During the first half-century of U.S.–Fiji relations, the United States government enabled this ironic development by encouraging these men to feel secure in their American identities. It was useful to have loyal Americans in such a faraway place as Fiji. But U.S. policy as made in Washington, D.C., and over time defined American borders more narrowly.

8 : Race and Indigeneity in the Life of Elisha Apes

Elisha Apes deserted from the New London, Connecticut, whaleship *Ann Maria* on its 1839–1841 voyage and spent the next fifty years, until his death in 1891, at Waikouaiti, or "Old Waikouaiti," New Zealand, now the seaside resort village of Karitane.[1] The younger brother of the radical Pequot Indian writer William Apess, Elisha Apes was native to North America, but when he settled in New Zealand, he became a foreigner and a settler, categorically "European" and "white." In Apes's case, it was not just that nineteenth-century New England and New Zealand employed different racial categorizing schemes but, more important, that colonialism used indigeneity to construct racial categories. In New Zealand, the indigenous and the settler became racialized opposites, initially natives and Europeans but eventually evolving into today's commonly used categories Maori and Pakeha. Because Apes was not indigenous, not native, to New Zealand, he fell into the same racial category as New Zealand's primarily British settler class.

In both the United States and New Zealand, racial hybridity characterized the Apes family, adding further ambiguity to racial categorization as cultural practice. Elisha Apes and William Apess, the writer, had the same father, also named William Apes. The writer added an extra "s" to his name later in life, which led Barry O'Connell, editor of the authoritative collection of Apess's writings, to adopt that spelling. I use "Apess" as well to distinguish the writer from his and Elisha's father.[2] A self-proclaimed Pequot Indian, William Apess gained notoriety as an ordained Methodist minister, lecturer and writer, and instigator of the 1833 Mashpee Revolt against the resident missionary and the Massachusetts Indian guardianship system. A minor celebrity in 1830s New England, Apess is even better known today because his vehement pleas for racial justice have become canonical works of early American literature. In the 1831 version of his autobiography, *A Son of the Forest*, Apess described his family origins in racial terms. His grandfather on his father's side was a "white man" who married a Pequot woman, making his father, William Apes, "of mixed blood." Apess's father also married a native woman, "a female of the tribe, in whose veins a single drop of the white man's blood never flowed."[3]

The Apes family may have been one of the families local historian John Avery had in mind when, speaking of the 1820s, he asserted that few of the neighboring Mashantucket Pequot Indians were "full-blooded." Most had "more or less white or negro blood in them," and "some had scarcely any Indian blood whatever." "Evidently," he concluded, "they were not very particular as to the race with which they commingled and amalgamated." One of Avery's examples of outlandish racial mixing—"one man, who was about half Indian and half white, had at one time a white woman (for, I believe he was never married), after that a full-blooded squaw, and finally, a full-blooded negress"—might even have been a reference to William Apes, but only if Avery had reversed the order of the wives to Indian, black, and then white.[4]

A shoemaker by trade, with roots in southeastern Connecticut, William Apes was living in the town of Colrain in northern Massachusetts when son William was born in 1798. The family moved to Colchester, Connecticut, at about the time that Apes and his wife separated. Some of their children may have remained in Colrain—records show that "a son of William Apes, an Indian," died there in a dysentery epidemic in 1803—while Apess went to live with his mother's parents in Colchester. Apess never lived with either parent again, for after he was beaten by his grandmother, an uncle took him to the town authorities, who bound him out as a servant to a succession of white men. Apess wrote of meeting his mother later in life but felt more attached to his father, whom he visited every few years.[5]

We never learn the names of William Apess's Indian grandparents or mother, but she was probably not Candace Apes, as others have assumed.[6] "Candis Apes," twenty-eight years old, appears in an 1805 emancipation order along with two others, all referred to as "Negro Slaves" and "blacks," owned by Joseph Taylor of Colchester.[7] William Apes apparently lived near the Taylors in Colchester up until the early 1810s, and so it seems plausible that the slave Candace Apes derived her surname from him even though there is no record of a marriage.[8] The Apes children born in Colchester in the early 1800s—Elias, Griswold, and Gilbert—and their children were later usually classified as "coloured," "mulatto," or "black." Candace and William Apes also must have separated after a few years of marriage. She moved to Hartford, Connecticut, and lived until at least 1838.[9]

However, sometime before May 1815, when Elisha Apes was born in Groton, Connecticut, William Apes had begun living with a woman named Mary, mother of the next round of Apes children: Elisha; Solomon, born in 1818 in Preston, Connecticut, also close to the Pequot Reservation; Leonard, born in 1820, who lived less than a year; Abby Ann, born in Colrain in 1822; Sally George (named after William Apess's favorite aunt, who lived in Groton near the Mashantucket Pequot reservation), born in Colrain, in 1823; and another Leonard, born in Leyden in 1824.[10] Mary Apes may have been white or mixed white and Indian, for her children appear in historical records as either Indian or white but never as black or mulatto. Moreover, in the 1820 U.S. census, taken when William and Mary Apes were living in Colrain, they and all their children were classified as white.[11]

Sometime in the late 1820s, the family returned to southeastern Connecticut, where Elisha, Solomon, and Leonard all became whalemen. Elisha went to sea at age seventeen on a whaleship out of Norwich and continued to whale on one voyage after another from 1832 to when he deserted the *Ann Maria* in late 1839. Solomon started whaling in 1832 as well but after one more voyage disappears from the records. The two brothers never went on a voyage together but off and on sailed with other men with connections to Connecticut's Indian reservations: Peter George from Groton, probably their cousin; Pequots Charles Brayton and Joseph Fagans; and Benjamin Uncas, Mohegan. Crew lists variously described Elisha, Solomon, and Peter George as "Indian" or "Dark." On the 1839 voyage of the *Ann Maria*, Elisha's complexion was "Florid."[12]

The youngest Apes, Leonard, had a life in some ways even more surprising than Elisha's, for he rose to bourgeois respectability. He ran away from home at age fourteen to go whaling, quickly rose to become first mate, and enjoyed a long and prosperous whaling career. In a memoir written about a voyage on the *Oriole* of New Bedford during the Civil War, greenhand George Zollers recalled each member of the crew to make a point about their great diversity. Although laced with racial observations—the Cape Verdean who "was black as jet," the "white Portuguese from the Azores Islands," and the "African cook, black as jet, full of antics and resembling a clown"—Zollers had only this to say about the "chief mate": "Leonard Apes had a bold, daring appearance; his eye was piercing, he had high cheek bones; in short, he was of grim and resolute mien."[13] A brief 1920 account of Leonard Apes's life in *The History of the State of Rhode Island and Providence Plantations* (1920) commented on how he had "sailed many seas, visited many strange lands, and in his home had a collection of rare and curious souvenirs of his adventurous life." It was not his whaling career that made him notable, however. It was his daughter Lillias who earned him mention in the local history, for she had married Alfred E. Lamoureux, a Rhode Island pharmacist, businessman, and state senator.[14] With a "Fair" and "Light" complexion on crew lists, later in life with a "Dark" complexion, Leonard Apes may have ignored his Indian heritage because he could. However, he did not reject his Indian ancestry outright; he kept his name and continued to reside in the Groton area, where acquaintances surely recognized the unusual Apes surname for its Pequot associations.[15]

The family's racial complexity would accumulate a few more kinks with Elisha's emigration to New Zealand. The story of how Elisha Apes ended up at Waikouaiti is in the memoir of Robert Gilbert, the son of William Gilbert, the English-born carpenter on the *Ann Maria*'s 1839–1841 voyage. Robert Gilbert misremembered some of the details. He called Apes "Jimmy," whereas other sources give Elisha's nickname as "Bill" or Billy.[16] And Gilbert called the whaleship *Ajax*, confusing the *Ann Maria* with either the South Island passenger and coastal trading vessel *Ajax* or the French whaleship *Ajax*, which a few years after Apes's desertion collided with the *Ann Maria* at sea, while on a subsequent voyage with the same captain, Nathaniel Middleton Jr. The *Ajax* took Captain Middleton and his crew aboard as the *Ann Maria* sank.[17]

If William Gilbert heard of the disaster, he may have thought it just revenge for Middleton's abuses. He told his son that in 1839, when the *Ann Maria* was on its way to New Zealand and in dangerously cold weather, Captain Middleton sent a young greenhand up into the rigging, where he nearly froze to death. When Gilbert protested against Middleton's treatment of the boy, Middleton tried to put Gilbert in irons. Gilbert armed himself with an ax and threatened anyone who came near him. Then "a fellow named Jimmy Apes, a North American half-caste Indian, an exceptionally big and also a very powerful man," came to Gilbert's defense by picking up a heavy piece of iron, scuffling with the first mate, and helping himself to weapons in the cabin. The rest of the crew refused the captain's request to put down the mutiny, and so to rid himself of the two men, Middleton agreed to head directly toward New Zealand as planned and drop them off there. A few days later, taking a whaleboat, guns, tools, and food, Gilbert and Apes landed near what is now Port Chalmers in Otago Harbor and headed toward the Maori *pa*, or fortified village, at Puketeraki, located on the Karitane Peninsula overlooking Waikouaiti Bay, which Gilbert knew about from a prior voyage. At Puketeraki, they made themselves useful with their whaleboat and Gilbert's carpentry skills, and so the Maori at Puketeraki treated them well. However, Gilbert soon fell in love with Te Marino, a Maori woman who would become Robert's mother but who in 1840 was a refugee from farther north living at Puketeraki in fear of Te Rauparaha's raids on the Ngai Tahu. Her protector, the charismatic and powerful Tuhawaiki, disapproved of Gilbert's interest in her, and so Gilbert secretly fled with her to join her people at Banks Peninsula, where he soon took up work as carpenter at the Piraki whaling station. Apes stayed at Waikouaiti.[18]

Gilbert's memoir barely hints at the great changes occurring at Waikouaiti and in all of New Zealand at the time of his father's and Apes's desertion from the *Ann Maria*. One such change was the influx of muskets, a frequent trade item imported by American whaling captains, among others. The first Maori to obtain muskets launched deadly invasions against neighboring peoples. Since the 1830s, the Ngai Tahu had been on the defensive, pushed farther down the South Island by Te Rauparaha's incursions. For all the peoples involved, European trade goods had become vital to their survival. Sealing, whaling, and trade with Australia also brought devastating new diseases, such as an 1835 measles epidemic, which along with the deaths and dislocations caused by war decimated the South Island's native population.[19]

Even more dramatic changes were afoot at Waikouaiti in that Europeans had already begun settling the area, conspicuously so. Gilbert and Apes headed to the Maori *pa* because as deserters they likely thought that they would not be welcome at the shore-whaling station adjacent to it, or perhaps they arrived in the off-season while the station was unoccupied. In any case, a whaling station had been built at Waikouaiti in 1837 by the Sydney, Australia, merchant firm Wright and Long. Another Sydney merchant, Johnny Jones, bought the station a year later and would eventually settle at Waikouaiti permanently. The Waikouaiti station was one of several dozen whaling operations active in New Zealand from the late 1820s to the mid-1840s, most of which were located along the coast of the South Island. Jones had some success initially but also had serious competition, especially from the Weller Brothers' Otago establishment, a mere twelve miles away and within a day's sail of Waikouaiti, and from other nearby stations at Taieri Heads and Moeraki. British, French, American, and German whalers visited the area, too. All targeted the southern right whale, which traveled up the South Island's eastern coast in winter, from about the beginning of May through October. The Waikouaiti station survived longer than those owned by the Weller Brothers but was still short-lived, its peak occurring in 1838 with forty-one whales captured. The poor returns of only nine whales in 1841, four in 1842, and five in 1843—a pattern of decline that all the South Island whaling stations faced with the depletion of the right whale population—led to the closing of Jones's Waikouaiti whaling establishment sometime in the mid-1840s.[20]

For such a fleeting industry, shore whaling had an extraordinary impact on South Island Maori. Relations were amicable, for the Maori saw economic benefits to having a whaling station near their residences. Station owners arranged with Maori leaders, Tuhawaiki and others, to purchase land for buildings and equipment, and the local villagers then traded goods or labor for cloth, tobacco, knives, and muskets. Adapting to whalers' needs, Maori sold pigs and potatoes to the shore stations and to the whaleships that stopped at the Weller Brothers' store in Otago or anchored in the roadstead at Waikouaiti Bay. Maori men supplemented the whaling gangs and worked at cleaning whalebone and building and repairing fences and houses. Maori women also contributed their labor to the whaling industry and took advantage of the new trading opportunities, such as European interest in New Zealand's native flax, but most Ngai Tahu women experienced the impact of whaling more intimately as wives of foreign whalemen.[21]

Whaling and sealing encouraged settlement of a class of men who would develop the closest ties to the Maori, through marriage and fatherhood, while other, more intrusive, foreign settlement had also begun at about the time of Apes's arrival. Sydney merchants like Johnny Jones had grander designs on New Zealand than merely whaling. An empire builder, Jones imported laborers and tenants from Australia to farm large tracts of land he had purchased from the Maori, and he solicited a Wesleyan Methodist missionary to come to Waikouaiti to minister to both the Maori and the European immigrants Jones had planted at Matanaika, on the opposite end of Waikouaiti Bay from the whaling station. The result was the first Christian missionary posted to the South Island, James Watkin, who arrived at Waikouaiti in May 1840, a few months after Apes and Gilbert. Watkin situated his homestead and church midway between the whalers' houses near the beach and the Maori village of Puketeraki.[22]

The most momentous development in New Zealand's history since the arrival of the Maori at Aotearoa several hundred years earlier also occurred shortly after Apes took up residence: the Treaty of Waitangi, by which Britain claimed dominion over New Zealand. The treaty ceremony took place in February 1840, in the far north at the Bay of Islands, the oldest and most popular whaling port in New Zealand. To obtain more signatures, British agents traveled throughout New Zealand. Tuhawaiki and others representing the South Island signed in June. Now treated as a sacred text—as the founding document that created a nation of two peoples, Maori and British— the Treaty of Waitangi left ambiguous the extent and limits of Maori sovereignty within the British Empire, opening it up to multiple, contested interpretations. Maori have held it up as a guarantee of protection from the state of both traditional rights and their rights as citizens of New Zealand, an interpretation at odds with the British understanding of the treaty in 1840, which assumed Maori subjection to British authority.[23]

The Treaty of Waitangi was partly a British effort to control a land rush, erupting from multiple directions. Older resident entrepreneurs such as the Weller Brothers and Johnny Jones began buying up huge tracts of land as speculation. Another speculator, Edward Wakefield, organized a land company in England to settle emigrants in New Zealand. And there was even a French emigration planned, partially realized at Banks Peninsula but squelched almost at its inception. The Treaty of Waitangi gave legal cover to British efforts to preempt private initiatives and centralize land acquisition under the control of the imperial state. Thus, within the first decade of Apes's life at Waikouaiti, with remarkable speed and ruthlessness, a series of British agents visited the area to investigate and settle the "monster claims" of pre-treaty land purchasers such as Johnny Jones, locate a land site for Scottish colonization, purchase from the Ngai Tahu all the land from Banks Peninsula to just north of Otago for a pittance (known as "Kemp's Purchase" of 1848), and set aside only the most obvious places of native habitation as native reserves.[24]

Although he was American and an American Indian, Elisha Apes was as much a part of these changes as the other foreign sealers and whalemen who arrived on the South Island a decade or two before rapid British settlement began in the mid-1840s. Many of these men, like Apes, had Maori wives and "half-caste" children. Whether they were the British-descended William Gilbert or Edwin Palmer, Portuguese Joseph Antoni, or Australian aboriginal "half-caste" Tommy Chaseland, their status as foreign men married to Maori women put them all in the same position within New Zealand society.[25]

Only one person in the paper trail of Apes's life in New Zealand showed special interest in Apes's racial distinctiveness as a "North American half-caste Indian": Robert Gilbert, the son of William Gilbert and Te Marino. His fascination with Apes spoke to his own ambivalence about his white father's racial attitudes. In the short memoir of his father's life, Robert twice referred to an incident that was the "one thing that my father had said and done that I had my doubts about." When Apes came to William Gilbert's defense on the *Ann Maria*, he "took the mate by the scruff of the neck and the seat of his trousers and had him up at arms length over his head," until Gilbert told him, "Stop. Put that man down. I will never stand and see a white man being slung overboard by a coloured man so put him down." When years later, Apes stopped by the Gilberts' house to visit, and Robert Gilbert met him, he asked his father again whether that had really happened: had he said that he could not bear to see a "white man being slung overboard by a coloured man"? Responding by saying only that he would not lie to him, William Gilbert confirmed his belief in white privilege, no doubt the source of his "coloured" son's unease. Robert Gilbert also claimed that when his father and Apes first came to Puketeraki, the Maori, wondering who the "dark man" was, "appeared to be much interested and were glad to meet him, he being a member of another coloured race." If Robert Gilbert believed that Apes's racial difference brought him closer to the Maori, then other Maori or other "half-castes," such as Apes's own children, might have thought so, too. Apes also may have seen himself as different from the other foreign whalemen because of his racial origins, but his experiences, as they appear in the documentary record, fully resembled those of whites who settled in New Zealand at the same time and under similar circumstances.[26]

New Zealand's emergent racial categories could not accommodate the minority of foreign men who were racial others in their own societies. On the North Island at midcentury, New Zealand's settler population had become Pakeha to the Maori. Of uncertain etymology but thought to refer to people who came in ships, "Pakeha" is best translated as "foreigner."[27] However, nineteenth-century translations variously interpreted it to mean foreigner, European, or white, with no one paying much attention to the possibility that not all foreigners coming to New Zealand considered themselves white or European. Thus, the painter and tourist Augustus Earle visiting northern New Zealand in the late 1820s wrote "packeahs (or white men)"; Edward Wakefield, in New Zealand two decades later as part of his family's colonial land scheme, wrote "*pakeha*, or 'White man'"; and U.S. consul John B. Williams, then stationed at the Bay of Islands in the 1840s, explained that "Pakeha" was "interpreted white men or foreigners."[28] In the far south of New Zealand, "Takata pora," according to Edward Shortland, was used instead of "Pakeha," and it meant "a man of a ship, or whiteman."[29] Even Robert Gilbert evaded the ambiguity of these terms in his memoir when he said that Tuhawaiki "was not going to allow a Pakeha or white man" to marry Te Marino.[30] From the Maori perspective, "Pakeha" may have had nothing to do with race originally but more to do with the larger package of cultural differences associated with foreign seamen—physical differences that included their ships, clothing, exotic languages, odd manners, and trade goods. But "Pakeha" quickly acquired racial meaning that was set in opposition to "Maori," with "white" the most common translation.

Apes's life history followed the same path as that of other Pakeha, or Takata pora, whalemen on the South Island. Initially, he worked for the whaling companies: cutting timber for the Weller Brothers and spending at least one season at their Taieri whaling station and the rest of the time at the Waikouaiti whaling establishment.[31] As his first child, Mary, was born in 1842, he must have formed an attachment to Mata Punahere shortly after he arrived at Waikouaiti.[32] A Ngai Tahu woman from Arowhenua to the north, Punahere, like Te Marino, was probably a war refugee driven south to Puketeraki to escape Te Rauparaha's raids.[33]

Apes's relationship with Punahere was not unusual; most of the native women at Waikouaiti lived with whalemen. In a list of Waikouaiti's "European Population," composed by Shortland during his 1843 visit, nearly all of the twenty-four men at Waikouaiti—except for Johnny Jones, his brother Thomas Jones, the Reverend James Watkin, and a few others—had "whaler" as their occupation and "Maori woman" or "native woman" as their family, perhaps with a few children as well. One man, Isaac Porter, appears on the list as a "man of color," but neither Apes nor Tommy Chaseland, the latter known from other sources to be of Aboriginal Australian and European descent, were ascribed a racial category. Apes was identified as the only "american." Alongside his name, it was written that Chaseland was "well acquainted with west coast."[34] Another visitor to Waikouaiti a few months later noted whaling's extraordinary influence on the life of the community, from the "strange mixture of white & native habitations, whale boats & canoes[,] barrels by the hundreds, cellars, whale shears, gigantic remains of whales & other evidences of a whaling station" to the "picturesque group [of natives] on the top of the cliff overhanging the beach," who "consisted entirely of men & boys the women having intermarried to a great extent with the whalers."[35]

Waikouaiti probably would have looked much like the Cook Strait shore-whaling stations that Wakefield described: ramshackle collections of buildings, with whalemen's houses usually made of Maori wattle-and-clay construction and inhabited by mixed families of foreign whalemen, native wives, and their children. According to Wakefield, most whalemen contracted with the woman's family, who might even have built a house for them and who expected a share of the profits in trade goods. When stations closed for the season, some men stayed to farm small plots of land that their wives' families allowed them. Wakefield thought these arrangements a mutually civilizing influence, for the "whalers' wives are generally distinguished by a strong affection for their companion; are very quick in acquiring habits of order and cleanliness; facilitate the intercourse between the whalers and their own countrymen; and often manage to obtain a strong influence over the wild passions of the formers."[36]

Apes and Punahere probably resided in the whaling shanty town that formed around the Waikouaiti shore station. Shortly after the birth of their second child, they married at the Wesleyan Methodist Mission Church in August 1844, on the same day as two other couples—Robert Mackintosh and Warero, James Stephens and Tarahape. These marriages occurred at the tail end of a rash of marriages between whalemen and the Maori women they lived with that had been taking place at Waikouaiti during the previous year, inspired by the missionary Watkin having "said strong things to those females who are living in concubinage with white men." If Apes stood out as different for any reason, it was because he was literate and able to sign his name in the church record when most of the other men with European names signed with x's, as did their Maori wives. Elisha Apes (figure 9) and Mata Punahere eventually had six children who lived to adulthood: Mary, William, George, James, Thomas, and Kitty. In 1848, christened Caroline, Punahere was baptized in this church, as were the couple's children.[37]

When the Waikouaiti whaling station shut down in the mid-1840s, Apes turned to small farming and wage work An 1851 census listed him as living in a clay house, with two acres of fenced land, growing crops of wheat and potatoes, and raising pigs and a few cattle. No doubt Punahere contributed important Maori foods and materials to the household, such as pounded fern root (a winter staple) and flax-woven goods for the family's use or for trade. Apes also supplemented their income by working as a farm laborer for Johnny Jones. On the 1851 census, Apes's occupation is "shepherd," and since he had no sheep himself, it seems likely that he was tending the 10,000 sheep that belonged to his neighbor on the census, Johnny Jones.[38]

With the demise of whaling, sheep came to dominate the New Zealand economy, and this is how most of Apes's sons made their living. They were migrant laborers, visiting one sheep run after another, in an industry that celebrated speed and skill through international competitions similar to the American rodeo. James Apes became renowned as one of New Zealand's greatest sheep shearers. He also became famous as a whaleman. Hints of a revived southern right whale population inspired the younger generation at Waikouaiti to try their hands at it. Advised by old-timers Elisha Apes and another former whaleman named Miller, the Maori sons of foreign whalemen tried whaling out of Waikouaiti Bay in the 1870s. Daniel Ellison and Thomas Pratt (Tame Parata), who would later become the South Island Maori representative to the New Zealand Parliament, invested in the whaleboats and gathered crews (figure 10). This second effort at whaling was short-lived and may have been more important for its nostalgic appeal than for any income

Figure 9. *Elisha Apes in New Zealand. On the back of this undated picture of Elisha Apes, his name appears as William, which is how he identified later in life, and his place of origin as "London," probably a mistake for New London, the port from which the* Ann Maria *sailed in 1839. Reproduced by permission of Hocken Collections, Uare Taoka o Hakena, University of Otago, S10-030a.*

Figure 10. *James Apes (Tiemi Hipi) is the tall man leaning on the* Maori Girl *whaleboat. Reproduced by permission of Otago Settlers Museum, Dunedin, New Zealand, F-609.*

it produced for the community.[39] Apes's sons George, James, and Thomas spent their lives mainly as sheep shearers. His son William had various occupations, including a brief venture operating a general store, which ended in bankruptcy.[40] Elisha, who later in life went more often by the name "William," ended his days as a fisherman.[41]

Except for Thomas, who spent more than thirty years shearing sheep on the North Island, they all lived out their lives at what had come to be called Karitane. Even Thomas returned there, and so he and the other children were buried near their mother in the cemetery at Puketeraki, on a hill above where the *marae*, or community building, is located, on what is today officially called Apes Road. Not every grave is marked with a headstone, but the family did erect a large and elaborately carved gravestone for Mata Punahere, who died in 1874. Elisha Apes is buried not with them, however, but instead down the hill in the graveyard near where the old mission church used to be.[42] Possibly this is because he married again, perhaps twice, his last marriage to a woman who appears to have been a Scottish immigrant.[43]

Even without the additional marriages, it seems probable that Apes would have been buried away from his children because in so many ways the family was divided by his being a foreigner while his wife and children were native to New Zealand.

They were not divided emotionally, for from what little evidence survives they all seem to have gotten along well. The most intimate and sympathetic account of the Apes family comes from the memoir of Thomas Kennard, which compiler Herries Beattie published in 1939 under the title *The First White Boy Born in Otago*. Kennard's family came to Waikouaiti in 1840 to work for Johnny Jones, and Thomas grew up with "half-caste" children of the old whalemen as "mates." He particularly liked Mary Apes, who "would visit my wife and me on occasions and have tea with us." He told two anecdotes about the family, the first about "Mrs Apes" paying off her account at the store and how she was considered "very honest, the storekeeper telling me he would give her unlimited credit." The second was about how he and his father-in-law ran into "Mr and Mrs Apes" in an old hut one evening. Returning from "a tangi or some celebration," Apes and Punahere had come in from the rain to dry off their clothes. Kennard's father-in-law invited them to his own house instead and "gave them a good bed," from which Kennard concluded, "That was over 80 years ago and there was no colour line then—the Maori was as good as the white man." Kennard is also the only source I have run across besides Gilbert's memoir to identify Apes's Indian ancestry: "he was said to have American Indian blood in him and when in a passion his eyes were as red as fire."[44]

American Indian was not a racial category in New Zealand, however. As Kennard and other contemporary accounts demonstrate, two racial categories developed in nineteenth-century New Zealand: Maori and white, with another transient, ambiguous category in between termed *half-caste*. Many of mixed descent drifted away from Maori communities, melting into the general population, while those "half-castes" or "quarter-castes" who continued to reside in Maori places came to be treated by the state as fully Maori in the management of Maori rights and restrictions in land ownership, parliamentary representation, vital records collection, and local governance.[45] The potency of foreign and native, white and Maori, as racial categories had real material and cultural implications in individuals' experiences and divided families in many ways—in the languages they used, their relationships to the bureaucratic state, and historical memory.

The Apes family was probably bilingual, but Elisha Apes was English-speaking first while his children favored the Maori language. Punahere's gravestone, for example, presents a Maori inscription to Mata Punahere first and then, below it, an English inscription: "Sacred to the Memory of Caroline Apes." Even more indicative of Maori primacy for the children are the names they commonly went by. So far, I have referred to Apes's children by their English names, but they also had Maori names, which they used interchangeably or in combination with their English names. Mary Apes went by Mere Hipi, and after she married William Harper, an Englishman, she became Mrs. Harper or Mere Hapa. James Apes, the most prominent of Elisha Apes's children, was more commonly known as Tiemi Hipi. Hipi may have been a Maori-inflected pronunciation of Apes, like Mere for Mary and Hapa for Harper, or it could have been a surname the Apes family acquired through work with sheep, as *hipi* is the Maori word for sheep.[46] In any case, the children seem to have used "Hipi" more than "Apes" and almost always used it in Maori contexts, such as before the Native Land Court.[47] In correspondence, the language divide was conspicuous. Both Elisha Apes and his son Tiemi Hipi wrote to inquire into the land claims of South Island "half-castes" in 1886. Apes wrote his letter to Thomas Pratt in English, signing it "William Apes Seinor [*sic*]," while Tiemi Hipi wrote his letter in Maori and addressed it to Tame Parata.[48]

These letters brought to completion a land claim dating back to 1845 according to one account.[49] Tracing the contours of the claim—or was it even more than one claim?—is complicated, partly because mixed families presented a quandary to colonial officials sent to dissolve Maori land rights through persuasion and purchase. To dissolve someone's title, one had to know first who had title, and so determining land rights precipitated the bureaucratic necessity of counting and categorizing, a process that gave race precedence over family as a social category. For example, the 1851 census of Waikouaiti, the same census that tells us that Elisha Apes was at that time a small farmer and shepherd, lists families with European surnames and what appear to be many single men, including Apes, with no intimation of the Maori wives and "half-caste" children they lived with.[50] Walter Mantell, commissioner of South Island Native Affairs, collected the information for this census. He was also behind the original Apes claim. In 1854, he recommended crown grants "in favour of the wives and half-caste families of Andrew Moore, Elisha Apes, J. Crocome," and eighteen other men of the Otago region and, in a fit of remorse over his earlier collusion in native dispossession, asked in 1863 that these outstanding claims be resolved. Some received their grants, but others, including that of Elisha Apes, never made it into the official record books. Nothing seems to have been done about it until 1877, when Parliament passed an act calling for final resolution of the "South Island half-caste claims." South Island Native Affairs commissioner

Alexander Mackay went on a scavenger hunt through records filled with gaps and contradictions, eventually certifying land deeds for several Puketeraki families, located at Hawksbury Bush. It was Elisha Apes's children, not Elisha Apes himself, who were seen as deserving a partial share of original Maori possession, the sons receiving ten acres each and the daughters eight acres each.[51]

Meanwhile, another land claim of even longer duration involved the Apes children, not as "half-castes," but as Ngai Tahu. Immediately after the New Zealand government's ruthless "block" purchases of the South Island, Ngai Tahu protested. Allowed only small tracts of land and denied access to traditional food-gathering sites, they demanded fairer compensation and restoration of rights of access. Tiemi Hipi, a political leader locally at Puketeraki, was active in the Ngai Tahu claim, with his name appearing first among the 917 signatures of a 1910 petition asking for "a final settlement of the claims of the Ngai Tahu Tribe, with reference to the purchase of the Ngai Tahu Block by Kemp in 1848."[52]

Although "half-castes" ambiguously fell between the cracks in the state's conception of the New Zealand population, Elisha Apes did not. He was not himself Maori even if the rest of his family was. In other ways, his non-Maori status was apparent. For instance, he appears on the electoral rolls, with rights to vote for parliamentary representation. Once they received their land claim tracts in Hawksbury Bush, Apes's Maori sons should have had this right, too, except that they do not appear in the Waikouaiti rolls for general representation. However, they had voting rights for a Maori representative that their father did not have.[53]

One of the most interesting distinctions between Apes's status as a "white" resident of New Zealand and his children's status as native and Maori is apparent in how the burgeoning industry of historical and ethnographic production at the turn of the twentieth century treated them in different ways. Newspapers, local historians, and "Early Settler" associations began collecting and disseminating the memoirs of the earliest foreign residents while at the same time ethnologists began seeking out aged Maori to salvage ethnographic data on ancient customs, place-names, and the Maori language. Apes became venerated as an "Early Settler" while his children aided ethnologists in their quest for Maori cultural information.

Among the oldest residents at Puketeraki in the early twentieth century, Apes's children—especially Mary and Thomas—became cultural informants. W. A. Taylor listed the "Apes Brothers" (probably James and Thomas) and "Mrs Harper (Big Mary)" among his "Old Waikouaiti" informants.[54] Henry Devenish Skinner received information on Maori house types and construction methods from Mary Apes Harper.[55] Herries Beattie conducted brief interviews with Apes's children Mary and Thomas.[56] Beattie left no notes on what Mary Harper may have said to him but described his conversation with Tamati, or Tame, Hipi (Thomas Apes), the topics of which were a North Island Maori expression for "Old Maid" that came from a word meaning "trapped eel," how he had heard (but never seen for himself) that the Maori used to make mats out of dogskin, and how as a boy he would see Mohi te Wahia grinding greenstone to shape it but never observed closely the process. In the end, Thomas Apes disappointed Beattie. Unable to satisfactorily answer Beattie's questions about moa bones and place-names, Thomas seemed to Beattie "very friendly but extremely ignorant of all Maori topics."[57]

That their father was a foreigner did not come up much in the gathering of ethnological data just as Elisha Apes's Maori wife and children were excised from stories about Apes as one of many "Early Settlers" to the Otago region celebrated in photographic displays and sought for interviews in the late nineteenth century. Most of the South Island's Early Settlers were whalemen, like William Haberfield, who recounted the old whaling days for a Dunedin newspaper and mentioned how "Mr Apes, of Waikouaiti" was coming soon for a visit to "have a chat about old times."[58] Other newspaper accounts put Elisha Apes ahead or behind other whalemen as they debated who was the earliest Early Settler. Letters to newspaper editors written by "An 1840 Settler" and "An 1850 Settler" disputed whether Thomas Kennard was the first white child born in the Otago area while also disagreeing as to whether Apes of Waikouaiti was indeed the "oldest settler" or whether that honor belonged to Carey or to McLauchlan.[59]

As founding fathers of Otago, the old whalemen with longevity, like Apes, were whitewashed, their Maori wives and children made invisible, their own racial backgrounds made irrelevant. As a relic of New Zealand's founding as a white nation, Apes had to be white. One of the earliest tourists to Karitane included among the "very interesting and quaint residents" he met "Mr Apes, who had then lived there for over 50 years." Apes regaled visitors with exciting stories about the "old whaling days, when he had been the chief harpooner." The tourist did not pigeonhole Apes into a racial, national, or ethnic category but implied that Apes was white: "With his flaxen-coloured hair and blue eyes, he reminded one of the Norsemen of old."[60] That Kennard had heard of Apes's Indian ancestry suggests that Apes himself must have told people of it, but his Indian heritage was irrelevant and did not fit the racial categorization in which his status as a foreigner in New Zealand placed him.[61]

Historians such as John Christie, a minister stationed at Waikouaiti in the late nineteenth century and author of its first full history, credited "W. Apes and W. McLachlan, the only two surviving representatives of the old whalers in the district," as his sources of historical information on the old whaling days. As for Apes's background, Christie included him in the list of "European fathers" of the eleven "half-caste" families at Waikouaiti in the late nineteenth century, along with the Sizemores, Lloyds, Pratts, and Ellisons. While anticipating an eventual "process of absorption going forward, which will, in a few years, extinguish the Maori" and acknowledging that there were "Europeans with skins as dark as a full half-caste," he expected that distinctively Maori "features and frizzled black hair and dark eyes will probably betray the native descent of individuals for several generations."[62] Apes's status as an old settler seemed to obviate recognition that he was, like his children, of mixed racial descent.

In both New Zealand and New England, racial categorization proceeded imperfectly, compelled on the one hand by the impulse to divide (into categories) and conquer and on the other hand by the impossibility of cleanly distinguishing people by complexion or descent or however else racial determinations were to be made. New England's racial history as experienced by the Apes family seems more complicated than that of New Zealand, complicated by the presence of three racial groups—Indian, black, and white—and by a culture of racial categorization that arose from the simultaneity of African enslavement and settler subjugation of North America's indigenous peoples. While local historian John Avery wished for a social order based on racial purity, he exposed a reality of blurred boundaries between racial categories as those deemed Indian, white, and black had children together. That Leonard Apes lived a life that seems more white than black or Indian adds even more diversity to the already racially complex history of the first William Apes's progeny. Leonard Apes did not have to move to New Zealand to achieve white respectability. In contrast, his brother Elisha probably did identify as Indian, perhaps not as vehemently so as his elder brother William Apess, but if Apes had not told people in New Zealand of his Native American ancestry, how would Kennard have heard of it? However, even if Apes had proclaimed his native identity, his being a Native American had no meaning in the New Zealand context. The racial infrastructure of colonial New Zealand was invested in the simpler juxtaposition of native and settler, Maori and Pakeha, making it impossible for Apes to assert the same kind of native identity that his wife and children could lay claim to.

9 : Beachcombers in New England

The American whaling industry put thousands of people from around the world on the move. Just as some American seafarers became temporary or permanent residents in the Bay of Islands, Hawai'i, Tahiti, or other places where whaleships stopped, numerous foreigners came to New England through whaling channels, and some married into native communities. In many ways, their experiences matched those of Americans who became beachcombers in the Pacific. They had to adapt to new ways of living and found some acceptance in their adopted homes, though they continued to be regarded as outsiders. Their children were considered Indian, but they were not. The similarities in experience ended there. No one called them beachcombers, they were not viewed as early settlers, and they had little impact and visibility in the places where they landed. Because the American whale fishery acted as a colonizing force in other places—by extracting resources, encouraging commerce, and initiating foreign settlement—American sailors and beachcombers in Fiji and New Zealand were on the front lines during the development of a racial matrix that aligned race and nativity as Indian/native/savage and white/foreigner/civilized. In contrast, the whaling diaspora had little effect on racial ideas in the United States. Foreign-born seafarers who married native New Englanders were not part of a vanguard hinting at more changes to come but found themselves enmeshed in a racial legacy two centuries old.

The colonization process made for equivalent trajectories in native affairs in New Zealand and the United States in particular. Both countries sequestered indigenous inhabitants to the margins through treaties and wars, consigning natives to small tracts called reserves in New Zealand and reservations in the United States. Reservation inhabitants fell subject to a colonial bureaucracy supervised by government agents: superintendents of native affairs, the Bureau of Indian Affairs, and, in New England, town- or state-appointed guardians, overseers, and trustees. But race emerged in New Zealand out of colonization alone, whereas American importation of African slave labor occurred alongside colonization. Consequently, the United

States had more racial categories, more reasons to categorize by race, more uncertainty about who belonged in which category, and more emphasis on race over other social hierarchies. Whereas colonial administrators in nineteenth-century New Zealand conceived of a society populated by Europeans, natives, and "half-castes," in the United States at that time three peoples—Native Americans, Europeans, and Africans—intermingled and intermarried, splintering race into myriad combinations. Instead of "half-caste," Americans often employed "mulatto" as a category denoting racial mixture between whites and blacks, while "people of color" became a handy label for all nonwhites: blacks, Indians, and "mulattoes."[1] So many racial permutations spawned confusion while heightening the supremacy of race in American society.

If native New Englanders had designed the racial categories of nineteenth-century America, they probably would have come up with a system much closer to New Zealand's with its simpler juxtaposition of natives and foreigners but without the ascription of racial labels such as Indian, black, mulatto, people of color, and white. But until immigration into the United States in the latter half of the nineteenth century added new racial anxieties to the mix, race had priority over nativity in determining how one was perceived. One sign of race's precedence over national origins is evident in how difficult it is to identify which nonnative spouses were born outside the United States. Crew lists for overseas voyages asked for a man's nationality, but inside the United States, few expressed interest in nativity. Vital records, censuses, and Indian overseer reports rarely mentioned the birthplace or citizenship of nonnative spouses but did assign them to a racial category as white, "Negro," or "mulatto."

Intermarriage of native New Englanders, mostly women, with whites and blacks from the region dated to early English settlement in the seventeenth century, long before the American whaling industry began to draw foreigners to New England.[2] In the eighteenth century, there were several well-known intermarriages between native women and men of other races, which also crossed continents. Paul Cuffe's father came to New England as a slave from Africa. A few years after his Quaker owner freed him, Cuffe married a Wampanoag woman from Gay Head in 1745.[3] And after the Revolutionary War, several Hessian and English soldiers in the British army found employment tending salt works on Cape Cod, where they met and married Wampanoag women. (One of these men appears to have been *Globe* mutiny survivor Anthony Hinson's father.)[4] By the nineteenth century, however, the majority of foreign-born, nonnative spouses came to New England on whaleships or as sailors on merchant vessels.

One of the earliest and best-documented marriages between a foreign-born sailor and a native woman is that of Thomas MacGregor (often spelled "McGrego") and Mercy Moses. English traveler Edward Augustus Kendall met MacGregor while touring the northeastern United States in 1807–1808 and recorded his history. MacGregor had left Manchester, England, as a boy and traveled the sea for ten years until at twenty he found himself at Mashpee. Like most European and American beachcombers on a Pacific island, he was "destitute" but for "a stock of clothes." MacGregor soon married Mercy Moses. Kendall visited their homestead twenty-seven years later and described MacGregor as one of "the wealthier members of the village" with a "very respectable farm and orchard." Kendall thought MacGregor an intriguing, romantic eccentric. Even though most Mashpee Wampanoag by then had European-style wooden houses, he lived in a wigwam for it "agrees with the taste of his wife"; "his enterprise, his situation, his wigwam, and the complete state of order observable around it, his straw hat, and general personal appearance, made me regard him as a second Robinson Crusoe." Adding to MacGregor's peculiarity, Kendall heard (probably from the family of missionary Gideon Hawley, with whom he was staying) that although MacGregor came to Mashpee bereft, his "situation was not so bad, but that he might have married into a respectable white family, almost as easily as into an Indian."[5] Clearly, MacGregor's neighbors thought him odd for crossing a racial boundary when white women were available as marriage partners.

Few of the foreign maritime laborers who married native women inspired as much commentary as MacGregor and thus are less easily traced in the historical record. Foreign seamen could not obtain certificates of protection, normally a useful source of biographical information, and their names were not always captured accurately or consistently in crew lists. Sometimes the only clue is a marriage record or the notice posted before a wedding, which was called an intention to marry. Thus, Lydia Chummuck of Herring Pond publicized her intention to marry a "transient Lascar Indian" named James McDonald in 1791.[6] Since India did not fall along whaling routes, McDonald had probably disembarked at New England from a Calcutta or China trader out of Boston, Salem, or Providence. Martha Williams's 1828 marriage notice gave Henry Tucker as the name of her intended, "a trancient man said to belong to East India" but whose birthplace on crew lists is given as Manila. He likely came to the United States on a merchantman, too, but after moving onto the Chappaquiddick reservation to live with his wife, he made at least one whaling voyage.[7]

Many of the foreign-born spouses I have been able to trace came from Cape Verde or the Hawaiian Islands, which suggests that they did indeed arrive in New England via a whaleship, as that would fit the demographic profile of the whaling workforce. For example, Mehitable DeGrass, whose Cape Verdean grandfather had married a Wampanoag woman, also wed a foreigner, Hawaiian whaleman William Allen in 1839.[8] Allen may have been the son of African American beachcomber Anthony Allen, who by the 1820s had established himself as a respected boardinghouse keeper and merchant in Honolulu and who with his Hawaiian wife had at least three children.[9] Or the odds are that he acquired the Allen surname on his first whaling voyage. The Chilmark marriage record stated only that Allen was from New Bedford. That he was Hawaiian comes from piecing together information on a crew list with an incidental comment in a journal kept by foremast hand Charles Goodall on the *Milo* of New Bedford. As 1845 drew to a close, the *Milo* was whaling in company with another New Bedford ship, the *Trident*, off the New Zealand coast. One day, the *Trident* lowered its boats for whales, and almost immediately the captain's boatsteerer "fell dead in the boat." Goodall was especially moved by the sudden death of "a man called from time into eternity who had a few minutes before been telling of his great success in whaling having sent home one ship full and shiped in the one he was now in he was an aged Kanaka having a wife on Gay Head." Crews of both vessels attended the funeral service the following day. With the American flag flying at half-mast, they buried Allen at sea, while Goodall further mulled over "the unfortunate life of one who has braved for 30 years the battle and the breeze." Allen's Gay Head wife would have been informed of the death, if not from the *Trident*'s captain or owners, then from one of the five Wampanoag whalemen aboard (Leander Bassett, Joseph Peters, George E. James, Harrison Cook, and Jeremiah Weeks). Allen was not on the original crew list and joined the *Trident* at Lahaina. Even though he had a wife at Gay Head, he may not have intended to change his residence permanently from Hawai'i to Massachusetts.[10]

A generation later, another Hawaiian whaleman married Rachel Anthony, a native woman from Christiantown. Her whaleman father, John, had been born in Sierra Leone, Africa.[11] Here is an instance where small clues point to how Rachel Anthony might have met her Hawaiian husband, John A. Luley (variously spelled Luly, Luluy, and Lewlo). Luley and Francis Spencer of Christiantown both went to sea on the *Draco* of New Bedford in 1862, Luley as boatsteerer and Spencer as fourth mate and boatsteerer.[12] When the voyage ended in 1865, Spencer must have brought Luley home to Christiantown, where he met the neighbors, since a few months later, in January 1866, Luley married Rachel Anthony. He embarked soon after on the *Benjamin Franklin*, which a year later shipwrecked off the coast of Africa. He survived the shipwreck, for he is listed among the crew members whom the U.S. consul at Zanzibar sent on to Bombay in an English vessel, but there is no evidence that he ever returned to New England.[13] While he was at sea, Rachel Anthony gave birth to a son, whom she named John.[14] Sadly, the son eventually fell victim to shipwreck, too. On what was apparently his first and only whaling voyage, he drowned at the age of nineteen with nearly the entire crew of the whaler *Atlantic* shortly after departing from San Francisco in 1886.[15] When he was a boy, his mother had remarried, again to a foreign whaleman, John Foster, from the island of Anabona off the west African coast. Foster eventually became a fisherman and remarried another woman from Gay Head shortly after Rachel died from cancer in 1884.[16]

Francis Spencer's Cape Verdean father appears to have met his mother, Mary James, in a similar way as the Luleys, through her whaleman brother Henry. One of thousands of Cape Verdean men hired by American whaling vessels, João Antonio Espencer from the Island of St. Nicholas arrived in New Bedford sometime before 1828, when he shipped aboard the *Hesper* for a three-year voyage. Henry James of Christiantown was among the crew. They both shipped again on the *Hesper* in 1831, Espencer having anglicized his name to John A. Spencer. After the *Hesper*'s return to New Bedford in 1834 and a few months before he left on another long voyage on the *Abigail*, Spencer married Mary James in August 1835. Their first child, Francis, was born in 1836 while John was at sea. Two more children followed. The children's birth notices referred to their father, or to the family generally, as "colored" but made no mention of his being Cape Verdean.[17] After Mary's 1848 death from consumption, twelve-year-old Francis shipped as "boy" on a whaling voyage with his father while the two youngest children moved in with their mother's parents, Judith and Thomas James.[18] When that voyage ended, Spencer remarried at Christiantown, to Martha Peters.[19] Two years after this second marriage, while second mate on the *Draco*, he became so ill with consumption that he was transferred to the U.S. *Macedonian* "for the purpose of medical aid, and to facilitate his return to the United States."[20] He died soon after.[21] Although whaling took Spencer away for three to four years at a time, Christiantown had become his home and the native community there his family.

As in Spencer's case, the longer lasting the relationship, the easier it is to discover more about the spouse who married in. Thomas Morse, for example, resided for several decades at Gay Head. Whaling crew lists give his birthplace as Madagascar and have him living on Martha's Vineyard by 1815. Long after his Wampanoag wife Betsy died, the Gay Head community allowed him to stay on as an occupant of the reservation.[22] Poor, elderly, and a nonproprietor at Gay Head, he became a state pauper on the rolls of the Commonwealth of Massachusetts, which funded his living expenses. As he left no descendants, his greatest impact on the community seems to have been his exoticism. Known as "Uncle Q . . . that man from Madagascar," he inspired ghost stories still told at Gay Head in the twentieth century.[23]

The foreign-born spouses who made the deepest imprint on native communities did so through their descendants. Two men who married Wampanoag women on Martha's Vineyard had particularly large families, Belains and Vanderhoops, many of whom numbered among the most influential and respected residents at Gay Head later in the century. Given the rarity of the Belain surname, Peter Belain was probably born in the French Caribbean.[24] When he married Sally Johnson of Chappaquiddick in 1805, the marriage record stated only that he was from Nantucket, so most likely whaling brought him to New England.[25] The Belains had eleven children, and all eight of their sons went whaling. George was the most successful at it, and before officer positions became routine for native men, he often held the rank of first mate.[26] A white Vineyarder who attended Peter Belain's funeral in 1833 described him as "a coloured man of great respectability . . . [and] a pious and worthy citizen" without mentioning where Belain originated.[27]

William Adrian Vanderhoop, born to a Dutch father and a Creole mother in Paramaribo, Suriname, in South America, probably came to New England not on a whaleship but on a merchant vessel. He arrived at the port of Gloucester in 1834, lived briefly in Boston, and then settled in New Bedford, where he married Beulah Salisbury of Gay Head in 1837 and worked as a barber. The Vanderhoops lived in the city for a few years and then relocated to Gay Head, where the majority of their nine children were born.[28] The three eldest sons—William Jr., John, and Edwin—went on several whaling voyages each in the 1860s and 1870s.[29]

Since most maritime laborers were male, so too were most of the non-native spouses who came from abroad. But sometimes, as in the case of William Wallace James's Norfolk Island wife (in chapter 7), a whaleman became attached to a woman in a foreign port and brought her home to New England with him. Such was the case with Evelina Redsdale of St. Helena, who became a permanent transplant at Gay Head several years after marrying Wampanoag whaleman Samuel Peters Jr. St. Helena was a frequent port of call for American shipping in the latter half of the nineteenth century. When exactly Peters first met Redsdale is unknown since he visited St. Helena on whalers often, but on 9 September 1880, while the *Niger* lay at anchor in Jamestown's harbor, a crew member recorded in his journal, "Mr. Peters was married to a lady named Everline Risdell of St. Helena."[30] Peters continued on the voyage but visited St. Helena every year or two, whenever the *Niger* stopped for provisions or repairs.[31] Sometime in 1886, Evelina moved to Gay Head and in June gave birth there to son Arthur. Three months later, her husband died at sea on another *Niger* voyage. She stayed on at Gay Head and after two years married another Wampanoag whaleman, Lewis Cook, now earning his living as a farmer and fisherman.[32]

In his 1861 report on Massachusetts Indians, John Milton Earle may have overstated the extent of Indian intermarriage with "sailors, from abroad, who, getting acquainted with the Gay Head men at sea, come here, and marry Gay Head women, and settle here for life."[33] His roll of the state's Indians shows that most married other Indians. Marriages with white and black Americans also appear to have been more common than those that crossed national borders, but because Earle did not specify whom among the nonnative spouses on his list were born outside the United States, such an analysis is impossible from the information he provided. Still, there was enough of a presence of immigrants from islands and seaside ports in the Atlantic, Indian, and Pacific Oceans to lead one African American seafarer resident at Mashpee to describe it as "a mixed township from all parts of the world."[34] Foreign-born spouses must have added to the worldliness of these small communities, bringing a diversity of languages and firsthand knowledge of distant places to family life and social gatherings. And yet, they seem to have become part of the community without disrupting or transforming it.

: : :

The nationality of nonnative spouses is nearly indistinguishable in the historical record because state authorities who handled Indian affairs viewed them foremost as people of color, most often grouping them with African Americans. Foreign-born seafarers who stayed on in New England would have learned quickly about its distinct racial landscape because they were so often classified by race. The U.S. customs office may have paid attention to crew members' national origins for overseas voyages, but domestically, inside the borders of the United States, race was of greater concern. Race was, however, a clumsy tool incapable of dividing the population into coherent categories applicable to every situation, and the conjunction of the two racial systems (one born from colonization and the other from African slavery) created much ambiguity. Should non-Indian spouses be treated like Indians? Should Indians be treated like blacks? In all these discussions, never at issue was the nationality of people who married Indians. Only their race mattered.

Various federal and state government laws and practices worked to demarcate racial boundaries and regulate race relations to favor the white race. Thus, the meager body of early federal law relating to U.S. citizenship limited naturalization to "free white persons" until 1870, when in keeping with the post–Civil War constitutional amendments extending civil rights to blacks, Congress opened up naturalization to residents of African descent but kept "white" in the wording of the law, which continued to deny naturalization to other foreigners whom courts deemed nonwhite.[35]

The federal census also emphasized race. The 1790 census, the first conducted at the federal level, broke the population down by race, gender, and age, establishing these as fundamental queries included in every census thereafter. In 1820, the census asked for the first time for "the number of foreigners not naturalized" in each household and in 1830 refined this query to limit it to whites only (since the law allowed only whites to be naturalized), but then the question disappeared from the form for several decades. Birthplace by "State, Territory, or Country" was introduced in 1850, and in 1870, renewed interest in nationality and ethnicity resulted in questions about foreign parentage and the citizenship status of males twenty-one years and older. Finally, in 1890, citizenship became a permanent question. This lack of curiosity about the number and status of foreign residents in the United States reveals greater anxiety about blacks than about immigrants for much of the nineteenth century.[36]

Racial anxiety found further expression in antimiscegenation laws. Massachusetts Bay Colony passed a law prohibiting marriage between blacks and whites in 1705, which did not mention Indians. But in 1786, as courts and legislatures in northern states began to move toward abolishing slavery, Massachusetts made it illegal for a minister to unite a white person and a "Negro, Indian or Mulatto" in marriage. Such unions would not be recognized, and the minister would be fined.[37] William Apess—whose marriage to "a good looking white woman, with whom he lived happily" (as reported in his death notice), probably took place in Connecticut—railed against Massachusetts's antimiscegenation law, so he must have believed it had teeth.[38] That might explain why the 1821 announcement of Wampanoag Eleanor Goodridge's intention to marry the Azorean Emanuel Joseph classified them both as "negroes," a salve perhaps for the conscience of the minister they would ask to marry them. In other documents, Joseph was classified as white, but performing that marriage would have been illegal.[39] The law would have made African Americans more viable than whites as native marriage partners.

On a more subtle level, race pervaded the bureaucratic surveillance of Indians. Massachusetts in particular excelled at periodically collecting data on Indians. Early lists of Massachusetts Indians were conducted under missionary auspices and divided each person into racial fractions. In 1792, Moses Howwoswee helped missionary patrons by describing each family at Gay Head according to "how much we are mixed."[40] Gideon Hawley, Mashpee's missionary who also served many years as a state-appointed Indian overseer, compiled a similar report for the Society for Propagating the Gospel (SPG) in 1800. Racial mixture was his great obsession. Numerous "Negroes" had married "full blooded squaws." A "Portugal Negro" had married a woman named Lois, who was of mixed "white, Negroe & Indian blood. The Negroe blood prevails." (This may have been whaleman James F. Pells's father and mother.) Another household consisted of a "white man of good family from Falmouth," who married a "wealthy good woman of these people." She was one-fourth Indian and three-fourths white and had previously been the "lawful wife of three full blooded Indians." She and her white husband "live happily." Other families' more riotous racial mixture led Hawley to observe "that Negroe and Indian mixt with white is bad blood."[41]

The SPG's interest in racial mixing continued to 1823, when minister Frederick Baylies submitted "The Names & Ages of the Indians on Martha's Vineyard." Baylies gave in addition each individual's sex and proportion of Indian, white, and black ancestry divided into halves, quarters, and eighths. Measuring blood quantum was an imperfect science, however. For Isaac Johnson of Gay Head, Baylies added the notation "1st born of mixed race, between Negro & Indian," but he miscalculated to arrive at an impossible three-quarters Indian, one-fourth black, and one-fourth white. Despite this and other errors (not recognizing that the Mingos living at Christiantown and Gay Head were of Narragansett descent, for example), the obvious trend across time was toward more intermarriage between blacks and Indians.[42] Howwoswee's 1792 roll listed as many Indian households as there were mixed, with white and Indian by far the most frequent mixture. Thirty years later, Baylies recorded nearly all but a handful of elderly individuals as mixed and the presence of numerous men with no Indian blood at all. Eight men at Gay Head were full blacks, four were half black and half white, and three were three-fourths black and one-quarter white.

Intermarriage was thus cast as entirely a racial issue. It made no difference whether a native woman's husband was born in Falmouth, Massachusetts, or the Cape Verde Islands. Hawley's account occasionally remarked on the foreign-born origins of some nonnative spouses, but nativity usually cannot be discerned from these surveys of Indian reservation populations. From Baylies's list, there is no way to know that Thomas Morse, one of the eight black men at Gay Head, was from Madagascar nor that Emanuel Salvary (Sylvia), half black and half white, and Emanuel Joseph, white, were Portuguese nationals. (Salvary was probably Cape Verdean and Joseph was Azorean.) For most of these men, a Portuguese surname or finding them on a crew list is the only way to know or speculate whether they were born abroad and came to New England as whalemen.[43]

Intermarriage across racial boundaries presented state administrators of Indian affairs with a quandary about who fell within their regulatory domain. "Indian Lands" were reserved for Indians, who retained certain proprietary rights rooted in Indians' status as aboriginal, or indigenous, people and who held an inferior status in law as state dependents. How was a guardian or legislature to determine each individual's political status when Indians married outside their category? The state response varied by the situation. Sometimes Indians, especially those not living on a reservation, were viewed as equivalent to blacks, as colored people, thus removing any entailments specific to Indians. Scholars have typically interpreted this enlargement of the category black to include Indians as a strategy aimed at Indian extinction.[44]

However, Indian marriages with whites more often threatened assertions of an Indian identity. Even though Earle listed the "Yarmouth Indians" in his 1861 report, it was only so that he could dismiss them as no longer Indian. They all descended from a single marriage between a white man and a native woman more than 100 years earlier; they had nearly all intermarried with whites; they associated primarily with whites; and they were "in possession of their civil right," free from "the unholy prejudice of caste and race," lived "in a condition of domestic ease and comfort," and had no land (only a dubious land claim that he would not help them pursue). They had brought their land claim to the attention of Massachusetts officials at least as far back as 1820, when governor John Brooks forwarded to the state legislature the complaint of "John Greenough and upwards of thirty other persons, who style themselves 'Indian Natives.'"[45] In short, Massachusetts officials thought the Yarmouth Indians were too white to be Indian.[46]

The state was more willing to equate Indians with people of African descent, premised on their shared status as subjugated, nonwhite peoples. Simple names for native communities at the start of the reservation system in the seventeenth century—Indian plantations, praying towns, and Indian lands—evolved by the late eighteenth century into cumbersome mouthfuls

of political entities identified in law as "the Indian, Mulatto, and Negro proprietors and inhabitants of the Plantation called Marshpee" and "Indians
and People of Colour" at Chappaquiddick and Christiantown.[47] Depending
on the place and circumstances, nonnative inhabitants of Indian reservations became state dependents, as Indians were. As the 1849 report of the
Massachusetts legislative committee headed by Francis Bird stated, "The
uniform legislation of the State has regarded all colored persons residing
upon the Indian lands, as Indians, and subject to all the disabilities of Indians."[48] These non-Indian residents were never called "Indian" explicitly,
and they did not share in the proprietary rights to common lands held by
Indians. But adding "mulatto," "Negro," and "people of colour" to the reservation's official title allowed the state to treat them as government wards in
certain situations.

Thus, the 1828 Massachusetts legislative acts that gave the state-appointed
overseer of "the Indians and People of Colour" at Chappaquiddick and Christiantown the powers of a legal guardian applied to all residents of these two
Indian communities, whether of Native American descent or not. In the
guardian's annual accounts appear his receipt and disbursement of native
whalemen's earnings and those of native women's nonnative spouses. Nothing in the accounts distinguishes spouses from Indians. The guardian acted
as intermediary for Henry Tucker of Manila; the Cape Verdean John A.
Spencer; African American James Williamson, who was originally from
Baltimore; and native whalemen (Belains, DeGrasses, Goodridges, and so
on). When Spencer died in 1854, Christiantown guardian Barnard C.
Marchant served as estate administrator and summed up Spencer's possessions as "one trunk" (probably his sea chest), a few pieces of furniture,
and $956.67 in cash "Rec'd from Bark *Draco* in hands of his guardian"
(meaning Marchant).[49] By marrying an Indian woman and residing with
her on Indian lands, Spencer was perceived of and treated as equivalent to
a minor in need of a guardian, not technically as an "Indian" but rather as
a person of color residing on Indian lands.[50]

: : :

Some nineteenth-century compilations of Massachusetts Indians separated
them not by explicit racial categories but by who had rights to reservation
residence and resources. When Charles Marston, the white man assigned
by the state to serve as Mashpee's treasurer, submitted an "enumeration" of
the "Plantation of Marshpee" in 1832, he generated two lists, one of Mashpee proprietors (what we today would call tribal members) and another,
shorter list of the nonproprietors who resided at Mashpee, usually because

of some family connection. In his list, nonproprietors may have had native ancestry but were not from Mashpee.

The 1849 Bird and 1861 Earle reports constructed similar distinctions with its two crucial categories, Indians and "foreigners," by which they meant foreign to the Indian community. African Americans born inside the United States and spouses born outside the United States were all "foreigners." This use of "foreigner" can be confusing, but it made sense to them and to native New Englanders as well. Earle defined "foreigner" three times in his report, so he must have been anticipating queries from readers about what a foreigner meant in this context. A foreigner was "not an Indian," "not one of 'kindred tribes,'" and "is used, throughout, in the Indian sense, simply to designate one not of Indian descent."[51] It thus encompassed all those without native ancestry who resided, for some reason, on an Indian reservation.

In defending his terminology, Earle attributed this language to Indians themselves, and indeed one of his main correspondents providing information on Gay Head, Zaccheus Howwoswee, made these distinctions. Saying that he spoke on behalf of the proprietors of Gay Head, Howwoswee laid out the rules that Gay Head's proprietors followed to prevent "foreigners & strangers" from claiming political and economic rights reserved for Indians. These foreigners had no "pole right on gayhead" and "when we set of[f] our planting fields we do not set of[f] any to the foreigner but to his wife if she is a proprietor." Nonnative spouses were conniving to gain access to the community's clay reserves and lands, Howwoswee complained, and in a subsequent letter reiterated that, if any change were to be made at Gay Head, it was to retain as voters "the native indians of the soil not foreigner you will understand what I mean by native Indian of the soil if [they] come from another indian settlement we do not call them foreigners."[52] In differentiating between native proprietors with inherent rights to Gay Head and foreigners, Howwoswee drew on the language of New England town governance.[53] Just as with state authorities, it made no difference to him whether these "foreigners" came from Cape Verde or Maryland. Exclusionary sentiment periodically surfaced in New England native communities as they struggled with how best to protect the integrity of their communities as Indian places when the natural forces of intermarriage and geographic mobility tugged at the boundaries of the category "Indian."[54]

By midcentury, Massachusetts officials were thinking about how to eliminate "Indian" as a political category altogether. The Bird report concluded that Indians' "peculiar and anomalous condition" was too unwieldy to manage, since "any of the descendants of these Indians, now scattered over the world, in whose veins shall run a single drop of Indian blood generations hence, may return to the Indian lands, and claim to be treated as the wards of the State." The committee looked forward to the day "when the social disabilities resting upon a conquered and servile race are removed" and recommended legislation to help the state move toward dissolving tribes and reservations in the name of civil "enfranchisement."[55] Twelve years later, Earle advocated eventual integration but at a more gradual pace. Despite his recommendations and spurred on by the post–Civil War ethos of racial equality, the Massachusetts legislature passed the Indian Enfranchisement Act in 1869, extinguishing the state's Indian tribes and reservations.[56] Rhode Island followed with a similar piece of legislation, "An act to abolish the tribal authority and tribal relations of the Narragansett Tribe of Indians," in 1880.[57]

U.S. citizenship was crucial to these debates but played out in different ways for natives, African Americans, and spouses born outside the United States, since now it did make a difference whether one was born inside or outside the United States. African Americans married to native women were among the most vocal advocates of tribal dissolution. At hearings held at Mashpee in 1869, African American Thomas Sewall was the first at this open hearing to speak. In language the commissioners sympathized with, he objected to how his "wife possesses land that *she* holds; if she dies to-morrow I can have no benefit from it, and all my labor and improvements go to somebody else." He believed he had rights to land, the vote, and "the privileges of a man." Another African American, Young Gouch, testified that he had been born a slave in Missouri, had fought in the Civil War, and wished "to be a man, with equal rights with every man." Samuel Godfrey, of African descent but born in Jamaica, also wanted to "live in a town where I can be recognized as a citizen."[58] Godfrey was unusual in voicing his views since foreign-born spouses typically did not make bold claims to possessing rights, especially considering that tribal dissolution would remove their quasi-Indian dependency status but would not make them U.S. citizens, only "foreigners" of a different sort.

Because many foreign-born spouses were of African descent, they did become eligible for naturalization at about the same time Massachusetts did away with tribal status. Whalemen William A. Vanderhoop Jr. and his brother Edwin were at sea when the momentum to change Gay Head from an Indian reservation into a Massachusetts town was building, and they automatically became U.S. citizens, perhaps without their knowledge, while they were on the other side of the globe. Meanwhile, their Suriname-born father chose U.S. citizenship. When U.S. naturalization law opened to those of African descent in 1870, the elder William Vanderhoop immediately applied, as did another man who had married into Gay Head, John P. Randolph of Haiti. They were both granted U.S. citizenship in the Dukes County Superior Court's May term, 1872.[59] When Vanderhoop senior died in 1893, his newspaper obituary described him as "a highly respected citizen," suggesting that he took pride in belonging to the larger community in which he lived.[60] His sons may also have looked favorably on their new status as American citizens, though the majority of natives were dubious of the new law. Tellingly, at the 1869 Mashpee Hearing, when the community put their opinions to a vote, nearly twice as many opposed rescinding Mashpee's protected status as those in favor of it.[61]

The enfranchisement of Massachusetts and Rhode Island Indians as U.S. citizens, purportedly freeing them from state supervision, was not as liberating as its few native advocates might have hoped for because race still continued as a force in people's lives. Moreover, the meaning of the racial category "Indian" became even more ambiguous, since state authority over colonized dependents had become an aspect of what defined the term "Indian." Once tribal status was eliminated, "Indian" became an identity one claimed, but it carried no element of its historic meaning as people with aboriginal rights to "Indian Lands."

∴ ∴ ∴

The landmark Massachusetts reports produced at midcentury did not fractionate individuals into racial hybrids as Hawley and Baylies had done but still regarded intermarriage as a diminishment of racial purity. Earle seemed to lament how "the Indian names have almost become extinct."[62] True, surnames changed, but apparently not much else did. Like state officials, native communities found it difficult to manage the fuzzy boundaries of political and social categories such as "Indian." However, natives were more likely to defer to lineal descent than to resort to state officials' language of racial and cultural purity.

When former whaleman Gideon Ammons died in 1899, his obituary in a Providence newspaper declared him the "Last of Narragansett Chiefs" and the tribe "extinct," for "what war and pestilence could not accomplish, the intermarriage with other races has done, and the race is no more."[63] Since 1847, Ammons had frequently been elected to the Narragansett Council, and while in that capacity in 1880 helped compile a list of tribal members as the state of Rhode Island prepared to dissolve the tribe and needed to determine who was entitled to a share in the $5,000 compensation for the tribe's common lands. At a series of meetings, claimants to tribal status who were not on the original list responded to queries about kin connections, residence, attendance at tribal meetings, and the marriages of their parents, especially in regards to a 1792 state law specifying that children of "Negro" women would follow the legal status of the mother, the object being to keep slave progeny in slavery. Ammons's and the other council members' initial list of eligible reservation residents quickly mushroomed as people returned to the tribe to claim a tribal inheritance. While animosities and accusations flared at these meetings, Ammons faithfully stuck by a single criterion for determining native rights that he said had been the councilors' standard practice: claimants had to bring a living witness who could prove that their descent could be traced back to the "stump of the tribe."[64] Ultimately, for Ammons, the only criterion that counted was descent from a single Narragansett parent.

At Gay Head, too, they prioritized lineal descent while acknowledging racial mixture. When Gay Head became a town in 1869, state record keeping and governance requirements fell to its native residents. Even before the 1869 change, Gay Head had its own town clerks, who had begun maintaining vital records for Massachusetts. Given the prominence of whaling in their history, not surprisingly nearly all the men holding the office of town clerk were former whalemen—Tristram Weeks, William A. Vanderhoop Jr., Isaac Rose, and others. Massachusetts vital records forms used "color" as the heading for the question on race, and Gay Head's responses show as much idiosyncrasy in determining "color" as occurred with complexions on crew lists: "I & A" [Indian and African], "col'd," "Mullato," "Ind," "Ne," "Col ind," "Indian & White," "Black," "Ind & Negro," "mixed," "Light," and "dark Collar."[65] Some of the clerks appear to have taken the term "color" literally. More revealing is the federal census. In 1870, immediately after enfranchisement, Henry H. Davis, who listed himself as white and from Edgartown, conducted the census for all of Martha's Vineyard. He did not find a single Indian anywhere, not even in the town of Gay Head. Even though the form listed "I" for Indian as an option, Davis put "B" (black) for all but a few whites living at Gay Head. In his mind, enfranchisement had not only dissolved the political boundaries of Indian lands, it had made all Indians in Massachusetts black. In 1880, another white enumerator from the town next to Gay Head, Beriah Hillman of Chilmark, collected the census for Gay Head. He listed a few people as black, but most were counted as either mulatto or Indian. In 1900, Edwin D. Vanderhoop served as Gay Head's enumerator, and as the first native to collect the data, he interpreted race very differently from his predecessors. He had been listed as black in 1870 and mulatto in 1880, but in 1900, when he held the power to determine race, he recorded himself and the majority of Gay Head's population as Indian. His wife Mary was one of the few people in the town he listed as black along with John Foster of Anabona and Evelina Cook of St. Helena. The Vanderhoop and Cook children were all listed as Indian.[66]

After two whaling voyages in the 1870s, Edwin Vanderhoop had left Gay Head to obtain a teaching degree in Washington, D.C., and then taught in Arkansas for several years. When he returned to Gay Head, he brought a new wife, Mary Cleggett, who had been born in Pennsylvania and raised in Wisconsin.[67] She later published a series of articles about Gay Head in a New Bedford newspaper that celebrated its beauty, history, and distinct culture as a native community. She asserted that foreigners—again, meaning those foreign to the tribe and not specifically those foreign to the United States—had had little impact on the culture and identity of Gay Head as a Wampanoag place. Disputing an 1870 Massachusetts report stating that "The marriage of a foreigner with a member of the tribe nearly obliterated all traces of the Indian," she proclaimed instead that "the foreigners are by marriage only 'transformed into Indians' to all intents and purposes— that is, they renounce their own and instead adopt the Indian customs and take up the Indian habits and views of life. In the offspring of these intermarriages the strongest blood may show externally, and the predominating features be those of either the white or the Negro, but the inner self, the ego, the soul, the mind, the living principle, is wholly and always and forever—Indian."[68]

Gladys Tantaquidgeon, the Mohegan anthropologist who published notes from her fieldwork at Gay Head in 1930, also dismissed the pretension that intermarriage had in any way diminished the native community's sense of itself as Wampanoag people. Attributing to whaling, especially in the period before 1860, a high number of marriages with "'foreigners,'" which she herself put in quotation marks, she concluded that "Despite the alien strain which is present in these Wampanoag descendants, they may still be regarded as Indians, inhabiting the sacred territory of their ancestors and living as nearly as possible in accord with their teachings."[69]

Since natives rarely had the opportunity to declare a racial identity in documents produced by missionaries, government agents, and other outsiders, the Vanderhoops and Tantaquidgeon seem more reliable windows into native perspectives on where they belonged in schemes of racial categorization. Although race and proprietorship could be divisive within native communities, the community ethic held to the principle of lineal descent. Whether spouses came from nearby or from halfway around the world, they could live on the reservation, and their children would come to be regarded as Indians who belonged fully to their communities.

In both the United States and New Zealand, the global migrations induced by the whaling industry's operations brought new people into native communities through marriage. But as was evident in the two Apes families, one in New Zealand and the other in New England, complexities inherent in the history of race in the United States compounded the ambiguity surrounding racial categorization efforts. In New England, three races—whites, blacks, and Indians—had intimate connections while the New Zealand state conceptualized mainly a nation with two races, European and native, and some mixed-race progeny. As a beachcomber who made New Zealand his permanent home, Apes did not become Maori or native, just as John A. Spencer at Christiantown or John Morse at Gay Head did not become Indian. They were nonproprietors living on Indian lands by marriage. No one, white or Indian, seems to have disputed that Apes's and Spencer's children belonged to the native community through descent from their mothers. The difference is that the colonial state had no separate category for someone like Apes and so claimed him as one of their own, as a "European" and a settler. The more variegated and ambiguous racial makeup of the United States allowed for those who married into native communities from abroad to be neither native nor settler but rather "colored people."

PART IV : THE RESERVATION

10 : Degradation and Respect

A decade after painting his homage to the explorer Bartholomew Gosnold, William Allen Wall exhibited another historical painting of New Bedford, *Birth of the Whaling Industry* (figure 11). Situated near the Smoking Rocks but set in time more than 150 years after Gosnold's landing, this depiction of men on the shore busily processing whale blubber includes an Indian and African American but only so as to write them out of whaling history. Wall himself explained what was happening in the scene. The "colored man" is asking directions of the "founder of New Bedford and the father of her whale-fishery, Joseph Russell" while "a fine-looking fellow is coopering a barrel, in conference with an Indian, who, with his baskets and mocassins for sale or barter, is seated upon a broken mast."[1] In the picture, we can make out the Indian not so much from the baskets at his feet but by the shawl-like blanket draped over his shoulders and the liquor jug in his hand. In portraying New Bedford's African Americans as transients passing through and the area's Indians as benign drunkards scraping by on traditional handiwork, Wall gave all credit for building New Bedford into a city of wealth and prosperity to industrious whites.

Wall's dismissal of Indian whaling work fit with the most common stereotype of Indians in nineteenth-century New England—that they were a degraded people. This new racial ideology was one outcome of a long colonizing process in which most of the land and political power in New England now belonged to whites. In earlier times, naive savagery on a beach had justified white perceptions of Indians as inferior peoples, but expectations that they would disappear once surrounded by white settlement had failed to materialize. Native people's enduring presence called for new perceptions of Indians, the dominant view being that they were a degenerate people incompetent to handle their own affairs. Indian degradation was expressed in a multitude of ways as racial impurity, economic dependence, and moral intemperance. These perspectives on what an Indian was intersected in complicated ways with the colonial state's policies related to the residual lands still remaining in native possession, the so-called Indian Lands or reservations. These small tracts of land, home to the largest of southern New

Figure 11. *William Allen Wall*, Birth of the Whaling Industry *(1853). Reproduced by permission of the New Bedford Free Public Library, gift of Samuel Rodman Morgan. Courtesy of the Trustees of the New Bedford Free Public Library.*

England's native communities, made tangible the colonial legacy, and many believed that they were thus sites of and abettors to Indian degradation. These images of Indians that prevailed on the home front contradicted the responsibilities and respected status held by many native men on whaleships, especially as officers. But the image of degraded Indians so appealed to white New Englanders, the stereotype thrived despite native whalemen's insistence that they had proven Indian competency through years of dedicated service to the whaling industry.

From idle travelers wandering through Indian reservations to state agents, white New Englanders painted in words the same picture as William Allen Wall of "the scanty remnant of the aboriginal inhabitants of the land," "this last remnant of an ancient race."[2] "How degraded are the descendants of Philip and Massasoit!" one writer exclaimed, decrying their "perpetual pupilage" as an "example of the poor results, that attend upon plans for Indian civilization."[3] Tourists rambled through Indian reservations, peeking into houses, asking about the native residents, often addressing their questions to white neighbors: How many could still speak the native language? How many were "pure blooded," "untainted aboriginals"?[4] They observed Indians attending reservation churches and Indian children in their schoolhouses. They expressed pleasant surprise upon entering a house that was orderly and well-furnished or sitting down to a dinner of good food and civil manners. And they spoke lamentably and abstractly about what they did not observe directly: the Indians' "intemperate use of ardent spirits."[5] Racial impurity and intemperance were symptoms of Indians' fall from an innocent and exotic past.

In the same vein, both Francis W. Bird's legislative subcommittee and commissioner John Milton Earle, whose reports were published in 1849 and 1861, respectively, made degradation their main theme when authorized by Massachusetts to investigate Indian "conditions" so that legislators could knowledgeably consider eliminating the reservation system. Discussing each tribal community one at a time, the Bird committee gave a mixed critique acknowledging that many Indian communities showed improvement in morals and industry. For instance, at Chappaquiddick, where twenty years earlier they had been "a degraded people, unchaste, intemperate, and, by consequence, improvident," they now had less illegitimacy and were as temperate and as "comfortable" in their domestic circumstances as their "white neighbors." The investigators believed that the 1828 legislative act that had divided the Chappaquiddick and Christiantown reservations into individually owned allotments (albeit still restricted from sale to tribal outsiders) and the 1834 allowance of more self-government at Mashpee (though still subject to oversight by a state-appointed "treasurer") had succeeded at making Indians on these three reservations less "indolent, ignorant, improvident, intemperate, and licentious."[6] Twelve years later, Earle observed that many were "idle, improvident, and, to a greater or less extent, immoral, and some among them are living in a state of more wretched poverty." But like the Bird committee, he also found many who were "frugal, industrious, temperate, and moral."[7] Whether complimenting Indians on their virtues or disparaging them for improvidence, both investigations assumed a baseline of degradation from which Indians would have to rise above.

The ideology of Indian degradation had practical application in that it justified state oversight. As a former guardian of two Martha's Vineyard Indian reservations phrased it, "the State is under a sacred obligation to protect them in all their interests, and care for them with parental solicitude."[8]

Thus, native lands could be sold to nonproprietors only with permission from the state, and guardians or the state could sell land without native permission. Natives had limited powers of self-government and complained often in petitions to their respective state legislatures about being denied control over communal resources, religious institutions, and schools. Although the precise nature of the constraints Indians faced as "Wards of the State" varied from reservation to reservation and even from individual to individual, theoretically their legal and political position resembled that of minors and other individuals deemed *non compos mentis* by the courts.[9]

Who exactly qualified as Indian under these terms was muddled, however, by permeable reservation boundaries. In chapter 9, I discussed how state authorities responded to the presence of nonnatives on reservations by applying to them some of Indians' "disabilities." Indians living off-reservation raised the same ambiguity as to their political status but from a different direction. Owning non–reservation land relieved them from the burden of guardianship in certain contexts and made possible claims to independence and citizenship not afforded reservation residents. Guardian Barnard Marchant told Earle about two men "of the Chappequiddic Tribe, (in one sense)" who owned land on the island but on the "'white side of the line,' so called." David Belain lived next to Chappaquiddick Indian Lands on a sixteen-acre tract his nonnative father Peter Belain purchased in 1825 for $172, valued at $500 at the time of Earle's survey thirty-five years later. David paid $2.81 annually in property tax for the land and a $1.50 poll tax as a voter. In 1848 and 1850, Isaac Joab purchased land in two sections from an Edgartown merchant for $180, now worth $400. Joab also paid property and poll taxes. Both men exercised "the same political rights as other citizens, & frequently vote." They "were always at the polls—at our fall elections—Joab occasionally goes to sea."[10] Most likely, Joab sailed on coastal traders, as I have found him on only one whaling voyage, as a boy.[11] If he did go whaling in the 1850s, presumably his earnings were not subject to guardian oversight because the nature of his land ownership qualified him for independence and citizenship rights as a voter in town, state, and federal elections.

Local and individual variability made for inconsistencies as to whether "Indian" referred to a racial category that traveled with the person or to a political status belonging to residents on designated Indian Lands. A Punkapog in the Canton, Massachusetts, area did not want the right to vote because it came with a tax burden. He held $1,000–$1,500 in property for which he had been paying taxes while also voting but "requested not to be taxed and ceased afterwards to vote."[12] Belain's and Joab's ownership of land in fee simple and exercise of the vote helped lay the foundation for Massa-chusetts to advocate the same for all Indians, thus eliminating ambiguities in their political status caused by mobility. Ridding the state of reservations simultaneously would do away with the lingering Indian presence that res-ervations represented.

The eventual result, Massachusetts's 1869 Enfranchisement Act, prom-ised civil rights but continued to diminish Indian capabilities by coating the enterprise in the language of Indian degradation. The Bird and Earle re-ports employed enlightened rhetoric emphasizing their compassion and be-nevolence. They also claimed responsibility for Indians' pitiable circum-stances, expressing regret at the ravages colonization had wrought on native peoples, a stance made possible by how native marginality in the region made them no longer a threat.[13] The Bird committee thought that the whites' mistake was keeping Indians, as conquered people, in a system of vassal-age: "We have brought them into their present condition. The disabilities under which we have placed them . . . have produced and perpetuated their unfitness to bear the burdens, of citizenship."[14] Earle advocated more grad-ual change but understood the problem and the long-term solution in the same way—that "we [should] treat the mental and moral weakness which our wrong has induced" by encouraging eventual citizenship and equality. He made white racism a fundamental cause of the Indians' problems in that "the prejudice of caste, social exclusion, and civil disfranchisement, have done a fearful work with the race." Condemning the colonialism that was employing him, Earle called natives the "unfortunate children of the State . . . unfortunate, because, for no fault of theirs, they have been despoiled of their property, robbed of their civil rights, shorn of their manhood, and made the unoffending and unresisting victims of a most cruel social pro-scription." Hyperbolically proclaiming Massachusetts "the most intelligent, free, and prosperous community on the face of the earth," Earle proposed legislation that would eventually bring Indians to "the full enjoyment of their civil rights." These humane solutions to the problem of Indian degradation kept whites in control, giving reservations' native residents (most of whom, when asked, opposed enfranchisement) few opportunities to change the course of legislative decision making.[15] White oppression supposedly had made Indians unable to think for themselves.

: : :

Because New England native men had for so long made a living by whal-ing work, one would expect their maritime labor to have figured more prominently in white attestations to Indian competence or incompetence, temperance or intemperance, industriousness or lack thereof. That so many men held positions as whaleship officers should have challenged whites' belief in Indian incapacity and dependence. But whites were uncertain about where Indian whaling labor fit in this schematic that bemoaned the degradation of Indians and the calls for their uplift into U.S. citizenship. Perhaps it was because men who traveled around the world for years at a time did not qualify, as farmers did, as model U.S. citizens. Or to acknowledge native whalemen's ability to earn an independent living, their leadership aboard ship, and their worldliness would require total rejection of whites' faith in Indian degradation.

Whether the outsider surveying Indian conditions was a tourist writing for popular magazines and newspapers or a government official, the influence of whaling work on the domestic life of native New Englanders was everywhere in evidence but still did not alter outsiders' opinions of Indians. The Bird report noted that whaling had left its mark not just on the great number of absent sons but also on the material culture of native communities. In assessing the quality of Indian houses, they noticed how, at Chappaquiddick, many had "their 'spare room' handsomely carpeted, and adorned with pictures and curiosities collected in the eastern and southern seas."[16] A travel writer accompanied by an illustrator explored Gay Head in 1860 and similarly encountered a cosmopolitanism in this small community, which derived from native men bringing their seafaring experiences home. They "met a man in the pathway, whose address indicated some acquaintance with the world." They said his name was "Roos," but it must have been George Belain, who was at that time the only Gay Head native who fit their description of "a professional sailor, who had made his last voyage as first mate of a whale-ship." Belain invited the pair to dinner at his house, after which they "retired to the parlor, where he spun us some sea-yarns, and traded us some pretty shells which he had gathered in the Indian seas." They thought Belain "a very intelligent and well-mannered person" and his house "altogether of a better sort than any we had yet seen. The parlor was respectably furnished, carpeted, and curtained; the mantle-piece and tables decorated with sea-shells, Daguerreotypes, and books." Yet, their article is otherwise full of disdain for Gay Head as a place, claiming "the appearance of every thing indicates a thriftless and inferior people."[17]

The historian and writer Charles Burr Todd showed the same blind spot, preferring to represent the Shinnecock Reservation not as he actually saw it but in terms already familiar in American popular culture. He visited the reservation in 1882 in company with a local, nonnative resident of Southampton, New York, who was "well versed in the affairs of the Indians." Todd's guide told him that the good agricultural land on the reservation "'is gone to waste through the indolence of the Indians in not cultivating it'" and that "'not two thirds of the tribe remain at home, the others leading a roving existence—whaling, fishing, wrecking, and as farm laborers.'" They then stopped at a small house that "bore a neater, more inviting appearance than its neighbors" to ask about the family's "five sons, every one a seaman, and several rising to be masters." This was the Lee family. They found William Garrison Lee, recently returned from a whaling voyage on the *Abbie Bradford*, at work in the garden. While "leaning on his plough handles," Lee recited his and his brothers' labors at sea. The eldest, Milton, had whaled for "sixteen or seventeen years, and died. Ferdinand rose to be mate, and then captain of the ship *Callao*, and made a good voyage of four years in her to the South Pacific about 1871." Robert "took to wrecking, and was drowned in the *Circassian* disaster [while salvaging a shipwreck off the Long Island shore]. As for myself," Lee recounted, "I shipped at sixteen in the *Pioneer*." A subsequent voyage was cut short when the Confederate privateer *Shenandoah* burned his ship on its passage home from the western Arctic. He eventually became first mate on the *Florida* of San Francisco and later on the *Abbie Bradford* to Hudson Bay, when "Eight months out the captain died of consumption, and I took command of the ship, and after completing the voyage brought the vessel into port." Only Notley could be describing as roving. He had become a Pacific beachcomber, and the family had not heard from him in ten years.[18]

William Garrison Lee might just as well have carried on with his plowing, for the sight of him hard at work in the garden and his stories of whaling in the far north since the age of sixteen did not make Todd question the credibility of his tour guide. Marveling that the Lee brothers had become "accomplished navigators, with no other education than that afforded by the tribal school," Todd did not use his own eyes and ears to conceive of Lee as representative of a hardworking, capable community of people whose employment took them away from the reservation for years at a time. Instead, Todd gave his companion the last word on Shinnecock character: "'Love of firewater, as with their fathers, is still their greatest failing. They are not industrious, despising the tilling of the soil, allowing their fine lands here to go to waste, as you see, but no better surfmen or sailors, especially whalemen, can be found. They are wandering and erratic in their habits . . . and negro and white blood being so intermixed that there is not a pure-blood Indian in the tribe.'"[19] Indian whaling was in this instance seen as a symptom of a larger social problem, Indians' instinct for wandering, intemperance, and indolence.

White commentators about native whalemen held different opinions as to whether whaling was indicative of Indian degradation (a by-product of their natural inclination for wandering and dissipation) or the Indians' salvation. One writer believed that the Mohegans exhibited the usual "indolence, intemperance, and improvidence of Indians" and the Mashpee Wampanoags much the same, "yet it is worthy of remark, that some of our best seamen, particularly for whaling, have proceeded from Massapee."[20] Another credited the Gay Head men out at sea on New Bedford whalers as "distinguished by their activity and expertness," in contrast to the general population at Gay Head, who were "palsied by inveterate indolence and ignorant of any occupation capable of affording them immediate subsistence."[21] More commonly, however, whites viewed whaling as indulging Indians' feckless natures. Whaling's windfall profits especially caused concern. Early in the nineteenth century, the guardian and minister on Martha's Vineyard complained of his Indian charges that "They are the most improvident beings." They sold shares in whaling voyages for less than they were worth, or they sold five quarters of a voyage to assorted middlemen, or when they made hundreds of dollars off a voyage, they ended up still in debt: in sum, "They are the most unsuitable to contract for themselves or to choose their own guardians."[22] Speaking of the neighboring Pequots, Connecticut town historian John Avery had the same impression. He recalled several he knew while growing up in Ledyard, who "became boat-steerers and harpooners on whale ships, and as such their services were highly prized by their employers. Sometimes one of them would return from a long voyage with several hundred dollars in his pocket, and frequently, instead of laying it away for future needs or investing it in a comfortable home, would spend it all in a few weeks in lavish generosity or gross dissipation."[23] Access to large amounts of money, it seemed, made Indians only more dissipated and resistant to self-improvement.

Some of the prejudices against whaling as an occupation had to do with the moral valence farming carried in nineteenth-century New England culture as a more stable, respectable occupation than life on the ocean wave. Thus, Gideon Hawley worried at Mashpee in 1802 that whaling "gets them into a distaste for tilling the ground."[24] Decades later, the Bird committee, assuming the same perspective as the guardians whom they had queried for information, claimed that those who "follow the sea" were "less thrifty, and more improvident, than those who depend upon agriculture for support" and that "by intercourse with the whites at sea and elsewhere, [they] have contracted vicious and improvident habits."[25] Earle believed that seafaring endangered Indian men by offering "temptations to a race naturally inclined to a roving and unsettled life" and inculcated "habits, uncongenial to steady application and industry in other pursuits."[26]

Even domestic service seemed more virtuous than whaling. Surveys of Indian economic activities often mentioned young men's whaling side-by-side with young women's domestic service. Both occupations required leaving the reservation. Men's work took them farther away, whereas women went to Edgartown or New Bedford as live-in servants, where they were "much esteemed as help."[27] Not only did they "obtain good wages. Their manners are hereby improved and their minds informed, especially when they are in respectable, intelligent and benevolent families."[28] The disreputable taint sailors bore as improvident people no doubt added to these expectations that whaling would lead Indians to vice, but one cannot help but wonder whether the independence whaling afforded Indian men, with its potential for large payments, was not an additional, underlying cause for white commentators' concerns.

Some observers did see how important whaling was to the reservation economy but did not always give just due to the life course. Just as in New England port towns more generally, native seafarers were usually younger than native farmers.[29] Whaling earnings provided the capital young men needed to build a home on the reservation and purchase livestock. A missionary agent, sent by the SPG to survey conditions at Gay Head in 1839, noted that "Many of the young men are absent on whaling voyages. This is the only way by which they get anything beforehand. Some are wasteful of their earnings. Others having obtained several hundred dollars by a good voyage, lay out their money in erecting houses for themselves and families for they generally choose to marry."[30] Women's work also followed a life course. He referred to the women who worked as domestic servants as "unmarried." Perhaps their earnings contributed to their ability to marry as well, but whaling could bring so much income in, most likely that was what made it viable for them to marry and settle on the reservation, tending to their own homes instead of living in and cleaning up after white households.

: : :

Asking "if degradation has not been heaped long enough upon the Indians," William Apess also blamed white racial prejudice along with the reservation system of common lands and paternalistic guardians for thwarting Indians' natural sense of industry and self-respect. While "their most sensible and active men are absent at sea," impoverished women turned to prostitution and drinking rum, contriving a meager living from their "baskets and brooms."[31] Whaling contributed to Indians' social problems through the prolonged absence of men but was also support for Apess's insistence that Indians were equal to whites in their natural intelligence and capabilities.

This, too, is how native communities understood seafaring. It was the touchstone for demonstrating competence. When the Gay Head community in 1816 protested against Massachusetts's attempt to appoint a guardian to oversee their affairs, a white neighbor acting on their behalf, Ebenezer Skiff, contacted Paul Cuffe in hopes that the intervention of a prosperous and respected citizen, with relatives at Gay Head, might help fend off the new initiative. Skiff acknowledged that the "proprietors of Gayhead and people of colour in general are to be considered as improvident people" but that some among them should be considered capable "when they the Gayhead people have among them good readers as well as those who can write & teach arithmatic or navigate a ship."[32] Cuffe was reluctant to intervene, for he shared in the wider view of reservations as sites of dependence and dissipation, of "excessive drinking and Idleness." He wondered whether Gay Head did not indeed "Stand in need of nursing farthers [sic] and mothers" since he had seen their fields left unweeded and trampled upon by livestock and the sale of precious clay reserves poorly managed. That Gay Head men had "obtained a Great place of fishery" only added to missed opportunities and lent further support to Cuffe's sense that "thare is Great need of Reformation among you As a moral people."[33] Gay Head won that battle and remained free from the oversight of guardians, although the people there were still regarded as wards of the state.

At the Massachusetts hearings held at Mashpee to discuss the pending Enfranchisement Act in 1869, several natives again explained competence by reference to seafaring abilities and experiences. This was a small gathering of perhaps several dozen people. Who precisely attended is difficult to determine. The legislature published the testimonies of ten men, only five of whom—Nathan S. Pocknett, Matthias Amos, William Simons, Joseph Amos (known in other records as "Blind Joe Amos"), and Solomon Attaquin— were native proprietors of Mashpee. The meeting ended with a poll in response to two questions. Fourteen voted in favor of removing the restrictions on Mashpee lands to allow sales to "strangers," a measure that twenty-six, nearly twice as many people, opposed. Asked how many wanted to be citizens, they were split, eighteen votes on each side. Why the two questions resulted in different total votes is unclear as is who exactly was allowed to vote on these matters. Among those who spoke at the hearings, Pocknett, Simons, and Joseph Amos were against changing Mashpee's status, though as Amos said, it was "a sore grief to me" that they were considered "not capable of taking care and managing our affairs and properties which belonged to us."[34] Matthias Amos and Attaquin wanted Mashpee opened up so that they could own their land in fee simple and sell it if they pleased.

Those on both sides of the issue referred to seafaring skills as evidence of intelligence and competence. Matthias Amos began his speech advocating reform by apologizing for having "come up uneducated" because "I went to sea very young." He then rested his rationale for supporting enfranchisement on his maritime accomplishments, saying first that "I have been, when absent, placed on the footing of quite a man, but while in Marshpee, I am rather below my friends around." He later came back to this point in a clearer reference to his days as first mate on a whaler:

> When I go abroad, there is a handle put to my name [Mr. Amos], and I can put on a stiff collar, and walk the ship's deck beside the master. I have done it, but here I am nothing, below everybody, the lowest they have. Now I feel as if I wanted to come out and be a man, and show my colors. If I owe a man a dollar and own an acre of land worth five dollars, I want him to have his pay. I have accumulated a trifle, and make a good comfortable living, wholesome and healthy. I have done it by going out. I could not have done it here, because my property was not worth anything.[35]

Pocknett opposed changing the status quo and saw little value in citizenship, especially in light of the tax burden that came with it. He believed that they were not yet ready for federal and state citizenship because Mashpee offered only "common school education," which prompted one of the panel of investigators to challenge him, "Don't you know that a good many men have made governors of States and members of congress, that never had anything more than a common school education?" Pocknett responded, "Yes, sir, just as a great many men have made navigators with only a knowledge of the three rules."[36] For those not having served as state legislators, abilities proven at sea demonstrated high levels of achievement at Mashpee.

Indeed, it was a common experience in the latter half of the nineteenth century, as Cape Cod and Long Island became resort destinations, for tourists to be regaled with sailors' yarns told by native whalemen proud of their seafaring knowledge and worldliness. Political bigwigs who visited Mashpee on hunting and fishing vacations heard Matthias Amos tell of how he learned about the start of the Civil War while on a Provincetown whaler taken as a prize by the Confederate privateer *John C. Calhoun.* Solomon

Attaquin, who owned and operated the Attaquin Hotel, also entertained his guests with stories from his seafaring and whaling years.[37] Amos and Attaquin were influential members of the Mashpee community, and like other prominent men from coastal native communities, they had grown up on whaleships and brought that experience home as a foundation for self-respect.

Because so many native men had been whaling, it is not clear how much the authority allowed them aboard ship influenced leadership at home. Many whalemen who succeeded at sea were politically active and highly respected in their communities. Absence on long voyages did not lessen their attachment. Even before his whaling days were over, in the thirty years that Gideon Ammons served off and on as a Narragansett councilor beginning in 1847, he pressured the state of Rhode Island to recognize Narragansett claims to land along the Rhode Island shore. He was also a church deacon. His 1899 obituary noted these achievements but belittled him, and through him the Narragansetts more generally, by memorializing him as a quaint relic of the "extinct" tribe that had once ruled the region. The obituary mentioned his whaling voyages, too, referring to him as a "famous boat steerer," when Ammons ended his whaling career as third mate on the *Emma C. Jones*.[38]

Other former whalemen who rose to political prominence were Edwin D. Vanderhoop of Gay Head and Watson F. Hammond of Mashpee. Once Massachusetts dissolved these communities' tribal status, as newly incorporated units of state government, they had a right and obligation to send representatives to the state legislature. In the 1880s, Hammond represented the first district of Barnstable County. Vanderhoop served as a representative for Dukes County.[39] Men with whaling pasts contributed in other ways than political leadership. The last remaining resident of Christiantown, Joseph Q. Mingo, spent his final decade working to preserve and restore the historic Christiantown meeting house. With enfranchisement, Chappaquiddick and Christiantown lost their identities as Indian communities. A few residents stayed on their historic lands, now owned in fee simple. The majority migrated to New Bedford or the burgeoning towns resulting from the rising tourist industry, such as Oak Bluffs on Martha's Vineyard. Mingo resided at Christiantown until his 1913 death, however.[40]

The responsibilities native whalemen had fulfilled so effectively at sea had parallels in tasks of local governance and made them balk at being characterized as inept and childlike. They could not understand why their extensive knowledge of the world and their having served in positions of command did not earn them the same respect on land that they had become accustomed to at sea. Maritime work equipped native men with a worldliness that brought them usable knowledge in their relations with the state and that brought complexity to the reservations as social spaces. The broader social and cultural history of native New England looks little different when whaling is made central to the story. However, highlighting whaling's impact on native communities shows how whaling labor presented a contradiction to some of the most deeply ingrained ideas about Indians in nineteenth-century New England.

The high regard whaling held for native New Englanders as employment crucial to the survival of native communities is still in evidence today. The Aquinnah Cultural Center at Gay Head, housed in the restored home of Edwin D. Vanderhoop, and the tourist shops on the Gay Head Cliffs, owned by tribal members, have on exhibit whaling memorabilia that pay homage to former whalemen. Best remembered are those whom people today knew personally, men who went whaling in the early twentieth century: Napoleon Bonaparte Madison and especially Amos Smalley, who died in 1961.[41] Photographs taken to accompany Smalley's memoir published in *Reader's Digest* in 1957 show an elderly Smalley wielding a harpoon, recreating his boatsteering days when he captured a white sperm whale.[42] As one of New England's last surviving whalemen, a Tashtego for modern times, Smalley attended the premiere of John Huston's 1856 production of *Moby Dick* as a special guest.[43] A prolific raconteur of his youthful whaling adventures, he has come to represent the Aquinnah community's memory of their whaling history. Although to some extent Smalley played up the Gay Head harpooner stereotype to meet popular expectations, as uncle, neighbor, or friend, all whom I have heard speak of him do so with deep affection and pride.

Other New England native museums recognize the significance of whaling history in their exhibits, and families remember stories passed down across three or four generations. The Tantaquidgeon Museum of the Mohegan Tribe, the Mashantucket Pequot Museum and Research Center, and the Mashpee Wampanoag Tribal Museum have on display mementoes that men picked up in their travels and information on the voyages taken by individuals from those communities.[44] The Shinnecock Nation Cultural Center and Museum in Southampton, Long Island, has extensive exhibits documenting this part of their history and consisting of photographs, newspaper articles, correspondence, fragments of whale specimens, and the brilliant murals of artist and museum director David Bunn Martine. These artistic renderings of Shinnecock history re-create the many different meanings and relationships whales have had in the lives of the Shinnecock people from before European contact up to the present day. In the same way that Amos Smalley has come to represent how important whaling was to the survival of the native community at Aquinnah, the few remaining "houses built with 'whaling money'" still standing on the Shinnecock reservation are ramshackle reminders of how families depended on this income.[45] These were at one time the roomiest and most substantial houses on the reservation, and their fortitude in the face of time, economic hardship, and hurricanes seems a fitting image of the enduring legacy left by the Shinnecocks' whaling past. As Holly Haile Davis has said of Shinnecock history, whaling meant that there would be "food on the table, and we can still live on our land, which has been our greatest accomplishment as Shinnecock people."[46]

Native communities' depictions of their whaling history and the stories they tell about it emphasize whaling as a centuries-old tradition that provided economic sustenance but not without sacrifice, for it was dangerous, risky labor requiring long absences from home. The memories seem, however, largely positive. While whaling earnings supported families and communities, native whalemen's specialized skills, commitment to their profession, and global travels gave them opportunities to earn respect that was otherwise denied them in the racial climate of nineteenth-century New England.

Conclusion

Scholars have long recognized that race is not embedded in the body but a fiction. More precisely, race consists of multiple fictions—a jumble of contradictory and illogical ideas and expectations—which can baffle and confound individual experience. In the case of nineteenth-century whalemen who identified as Indian or were identified by others as Indian in certain contexts, their lives intersected with racial ideas in different, often contradictory, ways depending on the situation.

Many of the racial ideas native New Englanders had to contend with originated in the white race's justifications for colonization, which allowed for different images of Indians at different stages of the colonization process. Racial ideas about Indians produced by colonization imagined a narrative that began with the presumption of discovery, led to volatile first encounters, and resulted eventually in settlers wresting the land away from unworthy native inhabitants, relegated to enclaves and swathed within an ideology of servitude and dependence. "Indians" thus began as a romantically savage people with exotic customs, who subscribed to an economy of work ruled by instinct, not by intellect, and who faced a fatal rendezvous with extinction. If they did survive the colonization process, it could only be as degenerate shadows of their former selves, dependents on the humanitarian largesse of their conquerors. However, the positions held by native New England whalemen as they traveled the world wreaked havoc on simple narratives of white encounters with natives from contact to conquest and expose the inherent flexibility of racial expectations to adapt to each situation.

Indians on the ship encountered disjuncture mainly in two ways. Those who served as officers occupied a higher social position than most of the white American men aboard, which was the opposite of their social status at home in New England. And their promotion into officer positions became common industry practice despite a race-based insistence that Indians' keen eyesight and hunting instincts made them ideal harpooners. The ship employed Native Americans in positions of responsibility and leadership that defied nineteenth-century expectations for Indians. The historiography on New England native whaling history has accepted subjugation as its most compelling aspect by emphasizing coercion and economic exploitation. In the 1830s and later, as more native men attained officer positions, whaling could still be considered economic exploitation in that its workforce—of all races—assumed so much personal risk on a long voyage while the wealth of the industry accumulated in the hands of its land-based investors. Undeniably an industry bent on profit with little regard for its workers, whaling had ironic consequences in how its harsh conditions drove the majority of white men away, creating a niche for native men to be measured foremost by ability and not wholly circumscribed by racial prejudice. Native men took full advantage of the opportunity offered. They tolerated whaling's dangers and deprivations, and they abided by its rules. Native whalemen were conceptualized racially as expert whalemen with natural abilities, but in practice, they assumed the role of skilled laborers valuable for their specialized, acquired knowledge, commitment, and trustworthiness. None of the tasks expected of whaleship officers—navigating the oceans, maintaining logbooks, ordering white men to stand watch or climb the rigging—were expected of Indians. To navigate the oceans, maintain logbooks, tell white men to stand watch or climb the rigging, none of these mundane tasks expected of whaleship officers were expected of Indians. Accustomed to a racial hierarchy on land that put them at the bottom, native whalemen who rose in the ranks at sea earned material rewards through higher lays and overturned the racial hierarchy they had known from childhood. As mates on the deck of a whaleship, they had the right, indeed the obligation, to tell white men what to do, and white men had to respect their authority.

For the English-speaking, literate, and Christian native New England whalemen arriving in the Pacific or Arctic on ships and engaging in cultural encounters on the beach, the role of the native, the Indian, fell to others. Native whalemen speaking English and dressed in duck pants, monkey jackets, and straw hats obtained from a New Bedford outfitter could claim to be Indians while in Hawai'i, New Zealand, or Fiji, but their actions did not match up with common notions of what an Indian was. For New England whalemen in general—white, black, and Native American—Pacific and Arctic peoples seemed their opposites: members of cultures of apparent simplicity and innocence but with the potential to rise up in a threatening, warlike manner in their unrestrained desire for trade goods. Even though nineteenth-century native New England whalemen knew firsthand the pressures of colonialism, they knew it most intimately as dispossession of homelands. In first encounters on the beach, land was not the issue. Even though the exchange of metal and cloth for food, water, and sex that American whalemen participated in on distant seas had parallels to the native history of seventeenth-century New England, similarities in the two experiences seem much more evident to us today, in retrospect, than they were to people involved in these events as they were happening. At the end of the colonization process, in the twentieth century, their Wampanoag, Maori, and Hawaiian descendants would recognize a common history. However, the beach was too powerful a divide. It contradicted racial expectations because the beach did not so neatly separate white from native as cultural encounter narratives depicted, but it did separate those who arrived by ship from native inhabitants of islands and coasts.

As immigrant settlers on islands in the Pacific, whalemen considered native in one part of the world were not considered native in their new homes but fell into the role of settlers. Elisha Apes was one of hundreds of foreign whalemen and runaway sailors with a Maori wife and family in nineteenth-century New Zealand. That he was native to North America made no difference from the perspective of the largely European population and government that grew up around him, which did not distinguish him from other foreigners: natives had to be indigenous by definition. That John Sparr allied with Williams, Whippy, and other Americans armed with deeds and backed up by warships in the Fiji land rush should not surprise us unless we are blinded by our own expectations about how Indians should behave and about what side Indians are supposed to stand on in the long, global history of colonization. That his American peers consistently recognized Sparr as a Seminole Indian and yet still claimed him as a fellow American seems a strategy borne of expediency, designed to meet the peculiar situation Americans in Fiji found themselves in. If Sparr had stayed in the United States, it seems impossible to imagine a situation in which U.S. warship officers would have so enthusiastically rushed to protect him and his property. That race had little impact on the experiences of Americans abroad stands in stark contrast to how race defined the place for immigrants settling in the United States, by categorizing them first and foremost as white or as people of color, disregarding their status as foreigners born outside the United States. While colonization could generate simpler juxtapositions that categorized all residents as either white settlers or Maori natives in New Zealand and either white settlers or Fijians in Fiji, in the United States African slavery joined colonization as a rationale for racial inequities. Race was consequently much more complicated and contingent on circumstances in the United States.

Native men believed their competencies proven at sea to be worthy of respect, but popular literature and policy makers treated Indians as degraded, amoral people. The reservation and the ship were two completely different spheres of interaction, each with its own social rules. The same individuals could be found in both places, but it was the situation, not the person, that established how race would function in that setting. In each of these four places where Indians lived, worked, and were imagined, formulations of race appear from a distance full of fundamental contradictions so obvious that it is a wonder so few in the time period remarked on the inherent illogic of racial ideas.

Appendix A
Native American Whalemen's Database

This project relies greatly on a database I created of over 2,000 whaling voyages for more than 600 individuals. Anyone wishing to obtain a copy may contact me; however, you will need *Filemaker Pro* software to access it. A vital resource for this database was the immense and nearly complete collection of crew lists in the New Bedford Port Records at the National Archives at Boston (NAB). The U.S. Customs crew list form, required for overseas voyages, has columns for birthplace, residence, nationality, age, height, complexion, and hair color that were filled in with information taken from whalemen's personal certificates of protection.

I also read Barnstable, Edgartown, and Newport crew lists at NAB, used National Archives microfilm of New London crew lists (the originals of which are at NAB), partially surveyed Bristol and Warren crew lists at the Rhode Island Historical Society, and happened upon a cache of crew lists for Edgartown and Nantucket at the Martha's Vineyard Museum (Thanks to Dana Street for finding these!). Judith Lund generously shared data she collected from Fall River crew lists at NAB; she has since posted her data online at the National Maritime Digital Library website. The Nantucket Historical Association's Ships' Papers and Stackpole Collections have some crew lists. However, much of Nantucket's whaling history was lost long ago by fire, and what few records exist in the National Archives, I was told at the time of my research, would be unavailable until conserved. Sag Harbor's crew lists may have survived somewhere in the National Archives at New York City or College Park, Maryland, but all I was able to locate were those for 1847 in the New Bedford Whaling Museum and a few others at the East Hampton Public Library. Two online databases helped at a preliminary stage because they can be digitally searched: New London crew lists are available through Mystic Seaport Museum's website, and an incomplete but still extensive collection of New Bedford area crew lists and shipping articles are on the New Bedford Free Public Library website. These databases have many transcription errors, especially in the spelling of names, and so I always confirmed information by checking the originals.

Enumerations of whaling crews can be found in other documents, too, but without the personal information that makes the official crew lists so valuable for identifying and tracing particular individuals. The contract called "whalemen's shipping papers" or "articles" gives each man's rank, lay (share of the profits), signature, and the signatures of witnesses. Business papers list advances for crew members' outfits of clothing and supplies, individual accounts for purchases each man made from the onboard slop chest, and final settlement accounts. The trade newspaper *The Whalemen's Shipping List and Merchants' Transcript* began publishing the name and rank of crew members sailing from the New Bedford area in 1852.[1] Occasionally, a logbook or journal lists the crew. The New Bedford Whaling Museum has the compilations of whaling crews maintained by the New Bedford Port Society, which they have transcribed into a searchable online database, but because the NAB crew lists are more complete and detailed, I had no need to pursue this alternative. Like shipping articles, business papers rarely give more than a name, rank, and lay, which makes identification of individuals difficult unless the name was distinctive to a native community, such as Pocknett or Webquish at Mashpee.

I used crew lists in conjunction with lists of Indians, which Massachusetts in particular excelled at producing. I found most useful Frederick Baylies's "The Names & Ages of the Indians on Martha's Vineyard; taken about the 1st of Jan. 1823"; Charles Marston's 1832 "Enumeration" of proprietors and non-proprietors at Mashpee; the legislative committee report of Bird, Griswold, and Weekes compiled in 1848 and published the following year; commissioner John Milton Earle's 1861 report based on information he collected circa 1859; and Richard Pease's 1871 Gay Head land report. The Rhode Island and Providence Plantations' *Report of Commission on the Affairs of the Narragansett Indians* appeared decades after whaling reached its peak, and so Narragansetts probably are underrepresented in my database. The Connecticut State Library has the Indian overseers' papers in the records of the county court system for New London County. Overseers periodically listed the people they considered Pequot and Mohegan, usually limiting themselves to those residing on lands reserved for these tribes. For the Shinnecocks on Long Island, I used the 1850 U.S. census for Southampton, New York. Households 358 through 381—Cuffees, Bunns, Lees, Eleazers, Walkers, Kellises, and others—are obviously residents of the Shinnecock Indian Reservation, even though the enumerator did not identify the place as such and racially identified them all as "M" for mulatto. I also referred to the 1865 New York State census and the 1900 U.S. census, which do demarcate a distinct community of people as the Shinnecock reservation.

Table 3

New Bedford Area Whaling Voyages with Native Americans Aboard, 1800–1889

Decade	Number of Native Americans				Total Voyages	Percentage with Natives
	0	1	2–3	4+		
1800–1809	6	7	4	1	18	67%
1810–1819	64	26	14	3	107	40%
1820–1829	280	86	54	14	434	35%
1830–1839	674	111	57	10	852	21%
1840–1849	939	89	36	10	1,074	13%
1850–1859	1,097	77	23	9	1,203	9%
1860–1869	575	46	32	6	659	13%
1870–1879	344	43	16	5	408	16%
1880–1889	196	17	10	2	225	13%

Source: DPT, New Bedford Port Records, NAB.

I added individuals to the database when other sources, such as newspaper death notices or whaling journals, referred to them as Indian but only when I could see how that individual might connect to a particular native community or family. Similarly, when perusing crew lists, I did not assume that "Indian" in the complexion column meant that an individual was a North American Indian, since "Indian" often was applied to men born in the Pacific or occasionally to men born in places like Minnesota or Maryland, for whom I had no substantiating information. I recorded voyages for non-Indian spouses in the database, but these are not included when I make summary comments about native whalemen. Because many crew lists are lost or inaccessible and because I maintained a high standard for entry in the database, it captures a bare minimum of Native American whalemen and their voyages.

When referring to individuals in the text, I have standardized the various surname spellings to a single surname: Pocket, Pognet, Pognit, and Pocknet are all Pocknett; Weepquish and Wepquish are Webquish; Jerard, Jerrod, Jerred, and Jerrett are Jared; Devine is Divine; and so on. I determined a standard surname by weighing frequency, individuals' preferences as revealed by their signatures, and how their descendants today spell the name.

To put Native American participation in the nineteenth-century whaling industry in perspective, I kept track of all New Bedford–area whaling departure crew lists to compare the number of voyages with Native American men to voyages without Native American men (table 3). Although Provincetown's crew lists are mixed in with New Bedford's, I excluded them from these calculations. (They rarely had natives aboard, anyhow.) However, I did include all ports closer to New Bedford, such as Fairhaven, Mattapoisett, Westport, Dartmouth, and Sippican.

Appendix B
Native American Logbooks and Journals

Nineteenth-century Native American whalemen sometimes kept a daily record of their whaling voyages, a few of which can be found today in archives.[1] First mates maintained official logbooks as part of their duties. Other native whalemen kept personal journals, which resemble logbooks in form and content. Table 4 lists native-authored logbooks and journals in approximate chronological order with their archival locations. Most of the several thousand surviving logbooks and journals from American whaling are available for viewing on microfilm or on the web. The Pacific Manuscripts Bureau (PAMBU) at the Australian National University microfilmed the majority of them in the New England Microfilming Project. Of the several hundred logbooks and journals I perused for this project, many were on PAMBU microfilm, which I read at the archives that held the original or acquired through interlibrary loan. Several archives—the East Hampton Public Library, Providence Public Library, Mystic Seaport Museum, and the Nantucket Historical Association—have scanned, open-access logbooks and journals online.

Native whalemen also produced memoirs, though the four I know of are all as-told-to accounts. Paul Cuffe Jr. told an upstate New York hotel keeper about his travels around the world, published as *Narrative of the Life and Adventures of Paul Cuffe, a Pequot Indian; During Thirty Years Spent at Sea and in Travelling in Foreign Lands* in 1839.[2] Ranald MacDonald, of Chinook descent and far from his birthplace in the Northwest when he boarded a whaler in Sag Harbor, collaborated with a family friend to write a book about his adventures as one of the rare foreigners in 1840s Japan.[3] Amos Smalley of Gay Head loved to regale visitors to Martha's Vineyard with sailors' yarns, most memorably the story of his having harpooned a great white whale in 1902 while boatsteerer on the *Platina*. The writer Max Eastman put Smalley's stories into print in the 1957 *Reader's Digest* essay "I Killed 'Moby Dick.'"[4] Another Gay Head Wampanoag, Napoleon Bonaparte Madison, told fellow Vineyarder Dorothy Cottle Poole about his voyage on the *Josephine* a few years later. Poole published a much-amended version of Madison's account in the Martha's Vineyard Museum's quarterly history journal in 1968.[5] Journals and logbooks reflect native authorship more directly than as-told-to memoirs, for they were mediated only by the demands of the genre.

The earliest daily record of a whaling voyage I have found is James F. Pells's journal kept while on the ship *Barclay* of Nantucket in 1835–1839. Pells was likely not the first native whalemen to produce a journal or logbook. In the late eighteenth century, whalemen Joseph Johnson (Mohegan) and Jeremiah Pharoah (Montauk) wrote diaries but started them upon their return from whaling voyages.[6] The surviving log Paul Cuffe Sr. kept for his 1810–1812 trading voyage from his home in Westport, Massachusetts, to Sierra Leone and England has a routine feel to it, suggesting that he and his protégés—Thomas Wainer, son William Cuffe, and others—probably were accustomed to keeping logs while at sea, but I have not located any for their whaling voyages.[7] The manuscript copy of Pells's journal appears to be privately held, but I was able to see a microfilm copy at the New Bedford Whaling Museum Research Library.[8] Although the title page and the first few pages of the journal are missing, Pells was clearly the author given how frequently he signed his name alongside entries about having raised whales. That signature, "James F. Pells," matches exactly his signature on several Mashpee petitions in the early 1840s.[9]

All the other whaling journals and most of the logbooks on this list were signed by the author, sometimes with additional confirmation of the author's identity, such as "Joseph Ammons Charlestown Nareganst."[10] Identifying to an Indian place is as close as these writers came to claiming a racial or tribal identity, and only a few even gave a birthplace or residence, leaving only their name as the clue to who they were. One cannot go to a maritime archives and expect to pull up a list of native-authored materials in its card catalog. Logbook collectors who amassed these materials and then donated their collections to archives did not have access to today's quick and easy genealogical research tools and probably would have assumed that the men who wrote these were white.

Given that native authorship is not self-evident in the documents, many more native-authored journals and logbooks are likely to be in archives than those listed here. For those official logbooks that do not give the log keeper's name, I concluded native authorship when I knew he was first mate (or, in Ferdinand Lee's case, a captain with first-mate problems) and thus the person expected to keep the official logbook. I then compared his handwriting and style of entry to a signed logbook or to another logbook where the same individual served as first mate. Unconfirmed, possible native authors are not on this list. Asa Wainer, first mate on the *Mercator* in 1850–1852, probably kept the logbook for part of the voyage, and David W. Bunn probably started keeping the *Lagoda*'s log when he joined the vessel as first mate in 1863. But in neither case can I substantiate their authorship with certainty.[11]

Like nearly everyone else aboard a whaleship, including captains' wives, native keepers of whaling logbooks and journals conformed to the norms of the genre.[12] Their daily entries describe the weather, vessel maneuvers, activities engaged in by the crew, ships spoken with and gammed, and vessel location. They lived a twenty-four-hour day that began and ended at noon. They rarely used the word "I," favoring instead an implied collective behind most actions. Here is a sampling of some typical entries:

> James F. Pells, 14 July 1836: "at 2 P.M. saw Whales loward And killed one At ½ past 8 A.M. got through cutting And began to Boil so ends the day."

> Joseph Ammons, 22 July 1843: "this day commences with light wind all hands imployed seting up riging middle and latter Part much the same at 8 A.M. loard the bow boat to giv the green seamon A little Excecize at oars at 9 oclock came on board."

> Joel G. Jared, 17 July 1847: "First part moderate breeze from S ship steering NNE At 3 P.M. spoke Bark Edward 13 months out 1050 bbls At 6 spoke ship charles Frederick 10 mths out 550 bbls Luffed ship to the wind At 7 for the night Latt 0 30 South Long 85 40."

A journal that looked like the official logbook would have been proof of one's whaling ability and could have been brought along to display to whaling agents when negotiating rank and rate of pay on subsequent voyages. Also, like charts or chronometers, logbooks had a practical purpose as they recorded where and at what time of year whales had been seen. They could serve as reference books on later cruises, and they helped whalemen accumulate knowledge about whale behavior and dangers at sea. Literary aspirations inspired some seafaring journals, influenced especially by the popular success of Richard Henry Dana's *Two Years before the Mast*, published in 1840. However, native whalemen did not write like those hoping to publish. Such accounts usually emphasized harrowing abuses of seamen in the style of Dana or the romance of travel to distant and exotic places in the style of Herman Melville's *Typee* (1846). Pells's journal is the most personal of the native-authored journals, exhibiting whaling professionalism in most entries but also personal thoughts delivered in a humorous style. The private journals of other native whalemen have so little self-expression in them, their purpose seems foremost to document the authors' whaling capabilities and support their ambitions to rise in the ranks to become officers.

The genre's form left little room for emotion but enough leeway to reveal distinctive personalities. Joel Jared was young, homesick, and ambitious. His journals are also a tour de force of whale imagery, with an impressive variety of whale stamps he must have carved himself, showing small, medium, and large sperm whales, right whales, blackfish (pilot whales), and even a porpoise as well as stamps for small and large whale flukes for the whales that got away. In colored inks, he added a deep blue sea at the bottom and a gushing fountain of red over the whale's head to show the spewing of blood during the whale's death throes. An accounting device that allowed for whalemen to quickly tally their progress, whale stamps also afforded ritual satisfaction affirming achievement. Samuel Mingo's journals show a fascination for sail handling, with entries detailing how the crew worked the ship that day and precise drawings of rigging. Joseph Ammons's most detailed entries narrate the excitement of the chase. The most professional and least interesting are Joseph G. Belain's, whose short entries tell us only the ship's course, where whales were caught, and occasionally some accident befalling one of the crew.

Note that throughout this book, when citing logbooks and journals, I refer to the years of the voyage, not the years covered by the documents. Also note that for those journals and logbooks I use information or quotations from and which I identify as being authored by whites, I have based those racial designations on self-identification in the document itself or on the crew list augmented by genealogical research on the author.

Table 4

Native American Logbooks and Journals

Name	Voyage (* denotes incomplete coverage of the voyage)	Rank	Log (L) or Journal (J); Archive
James F. Pells (Mashpee)	Ship *Barclay* of Nantucket, 1835–1839*	Unknown	J; Log 890, WMA
Joseph Ammons (Narragansett)	Ship *Roman* of New Bedford, 1843–1845	3rd mate	J; Log 792, MSM
	Ship *Roman* of New Bedford, 1845–1847	Unknown	J; Log 792, MSM
	Ship *Triton II* of New Bedford, 1849–1851	2nd mate	J; Log 791, MSM
	Ship *James Maury* of New Bedford, 1851–1855* (overlaps with Webquish)	2nd mate	J; Log 791, MSM
Joel G. Jared (Gay Head)	Ship *Amethyst* of New Bedford, 1846–1850	Boat-steerer	J; Log 633, NBW
	Bark *Samuel & Thomas*, of Mattapoisett, 1850–1852	3rd mate	J; Log 633, NBW
Thaddeus W. Cook (Gay Head)	Bark *Joseph Butler* of New Bedford, 1852–1856*	3rd mate	J; Log 226, NBW
Milton Lee (Shinnecock)	Bark *Amazon* of Fairhaven, 1856–1860* (Webquish kept log later in voyage)	1st mate	L; Log ODHS 337, NBW
Jesse Webquish Jr. (Mashpee)	Ship *James Maury* of New Bedford, 1851–1855*	1st mate	L; 2 Log 315 on microfilm, continues on another vol. in Special Collections only, NBL
	Bark *Amazon* of Fairhaven, 1856–1860* (Milton Lee kept log earlier in voyage)	1st mate	L; Log ODHS 337, NBW
William A. Vanderhoop Jr. (Gay Head)	Bark *Awashonks* of New Bedford, 1862–1865*	Boat-steerer	J; Log 53, MVM
	Bark *Abraham Barker* of New Bedford, 1866–1870	4th mate	J; Log 10, PPL

Ferdinand Lee (Shinnecock)	Ship *Eliza Adams* of New Bedford, 1867–1871	1st mate	L; Log ODHS 265, NBW
	Bark *Callao* of New Bedford, 1871–1875*	Captain	L; Log ODHS 667, NBW
Joseph G. Belain (Gay Head)	Bark *Palmetto* of New Bedford, 1875–1879	1st mate	L; Log ODHS 402, NBW
	Schooner *Arthur V.S. Woodruff* of New Bedford, 1917–1918	1st mate	L; Log 521, NBW
Timothy L. Belain (Chappaquiddick)	Bark *John Dawson* of New Bedford, 1879–1884*	2nd mate to 1st mate	J; Log 343, NBL
	Bark *John Dawson* of New Bedford, 1879–1884*	1st mate	L; Log 344, NBL
Samuel G. Mingo (Christiantown & Gay Head)	Ship *California* of New Bedford, 1881–1885	4th mate	J; Log 95, PPL
	Ship *California* of New Bedford, 1886–1889*	2nd mate	J; Log 95, PPL
Tristram A. Weeks (Gay Head)	Bark *Bartholomew Gosnold* of New Bedford, 1881–1885*	1st mate	L; Log ODHS 1028, NBW
	Bark *Platina* of New Bedford, 1887–1890*	1st mate	L; Log 555, PPL
Abram F. Cooper (Gay Head)	Bark *Swallow* of New Bedford, 1883–1887	Boat-steerer	J; Log 602, NBL
William W. James (Gay Head)	Ship *Niger* of New Bedford, 1886–1890*	1st mate	L; Log ODHS 212, NBW
William H. Morton (Gay Head)	Schooner *Abbie Bradford* of New Bedford, 1886–1888*	1st mate	L; Log ODHS 492, NBW

Notes

Abbreviations

AJHR *Appendix to the Journals of the House of Representatives* (New Zealand)

ANZ Archives New Zealand, Wellington, New Zealand

Baylies Frederick Baylies, "The Names & Ages of the Indians on Martha's Vineyard; taken about the 1st of Jan. 1823," Shattuck Collection, NEHGS

Bird Bird, Griswold, and Weekes, *Report of the Commissioners*

CSL Connecticut State Library, Hartford, Conn.

CVR New England Historic Genealogical Society, *Vital Records of Chilmark*

Despatches U.S. National Archives, General Records of the Department of State, RG59, *Despatches from United States Consuls in* . . . , with Microcopy Collection number

  Apia, Samoa, 1843–1906, T27

  Bay of Islands and Auckland, New Zealand 1839–1906, T49

  Fayal, Azores, Portugal, 1795–1897, T203

  Lauthala, Fiji Islands, 1844–1890, T25

  Levuka and Suva, 1891–1906, T108

  Paita, Peru, 1833–1874, T600

  Tahiti, Society Islands, French Oceania, 1836–1906, M465

  Valparaiso, Chile, 1812–1906, M146

  Zanzibar, Zanzibar, British Africa, 1836–1906, M468

DPT Departure crew list. U.S. Customs Office list of men departing on overseas voyages (DPT); a duplicate list, with missing men identified, created when the vessel returned (RTN). Unless otherwise stated in the note, the name of the port indicates the archival location of the crew list.

  Fairhaven: New Bedford Port Records, NAB

  Mattapoisett: New Bedford Port Records, NAB

  New Bedford: New Bedford Port Records, NAB

  New London: U.S. National Archives, *Records of the Collector of Customs*

  Newport: Newport Port Records, NAB

  Rochester: New Bedford Port Records, NAB

  Warren: U.S. Custom House Records, Rhode Island Historical Society

  Westport: New Bedford Port Records, NAB

Earle Earle, *Report to the Governor and Council*

Earle Papers	John Milton Earle Papers, American Antiquarian Society, Worcester, Mass.
EHPL	East Hampton Public Library, East Hampton, N.Y.
EVR	New England Historic Genealogical Society, *Vital Records of Edgartown*
FHS	Falmouth Historical Society, Falmouth, Mass.
HMCS	Hawaiian Mission Children's Society Library, Honolulu, Hawai'i
LCC	Land Claims Commission Records, National Archives of the Fiji Islands, Suva, Fiji
Lund	I used Lund's *Whaling Masters and Whaling Voyages*, but other versions are available, including the "American Offshore Whaling Voyages" database at the National Maritime Digital Library website.
Marston	Charles Marston, "Enumeration of the Proprietors on the Plantation of Marshpee" (1832), Indian Guardian Papers (microform), rl. 1, MSA
MAR	Massachusetts Acts and Resolves, State Library of Massachusetts, www.archives.lib.state.ma.us/handle/123456789/2
MAVR	Massachusetts Vital Records, 1841–1910 (database), NEHGS
MHS	Massachusetts Historical Society, Boston, Mass.
MSA	Massachusetts State Archives, Boston, Mass.
MSM	G. W. Blunt White Library, Mystic Seaport Museum, Mystic, Conn.
MVM	Martha's Vineyard Museum, Edgartown, Mass.
NAB	National Archives at Boston, Waltham, Mass.
NBL	New Bedford Free Public Library, New Bedford, Mass.
NBW	New Bedford Whaling Museum, New Bedford, Mass.
NEHGS	New England Historic Genealogical Society, Boston, Mass.
NHARL	Nantucket Historical Association Research Library, Nantucket, Mass.
PEM	Phillips Library, Peabody Essex Museum, Salem, Mass.
PLP	Passed Legislation Packet, MSA
PPL	Nicholson Whaling Collection, Providence Public Library, Providence, R.I.
RTN	Return crew list. See DPT.
SHP	Whalemen's Shipping Papers/Articles, at NBL unless otherwise stated
SPG	Society for Propagating the Gospel Among the Indians and Others in North America Records, PEM
TVR	New England Historic Genealogical Society, *Vital Records of Tisbury*
Turnbull	Alexander Turnbull Library (National Library of New Zealand/Te Puna Mātauranga o Aotearoa), Wellington, New Zealand
WMA	Whaling and Marine Manuscript Archives/International Marine Manuscript Archives (microform), NBW

WSL   *Whalemen's Shipping List and Merchants' Transcript*, available at the
National Maritime Digital Library website

Introduction

1. Jared, Journal, ship *Amethyst* of New Bedford, 1846–1850, Log 633, NBW. See
appendix A for how I constructed voyage histories and appendix B for more on native-
authored logbooks and journals. Jared appears under Gay Head in Bird ("Joel Jerrod,"
p. 63) and Earle ("Joel Jerard," p. xiii) and as greenhand on the ship *Adeline* of New
Bedford, 1843–1846; boatsteerer, ship *Amethyst* of New Bedford, 1846–1850; and third
mate, bark *Samuel & Thomas* of Mattapoisett, 1850–1852; see DPT, SHP. The DPT and
RTN of the bark *Mary Frances* of Warren, 1852–1856, do not list Jared, but his journal
suggests that he was aboard for at least part of the voyage.

2. Quotes from 19 Dec. 1846, second page of volume, and 12 Mar. 1847, Jared,
Journal.

3. I inferred these relationships based on what appear to be children of Patience Gershom in Baylies; "Jerrod," in Bird, 63; and the parentage of brother Abraham "Jerrett"
in Richard L. Pease, *Report*, 45, 47.

4. For James, see Bird, 61; for age and rank DPT and SHP, ship *Amethyst* of New
Bedford, 1846–1850.

5. Jared married Rosanna Gershom; see Richard L. Pease, *Report*, 45. "The Haymaker" comes after the 11 Feb. 1849 entry and "Rosenah . . . " on a nearly blank page
between the *Amethyst* and *Samuel & Thomas* voyages.

6. Gorham B. Howes, Journal, ship *Amethyst* of New Bedford, 1846–1850, Log 904,
WMA.

7. For race changing over time, see Smedley, *Race in North America*; Omi and Wi-
nant, *Racial Formation*; Baker, *From Savage to Negro*; and varying by place, Degler,
Neither Black nor White; Fredrickson, *White Supremacy*. Nightingale, "Before Race
Mattered," compares race's contingency by place given local conditions. Lake and
Reynolds compare race in different parts of the world to argue for a rise in global
whiteness, in *Drawing the Global Colour Line*.

8. For race varying by context, see Stoler, "Racial Histories and Their Regimes of
Truth," and Mehta's response, "Essential Ambiguities of Race and Racism." For "situa-
tional racism" in contemporary American law, see Wang, *Discrimination by Default*.

9. Hodes, "Mercurial Nature and Abiding Power of Race," 84, 104, and *Sea Captain's
Wife*.

10. For census forms and enumerator instructions, see U.S. Census Bureau, *Measur-
ing America*. For shifting racial categories and inconsistencies, see Nobles, *Shades of
Citizenship*; Hodes, "Fractions and Fictions"; Dominguez, "Exporting U.S. Concepts of
Race"; Rodríguéz, *Changing Race*. For idiosyncratic categorization of individuals, see
Melish, "Racial Vernacular."

11. Basson, *White Enough to Be American?*; Gross, *What Blood Won't Tell*; Pascoe, *What Comes Naturally.*

12. Anzaldúa, *Borderlands/La Frontera.* See also Alsultany, "Los Intersticios."

13. Rediker, *Slave Ship*, 260.

14. Jacobson, *Whiteness of a Different Color*; Roediger, *Working toward Whiteness*; Ignatiev, *How the Irish Became White.*

15. Deloria, *Indians in Unexpected Places*; see also Usner, *Indian Work*; Harmon, *Rich Indians.*

16. Dening, *Islands and Beaches.*

17. Veracini, *Settler Colonialism*; Wolfe, "Land, Labor, and Difference."

18. O'Brien, *Dispossession by Degrees*; Mandell, *Behind the Frontier* and *Tribe, Race, History*; Silverman, *Faith and Boundaries*; Fisher, *Indian Great Awakening*; Edward E. Andrews, *Native Apostles*; Simmons and Simmons, *Old Light on Separate Ways*; Gaynell Stone, *Shinnecock Indians*; Calloway, *After King Philip's War.*

19. On Mohegan minister Occom's financial worries, see Brooks, *Collected Writings of Samson Occom*, 72–82, 107–8; for Mashpee, see schoolteacher Reuben Cognehew to Gideon Hawley and Hawley's response, 3 Apr. 1764, Miscellaneous Bound Manuscripts, MHS

20. For Briant's debts, see Mashpee Petition to Commissioners for Indian Affairs in Boston, 4 Aug. 1757, Gideon Hawley Letters, MHS; for whaling, see Gideon Hawley to Rev'd. Dr. Thacher, 1 Jan. 1794, Gideon Hawley Letters, MHS.

21. John A. Strong, *Algonquian Peoples of Long Island*, ch. 11; "Pigskin Book," "Shinnecock and Montauk Whalemen," and *Unkechaug Indians*, 93–102; Breen, *Imagining the Past*; Braginton-Smith and Oliver, *Cape Cod Shore Whaling*; Vickers, "First Whalemen of Nantucket"; Little, "Indian Contribution to Along-Shore Whaling"; Philbrick, *Abram's Eyes*; Silverman, "Impact of Indentured Servitude." For overviews of American whaling history, see Dolin, *Leviathan*; Ellis, *Men and Whales.*

22. Reeves, Breiwick, and Mitchell, "History of Whaling"; Vickers, "Nantucket Whalemen in the Deep-Sea Fishery"; Philbrick, *Away off Shore*; Little, "Indian Sickness at Nantucket."

23. Camino, *Exploring the Explorers*; Salmond, *Aphrodite's Island*; Dunmore, *Visions & Realities*; Hiroa, *Explorers of the Pacific.*

24. Dodge, *Islands and Empires*; Gibson, *Yankees in Paradise*; Donald D. Johnson, *United States in the Pacific*; Strauss, *Americans in Polynesia.*

25. Elijah Durfy journal, ship *Rebecca* of New Bedford, 1791–1793, Log 50, MSM; Ricketson, *History of New Bedford*, 60–61; Stackpole, *Sea-Hunters*, 152–58.

26. Lance E. Davis, Gallman, and Gleiter, *In Pursuit of Leviathan*, 70; see also Starbuck, *History of the American Whale Fishery.*

27. Sahlins, *Anahulu*, ch. 5; Bockstoce, *Whales, Ice, and Men*, 172–73.

28. Whaling memoirs are the best source for the routines of whaling work. For example, see Beane, *From Forecastle to Cabin*; Bill, *Citizen*; Browne, *Etchings of a Whal-*

ing Cruise; Bullen, *Cruise of the Cachalot*; Camp, *Life and Adventures of a New England Boy*; Thomas Crapo, *Strange, but True*; William M. Davis, *Nimrod of the Sea*; Haley, *Whale Hunt*; Hazen, *Five Years before the Mast*; [Jones?], *Life and Adventure*; Osborn, *Reminiscences*; Paddack, *Life on the Ocean*; Sampson, *Three Times around the World*; Nathaniel W. Taylor, *Life on a Whaler*; Whitecar, *Four Years Aboard the Whaleship*; Harold Williams, *One Whaling Family*.

29. Mandell arrived at a population figure of 1,829 in 1865 for Indians in Connecticut, Rhode Island, and Massachusetts, in *Tribe, Race, History*, 4. Shoemaker, "Mr. Tashtego," gives an overview of Native American whaling in the first half of the nineteenth century. See also Nicholas, "Mashpee Wampanoags"; Barsh, "'Colored' Seamen"; Mancini, "Beyond Reservation"; Rapito-Wyppensenwah, "Eighteenth & Nineteenth Century Native American Whaling"; Silverman, *Faith and Boundaries*, 205–6; Farr, "Slow Boat to Nowhere." Maritime histories of African Americans refer to native people or people of mixed descent also, though not always identified as such by the author; see Bolster, *Black Jacks*, 234–39; Putney, *Black Sailors*; Cash, "African American Whalers."

30. See Appendix A for a breakdown by decade. For the rise and fall of the whaling industry, see Starbuck, *History of the American Whale Fishery*, which lists vessels by year and then by port, and Lance E. Davis, Gallman, and Gleiter, *In Pursuit of Leviathan*, 6.

31. Aiken & Swift of New Bedford operated vessels out of San Francisco, on which New England natives Joseph G. Belain, Johnson P. David, Joseph A. Peters, Abram L. Joab, and others served in the 1890s; see *Memoranda, 1880-1904*, vol. 1, Aiken & Swift Records, NBW.

32. Tønnessen and Johnsen, *History of Modern Whaling*.

33. Tripp, *"There Goes Flukes,"* 170–76, 253–55.

34. For a map of whaling grounds, see New Bedford Whaling Museum, "New Bedford: The City that Lit the World."

35. Robert Langdon, *Where the Whalers Went*. To identify contemporary names from historic place names in the Pacific, I relied mainly on Forster, *South Sea Whaler*, 141–42, and Quanchi, *Atlas of the Pacific Islands*.

36. For an overview of whaling record formats, see Sherman, *Voice of the Whaleman*. Whaling history has superb reference works, including Forster, *South Sea Whaler* and *More South Sea Whaling*; Sherman, Downey, Adams, and Pasternack, *Whaling Logbooks and Journals*; and Lund. For more on maritime memoirs and journals, see Schell, *"A Bold and Hardy Race of Men"*; Blum, *View from the Masthead*; Glenn, *Jack Tar's Story*.

37. See, for example, John Thompson, *Life of John Thompson*; letters Sojourner Truth's son wrote while on the ship *Zone* of Nantucket, 1839–1843, in *Narrative of Sojourner Truth*, 77–79; Abram C. Rice, Journal, ship *Roman* 1843–1845 of New Bedford, Log 578, PPL. I concluded Rice was of African American descent (perhaps also native) because he appears on crew lists and censuses as "yellow" in DPT, bark *Constitution* of Newport,

1836–1839, and ship *Roman* of New Bedford, 1843–1845; and as a "mulatto" cooper in households 548 and 1034, Newport, R.I., U.S. manuscript census, 1850 and 1860, www. ancestry.com.

38. Lebo, "Native Hawaiian Seamen's Accounts" and "Two Hawaiian Documents"; Eber, *When the Whalers Were up North*; Kiryaku, *Drifting toward the Southeast*. Warrin uses many Azorean and Cape Verdean whalemen's writings in *So Ends This Day*.

39. For New England, see Sweet, *Bodies Politic*, ch. 7, and more generally Stepan, *Idea of Race*.

Chapter 1

1. Number of voyages from Lance E. Davis, Gallman, and Gleiter, *In Pursuit of Leviathan*, 44.

2. See Rockman, *Scraping By*, on the ramifications of a flexible workforce in the early Republic period.

3. Freeman, "Notes on Nantucket"; "Black hands of Ship Galen," final settlement papers, ship *Galen* of Nantucket, 1820–1823, Folder 992, and A. Paddock to Dear Brother, 10 Sept. 1815, ship *Thomas* of Nantucket, 1815–1817, Folder 1014, Edouard A. Stackpole Collection, MS335, NHARL; "Ship Hero, of Nantucket," *New Bedford Mercury*, 22 June 1821; Richard W. Hixson, journal, ship *Maria* of Nantucket, 1832–1836, Daniel B. Fearing Logbook Collection, Houghton Library, Harvard University, Cambridge, Mass. For a New Bedford example, see DPT, ship *Martha* of New Bedford, 1818–1819.

4. 29 Aug., [date illeg.] Nov., 22 Dec., [date illeg.] Dec. 1801, in Gideon Hawley Letterbook, vol. 3, Gideon Hawley Journals and Letters, Congregational Library, Boston, Mass.

5. Indian Inhabitants of Christiantown to the General Court of the Commonwealth of Massachusetts, n.d., PLP for Acts 1804, ch. 84, "Act for the Protection of the Indians and their Property in that Part of Dukes County known by the Name of Christian Town," approved 8 Mar. 1805.

6. Gideon Hawley to James Freeman, 15 Nov. 1802, Gideon Hawley Letters, MHS. The Edouard A. Stackpole Collection, MS335, NHARL, has many receipts, shipping papers, and wharf books listing men who sold shares in their voyages, for example, on Nantucket ships *Minerva*, 1815–1817; *Renown*, 1803–1805; *States*, 1880–1820, 1820–1823; and *Thomas*, 1815–1817, 1817–1820.

7. Keeter contract, ship *Dauphin* of Nantucket, 1820–1823, Ships' Papers Collection, MS15, NHARL; his age is from Marston.

8. Kendall, *Travels through the Northern Parts*, 2:194.

9. "An Act for the Better Regulation, Instruction, and Government of the Indians and People of Colour in the County of Dukes County," Acts 1827, ch. 114, approved 10 Mar. 1828, MAR.

10. Chappaquiddick and Christiantown annual accounts conveniently give native whaling earnings from 1828 to 1869; some years are in Indian Guardian Papers, on

microfilm rl. 2, MSA; others are in Dukes County Probate Records, on microfilm r rl. 1, MSA.

11. *Leavitt Thaxter, Administrator vs. Lawrence Grinnell & Others.*

12. Isaiah Belain, Abram Brown, and Lawrence Prince to the Senate and House of Representatives in General Court Assembled, 9 Mar. 1840, Unpassed Indian Legislation, on microfilm, rl. 2, MSA. Natives more frequently complained about guardians; see Mandell, *Tribe, Race, History*, ch. 3.

13. Bird, 51–52; Grandin, *Empire of Necessity*, 161–64.

14. Howwoswee's voyages: DPT, ship *Martha* of New Bedford, 1816–1817, 1817–1818, 1818–1819; ship *George and Susan* of New Bedford, 1819–1820, 1824–1827; ship *Milwood* of New Bedford, 1820–1821; brig *President* of New Bedford, 1821–1822; ship *Maria Theresa* of New Bedford, 1822–1823, 1823–1824; ship *Java* of New Bedford, 1829–1830, 1830–1831, 1831–1832, 1832–1833; bark *Equator* of New Bedford, 1833–1836; ship *Hercules* of New Bedford, 1837–1840. Howwoswee's rank and death reported on SHP and RTN, ship *Massachusetts* of New Bedford, 1840–1844. Hillman's rank as third and first mate estimated from where his name falls on crew lists. For Hillman as captain, see Lund, 173.

15. SHP, ship *Adeline* of New Bedford, 1843–1846; ship *Amethyst* of New Bedford, 1846–1850; bark *Samuel & Thomas* of Mattapoisett, 1850–1852; bark *Anaconda* of New Bedford, 1856–1860. "Died," *Vineyard Gazette*, 11 Jan. 1861.

16. Some voyages with native officers (from SHP unless otherwise stated): Asa Belain, second mate, ship *Phocion* of New Bedford, 1846–1849; Philip Goodridge, third mate, ship *America* of New Bedford, 1845–1848; Richard Gould, second mate, ship *Condor* of New Bedford, 1853–1856; George DeGrass, third mate, bark *Columbus* of New Bedford, 1855–1859; William Jeffers, third mate, ship *John* of New Bedford, 1844–1848; Simon Johnson, second mate, bark *Mermaid* of New Bedford, 1855–1860; Thomas Cook, third mate, ship *John Coggeshall* of New Bedford, 1847–1850; Nathan S. Webquish, second mate, ship *Bartholomew Gosnold* of New Bedford, 1844–1847, from death notice, *Sandwich Observer*, 17 Apr. 1847; Jesse Webquish Jr., first mate, bark *Fortune* of New Bedford, 1856–1858; Levi Webquish, second mate, ship *Bartholomew Gosnold* of New Bedford, 1858–1862; William S. Webquish, second mate, ship *George Washington* of New Bedford, 1855–1856; Asa Wainer, first mate, brig *Rodman* of New Bedford, 1845–1846; Rodney Wainer, second mate, bark *President* of Westport, 1849–1850 and 1850–1851; Joseph Ammons, second mate, ship *James Maury* of New Bedford, 1851–1855; Gideon Ammons, third mate, ship *Emma C. Jones* of New Bedford, 1849–1852; Milton Lee, first mate, bark *Amazon* of New Bedford, 1856–1860; Ferdinand Lee, first mate, ship *Roman* of New Bedford, 1864–1868, in crew list, WSL, 19 July 1864; William Garrison Lee, schooner *Abbie Bradford* of New Bedford, 1880–1881, crew list, WSL, 11 May 1880.

17. Crew list, bark *Sunbeam* of New Bedford, 1868–1871, WSL, 9 June 1868.

18. Crew list, bark *Kathleen* of New Bedford, 1871–1875, WSL, 24 Oct. 1871; crew list, bark *Atlantic* of New Bedford, 1872–1876, WSL, 2 July 1872.

19. Belain on crew list, bark *Triton* of New Bedford, 1876–1880, WSL, 5 Sept. 1876; Peters's rank in crew list, Logbook, bark *Atlantic* of New Bedford, 1876–1879, Log ODHS 798, NBW

20. "Died," WSL, 7 Aug. 1877; 13 Mar. 1877, Deaths, Gay Head, MAVR.

21. "Bark Atlantic," WSL, 6 Aug. 1878: "Frank Waters [Peters], Gay Head, 3d mate"; also lost, Frank E. Mashow of Mashpee descent (Earle, xxix).

22. Wiggins, *Captain Paul Cuffe's Logs and Letters*, 50; Lamont D. Thomas, *Rise to Be a People*, 15; Putney, *Black Sailors*, 60, 72.

23. Karttunen, *Other Islanders*, 69.

24. "Two Men Missing," *Vineyard Gazette*, 15 July 1847. Samuel E. Pharaoh was rumored to have declined an offer to command a voyage; Rapito-Wyppensenwah, "Eighteenth & Nineteenth Century Native American Whaling," 444.

25. In a rare mistake, Lund, 165, credits Amos Haskins with three voyages as master, but DPT, ship *Charles Frederick* of New Bedford, 1850–1854, has Abiel Haskins as captain, no relation to Amos; SHP, bark *Elizabeth* of Mattapoisett, 1849–1850; "Memoranda," WSL, 1 Oct. 1850; oil returns, bark *Massasoit* of Mattapoisett, 1851–1852 and 1852–1853, "American Offshore Whaling Voyages: A Database," www.nmdl.org; "Mortality on Shipboard," WSL, 26 July 1853. For more on Haskins, see Shoemaker, "Mr. Tashtego," 128–31.

26. Crew list, brig *March* of Mattapoisett, WSL, 5 June 1860; "Missing Vessel," WSL, 25 Feb. 1862.

27. Crew list, ship *Eliza Adams* of New Bedford, WSL, 30 July 1867; "The First of the Season," WSL, 7 Feb. 1871.

28. Moment, "Business of Whaling," 271–73.

29. "The Lost Amethyst: Little Hope of Ever Finding Vessel or Crew," *Sag Harbor Corrector*, 2 Oct. 1886; Ferdinand's brother William Garrison Lee, first mate on the *Rainbow*, was rumored to have died on the *Amethyst*, which had saved him and four others from the wreck of the *Rainbow* shortly before, in "The Lost Whaler Amethyst Found," WSL, 20 Sept. 1887.

30. Lance E. Davis, Gallman, and Gleiter, *In Pursuit of Leviathan*, 386–88.

31. Crew list, bark *Palmetto* of New Bedford, WSL, 30 Nov. 1875; Lund, 34. For his long whaling career, see "Indian Chief's Scion Is Dead," *New Bedford Evening Standard*, 20 Oct. 1926.

32. William H. Cook, bark *Reindeer* of New Bedford: crew list, WSL, 19 June 1877; "From Our Correspondent," WSL, 9 Sept. 1879. Samuel Peters, ship *Niger* of New Bedford, 1882–1886: crew list, WSL, 10 Oct. 1882; "Letters," WSL, 22 Apr. 1884; "Letters," WSL, 14 Oct. 1884; William Garrison Lee took over after the captain's death, schooner *Abbie Bradford* of New Bedford, 1880–1881, in Todd, *In Olde New York*, 222.

33. Lund, 89; as son-in-law, see Lamont D. Thomas, *Rise to Be a People*, 161.

34. Lund, 219; "Passed Their Fiftieth Wedding Anniversary," *Vineyard Gazette*, 11 July 1907; Weintraub, *Lighting the Trail*, 38–51.

35. "Worthy of Record," *Barnstable Patriot and Commercial Advertiser*, 4 Oct. 1837; DPT, ship *Good Return* of New Bedford, 1825–1826. For Benjamin Attaquin also, see Ramona Peters's oral history in Shoemaker, *Living with Whales*, 153.

36. Warren P. Strong, "Wharves of Plymouth," 7.

37. Red Thunder Cloud, caption on back of "Captain Aaron Cuffee," album 11, photo 477, Long Island Collection, EHPL. He was on at least two whaling voyages: rescued from shipwreck of ship *William Tell* of Sag Harbor in the Arctic in July 1859, in P. C. Edwards to Judge Pratt, 14 Oct. 1859, Records of Foreign Service Posts, Consular Posts, Honolulu, Hawai'i, State Department, RG 84, National Archives, College Park, Maryland; DPT, bark *E. Corning* of New Bedford, 1860–1866. For scrimshaw, see Frank, *Dictionary of Scrimshaw Artists*, 41. For scrimshaw artists whose work is not in museum collections, see Frank, *Dictionary of Scrimshaw Artists*, 93, on Samuel G. Mingo; Peters's and David Bunn Martine's oral histories in Shoemaker, *Living with Whales*, 144–45, 182, 184–85.

38. 1 Jan. 1831, Dwight Baldwin, Journal, ship *New England* of New Bedford, 1830–1834, Journal Collection, HMCS. In the 1850s, "the typical New Bedford whaling venture" cost $20,000–30,000 and was four to five times more costly an investment than a farm or factory, in Lance E. Davis, Gallman, and Gleiter, *In Pursuit of Leviathan*, 384.

39. Osborn, *Reminiscences*, 5; Camp, *Life and Adventures*, 123; Nevens, *Forty Years at Sea*, 189; Hohman, *American Whaleman*, 217–19.

40. "Memoranda," WSL, 28 Jan. 1851; U.S. National Archives Project, *Ship Registers of New Bedford*, 2:165–66.

41. SHP, bark *Massasoit* of Mattapoisett, 1852–1853; U.S. National Archives Project, *Ship Registers of New Bedford*, 2:166.

42. DPT, brig *Elizabeth* of Westport, 1839–1840, 1840–1840, and SHP, 1841–1842; U.S. National Archives Project, *Ship Registers of New Bedford*, 1:85.

43. Isaac's earnings covered four years of the five-year voyage since he received his discharge in 1858 (RTN); for earnings, see crew and owner final settlement accounts for Aug. 1859, Account Book, bark *Benjamin Cummings* of Dartmouth, 1854–1861, Cummings Family Papers, NBW. The partnership Alonzo Matthews, John Mashow, and James M. Babbitt owned shares in the *A. R. Tucker*, *Benjamin Cummings*, *Cape Horn Pigeon*, *Matilda Sears*, and other whalers; U.S. National Archives Project, *Ship Registers of New Bedford*, 2:1, 28, 38–39, 166–67. See also Sidney Kaplan, *American Studies in Black and White*, 235–36.

44. Bird, 14–15. Unnamed, George E. James is the only twenty-two-year-old man from Christiantown (p. 61) with a blind elder brother at the time of the investigation.

45. Creighton, *Rites and Passages*, ch. 2.

46. See, for example, captains' memoirs: Bodfish, *Chasing the Bowhead*; Cook, *Pursuing the Whale*; Gardner, *Captain Edmund Gardner*; Gelett, *Life on the Ocean*.

47. Corduda in Little, "Indian Contribution to Along-Shore Whaling," 67. "Cadoody," Chappaquiddick, in Baylies. Laban "Caduba," "Ship Oeno," *Canal of Intelligence*

(Norwich, Conn.), 15 Oct. 1828; Levi "Cordoody," DPT, ship *Meridian* of Edgartown, 1834–1836, MVM; "The Sperm Whale Fishery," *New Bedford Mercury*, 12 Jan. 1838. Joseph "Kudordy," DPT, ship *Hector* of New Bedford, 1852–1856.

48. Summary conclusions about native men's voyages are based on my database; see Appendix A.

49. His last voyage was as third mate; see SHP, ship *Emma C. Jones*, 1849–1852; "Last of Narragansett Chiefs," *Providence Journal*, 4 Dec. 1899.

50. 9 June and 24 June 1838, 22 May 1839, Pells, Journal, ship *Barclay* of Nantucket, 1835–1839, Log 890, WMA.

51. Poole, "Full Circle," 128.

52. Mandell, *Tribe, Race, History*, ch. 1, ch. 5, especially 160–63.

53. Final pages of Joseph Ammons, Journal, ship *Roman* of New Bedford, 1843–1845 and 1845–1847, Log 792, MSM.

54. Thaddeus W. Cook, Journal, bark *Joseph Butler* of New Bedford, 1852–1856, Log 226, NBW. The accounts appear on pages 20–23 of the unpaginated journal. Indian Guardian Accounts for Chappaquiddick and Christiantown, MSA, cite similarly small sums paid to native men for building stone walls and carting wood interspersed with several hundred dollars paid to whalemen returning from voyages.

55. Hohman, *American Whaleman*, chs. 10–11; Lance E. Davis, Gallman, and Gleiter, *In Pursuit of Leviathan*, ch. 5.

56. 19 June 1866, William A. Vanderhoop Jr., Journal, bark *Abraham Barker* of New Bedford, 1866–1870, Log 10, PPL.

57. Bark *Abraham Barker* of New Bedford, 1866–1870, Agent's Accounts, p. 14, 22, J. & W. R. Wing Business Records, NBL.

58. Vanderhoop's personal accounts and memoranda in his *Abraham Barker* journal, after voyage entries and before his crew list, show his activities at Gay Head postwhaling; marriage to Louisa Wood, 23 Feb. 1871, New Bedford, MAVR; Earle, xli, lists Wood with Herring Pond.

59. "Ship outfits, cargos, and crew list book; 1836–1843," pp. 74–75, Charles W. Morgan Collection, MSM.

60. Final Settlement Accounts, bark *Atlantic* of New Bedford, 1876–1879, J. & W. R. Wing Papers, NBL.

61. Norling, *Captain Ahab Had a Wife*, 144–47.

62. Elizabeth P. Haskins to Josiah Holmes Jr., 19 July 1859 and 27 July 1859, Records of the Holmes's Shipyard, MSM, with similar letters in same file from Sophia L. Clarke, 4 Dec. 1857, and Rosetta M. Camp, 12 April 1859.

63. Amos Haskins, household 1581, Ward 4, New Bedford, Mass., U.S. manuscript census, 1860, www.ancestry.com.

64. Accounts for 1850, Indian Guardian Papers, rl. 2, MSA; 16 Mar. 1850, logbook, ship *Erie* of Fairhaven, 1847–1850, Log ODHS 382, NBW.

65. For example, Daniel Belain fell from aloft: "Letters," WSL, 25 June 1878. Ebenezer Pharaoh fell overboard and drowned: RTN, bark *Washington* of New Bedford, 1861–1865. James Francis died of scurvy as reported in the Honolulu newspaper, *Friend*, 1 Nov. 1844. James David was killed by a whale: RTN, ship *George and Susan* of New Bedford, 1820–1821. Alexander David was attacked by a shark: WSL, 10 Sept. 1867.

66. RTN, bark *Benjamin Cummings* of New Bedford, 1875–1876; DPT, bark *Vigilant* of New Bedford, 1879–1879; WSL: "From the Arctic," 19 July 1881; "The Wrecked Whalers," 23 Aug. 1881; "Loss of Bark Daniel Webster, of this Port," 27 Sept. 1881.

67. William Amos in Gulf Stream, "Loss of Ship Henry, of Nantucket," *New Bedford Mercury*, 1 Oct. 1813; Charles F. Alves, DPT, ship *Israel* of New Bedford, 1846–1847, wrecked at Table Bay, "The Cape Good Hope Shipping Gazette of April 16," WSL, 27 July 1847; Anthony Hinson, DPT, brig *Helen* of Mattapoisett, 1848–1848, Charles W. Dabney to James Buchanan, 24 Dec. 1848, rl. 3, *Despatches*, Fayal; Spencer Edwards, DPT, ship *Huntress* of New Bedford, 1850–1852; "Wrecks in the North Pacific in 1852," WSL, 11 Jan. 1853; DPT, ship *Liverpool II* of New Bedford, 1851–1853, has Isaac F. Hendricks, Walter R. Mingo, Watson F. T. Hammond, Kilbourn Webquish, Grafton Pocknett, and Nicholas Pocknett; wreck in Bering Strait, in "Loss of Whalers," WSL, 1 Nov. 1853.

68. SHP and RTN, ship *George Washington* of New Bedford, 1851–1855; "A Successful Voyage," WSL, 5 June 1855. Starbuck called this "an extraordinary voyage" in *History of the American Whale Fishery*, 479.

69. DPT and SHP, ship *George Washington* of New Bedford, 1855–1856.

70. "Burning of Ship George Washington of this Port," WSL, 20 May 1856; "The Junior Mutineer," WSL, 12 July 1859.

71. DPT, ship *Mary* of New Bedford, 1856–1860. Pells and Webquish are "mariner" by occupation in Earle (1861), xxxv–xxxvi, and in the federal census taken around the same time: households 49 and 54, District of Mashpee, Falmouth, Mass., U.S. manuscript census, 1860, www.ancestry.com.

72. Charles Lee and Francis H. Hicks, DPT, ship *Factor* of New Bedford, 1844–1847, condemned at Tahiti, "By Last Night's Mail," *Vineyard Gazette*, 25 Nov. 1847; Uriah Low and Thomas L. Hicks, DPT, bark *Congaree* of New Bedford, 1859–1863, condemned at Valparaiso, "Protest of Weston J. Swift, Master," 28 May 1863, Miscellaneous Whaling Ships, Nicholson Collection, PPL; James S. Mills (also aboard William P. Johnson of Gay Head), DPT, bark *Laetitia* of New Bedford, 1875–1879; condemned at Mauritius, 1 July 1879, Logbook, Log 383, NBL.

73. "Ship Hero, of Nantucket," *New Bedford Mercury*, 22 June 1821; Philbrick and Philbrick, *Loss of the Ship* Essex, 21, 110–11, 188–89.

74. Deposition of Five Subscribers, 21 Dec. 1821, in Michael Hogan to John Quincy Adams, 15 Jan. 1822, rl. 1, *Despatches*, Valparaiso. On Benavides, see Basil Hall, *Extracts from a Journal*, 1:321–62. I have not found Cowet on later crew lists, and he is not in Marston. Two Pocknetts on the *Hero* with Cowet also may not have returned.

75. William A. Vanderhoop, bark *Awashonks* of New Bedford, 1862–1865, Log 53, MVM.

76. William A. Vanderhoop, bark *Abraham Barker* of New Bedford, 1866–1870, Log 10, PPL.

77. 21 and 25 Sept. 1862, Vanderhoop, Journal, *Awashonks*.

78. See Appendix B for more on Ammons's journals. Webquish's first entry is 14 Jan. 1854, Logbook, ship *James Maury* of New Bedford, 1851–1855, Log 315 on microfilm continues in a volume available in Special Collections only, NBL. Webquish's logbook overlaps with Ammons's journal briefly, but Ammons appears to have run out of pages and was then discharged at Lahaina, 2 Apr. 1854, Logbook, *James Maury*.

79. 10 Aug. 1855, 10 Feb. 1855, 6 Mar. 1855, 11 Sept. 1855, Logbook, *James Maury*.

80. Final Settlement, ship *James Maury* of New Bedford, 1851–1855, "Ship Accounts, 1845–1876," p. 97, Voyage Accounts of C. R. Tucker, NBL. Ammons's large, frequent advances kept him in debt to the ship (p. 67).

81. Reuben Tinker, "Voyage to the Sandwich Islands," 15 Jan. 1831, Journal Collection, HMCS; DPT, ship *New England* of New Bedford, 1830–1834.

82. Reference to a "half breed Indian" in Cyrene M. Clarke, *Glances at Life upon the Sea*, 57.

83. Sampson, *Three Times around the World*, 53.

84. Cheever, *Whale and His Captors*, 189. See also Comstock, *Voyage to the Pacific*, 17.

85. Melville, *Moby-Dick*, 25, 124.

86. Earle, 27.

87. Earle, v–vii. Peters began whaling at age 15: DPT, ship *Richmond* of New Bedford, 1826–1827. On his last two voyages, he was boatsteerer: SHP, bark *Lafayette* of New Bedford, 1840–1844, and ship *James Maury* of New Bedford, 1845–1848.

88. Ages in Earle, vi–vii; crew lists, ship *Minerva Smyth* of New Bedford, 1858–1862, WSL, 30 Nov. 1858, and bark *Dominga* of New Bedford, 1858–1861, WSL, 26 Oct. 1858.

89. Earle, v–vi. James W. DeGrass: SHP, bark *Draco* of New Bedford, 1847–1850. Mingo was promoted to second mate by the end of the voyage: "Joseph Mingo Dead," *Vineyard Gazette*, 10 Apr. 1913. George DeGrass: SHP, bark *Columbus* of New Bedford, 1855–1859. James: SHP, bark *Mermaid* of New Bedford, 1855–1860.

90. SHP, bark *Osceola* of New Bedford, 1851–1853.

91. See earlier quotation of George E. James from Bird, 14.

92. Goode and Collins, *Fishermen of the United States*, 14; Morison, *Maritime History of Massachusetts*, 158; Hohman, *American Whaleman*, 50.

93. Thomas Perkins, *Whaling Voyage in the Bark "Willis,"* 8.

94. Hazen, *Five Years before the Mast*, 95.

95. Nordhoff, *Nine Years a Sailor: Whaling and Fishing*, 156–57, 248–50.

Chapter 2

1. On crew diversity, see Busch, *"Whaling Will Never Do for Me,"* ch. 3; Schell, *"A Bold and Hardy Race of Men,"* ch. 6.

2. Examples include six Mashpee men (Isaac F. Hendricks, Walter R. Mingo, Watson F. T. Hammond, Kilbourn Webquish, and Grafton and Nicholas Pocknett), DPT, ship *Liverpool II* of New Bedford, 1851–1853; seven Gay Head men (George and William Belain, Jonathan Cuff, Zaccheus Cooper, Joel Jared, William Weeks, and Thomas Jeffers), DPT, ship *Adeline* of New Bedford, 1843–1846; and ten Shinnecocks (Andrew, Wickham, Elias, and two James Cuffees, David and Alonzo Eleazer, Russell and William Bunn, and Milton Lee), ship *Panama* of Sag Harbor, 1847–1850, departure crew list at NBW.

3. Stein, *American Maritime Documents,* 50–58, 145–48, 154; Sherman, *Voice of the Whaleman,* 59–65; Dana, *Seaman's Friend,* 177–78.

4. Bradburn, *Citizenship Revolution,* ch. 7; Kettner, *Development of American Citizenship,* ch. 10.

5. For example, RTN, ship *Jason* of New London, 1842–1844, and ship *Robert Browne* of New London, 1842–1845.

6. Silverman, *Faith and Boundaries,* appendix B. Bolster, *Black Jacks,* 234–39, divides complexions into two categories, black and white; Putney's *Black Sailors* similarly treats those with "yellow," "coloured," "mulatto," and "black" complexions as African American.

7. Amos: DPT, bark *Dryade* of Rochester, 1834–1835; brig *Mattapoisett* of Rochester, 1839–1840; the aborted voyage on the brig *Chase* of Mattapoisett, 1841–1841; brig *Annawan* of Mattapoisett, 1843–1844; bark *Cachalot* of Mattapoisett, 1845–1847; bark *Willis* of Mattapoisett, 1847–1848; bark *Elizabeth* of Mattapoisett, 1849–1850; bark *Massasoit* of Mattapoisett, 1851–1852 and 1852–1853; bark *Oscar* of Mattapoisett, 1857–1861; his personal information is blank on brig *March* of Mattapoisett, 1860–1861. Samuel: DPT, brig *Annawan* of Mattapoisett, 1844–1846; bark *Valparaiso* of New Bedford, 1852–1856; schooner *Palmyra* of Mattapoisett, 1856–1857; brig *Elvira* of Mattapoisett, 1858–1859; bark *Sarah* of New Bedford, 1865–1867; for bark *Samuel & Thomas* of Mattapoisett, 1850–1852, complexion is blank. On their family relationship, see Shoemaker, "Mr. Tashtego," 128.

8. S. Macy to Owners & Captain of Ship *Thomas,* 27 Sept. 1815, Edouard A. Stackpole Collection, MS335, Folder 1014, NHARL; DPT, ship *Walker* of New Bedford, 1808–1810, and ship *Martha* of New Bedford, 1810–1811.

9. Pratt, *Journals,* 15–16.

10. Philbrick and Philbrick, *Loss of the Ship* Essex, 71, 73, 88 (quotation); Philbrick, *In the Heart of the Sea,* 165–67.

11. Bullen, *Cruise of the Cachalot,* 4.

12. Smalley, "I Killed 'Moby Dick,'" 172–74; Samuel Smalley, 26 Jan. 1861, Marriages, Tisbury, and 9 Oct. 1893, Deaths, Gay Head, MAVR.

13. Bolster, *Black Jacks,* 167; Busch, *"Whaling Will Never Do for Me,"* 34–41.

14. SHP, bark *Draco* of New Bedford, 1847–1850; 15 Jan. 1850, James V. Cox, Journal, bark *Draco* of New Bedford, 1847–1850, Log 201, PPL; Baylies, Christiantown section.

15. Olmsted, *Incidents of a Whaling Voyage*, 45–47, 84. See also Reilly, *Journal of George Attwater*, 372; William M. Davis, *Nimrod of the Sea*, 30–31, 211; [Jones?], *Life and Adventure*, 201–2; Zollers, *Thrilling Incidents*, 174, 274; Edward T. Perkins, *Na Motu*, 81.

16. Whitecar, *Four Years Aboard the Whaleship*, 196.

17. Charles Francis Hall, *Life with the Esquimaux*, 2:199.

18. Druett, *In the Wake of Madness*.

19. Reilly, *Journal of George Attwater*, 106, 144, 224, 273, 286, 444. On Attwater's beatings, see 16, 434.

20. Browne, *Etchings of a Whaling Cruise*, 108. For its reception, see Seelye's introduction, 12–15.

21. Roediger, *Wages of Whiteness*.

22. Browne, *Etchings of a Whaling Cruise*, 315. See also 2 Aug. 1842, William A. Allen, Journal, ship *Samuel Robertson* of New Bedford, 1841–1846, Log ODHS 1040, NBW; Ely, *"There She Blows,"* 40; Nordhoff, *Nine Years a Sailor: Whaling and Fishing*, 250, 272; Bolster, *Black Jacks*, 219: Raffety, *Republic Afloat*, ch. 3.

23. John Thompson, *Life of John Thompson*, 117.

24. Whitecar, *Four Years Aboard the Whaleship*, 37, 42; Browne, *Etchings of a Whaling Cruise*, 24, 43, 151, 214; 26 July 1859, William A. Abbe, Journal, bark *Atkins Adams* of Fairhaven, 1858–1863, Log ODHS 485, NBW; Burns, *Year with a Whaler*, 32.

25. On Portuguese and Kanaka performances, see Zollers, *Thrilling Incidents*, 139; [Jones?], *Life and Adventure*, 90, 98; Whitecar, *Four Years Aboard the Whaleship*, 163, 172; Browne, *Etchings of a Whaling Cruise*, 44, 46; 24 Jan. 1859, 16 & 24 Apr. 1859, 10 May 1859, William A. Abbe, Journal, bark *Atkins Adams* of Fairhaven, 1858–1863, Log ODHS 485, NBW. On Kanakas running amok, see Harold Williams, *One Whaling Family*, 292–96; 21 Aug. 1853, William H. Chappell, Journal, ship *Saratoga* of New Bedford, 1852–1856. As mutineers, see Paddack, *Life on the Ocean*, 152; Druett, *In the Wake of Madness*. On Portuguese pulling knives, see William M. Davis, *Nimrod of the Sea*, 198; Browne, *Etchings of a Whaling Cruise*, 310–11; 6 Nov. 1887, Logbook, bark *Wave* of New Bedford, 1887–1889, Log ODHS 220, NBW. On vengeful Portuguese with knives and insane Kanakas, see Gelett, *Life on the Ocean*, 19, 30–31.

26. For Azoreans and Cape Verdeans in the whaling industry, see Warrin, *So Ends This Day*. For Pacific Islanders on whalers and other European and American sailing vessels, see Lebo, "Native Hawaiian Whalers"; Chappell, *Double Ghosts*; Diamond, "Queequeg's Crewmates."

27. RTN, ship *Abigail* of New Bedford, 1821–1823; and DPT, ship *Amazon* of Fairhaven, 1822–1823.

28. Gilje, *Liberty on the Waterfront*, 156–61.

29. U.S. Congress, "Act for the Regulation of Seamen" (1813), "Act Concerning the Navigation of the United States" (1817), and "Act Repealing Certain Provisions of Law Concerning Seamen" (1864); Dana, *Seaman's Friend*, 178.

30. Plane and Button, "Massachusetts Indian Enfranchisement Act"; Boissevain, "Detribalization of the Narragansett Indians."

31. U.S. Congress, "Act for the Regulation of Seamen" (1813).

32. Cyrene M. Clarke, *Glances at Life upon the Sea*, 78.

33. See, for example, Frederick Dabney to James Buchanan, 20 Oct. 1848, rl. 3, *Despatches*, Fayal; see also Dana, *Seaman's Friend*, 178; Busch, *"Whaling Will Never Do for Me,"* ch. 5; Creighton, *Rites and Passages*, 107, appendix VI.

34. Cloud, *Enoch's Voyage*, 38, 74. The lead Portuguese in the fight was a "colored" Cape Verdean: 23 Jan. 1852, William Farmer, Journal, ship *Montreal* of New Bedford, 1850–1853, Log ODHS 146, NBW.

35. Bullen, *Cruise of the Cachalot*, 4–5, 31, 56.

36. Haley, *Whale Hunt*, 36.

37. William M. Davis, *Nimrod of the Sea*, 250, 253–54.

38. [Jones?], *Life and Adventure*, 199, 314.

39. Bullen, *Cruise of the Cachalot*, 214, 368.

40. Burns, *Year with a Whaler*, 73. Burns named vessel and captain but not the year; Lund, 286, lists three one-year voyages for the *Alexander* with Shorey as captain from 1889 to 1891.

41. Beasley, *Negro Trail Blazers of California*, 125–27; Tompkins, "Black Ahab."

42. 22 June 1862, 22 Mar. 1863, William A. Vanderhoop, Journal, bark *Awashonks* of New Bedford, 1862–1865, Log 53, MVM.

43. DPT, SHP, and 14 Nov. 1850, Logbook, bark *Mercator* of Westport, 1850–1852, Log 838, NBW.

44. 17 June 1859, William A. Abbe, Journal, bark *Atkins Adams* of Fairhaven, 1858–1863, Log ODHS 485, NBW; William F. Wyatt Jr., "Introduction to William A. Abbe's Journal Aboard Ship *Atkins Adams* of Fairhaven, Mass., 1858–1859," *Bulletin from Johnny Cake Hill*, Fall 2011, 8–9.

45. Schell, *"Bold and Hardy Race of Men"*; Creighton, "Davy Jones' Locker Room" and *Rites and Passages*; Norling, *Captain Ahab Had a Wife*; Glenn, *Jack Tar's Story*, ch. 5.

46. For Vanderhoop and Pells, see chapter 1.

47. The best-documented cross-dressing woman was on the ship *Christopher Mitchell* of Nantucket, 1848–1852: "Memoranda," WSL, 21 Aug. 1849; Haley, *Whale Hunt*, 60–70; Little, "Female Sailor."

48. Sampson, *Three Times around the World*, 79; Nathaniel W. Taylor, *Life on a Whaler*, 94–95; second to last page, n.d., Marshall Keith, journal, bark *Brewster* of New Bedford, 1863–1865, Log 84, PPL; Creighton, *Rites and Passages*, ch. 7; Norling, *Captain Ahab Had a Wife*, ch. 6; Druett, *Hen Frigates*.

49. Brower, *Fifty Years below Zero*, 186–88, misspelling their names "Whitesides" and "Belaine."

50. 2 Apr. 1855, 18 Apr. 1855, William H. Chappell, Journal, ship *Saratoga* of New Bedford, 1852–1856, Log 597, PPL.

51. Camp, *Life and Adventures*, 68.

52. "Songs That Resounded in the Fo'castles and Cabins," *Vineyard Gazette*, 11 May 1856; Huntington, *Songs the Whalemen Sang*, 148–51; see that volume's "Introduction" by Rick Spencer for Samuel Mingo as the author of the journal Huntington discusses on those pages. See also Malloy, "Sailor's Fantasy."

53. Kiryaku, *Drifting toward the Southeast*, 50, 69, 82, 85.

54. Ely, *"There She Blows,"* 98.

55. Busch, *"Whaling Will Never Do for Me,"* 147–48; Creighton, *Rites and Passages*, 190–91; Warrin, *So Ends This Day*, 207–9; for incidents not mentioned by previous authors, see 26 Jan. 1847, Logbook, ship *Frances* of New Bedford, 1843–1847, Log 91, NBW; RTN, ship *Hope* of New Bedford, 1857–1863; C. F. Winslow, consulate attachment (copy), 10 Dec. 1862, in C. F. Winslow to William H. Seward, 30 June 1863, rl. 2, *Despatches*, Paita.

56. 7 Sept. 1839, and protest at end of volume (signed "Hosear Pocknet"), n.d., Logbook, ship *Joseph Starbuck* of Nantucket, 1838–1842, MS220, Log 224, NHARL.

57. Haley, *Whale Hunt*, 41. On the ritual more generally, see Nevens, *Forty Years at Sea*, 19–20; Bill, *Citizen*, 18–23; Gelett, *Life on the Ocean*, 10; Creighton, *Rites and Passages*, 117–21.

58. George W. Kennedy, "A Whaleman's Story: The Diary of George W. Kennedy, 1851–1853," on ship *New England* of New London, 1851–1854, MSM.

59. 17 Oct. 1879, Timothy Belain, Journal, bark *John Dawson* of New Bedford, NBL.

60. 28 Nov. 1881, Logbook, bark *John Dawson* of New Bedford, 1879–1884, NBL.

61. Whitecar, *Four Years Aboard the Whaleship*, 131, 156.

Chapter 3

1. Ditty comes after 31 Apr. 1880 entry; 13 June 1879, 25 Sept. 1879, 29 Sept. 1880, 8 Aug. 1881, Ellenwood B. Coleman, Journal, ship *Niger* of New Bedford, 1878–1882, WMA.

2. Coleman's crew list between years 1880 and 1881 in his journal and crew list, WSL, 13 Aug. 1878, give ranks, Peters's residence as Gay Head, and Walker's as Sag Harbor. Walker headed household 253, Shinnecock Reservation, New York State manuscript census for 1865, on microfilm, EHPL.

3. Rediker, *Between the Devil and the Deep Blue Sea*; Linebaugh and Rediker, *Many-Headed Hydra*.

4. Final settlement papers, ship *Galen* of Nantucket, 1820–1823, Folder 992, Edouard A. Stackpole Collection, MS335, NHARL; Bolster, *Black Jacks*, 75–76.

5. Hohman, *American Whaleman*, 232–33; Lance E. Davis, Gallman, and Gleiter, *In Pursuit of Leviathan*, 154–69.

6. John P. Vanderhoop, 1/45, Accounts of bark *A. R. Tucker* of New Bedford, 1871–1874; Thomas C. Jeffers, 1/40, same vessel, 1876–1879; Edwin D. Vanderhoop, 1/50, Accounts of bark *Atlantic* of New Bedford, 1872–1876; Abram F. Cooper promoted during the voyage to 1/50, same vessel, 1876–1879, J. & W. R. Wing Papers, NBL. The last year for which Lance E. Davis, Gallman, and Gleiter, *In Pursuit of Leviathan*, 162, give an average lay for third mates is 1866: 1/54.

7. SHP, bark *Cachalot*, 1851–1854, Charles B. Hosmer, lay 1/12; bark *LaGrange*, 1851–1854, Elisha C. Jenney, lay 1/12; bark *Massasoit*, 1851–1852, Amos Haskins, lay 1/14; bark *Oscar*, 1851–1854, Ebenezer Dexter, lay 1/15; bark *R.L. Barstow*, 1851–1853, Joseph R. Taber, Jr., lay 1/14; ship *Sarah*, 1851–1855, Ezra Smalley, lay 1/15; bark *Sun*, 1851–1853, Richard Flanders, lay 1/12; Mattapoisett vessels of 1851 from "American Offshore Whaling Voyages: A Database," www.nmdl.org.

8. William M. Davis, *Nimrod of the Sea*, 23.

9. Smalley, "I Killed 'Moby Dick,'" 176.

10. Crew list, WSL, 2 June 1868; 2 Nov. 1869, Warren Gifford, Journal, bark *Napoleon* of New Bedford, 1868–1872, Log 53, NBW.

11. "Memoranda," WSL, 1 Oct. 1850 and 28 Jan. 1851. The WSL similarly did not mark John Mashow as African American when reporting his firm's building of new ships; see, for example, "Launch," 18 Mar. 1851; "New Clipper Whaler," 20 May 1851.

12. Delano, *Wanderings and Adventures*, 74. I inferred the identity of the unnamed vessel and Page's identity from clues in Delano's account that match up with the DPT and RTN, ship *Sophia* of New Bedford, 1830–1831, particularly the death of Benjamin Blake. DPT has "Lily Page," "Indian" complexion, birthplace Troy (an Indian reservation in Fall River, Massachusetts). I inferred Page's rank from Delano's comments and crew accounts, which list Page fourth and with the fourth highest lay: William R. Rotch Account Book, vol. 1, 59–67, Rotch Collection, NBW.

13. Delano, *Wanderings and Adventures*, 21, 74–76; for a similar whale hunt account, see Densmore, *Halo*, 80–82; for officer rivalry and lancing, see Nordhoff, *Nine Years a Sailor: Whaling and Fishing*, 119.

14. Browne, *Etchings of a Whaling Cruise*, 53.

15. 20 Sept. 1882, George F. Brightman, Journal, ship *California* of New Bedford, 1881–1885, Log 94, PPL; rank from crew list, WSL, 24 May 1881. See also Bullen, *Cruise of the Cachalot*, 68.

16. Rank on crew list, *California*, WSL, 24 May 1881.

17. 24 Aug. 1882, Logbook, bark *Bartholomew Gosnold* of New Bedford, Log ODHS 668, NBW.

18. Burns, *Year with a Whaler*, 120.

19. Nordhoff, *Nine Years a Sailor: Whaling and Fishing*, 52.

20. Paddack, *Life on the Ocean*, 7–8; Osborn, *Reminiscences*, 25–26; Hazen, *Five Years before the Mast*, 111–12; Harold Williams, *One Whaling Family*, 248–49; Camp, *Life and Adventures*, 95; Browne, *Etchings of a Whaling Cruise*, 42, 302; 23 Aug.

1859, William A. Abbe, Journal, bark *Atkins Adams* of Fairhaven, 1858–1863, Log ODHS 485, NBW.

21. Lightcraft, *Scraps from the Log Book*, 58. The author signed the preface "G. L. Colburn" and is George Lightcraft Colburn on DPT, bark *Hesper* of New Bedford, 1831–1834. Colburn did not identify the name of the bark, but Van Lone is also on the DPT, and the loss of one of the crew at the Galapagos, "last seen with a large terrapin lashed to his back" (p. 86), matches information on the RTN.

22. Lightcraft, *Scraps from the Log Book*, 56–57.

23. DPT, bark *Hesper* of New Bedford, 1828–1830 (Jno. Antonio Espencer) and 1831–1834 (John A. Spencer). For Christiantown connections, see Baylies; Bird, 61; Francis Spencer's parents, Richard L. Pease, *Report*, 47. For ranks, see shipping articles, bark *Hesper* of New Bedford, 1831–1834, Charles Waln Morgan Papers, NBW.

24. Lightcraft, *Scraps from the Log Book*, 69. The two surviving journals for the 1831–1834 *Hesper* voyage—kept by the two protagonists in the falling out, second mate William P. Bunker (Log 609, NBW) and boatsteerer Joseph Grant (Log ODHS 118, NBW)—do not mention this conflict.

25. Lightcraft, *Scraps from the Log Book*, 75.

26. Sampson, *Three Times around the World*, 15; Burns, *Year with a Whaler*, 35, 41, 54; Thomas Crapo, *Strange, but True*, 13–15; Zollers, *Thrilling Incidents*, 176; 22 and 27 Oct. 1858, 23 Nov. 1858, 18 Jan. 1859, William A. Abbe, Journal, bark *Atkins Adams* of Fairhaven, 1858–1863, Log ODHS 485, NBW.

27. William M. Davis, *Nimrod of the Sea*, 283–84.

28. Vickers, *Young Men and the Sea*, ch. 7.

29. Busch, *"Whaling Will Never Do for Me"*; Creighton, *Rites and Passages*, 106–11, 223–24; Raffety, *Republic Afloat*.

30. Glenn, *Campaigns against Corporal Punishment*; for the size of the flogging instrument and use of reason, see a case in which Abel Manning of Gay Head, third mate on the ship *James Maury* of New Bedford, 1845–1848, assisted the captain in punishing insubordination: *Antone Fales vs. Alexander Whelden*, Special Court, June 1848, Case Files, U.S. District Court of Massachusetts. Whelden settled by paying Fales $200 and court costs.

31. WSL, 7 Apr. 1862. Jourdain's mother was from Gay Head: Earle, xviii; Grover, *Fugitive's Gibraltar*, 54–55, 277.

32. DPT, SHP, and 30 May 1841, Cornelius Howland Jr., Journal, bark *Lafayette* of New Bedford, 1840–1844, Log 386, NBL.

33. "Joseph Mingo Dead," *Vineyard Gazette*, 10 Apr. 1913.

34. RTN and 17 Aug. and 12 Sept. 1824, Logbook, ship *Ann Alexander* of New Bedford, 1824–1825, Log ODHS 291, NBW.

35. RTN, brig *Columbus* of New London, 1842–1844.

36. 23 Dec. 1839 and 11 Jan. 1840, Logbook, ship *Rousseau* of New Bedford, 1837–1840, Log ODHS 484, NBW; relationship inferred from Gay Head section, Baylies.

37. RTN, ship *Massachusetts* of New Bedford, 1848–1851.

38. 25 Feb. 1867 and 29 June 1868, Logbook, bark *Cape Horn Pigeon* of Dartmouth, 1866–1869, Log 698, NBW. Also from Gay Head on DPT are John P. Vanderhoop, Joseph A. Peters, and Joseph G. Belain.

39. Earle, xxiii, xxvi–xxviii, xxxi ("Ockry"); Final Settlement Account Book, bark *Almira* of Edgartown, 1869–1870, Log 34, PPL.

40. 12 Oct. 1869, Logbook, bark *Almira* of Edgartown, 1869–1870, Log 35, PPL; J. C. Cover to J. C. Bancroft Davis, 1 Apr. 1870, includes English translation of the deserters' affidavit taken 14 Oct. at Graciosa and Captain Cornelius H. Marchant's protest of 2 Nov. 1869, rl. 7, *Despatches*, Fayal.

41. Affidavit in Cover to Davis, 1 Apr. 1870; jail quotation from J. C. Cover to J. C. Bancroft Davis, 13 July 1870; see also dispatches dated 31 Mar. 1870, 7 Apr. 1870, 14 Apr. 1870, rl. 7, *Despatches*, Fayal.

42. "Mutiny on Whaling Bark Almira, of Edgartown," WSL 3 May 1870; "The Alleged Mutiny on the American Bark Almira," 10 May 1870. See also "The Alleged Mutiny on the Barque Almira," *Boston Journal*, 30 Apr. and 4 May 1870.

43. Cover to Davis, 1 Apr. 1870.

44. "Letters," WSL, 28 June 1870; other Marchant correspondence excerpted in "Letters," WSL, 30 Nov. 1869 and 21 Dec. 1869.

45. 26 Aug. 1870, Logbook, *Almira*.

46. Account Book, bark *Perry* of Edgartown, 1877–1880, Log 545, PPL; 31 Aug. 1880, Logbook, bark *Perry* of Edgartown, 1877–1880, Log 546, PPL.

47. B. C. Marchant to J. M. Earle, 17 Sept. 1859 and 9 Mar. 1860, Earle Papers. Marchant was guardian from 1853 to 1869, rl. 2, Indian Guardian Papers, MSA; Cornelius in household 158 headed by Barnard C. Marchant, Edgartown, Mass., U.S. manuscript census, 1850, www.ancestry.com; Cornelius Marchant as Barnard's son, EVR, 45.

48. "Mutiny at Sea," WSL, 23 Jan. 1849.

49. Annie Holmes Ricketson, *Journal*, 74, 78; crew list, *A. R. Tucker*, WSL, 9 May 1871.

50. 26 Apr. to 1 May 1873, 7–14 Apr. 1874, 12 June 1874, Logbook, bark *Palmetto* of New Bedford, 1872–1875, Log 512, NBL; for Belain's rank, see crew list, WSL, 15 Oct. 1872.

51. 14 May, 29 Sept., 1 Oct., 4 Oct. 1857, and Lee's last entry on 3 Mar. 1858, Logbook, bark *Amazon* of Fairhaven, 1856–1860, Log ODHS 337, NBW.

52. 30 Aug. 1873 and 14 Feb., 30 Apr., 16–17 Sept. 1874, Logbook, bark *Callao* of New Bedford, 1871–1875, Log ODHS 667, NBW.

53. 11 Dec. 1869, Logbook ship, *Eliza Adams* of New Bedford, 1867–1871, Log ODHS 265, NBW.

54. "Communicated," *Barnstable Patriot & Commercial Advertiser*, 16 May 1832.

55. DPT, ship *Flora* of New London, 1843–1845; Camp, *Life and Adventures*, 115–16. By his placement on the crew list, this must have been James L. Rogers, who is not on

the "Mohegan Census, 1830," Yale Indian Papers Project, http://www.library.yale.edu /yipp/. However, "Rogers" was a Mohegan surname. Or this third mate could have been Alpheus Matthews, who is in the 1830 census and falls on the crew list as most likely a boatsteerer.

56. West, *Captain's Papers*, 29.

57. RTN and SHP, bark *Massasoit* of Mattapoisett, 1851–1852, 1852–1853.

58. Logbook, *Callao*.

59. "Memorandum of Captains officers coopers Boatstearers &c That came home in Whalers from 1860 to June 1st 1870," Misc. Vol. 37, MSM. On Jared, see Earle, xiii.

60. Crew list, WSL, 25 Nov. 1862; Charles Bailey to Wood & Nye, 10 Dec. 1863, and James M. Willis to Wood & Nye, 30 Nov./7 Dec. 1863, Wood & Nye Papers, NBW.

61. Camp, *Life and Adventures*, 40–41.

62. Glenn, *Jack Tar's Story*, ch. 5; Gilje, *Liberty on the Waterfront*, 7–9, 215–16.

63. Lightcraft, *Scraps from the Log Book*, 56.

64. Delano, *Wanderings and Adventures*, 87.

65. Memoranda, 1880–1904, vol. 1, pp. 24–25, 168–69, 220, Aiken & Swift Records, NBW.

66. West, *Captain's Papers*, 29.

67. Memoranda, 1880–1904, vol. 1, pp. 66–67, 168–69, Aiken & Swift Records, NBW.

Chapter 4

1. Hawley, "Biographical and Topographical Anecdotes," 189; Hutchins, *Mashpee*, 47–49; Hinson in Bird, 65.

2. SHP and Wharf Book, ship *Sally* of Nantucket, 1820–1823, Edouard A. Stackpole Collection, NHA.

3. Anthony Hanson Testimony, 30 June 1824, rl. 1, *Despatches*, Valparaiso. For histories of the mutiny, see Heffernan, *Mutiny on the Globe*; Gregory Gibson, *Demon of the Waters*; Stackpole, *Sea-Hunters*, 413–33.

4. Paulding, *Journal of a Cruise*, 124–25.

5. Lay and Hussey, *Narrative of the Mutiny*, 69, 70, 75, 80, 87, 114; for "Indians," see 65, 67, 101. Paulding also used "Indian," "savage," and "native" interchangeably, in *Journal of a Cruise*, 39, 42, 56, 63, 96, and referred to Pacific Islanders as "untutored" and "people in a state of nature," 40. For captivity narratives, see Salisbury, *Sovereignty and Goodness of God*; Colley, *Captives*.

6. Lay and Hussey, *Narrative of the Mutiny*, 19–20.

7. Gilbert Smith Deposition, 15 June 1824, rl. 1, *Despatches*, Valparaiso.

8. "George Comstock, 'Narrative,'" appendix B, in Heffernan, *Mutiny on the Globe*, 223.

9. Comstock, *Life of Samuel Comstock*, 92. William was not on the *Globe* with his brothers, so his is not an eyewitness account.

10. "George Comstock, 'Narrative,'" 224.

11. Gilbert Smith Deposition.

12. For the earliest Europeans at Tahiti, see Salmond, *Aphrodite's Island*.

13. "Captain Wallis's Voyage Round the World," in Hawkesworth, *Account of the Voyages*, 1:218–19.

14. "Samuel Wallis: The Discovery of Tahiti," in Lamb, Smith, and Thomas, *Exploration & Exchange*, 65.

15. Beaglehole, *Journals of Captain James Cook*, 1:89, 108, 112.

16. Quoted and translated in Dunmore, *Storms and Dreams*, 37. For original French, see Bougainville, *Écrits sur le Canada*, 109.

17. Dunmore, *Pacific Journal of Louis-Antoine de Bougainville*, 61.

18. Avery, *History of the Town of Ledyard*, 30, 252. On Ledyard's life, see Gray, *Making of John Ledyard*.

19. Samson Occom to John Bailey, 1784, in Brooks, *Collected Writings of Samson Occom*, 121–23.

20. Gray, *Making of John Ledyard*, 35–37.

21. Munford, *John Ledyard's Journal*, 145–51.

22. Douglas, "Slippery Word, Ambiguous Praxis"; Nicholas Thomas, "'On the Varieties of the Human Species,'" xxii–xl; Smith, *Imagining the Pacific*, ch. 7. For "Negro" as a more common analogy in the southwestern Pacific, see Douglas, "'Novus Orbis Australis,'" and Ballard, "'Oceanic Negroes.'"

23. For the North American noble and brutal savage, see Pearce, *Savagism and Civilization*; Berkhofer, *White Man's Indian*; for the Pacific, see McCormick, *Omai*; for both, see Ellingson, *Myth of the Noble Savage*.

24. Ryan, "'Le Président des Terres Australes'"; Edmond, *Representing the South Pacific*, 104–13.

25. See special issue, Geoffrey Clark, "Dumont D'Urville's Divisions of Oceania," especially Tcherkézoff's "Long and Unfortunate Voyage"; also Tcherkézoff, *Polynésie/ Mélanésie*.

26. Hau'ofa, "Our Sea of Islands"; Nicholas Thomas, *In Oceania*, 133–55; Jolly, "Imagining Oceania"; Geoffrey Clark, "Dumont d'Urville's Oceania."

27. Lorrin Andrews, *Dictionary of the Hawaiian Language*, 257, 508.

28. Altick, *Shows of London*, 45–48; Fullagar, *Savage Visit*. On North American visitors to Europe, see Vaughan, *Transatlantic Encounters*; on Omai with Cook, see Salmond, *Aphrodite's Island*, chs. 18–20; and on the salon circuit, McCormick, *Omai*, 111–34.

29. Dwight, *Memoirs of Henry Obookiah*, 109; for another famous Hawaiian at the Cornwall school, see Spoehr, "George Prince Tamoree."

30. Harlan Page, *Memoir of Thomas H. Patoo*.

31. Phillips, *Protestant America and the Pagan World*, 57–132; Demos, *Heathen School*.

32. Gaul, *To Marry an Indian*.

33. William Ellsworth Strong, *Story of the American Board*, 145.

34. Dwight, *Memoirs of Henry Obookiah*, 35–36, 94; Sánchez-Eppler, "Copying and Conversion," 302.

35. For "canoe" and "tomahawk," see Holden, *Narrative*, 31–32; Annie Holmes Ricketson, *Journal*, 45. For "wigwam," see A. C. C. Thompson, *Incidents of a Whaling Voyage*, 32. For "squaw," see a "canoe of Indians & squars [squaws]," in Reilly, *Journal of George Attwater*, 193; Whitecar, *Four Years Aboard the Whaleship*, 312; Beane, *From Forecastle to Cabin*, 245; Edward T. Perkins, *Na Motu*, 100. See also Joyce, *Shaping of American Ethnography*; Rouleau, "Maritime Destiny as Manifest Destiny"; Lyons, *American Pacificism*, 30–31.

36. 17 Oct. 1842, William Allen White, Journal, ship *Samuel Robertson* of New Bedford, 1841–1846, Log ODHS 1040, NBW.

37. Entries for "canoe," "wigwam," "tomahawk," and "squaw," *Oxford English Dictionary Online*, http://dictionary.oed.com, show that these words originated in European exploration accounts of sixteenth- and seventeenth-century North America. In Narragansett, "squaw" simply meant "woman"; speakers of English gave it its derogatory connotations; see Roger Williams, *Key into the Language of America*, 27; Smits, "'Squaw Drudge'"; King, "De/Scribing Squ*w." For more on tomahawks, see Shannon, "Queequeg's Tomahawk."

38. Endicott, *Wrecked among Cannibals*, 19; Whitecar, *Four Years Aboard the Whaleship*, 106; Holden, *Narrative*, 32. See also Osborn, *Reminiscences*, 53–54.

39. [Jones?], *Life and Adventure*, 98.

40. Harold W. Thompson, *Last of the "Logan,"* 39.

41. Whitecar, *Four Years Aboard*, 85; George R. West to Lewis Cass, 15 July 1858, rl. 3, *Despatches*, Bay of Islands, New Zealand.

42. [Jones?], *Life and Adventure*, 103–4; see also Joseph G. Clark, *Lights and Shadows*, 154–55.

43. Speaking of the Maoris, see Cloud, *Enoch's Voyage*, 72; speaking of Hawaiians, see Olmsted, *Incidents of a Whaling Voyage*, 263; speaking of "the Polynesian people," Osborn, *Reminiscences*, 54.

44. Haley, *Whale Hunt*, 233.

45. On betel nut juice and native dress, see Martin, *"Naked and a Prisoner,"* 12; Holden, *Narrative*, 32. For clothing at the Marquesas, see A. C. C. Thompson, *Incidents of a Whaling Voyage*, 33–34; on eating poi, see Beane, *From Forecastle to Cabin*, 225–26; on baking underground and poi, see Newhall, *Adventures of Jack*, 52–53; on kava ceremony and underground ovens, see Harold W. Thompson, *Last of the "Logan,"* 76–77; for kava, see John G. Williams, *Adventures of a Seventeen-Year-Old Lad*, 117–19, and Camp, *Life and Adventures*, 97. For typical Pacific whaling ethnographies with taboos, tattoos, and other exotic customs described, see [Jones?], *Life and Adventure*, 126–39, and Torrey's semi-fictionalized *Torrey's Narrative*, 117–56.

Chapter 5

1. Hawaiian Mission Children's Society, *Missionary Album*, 7.

2. Spicer, *Cycles of Conquest*.

3. O'Brien, *Firsting and Lasting*; Rubertone, *Grave Undertakings*; Lepore, *The Name of War*.

4. For the names of all known American whaling vessels, see Lund.

5. For Annawan, see Drake, *Book of the Indians*, book III, p. 54. For the antebellum claiming of Metacom as a kind of founding father, see Lepore, *Name of War*, 191–226.

6. Lund, 611–12.

7. First published as *Indian Biography* with a New England focus, other editions (e.g., *Book of the Indians*, 9th ed.) were expanded to include more recent U.S.–Indian wars in the Southeast and Midwest.

8. RTN, ship *Bartholomew Gosnold* of New Bedford, 1844–1847; Webquish's rank comes from his death notice in *Sandwich Observer*, 17 Apr. 1847. For the family relationship, see EVR, 136, 233, and Baylies (Nathan's sister Clarissa married Eliakim Jonas and gave birth to Henry).

9. Deyo, *History of Barnstable County*, 666–67; Starbuck, *History of the American Whale Fishery*; Worth, "Voyages of Ship 'Bartholomew Gosnold,'" 11–12.

10. Prince, *Chronological History*.

11. "Visit to the Elizabeth Islands," 316–17; Daniel Ricketson, *History of New Bedford*, 25, 119–26, 374–77; Tucker, *Clio's Consort*, 55–57.

12. Kugler, *William Allen Wall*, 9, 19.

13. Gabriel Archer, "The Relation of Captaine Gosnols Voyage to the North part of Virginia," 125, 133–134, and John Brereton, "A Briefe and Trve Relation of the Discouerie of the North Part of Virginia," 156, in Quinn and Quinn, *English New England Voyages*. I modernized the print styles of "u" and "v" for readability.

14. Archer, "Relation of Captaine Gosnols Voyage," 126–27, 136; Brereton, "A Briefe and Trve Relation," 157–59.

15. "The Memorial of the Indian natives and colour'd People inhabiting the Indian Lands so called on the Island of Chapoquiddick," n.d., and see also Subscribers Hannah Joel et al., Petition, 24 Mar. 1812, Indian Guardian Papers, rl. 2, MSA; Daniel Fellows, Guardian of sd. Indians, to the Senate and House of Representatives of the Commonwealth of Massachusetts, 23 May 1829, Unpassed Legislation, rl. 2, MSA; Petition of the Indians on Chabaquidic, 24(?) May 1826, and Remonstrance of Mary Cooke and Others [June 1827?], PLP, Acts 1827, chap. 114, MSA; Bird, 11; Earle, 15, 17, 21.

16. On factors behind choosing a ship, see Sampson, *Three Times around the World*, 9, 78, 116–17; Whitecar, *Four Years Aboard the Whaleship*, 15; Philbrick and Philbrick, *Loss of the Ship* Essex, 85.

17. WSL, 24 Aug. 1852; Lund, 486; DPT, ship *Gay Head* of New Bedford, 1851–1856, 1856–1860, 1860–1865, 1865–1870, and refitted as a bark, 1870–1871. Lost in the Arctic disaster of 1871, another bark named *Gay Head* operated out of New Bedford until 1894

and then out of San Francisco. Samuel E. Pharoah, Montaukett, served as its second mate in 1888–1892, DPT; crew list in WSL, 18 Sept. 1888.

18. O'Connell, *On Our Own Ground*, 3.

19. Peirce, *Indian History, Biography, and Genealogy*, iii; genealogy on 210–19; see also Walter Gilman Page, "Descendant of Massasoit."

20. For Falmouth vessels, see Henry H. Crapo, *New-Bedford Directory*, 100. For Swift and Lawrence shipbuilding, see "Launch," *New Bedford Mercury*, 3 Oct. 1828; "Launch," *Nantucket Inquirer*, 25 Sept. 1830; for more on Swift and Falmouth whaling and shipbuilding, see Deyo, *History of Barnstable County*, 666–70; Geoffrey, *Suckanesset*, chs. 10–12; Wood, *Live Oaking*, ch. 4.

21. S. Dillingham, "Instructions to the Master of the Ship William Penn," 1 Jan. 1833, Maritime Collection, FHS, suggests that Dillingham was the ship's agent and a Quaker ("Esteemed Freind" and "1 mo. 5th 1833"); Henry H. Crapo's *New-Bedford Directory*, p. 100, lists Elijah Swift as its agent in 1836.

22. Abrams, "Benjamin West's Documentation"; Tobin, "Native Land and Foreign Desire"; for an equivalent depiction in a New Zealand context, see Bell, "Augustus Earle's *The Meeting of the Artist and the Wounded Chief Hongi*."

23. Besides selling land, Popmonet appears to have bought land to make the praying town of Mashpee accord with English landholding practices; Bangs, *Indian Deeds*, 111–12, 117, 122, 125–26, 134, 149, 154–55, 187, 211; Hutchins, *Mashpee*, 35, 41–42, 63–65; Cesarini, "Sources and Interpretations," 126.

24. Barber, *Historical Collections*, 48.

25. *Commonwealth of Massachusetts vs. William Apes et al.*, Sept. 1834, Records of the Court of Common Pleas, vol. 1, p. 488, Barnstable County Courthouse, Barnstable, Mass.

26. Apess, "Indian Nullification of the Unconstitutional Laws of Massachusetts Relative to the Marshpee Tribe; or, The Pretended Riot Explained," in O'Connell, *On Our Own Ground*, 163–274.

27. Minutes of the Governor's Council, 19 Dec. 1833, Executive Records 1830–1835, MSA. The governor's appointment of Fiske and his report are in Commonwealth of Massachusetts, *Documents Relative to the Marshpee Indians*.

28. "An Act to Establish the District of Marshpee" (approved 31 Mar. 1834), Acts 1834, chap. 166, approved 31 Mar. 1834, MAR. See the PLP for this act for the "Petition of the Proprietors and Inhabitants of the Marshpee Plantation." See also O'Connell, *On Our Own Ground*, xxxv–xxxviii; Hutchins, *Mashpee*, chs. 5–6.

29. According to the Minutes of the Governor's Council, from 1832 to 1834, Swift attended most meetings, including 30 Aug. 1833, when Fiske presented his initial report, but not 25–26 June 1833, 19 Dec. 1833, or 2 Apr. 1834, when the Mashpee case came up for discussion.

30. O'Connell, *On Our Own Ground*, 229.

31. "Launched at Waquaett," *New Bedford Mercury*, 22 Apr. 1836.

32. Newspapers in Baltimore, Philadelphia, New York State, Virginia, and elsewhere (see Early American Newspapers database) reprinted stories of the *Awashonks* incident that appeared first as "Horrible Massacre," *Nantucket Inquirer*, 23 Apr. 1836; "Massacre at the Fegee Islands," *New Bedford Gazette*, 25 Apr. 1836; "Particulars of the Massacre on Board the Ship Awashonks," *New Bedford Mercury*, 13 May 1836. "Ship William Penn," *Nantucket Inquirer*, 16 May 1835, also spawned many reprintings.

33. 21 Nov. 1833, 6 Jan. 1834, Logbook, ship *William Penn* of Falmouth, FHS.

34. 26–29 Sept. 1834, Logbook, *William Penn*.

35. "Ship William Penn," *Nantucket Inquirer*, 16 May 1835. Other newspapers picked up Worth's account and also published a separate article in which Worth emphasized Samoa's convenience for American ships needing provisions; "Navigator Islands," *New Bedford Mercury*, 22 May 1835. One of the men taken captive (a Hawaiian perhaps) later told Charles H. Robbins that Captain Lewis Tobey of the *Swift* had rescued him from the island as the sole survivor sometime before 1837, in Robbins, *Gam*, 57–59.

36. John H. Aulick to Mahlon Dickerson, 26 Jan. 1836, rl. 21, U.S. National Archives, *Letters Received by the Secretary of the Navy*.

37. Browning, "Cruise of the United States Sloop-of-War 'Vincennes'"; for the *William Penn* incident, see 13:576. For the events at Quallah Battoo, see Warriner, *Cruise of the United States Frigate Potomac*, 11, 66–85.

38. Browning, "Cruise of the United States Sloop-of-War 'Vincennes,'" 14:194–95, 197, 199. See also "Cruise of the Vincennes."

39. 6 Oct. 1835, Logbook, ship *Awashonks* of Falmouth, 1833–1836, FHS; Silas Jones, "Narrative"; "Particulars of the Massacre on Board the Ship Awashonks," *New Bedford Mercury*, 13 May 1836.

40. J. N. Reynolds, *Address*, 25, 68. For the U.S. Ex Ex, see Joyce, *Shaping of American Ethnography*; Philbrick, *Sea of Glory*; Viola and Margolis, *Magnificent Voyagers*. On the U.S. Pacific Squadron, see Robert Erwin Johnson, *Thence Round Cape Horn*.

41. Wilkes, *Narrative of the United States Exploring Expedition*; Papatoono is Opotuno in Wilkes, 2:96–111. The Fiji events are in 3:103–5, 126–38, 412–14. For *Charles Doggett*, see "Distressing Outrage," *Salem Gazette*, 23 Sept. 1834. For Veidovi, see Fabian, *Skull Collectors*, ch. 4.

42. Wilkes, *Narrative of the United States Exploring Expedition*, 3:242–244, 262–315; William Reynolds, *Private Journal*, 190–202.

43. William Reynolds, *Private Journal*, 228; for the search for "Popotuna," see 229–33, 243.

44. William Reynolds, *Private Journal*, 65, 193, 198, 199, 226; for whites versus natives, see, for example, 200–2.

45. For the Tahitians, see Silas Jones, "Narrative." For the Mashpee whalemen, see Abstract account and Slop Chest Account Book, *William Penn*, 1833–1836, FHS. Marston's 1832 census gives Joshua Pocknett's age as seventeen and John Mye's as fifteen.

Alexander Williams of Mashpee was possibly also on the *William Penn*, but the common surname makes his presence not as certain as Pocknett's and Mye's.

46. "Petition of the Proprietors and Inhabitants of the Marshpee Plantation."

47. 25 July 1851, Journal (keeper unknown), bark *Wolga* of Fairhaven, 1846–1852, Log 688, PPL. See also 5 Aug. 1851, William Farmer, Journal, ship *Montreal* of New Bedford, 1850–1853, Log ODHS 146, NBW; 21 July 1851, Logbook, bark *Cossack* of New Bedford, 1850–1853, Log ODHS 92, NBW; 21 July 1851, B. F. Homan, Journal, bark *Cossack* of New Bedford, 1850–1853, Log 968, NBW; 14 July 1851, Logbook, ship *Tamerlane* of New Bedford, 1850–1854, Log NBW 1227, NBW.

48. Sampson, *Three Times around the World*, 53, heard the story of the Narragansett Indian but garbled the name of the vessel; the timing, location, and description of the incident suggest it was the *Armata*; DPT, ship *Armata* of New London, 1849–1851.

49. De Varigny, *Fourteen Years*, 4–7, 66, 105; Sahlins, *Anahulu*, ch. 5; Kuykendall, *Hawaiian Kingdom*, 1:92–95, 305–15.

50. Kame'eleihiwa, *Native Land and Foreign Desires*; Banner, *Possessing the Pacific*, ch. 4.

51. Liholiho, *Journal of Prince Alexander Liholiho*, 3–4, 113.

Chapter 6

1. Chappell, *Double Ghosts*, 75.

2. James F. Pells, Journal, ship *Barclay* of Nantucket, 1835–1839, Log 890, WMA; Joseph Ammons, Journals, ship *Roman* of New Bedford, 1843–1845 and 1845–1847, Log 792, and ship *Triton II* of New Bedford, 1849–1851, and ship *James Maury* of New Bedford, 1851–1855, Log 791, MSM. For more on native-authored journals and logbooks, see appendix B.

3. 7 and 29 July 1846, Ammons, Journals.

4. Geiger, *Facing the Pacific*; Lyons, *American Pacificism*; Edmond, *Representing the South Pacific*; Smith, *Imagining the Pacific*.

5. Wharf Book, ship *Washington* of Nantucket, 1819–1822, Edouard A. Stackpole Collection, NHA; DPT, ship *Triton* of New Bedford, 1825–1827; DPT, ship *Ann* of Nantucket, 1827–1830, in New Bedford Port Records, NAB.

6. 11 Jan. and 26 Apr. 1838, Pells, Journal.

7. "Newheaver," 5 Oct. 1842, William A. Allen, Journal, ship *Samuel Robertson* of New Bedford, 1841–1846, Log ODHS 1040, NBW; "Newheavour" in John Richards Child, Journal, ship *Hunter* of Boston, 1810–1814, in John Richards Child Papers, MHS.

8. Kaplanoff, *Joseph Ingraham's Journal*, 59–60; see also Hiroa, *Explorers of the Pacific*, 63–67. For nineteenth-century Marquesan history, see Dening, *Islands and Beaches*; Nicholas Thomas, *Marquesan Societies*; Herbert, *Marquesan Encounters*.

9. Ingraham, "Account of a Recent Discovery," 20. For the larger context of such ceremonies, see Seed, *Ceremonies of Possession*.

10. Belknap, "Discovery and Description of the Islands Called the Marquesas."

11. Porter, *Voyage in the South Seas*, 76.

12. For violent trading negotiations in the Marquesas, see Robbins, *Gam*, 51–53; Coan, *Life in Hawaii*, 177–78. For food shortages because of ship traffic, see 7 Mar. 1855, Gilbert L. Smith, Journal, ship *Cornelius Howland* of New Bedford, 1854–1858, Log 780, NBW.

13. Stewart, *Visit to the South Seas*, 183, 194; Browning, "Cruise of the United States Sloop-of-War 'Vincennes,'" 13:726–27. See also Calkin, *Last Voyage of the Independence*, 1–17.

14. Olmsted, *Incidents of a Whaling Voyage*, 197–98; 21 Apr. 1840, John Brown, Journal, ship *Catharine* of Nantucket, 1839–1840, Log ODHS 775, NBW.

15. Charles Roberts Anderson, *Melville in the South Seas*, chs. 5–8; Heflin, *Herman Melville's Whaling Years*, chs. 15–16.

16. "Marine News," *Nantucket Inquirer*, 7 June 1837; J. A. Moerenhoet to John Forsyth, 25 March 1837, rl. 1, *Despatches*, Tahiti.

17. Melville, *Typee*, 276.

18. 11 Sept. 1836, Logbook, ship *Leonidas* of Bristol, 1833–1837, Daniel B. Fearing Logbook Collection, Houghton Library, Cambridge, Mass.

19. 22 and 25 Aug. 1836, Pells, Journal.

20. Stewart, *Visit to the South Seas*, 142–43; Alexander, *William Patterson Alexander*, 120–21, 142, 166; Woodhouse, *Autobiography*, 57–58. See also Heflin, *Herman Melville's Whaling Years*, 127–130, and for the larger context, Chappell, "Shipboard Relations"; Wallace, *Sexual Encounters*, ch. 3.

21. Browning, "Cruise of the United States Sloop-of-War 'Vincennes,'" 13:718, 722.

22. Porter, *Voyage in the South Seas*, 83, see also pp. 79–82; Tcherkézoff, *Tahiti—1768*, "Reconsideration of the Role of Polynesian Women," and *"First Contacts" in Polynesia*; Dening, *Islands and Beaches*, 126–27.

23. Alexander, *William Patterson Alexander*, 166.

24. 13 Sept. 1842, Allen, Journal. For the impact of venereal disease on the nineteenth-century Pacific in light of the sex trade, see Igler, *Great Ocean*, ch. 2.

25. 16–22 Mar. 1837, Pells, Journal. On rum and the law in Tahiti in the late 1830s, see Robbins, *Gam*, 82–85; on women "tabooed" from coming aboard ship at Tahiti, see 17 Oct. 1842, Allen, Journal.

26. 17 Dec. 1838 and 1 Nov. 1837, Pells, Journal. Pells's account matches a contemporary description of Honolulu in Jarves, *Scenes and Scenery*, 39–42. For temperance efforts, see Dwight Baldwin, "Temperance Report for Maui, 1837," Dwight Baldwin Papers, Missionary Letters Collection, HMCS; "Grog Shops," 17 Mar. 1838, and Kamehameha III, "A Law Regulating the Sale of Ardent Spirits," *Sandwich Islands Gazette*, 31 Mar. 1838; Kuykendall, *Hawaiian Kingdom*, 1:134–36, 161–63.

27. Kamakau, *Ruling Chiefs of Hawaii*, 280.

28. 21–22 Oct. 1837, Pells, Journal.

29. Coan, *Life in Hawaii*, 128.

30. "The Career of Boki," and "Premiership of Kinaʻu," in Kamakau, *Ruling Chiefs of Hawaii*, 270–96, 334–49; Bingham, *Residence of Twenty-One Years*, 274, 283–89; Stephen Reynolds, *Journal*, 108–10, 123–24, 206; Greer, "Trouble on the Waterfront," 28–29; Kashay, "Competing Imperialisms"; Ralston, "Changes in the Lives of Ordinary Women."

31. Schmitt, "Early Crime Statistics of Hawaii." On the ineffectiveness of fines, see C. F. Winslow to S. C. Damon, 26 Jan. 1846, Damon Papers, HMCS; and for the extensive prostitution in 1850s Hawaiʻi, see Lyman, *Around the Horn*, 151, 179.

32. 12–22 Dec. 1838, Pells, Journal, 12–22.

33. DPT, ship *Constitution* of Newport, 1833–1836, and rerigged as a bark, 1836–1839; ship *Roman* of New Bedford, 1839–1842, 1843–1845, 1845–1847; ship *Triton II* of New Bedford, 1849–1851; ship *James Maury* of New Bedford, 1851–1855 (second mate, SHP).

34. Dwight Baldwin to "Brother Hall," 20 Mar. 1844, Dwight Baldwin Papers, Missionary Letters Collection, HMCS.

35. Sampson, *Three Times around the World*, 57–58; "Order Restored," *The Friend* (Honolulu) 17 Nov. 1852; Parke, *Personal Reminiscences*, 35–44; Busch, "*Whaling Will Never Do for Me*," 177–85.

36. "Marine Intelligence: Vessels in Port," *Sandwich Island Gazette*, 4 Nov. 1837.

37. "Marine Journal: Port of Honolulu," *The Friend* (Honolulu), 2 Nov. 1852. Coan estimated that 4,000 ships and 40,000 seamen had visited Hilo in the forty years since 1835 that he had resided there, *Life in Hawaii*, 65–66.

38. "History of 'The Bethel Flag,'" *The Friend* (Honolulu), 1 June 1846; Cheever, *Whale and His Captors*, 230–64; Gelett, *Life on the Ocean*, 41–47; Kverndal, *Seamen's Missions*, 151–65, 211–12; Gilje, *Liberty on the Waterfront*, ch. 7.

39. 14 and 28 Aug. 1843, Ammons, Journals.

40. 6–14 Mar. and 16 Sept. 1844, Ammons, Journals. Ammons mistook Andrews's name as "Anderson." For Andrews as seaman's chaplain at Lahaina, see Lorrin Andrews to Brother Damon, 18 June 1845, 23 May 1845, Damon Collection, HMCS; "Seamen's Chaplaincy—Lahaina, Maui," *The Friend* (Honolulu), 4 Sept. 1844; Hawaiian Mission Children's Society, *Missionary Album*, 24–25.

41. 15 Mar. 1846, Ammons, Journals.

42. 23 Jan., 4 and 11 Feb. 1831, Dwight Baldwin, "Journal on Board the Ship New England," 1830–1831, HMCS; Hawaiian Mission Children's Society, *Missionary Album*, 8–9; DPT, ship *New England* of New Bedford, 1831–1834. See also Reuben Tinker, "Voyage to the Sandwich Islands," 1830–1831, HMCS.

43. Until discharged at Maui in 1844, Gideon was on every voyage with his older brother Joseph: DPTs, ship *Constitution* of Newport, 1833-1836; bark *Constitution* of Newport, 1836-1839; ship *Roman* of New Bedford, 1839-1842; DPT and SHP, ship Roman of New Bedford, 1843-1845. For Gideon Ammons's obituary, see "Last of Narragansett Chiefs," *Providence Journal*, 4 Dec. 1899.

44. 16 Sept., 6 Oct., 6 Dec., and 28 Oct. 1846, Ammons, Journals.

45. 12 Feb. 1846 and 18 Jan. 1847, Ammons, Journals.

46. Edward T. Perkins, *Na Motu*, 379. See also Cary, *Wrecked on the Feejees*, 87–88; Endicott, *Wrecked among Cannibals*, 30–31; Lucett, *Rovings in the Pacific*, 2:252–53.

47. 28 July–2 Aug. 1852, Ammons, Journals.

48. Cook, *Pursuing the Whale*, 47, 119. For interactions with natives on Arctic whaling grounds, see Bockstoce, *Whales, Ice, and Men*, ch. 9; Ross, *Whaling and Eskimos*.

49. William Garrison Lee probably kept the logbook on schooner *Abbie Bradford* of New Bedford, 1880–1881, but it is unsigned, Log ODHS 489B, NBW; Todd, *In Olde New York*, 222; Sluby, *Family Recollections*, 44.

50. Logbook, schooner *Abbie Bradford* of New Bedford, 1886–1888, Log ODHS 492, NBW. Daily entries mention only "fresh meat," but the back of the logbook lists the quantities of meat received.

51. Ross, *Arctic Whaling Diary*, 101, 102, 105; Eber, *When the Whalers Were up North*, 114–23. See also Pálsson, "Race and the Intimate."

52. Burns, *Year with a Whaler*, 158–61.

53. Ross, *Whaling and Eskimos*, 119–21.

54. Eber, *When the Whalers Were up North*.

55. Ammons, Journals, Log 791.

Chapter 7

1. Robbins, *Gam*, 57. See also [Jones?], *Life and Adventure*, 204–5; Nevens, *Forty Years at Sea*, 299.

2. Maude, *Of Islands and Men*, ch. 4; Campbell, *"Gone Native" in Polynesia*; Ralston, *Grass Huts and Warehouses*; Chappell, *Double Ghosts*, ch. 5. For "squaw man," see Dippie, *Vanishing American*, 257–62; Hagan, "Squaw Men," 171–202.

3. Anonymous Gay Head resident quoted in Burgess, "Old South Road," 30.

4. Vanderhoop, "Gay Head Indians," 6 Aug. 1904.

5. Hebron Hicks and William Jones of Mashpee, miners in California, and Sylvanus E. Wainer, miner, Australia, in Earle, xxvi, xxvii, lxix. Wainer probably arrived in Australia on a whaler; he was on at least one earlier voyage, DPT, bark *R. L. Barstow* of Mattapoisett, 1851–1853. Sylvanus E. Wainer, farmer, households 182 and 142, Westport, Mass., U.S. manuscript census, 1880 and 1900, www.ancestry.com.

6. Cuffe, *Narrative*, 17–20. See appendix B for more on Cuffe's memoir. For similar contemporary descriptions of Tahitians, see William Reynolds, *Private Journal*, 93.

7. Quoted in Todd, *In Olde New York*, 222. W. L. G. Lee was on the voyage with Notley when he deserted at Tongatabu in 1872; crew list, WSL, 23 May 1871; RTN, 20 and 28 Oct. 1872, Logbook, bark *Abraham Barker* of New Bedford, 1871–1875, Log 3, NBW.

8. 16 Aug. and 1 Sept. 1874, Logbook, bark *Callao* of New Bedford, 1871–1875, Log ODHS 667, NBW.

9. Shoemaker, *Living with Whales*, 187.

10. RTN, bark *Swallow* of New Bedford, 1883–1887. For descendant discussions, see http://boards.ancestry.com (searching Marcellus Cook New Zealand), ancestry.com. June Manning, former membership director for the Wampanoag Tribe of Gay Head (Aquinnah), contributed to these postings and, during a presentation I gave at the Aquinnah Cultural Center in August 2011, told of descendants visiting Aquinnah.

11. James's first wife, Priscilla Wamsley of Gay Head, died while he was on this voyage: 27 Aug. 1886, Marriages, Gay Head, MAVR; "Died," WSL, 22 Feb. 1887; William Wallace James and Annie Mabel Allen, 10 Mar. 1890, Registration Number 1890/698, Births, Deaths, & Marriages Online, www.bdmhistoricalrecords.dia.govt.nz. In the 19 May 1888 entry, he assumed logbook duty when promoted to first mate; "mate on a run," 11 Mar. 1890, Logbook, ship *Niger* of New Bedford, 1886–1890, Log ODHS 212, NBW.

12. "Obituary" of her mother Esther Allen, *Evening Post*, 12 May 1926, www.paperspast.natlib.govt.nz. For her father, Dwight Allen, see obituary of his granddaughter Avis Dunning, Norfolk Island Hansard, 18 Oct. 2000, p. 468, Norfolk Island Government Information, ISYS: Administration Files, www.info.gov.nf/hansard/9th%20Assembly%209%20Feb%202000/.

13. "Annie Mabail James," 28 June 1891, Births, Gay Head, Mass., MAVR.

14. See *Charles W. Morgan* crew lists for 1890–1891, 1891–1892, 1892–1893, and 1893–1895; Leavitt, *Charles W. Morgan*, 112–13. Captain James A. M. Earle's wife was a New Zealander, and many *Bounty* mutineer descendants from Norfolk Island were in the crew (p. 57).

15. "Certificate of Registration of American Citizen" for William Wallace James, n.d., in "U.S. Consular Registration Certificates, 1907–1918," www.ancestry.com.

16. William Wallace James, naturalized 19 July 1935, in "New Zealand, Naturalisations, 1843–1981," www.ancestry.com; "Born in Christiantown: Mrs. Samuel Smalley Was One of Last of That Colony," obituary from *Vineyard Gazette*, 20 Feb. 1942, Indian Papers, MVM.

17. John W. Belain et al., to T. Y. Brown, Edgartown, Chappaquiddick, North Neck, Lot #50, signed 30 Jan. 1899, Land Records, Book 96, 524–525, Registry of Deeds, Dukes County Courthouse, Edgartown, Mass.

18. 15 Feb. 1861, Marriages, Edgartown, Mass., MAVR; Elijah & Lucretia W. Johnson to Isaiah Belain, Chappaquiddick, Edgartown, 23 Feb. 1861, Land Records, Book 39, 471–72, Registry of Deeds, Dukes County Courthouse, Edgartown, Mass.

19. Final Settlement Accounts, ship *Almira* of Edgartown, 1864–1868, Log 33, PPL.

20. Journal or Logbook, ship *Almira* of Edgartown, 1864–1868, Log ODHS 448A, NBW.

21. On Sparr's discharge from an unnamed American whaleship, see "W.H.B." marginal notation on the attached petition to "Mr. President of the United States of North America, Washington," *Polynesian Gazette* (Levuka, Fiji), 1 July 1887, in Andrews A. St. John to James D. Porter, 1 July 1887, rl. 7, *Despatches*, Lauthala, Fiji.

22. Cary, *Wrecked on the Feejees*, 38–39; Cargill, *Diaries and Correspondence*, 165–66; Waterhouse, *King and People*, 16–17; Wilkes, *Narrative of the United States Exploring Expedition*, 3:62, 68–70; Stanley Brown, *Men from under the Sky*, ch. 3.

23. Stanley Brown, *Men from under the Sky*, ch. 4; Campbell, *"Gone Native" in Polynesia*, 62–68; Stackpole, "Story of David Whippey." (The surname is usually spelled "Whippey" on Nantucket.) For more on bêche-de-mer, see R. Gerard Ward, "Pacific *Bêche-de-Mer* Trade."

24. Cary, *Wrecked on the Feejees*, 35; "Ship Oeno," *Canal of Intelligence*, 15 Oct. 1828.

25. For nineteenth-century Fiji political history, see Waterhouse, *King and People*; Routledge, *Matanitū*; Derrick, *History of Fiji*.

26. Cary, *Wrecked on the Feejees*, 35, 58; Wilkes, *Narrative of the United States Exploring Expedition*, 3:47–48. By 1855, the son of Whippy's benefactor had inherited the title Tui Levuka, so Robert Coffin called "Dorcas" Whippy Tui Levuka's sister in Harold W. Thompson, *Last of the "Logan*," 81; her son Samuel gave her name as "Delia" in "Naisogobuli, Ovalau," Report 989, LCC. On Whippy as "chief" of all the "white men," see 6 June 1834, Joseph W. Osborn, Journal, ship *Emerald* of Salem, 1833–1836, PEM.

27. Guernsey, "Cruise after and among the Cannibals," 462.

28. Charles Wilkes to John C. Calhoun, 29 July 1844, rl. 1, *Despatches*, Bay of Islands; John B. Williams to James Buchanan, 13 Feb. 1846, rl. 1, *Despatches*, Lauthala, Fiji; David Whippy to John B. Williams, 22 Aug. 1856, rl. 2, *Despatches*, Lauthala, Fiji. For more on Williams, see Kenny, *New Zealand Journal*.

29. Wallis, *Life in Feejee*, 225, 230.

30. John B. Williams, "Feejee Islands," *Empire* (Sydney), 30 Dec. 1853. Williams begged for a ship of war in every dispatch, rls. 1–3, *Despatches*, Lauthala, Fiji, and enlisted his brother to lobby for a warship to visit: John B. Williams to Henry L. Williams, 22 Feb. 1851, 5 Mar. 1851, John B. Williams Papers, PEM.

31. John B. Williams to James Buchanan, 25 July 1849, and attachments, rl. 1, *Despatches*, Lauthala, Fiji. For an overview of the claims' history, see Dorrance, "John Brown Williams."

32. John B. Williams to "Sir" [Petigru], 4 Mar. 1851 (copy), attachment in dispatch dated 6 Mar. 1851, rl. 2, *Despatches*, Lauthala, Fiji. Thomas Williams, *Fiji and the Fijians*, 33–34, attributed the title "Tui Viti" to a mistake in a letter to Cakobau by the British consul at Hawai'i; foreigners in Fiji picked up its usage.

33. John B. Williams to W. L. Marcy, 16 Oct. 1855, and attachments, Dispatch 75, rl. 2, *Despatches*, Lauthala, Fiji; U.S. Congress, "Sloop of War 'John Adams,'" 12, 48–49; Miller, *Treaties and Other International Acts of the United States*, 283–324.

34. Calvert, *Fiji and the Fijians*, 333.

35. John B. Williams to Lewis Cass, 30 June and 13 July 1858, and attachments, rl. 3, *Despatches*, Lauthala, Fiji. On the coalitions of the 1850s, see Waterhouse, *King and People of Fiji*, ch. 10.

36. John B. Williams to W. L. Marcy, 31 Mar. 1856, rl. 2, *Despatches*, Lauthala, Fiji.

37. James Calvert to W. L. Marcy, 1 Jan. 1856, rl. 2, *Despatches*, Lauthala, Fiji.

38. "Doings in the South Sea Islands," *Empire* (Sydney), 5 May 1853.

39. John B. Williams to Henry L. Williams, 20 Nov. 1851, Williams Papers.

40. "John Douglas Bemo," 329–30; Ely, *"There She Blows,"* 125–31.

41. Calvert to Marcy. Calvert was paraphrasing a comment about two English beach-combers converting natives to Christianity— "makes 'em religion, and baptizes 'em"—in John Williams, *Narrative of Missionary Enterprises*, 421.

42. 8 Nov. 1855, Logbook, U.S. sloop of war *John Adams*, 20 Oct. 1854–9 Nov. 1855, Records of the Bureau of Naval Personnel, RG 24, U.S. National Archives, Washington, D.C.

43. U.S. Congress, "Sloop of War 'John Adams,'" 5, 71–72.

44. U.S. Congress, "Sloop of War 'John Adams,'" 6–7.

45. "Kenia, Kadavu," Report 1291, LCC.

46. John B. Williams to Henry L. Williams, 23 Nov. 1858, Williams Papers; "Lands Purchased in the Feegee Islands by J. B. Williams," in John B. Williams to W. L. Marcy, 31 Dec. 1856, rl. 2, *Despatches*, Lauthala, Fiji. For rumors of British or French colonization, see John B. Williams to Lewis Cass, 17 Sept. 1858, rl. 3, *Despatches*, Lauthala, Fiji. For land issues in nineteenth-century Fiji, see France, *Charter of the Land*; R. Gerard Ward, "Land Use and Land Alienation."

47. [Smythe], *Ten Months in the Fiji Islands*, 40–41.

48. For the document (Sparr signed with an X) Williams's voucher, and Smith's involvement, see "Tawadromu, Kadavu," Report 1267, LCC. For Smith's living with Sparr, see Report 1291, LCC. Royce's Diary, 28 Feb. 1860, spells Williams's "Na Thebu" as "Na Cevu" in keeping with missionary orthography, and Navulivuli is "Nabulibuli" in the documents. For Williams's process and his other agents, see "Island of Naqara (Serua)," Report 580, LCC.

49. Tui Nabulibuli to John B. Williams, 22 Jan. 1857 (copy) in John B. Williams to W. L. Marcy, 31 Mar. 1857, rl. 3, *Despatches*, Lauthala, Fiji.

50. John B. Williams to Tui Nabulibuli, 18 Feb. 1857 (copy), in Williams to Marcy, 31 Mar. 1857, rl. 3, *Despatches*, Lauthala, Fiji. See also attachments in this dispatch, including John B. Williams to "Mr. John Sparr," Ono, 17 Feb. 1857 (copy).

51. Royce, Diary, 26 Feb. 1860.

52. Seemann, *Viti*, 142–43.

53. Sparr signed the transfer with an X, 2 Sept. 1864, in "Tawadromu, Kadavu," Report 1267, LCC.

54. "Visa Island, Kadavu," Report 1296, LCC; Deed for Vesa Island, Vecely and Abraham to John Esparr, 27 July 1864 (copy), and Deed for island of Tanua Lambu, Ratu Davita to John Esparr, 27 July 1864 (copy), for another Sparr land purchase, in Andrews A. St. John to the Department of State, 5 June 1889, rl. 7, *Despatches*, Lauthala, Fiji.

55. Fourth Day of Court of Arbitration, U.S.S. *Jamestown*, 1 Nov. 1869, rl. 4, *Despatches*, Lauthala, Fiji.

56. W. T. Truxtun to Thakombau, 1 Nov. 1869; Cakobau to Truxtun, 2 Nov. 1869 ("translation"); W. T. Truxtun to J. Nettleton, 3 Nov. 1869, rl. 4, *Despatches*, Lauthala, Fiji.

57. Williams's pursuit of American claims was one factor in Fiji's cession to Britain: 18 Oct. 1858, Royce, Diary; McIntyre, "Anglo-American Rivalry." On planter immigration, see Young, *Adventurous Spirits*.

58. I. M. Brower to Secretary of State, 12 June 1860, rl. 4, *Despatches*, Lauthala, Fiji.

59. Obituary of David Whippy, *Fiji Times*, 8 Nov. 1871; for resolution of his claim, see Miller, *Treaties and Other International Acts of the United States*, 319; I. M. Brower to Secretary of State, 31 Dec. 1870, Dispatch 32, rl. 5, *Despatches*, Lauthala, Fiji. For some Whippy family land purchases, see "Yadali, Wainunu," Report 588, and "Lovonisikese," Report 875, LCC; Annelise Riles's "Law as Object" and "Division within the Boundaries."

60. Legge, *Britain in Fiji*, ch. 8; Kelly, "Gordon Was No Amateur"; Heartfield, *Aborigines' Protection Society*, 158–203; France, *Charter of the Land*.

61. Reports 1291 and 1296, LCC. References to "tapioca" mean arrowroot.

62. Reports 1291, 1296, 1267, LCC. See also "Kenia, Kandavu, claimed by Abraham Ryder," Report 1291A, and "Tawadromu, Kadavu, claimed by I. M. Brower, Levuka," Report 1268, LCC.

63. For the 1887 petitioners, see petition to "Mr. President," though the number of petitions would increase over the years to include other beachcombers' descendants. For Farrell, see "Ucu ni Vatu," Report 744, LCC. Reel 7 of the *Despatches* has many reports on individual claims and forwards evidence brought before the land commission; the Sparr family report is in Andrews A. St. Johns to Assistant Secretary of State, 5 June 1889. For Berwick's and the Whippys' disallowed claims, see Andrews A. St. John to Assistant Secretary of State, 13 Feb. 1889, and to the Department of State, 9 Apr. 1889, rl. 7, *Despatches*, Lauthala, Fiji.

64. I. M. Brower to Secretary of State, 20 July 1867, rl. 4, *Despatches*, Lauthala, Fiji.

65. The "pioneer settlers of Fiji" comes from Henry S. Lasar to Charles Payson, 3 May 1880, rl. 6, *Despatches*, Lauthala, Fiji.

66. Oaths of William Sparr and Velise Sparr, 16 Apr. 1889, rl. 7, *Despatches*, Lauthala, Fiji.

67. Oath of Samuel Whippy, 28 Feb. 1889, rl. 7, *Despatches*, Lauthala, Fiji.

68. Petition to "Mr. President," 1 July 1887, rl. 7, *Despatches*, Lauthala, Fiji

69. W. H. Bruce to John Davies, 29 Oct. 1884 (Despatch #5 of that date), rl. 6, *Despatches*, Lauthala, Fiji.

70. See attachments in Samuel E. Belford to Third Asst. Secretary of State, 30 June 1885, rl. 6, *Despatches*, Lauthala, Fiji.

71. Henry S. Lasar to J. B. Thurston (copy), 3 Nov. 1879, attachment in Henry S. Lasar to Charles Payson, 17 Mar. 1880, rl. 6, *Despatches*, Lauthala, Fiji.

72. Salesa, "Samoa's Half-Castes," 82.

73. "Claims of B. H. Henry and Others," 54th Congress, 1st Sess., Senate Report No. 934, U.S. Serial Set #3366 (1895–96), 17. For Berwick helping Scidmore, see Benjamin Morris to George H. Scidmore, 31 Oct. 1896, *Despatches*, Levuka and Suva, Fiji.

74. W. Berwick et al., to the President of the United States of America, 15 Dec. 1896, *Despatches*, Levuka and Suva, Fiji.

75. U.S. Department of State, *Memorandum on Fiji Land Claims*.

76. William Roy Vallance to President Calvin Coolidge (copy), n.d., and other correspondence of Nov. 1923, in William Roy Vallance Papers, Rare Books & Special Collections, Rush Rhees Library, University of Rochester, N.Y.

77. Tent and Geraghty, "Exploding Sky or Exploded Myth?"; Tcherkézoff, *"First Contacts" in Polynesia*, 182–96.

78. Endicott, *Wrecked among Cannibals*, 71.

79. Wallis, *Life in Feejee*, 200.

80. For Allen, see Stewart, *Journal of a Residence*, 115–16, and Scruggs, "Anthony D. Allen"; for another example, see Tui Tongoa, alias Sam at Futuna, in Bullen, *Cruise of the Cachalot*, 291–98, 368–69.

81. "Statement of William Berwick re cutter 'Psyche' (register No 489)," attachment, in Andrews A. St. John to Assistant Secretary of State, 13 Feb. 1889, rl. 7, *Despatches*, Lauthala, Fiji.

Chapter 8

1. Robert Gilbert Memoir, 1939, Akaroa Museum Collection, Banks Peninsula, New Zealand. For the correct name of the vessel, see DPT, ship *Ann Maria* of New London, 1839–1841. I thank Betty Apes for a copy of "Registrar's Return of all Entries of Deaths in the District of Waikouaiti during the quarter ending the 31st day of March, 1892." For a history of Old Waikouaiti, see Church, *Karitane by the Sea*.

2. Betty Apes found the critical reference to the document that links Elisha Apes to the writer Apess's father, William Apes: "A Book of Records of Births and Deaths," p. 98, *Massachusetts Vital Records: Leyden, 1756–1899*, Fiche 15, Holbrook Research Institute Microfiche Collection, which I used at the Boston Public Library, Boston, Mass. Leyden is the town next to Colrain, where William Apes Sr. appears in the 1820 U.S. manuscript census form and where the writer William visited his father shortly before the census was taken; "William Apes," manuscript page 57, Colrain, Mass. in www.ancestry.com. When Elisha was born in 1815 in Groton, Connecticut, seventeen-year-old William had just completed military service and was living at the Bay of Quinte; see O'Connell, *On Our Own Ground*, 32–33, 43, xiv.

3. O'Connell, *On Our Own Ground*, 3–4.

4. Avery, *History of the Town of Ledyard*, 257.

5. O'Connell, *On Our Own Ground*, 4–6, 23, 42–43, 47, 120. *Greenfield Gazette* death notice, 12 Sept. 1803. Apess's uncle was probably Lemuel Ashbo, whom the Town

of Colchester compensated for taking care of him for ten days in 1802; see items 18 and 32, 1802 accounts, Town Records, 1797–1805, Town Clerk's Office, Colchester, Conn.

6. O'Connell, *On Our Own Ground*, xxvii, accepted, with doubts, the rush to connect the dots in the otherwise impressive genealogical research of Barbara W. Brown and Rose, *Black Roots*, 11.

7. Emancipation of Candis Apes, Robin Freeman, and Jane Johnson, 18 Feb. 1805, Vital Records, vol. 2, p. 361, Colchester Town Records (microform), CSL.

8. In 1811, William Apes sold rights to thirteen acres of land in Colchester to Daniel Taylor, neighbor to Candace Apes's former owner; William Apes, grantor, to Daniel Taylor, grantee, 29 July 1811, Land Records, vol. 17, p. 293, Town Clerk's Office, Colchester, Conn.

9. Incomplete records suggest that William and Candace Apes had at least three sons: Elias married Louisa Worthington, "colored," in 1827, Hartford Vital Records, Barbour Collection, CSL; Gilbert eventually moved to Brooklyn, New York, where the 1850 U.S. census, household 184, lists him as "M" for mulatto; Griswold stayed in Colchester, where he is "B" for black, household 179, in the 1870 U.S. census and "W" for white in the 1880 U.S. census, household 183; Griswold's sons Elias G. and Gad W. served in "Colored" units in the U.S. Civil War; www.ancestry.com. Candace Apes, grantor, to Gilbert Apes, grantee, 22 Sept. 1838, Hartford Land Records, CSL.

10. "Book of Records." On Sally George, see O'Connell, *On Our Own Ground*, 148–51. She appears to have been William Apes's sister, though the closest possible marriage record has "Poll Apes" marrying Peter "Gorge" in 1789, both of Groton, "Church Records of Preston, Connecticut," 26.

11. Manuscript page 57, 1820 U.S. census, Colrain.

12. Elisha: DPT, ship *Connecticut* of Norwich, 1832–1833; ship *Neptune* of New London, 1834–1836 and 1836–1837; ship *Ann Maria* of New London, 1837–1839 and 1839–1841. He left the 1837–1839 *Ann Maria* voyage at sea to join the ship *Neptune* of New London; see logbook, *Ann Maria*, 1837–1839, MSM. Solomon: DPT and RTN, ship *Palladium* of New London, 1832–1833; and bark *Jason* of New London, 1837–1839. The Apes family must not have lived on the reservation since the overseers of the Mashantucket Pequot tribe do not mention them, but Fagans, Braytons, and Georges regularly appear in overseer accounts and lists of tribal members in New London County Court Records, Papers by Subject: Indians, Mashantucket Pequot, 1758–1855; and New London County Superior Court Records, Papers by Subject: Indians, Mashantucket Pequot, 1758–1887, and Other Indian Papers, 1826–1907, CSL.

13. Zollers, *Thrilling Incidents*, 72–73.

14. Bicknell, *History of the State of Rhode Island*, 5–6. See also Cole, *History of Washington and Kent Counties*, 1324.

15. Later in life, he reported his birth year as 1829, but the earliest crew lists have him born in 1824. Voyages: DPT, ship *Armata* of New London, 1840–1842, 1842–1844, 1844–1846; ship *Benjamin Morgan* of New London, 1846–1848, 1848–1851;

bark *General Scott* of New London, 1851–1854; ship *New England* of New London, 1854–1857; ship *Erie* of Fairhaven, 1857–1861; bark *Oriole* of New Bedford, 1863–1866.

16. Gilbert Memoir; Beattie, *First White Boy Born in Otago*, 28.

17. "Loss of Ship Ann Maria, of New London," *New Bedford Mercury*, 3 March 1843.

18. Gilbert Memoir.

19. A conversation with Tuhawaiki, remembered by George Clarke, *Notes on Early Life*, 62–63; for Te Rauparaha and his musket-driven war against the Ngai Tahu in 1839, the year Apes arrived, see Wakefield, *Adventure in New Zealand*, 1:110–22. For general histories of South Island Maori and Maori–European relations in the nineteenth century, see Evison, *Te Wai Pounamu*; Entwisle, *Behold the Moon*.

20. Edward Shortland, "Journal Notes Kept While in the Middle Island" (Jan. 1844), Edward Shortland Papers, Hocken Library, Dunedin, New Zealand, and *Southern Districts of New Zealand*, 105–16, 300–301. J. F. H. Wohlers suggested that Jones was still operating the Waikouaiti station in 1844, in "First Report on Ruapuke" (June 1844), p. 4, typescript, Turnbull; local historian John Christie gave 1848 as the date of the Waikouaiti station's closing in *History of Waikouaiti*, 62. The best manuscript collection for New Zealand's shore whaling industry is the Weller Brother Papers at Mitchell Library, Sydney, Australia; I read photocopies at Turnbull. For the whaling season and a good account of how shore whaling worked at New Zealand's Cook Strait stations, see Wakefield, *Adventure in New Zealand*, 1:44–51, 312–43. For general histories of New Zealand whaling, see Morton, *Whale's Wake*; McNab, *Old Whaling Days*; Richards, *Murihiku Re-Viewed*.

21. For Maori labor and trade activity at the Otago station, see Octavius Harwood Journals, 1838–1840, 1840–1842; Notebooks, 1838, 1839–1840, 1841; and Day Books, 1842, 1842–1843, in George Craig Thomson Papers, Hocken Library, Dunedin, New Zealand.

22. Jones sponsored the Kennard family; see Beattie, *First White Boy in Otago*. For Watkin and Jones, see entries for May 1840, James Watkin's Journal, photocopy, Turnbull (original in the Mitchell Library, Sydney, Australia). For a history of the South Island missions, see Pybus, *Maori and Missionary*.

23. Orange, *Treaty of Waitangi*; Alan Ward, *Unsettled History*.

24. Shortland, *Southern Districts*, 86; see also 1, 83–91, 284–91; Evison, *Ngai Tahu Deeds*; Jane Jones, "Purchase of the Southern Blocks."

25. Wanhalla, *In/visible Sight*; Haines, "In Search of the 'Whaheen'"; Atholl Anderson, *Race against Time*; Russell, "'A New Holland Half-Caste'"; "Casual Allusions to the Whalers Made by Maoris in Interviews Given to Herries Beattie Between 1900 and 1950," 1–15, in James Herries Beattie Papers, Hocken Library, Dunedin, New Zealand.

26. Gilbert Memoir, 4, 6, 17–18. In "Te Anu's Story," Tony Ballantyne suggests that Maori readily incorporated foreign men of color in the case of a South Asian emigrant; Te Anu arrived in New Zealand a generation before Apes and Gilbert and experienced

adoptive practices (tattoos, joining in warfare) like those described in Bentley, *Pakeha Maori*, that do not appear in accounts of Apes and others who came in the 1830s and later.

27. One definition of "Pakeha" attributed its origins to sailing ships having wings like birds; see Mamaru Te Au to James Herries Beattie, 9 Sept. 1946, "Letters from Maoris and halfcastes," Beattie Papers. Pakeha translates as "foreigner" in William Williams, *Dictionary of the New Zealand Language*, 106.

28. Augustus Earle, *Narrative of a Nine Months' Residence*, 146; Wakefield, *Adventure in New Zealand*, 1:148; Kenny, *New Zealand Journal*, 32.

29. Shortland, *Southern Districts*, 312. John Boultbee distinguished north and south variants of "white man" in this way also; see Starke, *Journal of a Rambler*, 109. See also Ballantyne, "Te Anu's Story."

30. Gilbert Memoir, 7.

31. Apes cut timber for the Weller Brothers in the off-season and then joined their whaling gang at Taieri station for the 1841 season; 9–10 Dec. 1840, 21 Dec. 1840, Octavius Harwood Journal (Oct. 1840–July 1842), Thomson Papers; "Giant of the Past: James Apes, Whaler and Shearer," *Dunedin Evening Star*, 10 Sept. 1938, reports that Elisha Apes (James's father) worked out of the Waikouaiti whaling station.

32. Mary Apes, six years old, baptized Wesleyan mission church, Waikouaiti, 18 July 1848; baptism entry 524, "Typescript of Burial, Marriage and Baptismal Registers of Methodist Church, Waikouaiti, 1840–1859," Thomson Papers.

33. "Enclosure 5 in No. 15," in "Half-Caste Claims in the South and Stewart Island (Papers Relative to)," AJHR (1876), session I, G-9, p. 24.

34. Shortland, "Journal Notes," under section "Waikouaiti." Lynette Russell makes the same observation about Tommy Chaseland: the longer Chaseland was in New Zealand, the more his aboriginal descent came to be disregarded, in "'A New Holland Half-Caste,'" 7–8.

35. 19 Apr. 1844, J. W. Barnicoat, Diary, 1843–1844, Hocken Library, Dunedin, New Zealand. See also "Mr. Tuckett's Diary," appendix A, in Hocken, *Contributions*, 222–23.

36. Wakefield, *Adventure in New Zealand*, 1:324. For intermarriage issue, see Salesa, *Racial Crossings*, especially ch. 1.

37. Watkin's Journal, quoted on 14 Aug. 1843. He mentions other marriages occurring on 9 Sept. 1843, 13 Oct. 1843, 16 Dec. 1843, but in mid-1844 was replaced by Charles Creed, who married "Elisha Apes to Punahere," marriage 43, 10 Aug. 1844; baptism entries for Karoraina Punahere, 523; Mary and William Apes, 524; John, 544 (who died young); George, 650; James, 767; and Thomas, 888, all in "Typescript of Burial, Marriage and Baptismal Registers of Methodist Church, Waikouaiti." Kitty, born too late to appear in this register, is listed as the last of the Apes's six children in the *whakapapa* of Tera Namieha, Native Land Court at Puketeraki, 1908, vol. 11, p. 198, 205, South Island Maori Land Court Records Minute Book, rl. 3021, ANZ.

38. "Census Return for Waikouaiti, Moeraki, 1851," in folder with "South Island Maori Census," Mantell Family Papers, rl. 17, Turnbull. For Apes as Jones's farm laborer in the 1850s, see Gordon, *Waikouaiti and Dunedin*, 59–62.

39. "Giant of the Past"; Beattie, *First White Boy in Otago*, 29, 53.

40. Bankruptcy notice, 189, William Apes, *Otago Daily Times*, 28 Mar. 1878, in *Papers Past*, http://paperspast.natlib.govt.nz/cgi-bin/paperspast; Paterson, "*Hāwhekaihe*," 139.

41. John Stone, *Stones Otago & Southland Directory*, 131–132.

42. I visited the Karitane and Puketeraki cemeteries on 14 Jan. 2011 with Betty Apes, Jim Apes, and other Apes descendants. I thank them for their welcome and tour of the area.

43. I thank Betty Apes and John Scragg for their notes on Waikouaiti marriage records, which give two marriages in the 1870s for William Apes, but with an age that falls in between Elisha's and son William's ages. The Waikouaiti marriage register given me by John Scragg suggests that the 1879 marriage to Fanny Morris, a dressmaker of Hawksbury, involved Elisha and not his son William because the groom is listed as a "settler." Betty Apes suggested to me that his other marriages would explain why Elisha Apes was not buried at the Puketeraki cemetery.

44. Beattie, *First White Boy in Otago*, 24–25, 47–48.

45. Binney, "'In-Between' Lives'"; Paterson, "*Hāwhekaihe*"; Wanhalla, *In/visible Sight*; Salesa, *Racial Crossings*.

46. Interview with Betty Apes, Dunedin, New Zealand, 9 Jan. 2011.

47. See, for example, South Island Maori Land Court Records Minute Book, vol. 11, 197, 205, rl. 3021; vol. 23, 317–18, rl. 3024.

48. William Apes "Seinor" to Thos. Pratt, 29 July 1885, and Tiemi Hipi to Tame Parata, 30 Jan. 1885, Land Claims of South Island Half Castes, Special File 10, ANZ. I thank Lachy Paterson for translating Tiemi Hipi's letter.

49. Memos of 4 Sept. 1885 (author unknown) and from "CCL," 28 Aug. 1885, in Folder 12a, Land Claims of South Island Half Castes, ANZ.

50. "Census Return for Waikouaiti, Moeraki, 1851." It is unclear whether Punahere and the children were included in the nearby document "Southern Maories" (1852) because it is a statistical summary only; see South Island Maori Census folder, rl. 17, Mantell Family Papers, Turnbull.

51. "House of Representatives" (New Zealand Parliament), 20 Nov. 1863, p. 910; "Half-Caste Claims in the South and Stewart Island"; Alexander Mackay, to the Under Secretary, Native Department, Wellington, 21 Nov. 1878, Claims of South Island Half Castes, Special File No. 10, ANZ. The Apes children owned more land than this, from Kiti Hipi Pohio with twenty-three acres to Tiemi Hipi with fifty-three acres in 1891, but the land that preoccupied the native commissioners over the years appears to be just this Mantell promise brought to a conclusion in 1886 with the eight- and ten-acre grants. See

"Middle Island Native Claims, (Report by Mr. Commissioner Mackay Relating to)," AJHR (1891), G.-7, p. 25, 31.

52. "Native Affairs Committee: Ngaitahu Block (Kemp's Purchase), Petition of Tiemi Hipi and 916 others RE (Report on): Together with Minutes of Proceedings and Evidence," AJHR (1910) I.-3B, p. 1.

53. A search on "Apes" in Otago Nominal Index, University of Otago, New Zealand, http://marvin.otago.ac.nz/oni, accessed 8 Dec. 2010, lists William Apes on the general (non-Maori) electoral rolls from 1856 to 1890 but lists none of his sons.

54. William Arthur Taylor, *Lore and History*, 113, 115.

55. "Mrs Harper, Karitane," in "Otago Maoris: Notes by Rehu King, Mrs. Harper, etc.," Henry Devenish Skinner Papers, Hocken Library, Dunedin, New Zealand.

56. The interview with Tame Wiremu Hipi/Tommy Apes, is mentioned in "Summary of Maoris & Halfcastes Interviewed by me Between January 1, 1921 and December 31, 1942," p. 35, and Mere Harper or "Big Mary" is mentioned in "Summary of Maoris & Halfcastes Interviewed by me between January 1, 1900 & December 31, 1920," p. 38, "General Maori Information #3" Notebook; 20 Apr. 1920 entry, "Trips to Maoris" (1920), Beattie Papers.

57. "Nature and General Maori Information Gathered Between 1920 and 1940 from Maories, Supplementary to Previous Notes Printed," book 1 (July 1941), p. 9, 13, 15; "Thomas Apes," in "General Maori Information," book 2, p. 12, Beattie Papers.

58. "William Haberfield of Moeraki from 1836," in Richards, *Murihiku Re-Viewed*, 121–22, originally from the *Dunedin Evening Star*, 14 Feb. 1891.

59. "A Bit of Early History," *Otago Witness*, 23 Jan. 1890, in *Papers Past,* http://paperspast.natlib.govt.nz.

60. Aroha [pseudonym for anonymous author], "Our First Visit to Karitane," *Otago Witness*, 24 Mar. 1925.

61. For other accounts in which Apes is mentioned as an "Early Settler" and historical informant, see "Rejoicings at Waikouaiti," 20 Mar. 1901, and "Early Waikouaiti: A Correction," *Otago Witness*, 20 Mar. 1901, in *Papers Past*, http://paperspast.natlib.govt.nz.

62. Christie, *History of Waikouaiti*, 51–52.

Chapter 9

1. Herndon and Sekatau, "Right to a Name"; Melish, "Racial Vernacular"; Forbes, *Africans and Native Americans*; Sweet, *Bodies Politic*.

2. Pierce, "Joseph Daggett of Martha's Vineyard"; Plane, *Colonial Intimacies*, 143–48; Mandell, "Saga of Sarah Muckamugg" and *Tribe, Race, History*, ch. 2; Silverman, *Faith and Boundaries*, ch. 7.

3. Marriage certificate in Paul Cuffe Papers, NBL; Lamont D. Thomas, *Rise to Be a People*, 3–4.

4. Kendall, *Travels*, 2:179; Mitchell, "Cape Cod," 656–57; Gideon Hawley to Peter Thacher, 6 Nov. 1800, SPG (for Hinson's likely father, see Anthony Hinchins, family 11).

5. Kendall, *Travels*, 2:180–81.

6. Kardell and Lovell, *Vital Records of Sandwich*, 1:543.

7. EVR, 192; DPT, ship *Java* of New Bedford, 1831–1832, confirmed as same man in Indian Guardian Accounts for Christiantown and Chappaquiddick for 1832, rl. 1, Dukes County Probate Records, MSA.

8. CVR, 41. On grandfather Joseph DeGrass and father Recall DeGrass, see Segel and Pierce, *Wampanoag Genealogical History*, 388; as daughter of Recall DeGrass, see Christiantown section, Baylies.

9. Stewart, *Journal of a Residence*, 115–16; Scruggs, "Anthony D. Allen." Susan Lebo pointed out this possibility to me.

10. Charles Goodall, Journal, 22–23 Nov. 1845, ship *Milo* of New Bedford, 1843–1846, Huntington Library, San Marino, Calif.; RTN, ship *Trident* of New Bedford, 1843–1846, gives date of Allen's death as 1 Jan. 1846, probably the date it was reported to a U.S. consul; an undated attachment with the RTN says that he joined in Lahaina, had a "copper" complexion, and was thirty years old.

11. DPTs, bark *Valparaiso* of New Bedford, 1852–1856 and 1856–1861, give John Anthony's birthplace as Sierra Leone (residence Martha's Vineyard and Gay Head), which in their greater detail seem more accurate than Earle, viii, which lists him as Portuguese.

12. Luley was also on that vessel's prior voyage: crew lists, bark *Draco* of New Bedford, 1858–1862 and 1862–1865, WSL, 27 Apr. 1858 and 24 June 1862.

13. Crew list, bark *Benjamin Franklin* of New Bedford, 1866–1867, WSL, 15 May 1866; "Loss of Bark Benjamin Franklin, of this Port," WSL, 29 Oct. 1867; 31 Aug. 1867, Samuel T. Braley, Journal, bark *Benjamin Franklin* of New Bedford, 1866–1867, Log 260, NBW; Francis R. Webb to Wm. H. Seward, 30 Sept. 1867, rl. 2, *Despatches*, Zanzibar.

14. Richard L. Pease, *Report*, 40.

15. John A. Lewlo, 14 Dec. 1886, Deaths, Gay Head, MAVR; "Bark Atlantic Wrecked," WSL, 21 Dec. 1886; under name John Anthony, in "Wrecked Bark Atlantic," WSL, 4 Jan. 1887.

16. John and Rachel Foster, household 125, Gay Head, Mass., U.S. Manuscript Census, 1880, www.ancestry.com; Rachel Foster, 12 Apr. 1884, Deaths, Gay Head, MAVR. For Foster as a fisherman and his remarriage, see household 16, Gay Head, Mass., 1900 U.S. census, www.ancestry.com; marriage of John Foster and Ann David, 14 Oct. 1884, Marriages, Gay Head, MAVR.

17. DPTs, bark *Hesper* of New Bedford, 1828–1830 and 1831–1834; ship *Abigail* of New Bedford, 1835–1838; marriage in CVR, 73; Richard L. Pease, *Report*, 45, 47; "colored," TVR, 87.

18. TVR, 239; on James family, see Bird, 61; Earle, vi–vii. For their ranks, see SHP, ship *L. C. Richmond* of New Bedford, 1848–1851.

19. 4 May 1851, Marriages, Tisbury, MAVR.

20. "A letter from Capt Abbott," WSL, 29 Nov. 1853; see also single entry summarizing 29 July–10 Aug. 1853 while anchored at Java, Logbook, bark *Draco* of New Bedford, 1851–1854, Log 202, PPL.

21. John A. Spencer, Probate Records, 22 May and 2 June 1854, rl. 10, Dukes County Probate Records, MSA.

22. Morse's known voyages: DPTs, ship *Winslow* of New Bedford, 1808–1810; ship *Maria* of New Bedford, 1810–1812; ship *Phoebe Ann* of New Bedford, 1815–1817; ship *Martha* of New Bedford, 1819–1820; ship *Frances* of New Bedford, 1820–1823; wife Betsy from Baylies.

23. Commonwealth of Massachusetts, "Pauper Accounts," in *Resolves . . . Commencing January, 1835, and Ending April, 1838*, 679; *Acts and Resolves . . . Second Session in the Year 1842*, 579; *Acts and Resolves . . . 1843, 1844, 1845*, 92; Burgess, "Old South Road," 8.

24. A 24 Oct. 2012 Google search on "Belain" returned only histories of Pierre Belain d'Esnambuc's claiming Martinique for France in the early seventeenth century and the Chappaquiddick family's genealogy.

25. EVR, 97 ("Belin").

26. Family reconstructed with Baylies; Bird, 60–63; Richard L. Pease, *Report*, 33–35. Isaiah went on at least two voyages: crew list, ship *Meridian* of Edgartown, 1828–1831, MVM; DPT, ship *Emerald* of New Bedford, 1831–1832. The earliest record I have found for George is DPT, ship *Hercules* of New Bedford, 1830–1831; his last voyage was as first mate on bark *Pioneer* of New Bedford, 1854–1858, SHP. David made at least three voyages: DPT, ship *Commodore Decatur* of New Bedford, 1831–1832; DPT, ship *Marcia* of Fairhaven, 1832–1833; crew list, ship *Three Brothers* of Nantucket, 1833–1836, MVM. Asa was probably on more than the three voyages I have found for him: DPTs, ship *Columbus* of Fairhaven, 1833–1835; ship *Benjamin Tucker* of New Bedford, 1843–1846; ship *Phocion* of New Bedford, 1846–1849. Peter Jr. made at least two voyages: DPT, ship *Ansel Gibbs* of Fairhaven, 1835–1839; crew list, ship *Almira* of Edgartown, 1839–1843, MVM. Thomas died at sea while on ship *Mercury* of New Bedford, 1844–1848; see RTN. William made several voyages, first on ship *Adeline* of New Bedford, 1843–1846 (DPT), and is last found as second mate, SHP, bark *Pioneer* of New Bedford, 1854–1858. Joseph died before receiving earnings from ship *Amethyst* of New Bedford, 1846–1850; see Indian Guardian Accounts for Christiantown and Chappaquiddick for 1850, rl. 2, Indian Guardian Papers, MSA.

27. Jeremiah Pease, "Jeremiah Pease's Diary," 4 and 5 Aug. 1833, 26.

28. William A. Vanderhoop, Petition for Naturalization, 31 May 1870, May Term, 1870, Superior Court Records for the Commonwealth of Massachusetts, vol. 2, p. 138, Superior Court Clerk's Office, Dukes County Courthouse, Edgartown, Mass.; marriage and children's birthplaces in Richard L. Pease, *Report*, 37; marriage, 22 Mar. 1837, in New England Historic Genealogical Society, *Vital Records of New Bedford*, 2:461;

New Bedford City Directory, 1838, p. 114, in *U.S. City Directories, 1821–1989*, database, www.ancestry.com. The Vanderhoops were friends and associates with Anthony Jourdain, a New Bedford barber from Suriname, and his Gay Head wife, Hepsibah Johnson, in Grover, *Fugitive's Gibraltar*, 54, 248.

29. William A. Vanderhoop Jr.: DPTs, bark *Valparaiso* of New Bedford 1856–1861; bark *Awashonks* of New Bedford, 1862–1865; bark *Abraham Barker* of New Bedford, 1866–1870. John: DPTs, bark *Cape Horn Pigeon* of Dartmouth, 1866–1869; bark *A. R. Tucker* of New Bedford, 1871–1874. Edwin: DPTs, bark *Sunbeam* of New Bedford, 1868–1871; bark *Atlantic* of New Bedford, 1872–1876.

30. 9 Sept. 1880, Ellinwood B. Coleman, Journal, ship *Niger* of New Bedford, 1878–1882, Log 544, MWA. Her maiden name is Redsdale in 6 Oct. 1888, Marriages, Gay Head, MAVR.

31. *Niger* at St. Helena, 22 Oct. 1881 and end of March 1882, in Coleman, Journal; "Letters," WSL, 22 Apr. 1884; "Letters," WSL, 14 Oct. 1884.

32. Evelina Cook's arrival in the United States is given as 1886, household 19, Gay Head, Mass., U.S. manuscript census, 1900, www.ancestry.com; Arthur Peters, 12 June 1886, Births, Gay Head, MAVR; Samuel Peters Jr.'s death date reported as 28 Sept. 1886, in "Letters," WSL, 14 Dec. 1886; 6 Oct. 1888, Marriages, Gay Head, MAVR.

33. Earle, 34.

34. John D. Brown testimony, Commonwealth of Massachusetts, *Hearing before the Committee on Indians, at Marshpee*, 26.

35. Kettner, *Development of American Citizenship*, 236, 345; Bradburn, *Citizenship Revolution*, 260. The historiography of naturalization and race focuses on immigration and late nineteenth- to twentieth-century immigration history; see Tehranian, "Performing Whiteness"; López, *White by Law*.

36. U.S. Census Bureau, *Measuring America*, 6–7, 119–24.

37. "An Act for the Better Preventing of a Spurious and Mixt Issue," Province Laws 1705–6, chap. 10, approved 5 Dec. 1705, and "An Act for the Orderly Solemnization of Marriages," Acts 1786, chap. 3, approved 22 June 1786, MAR. See also Rosen, *American Indians and State Law*, 110–11; Woods, "'Wicked and Mischievous Connection,'" 58–60; Weierman, "'For the Better Government of Servants and Slaves,'" 144–51.

38. "Death of a Poquod Indian," *Albany Evening Journal*, 13 Apr. 1839; O'Connell, *On Our Own Ground*, 159.

39. Joseph's race is white in Baylies, Chappaquiddick section. In Baylies, she appears as Penelope Joseph, but Leavitt Thaxter to John Milton Earle, 28 Jan. 1860, John Milton Earle Papers, wrote that Nelly was short for Eleanor; Nelly Gudly and Emanuel Joseph, EVR, 129.

40. Moses "Hawwoswee," "Census of Wampanoag Indians," 19 Mar. 1792, Misc. Manuscripts, MHS.

41. Gideon Hawley to Peter Thacher, 6 Nov. 1800, SPG (see family 37 for what may be Pells' family; family 26, named Hatch; family 61, Ceesar). See also Hawley's 1776 list

of Mashpee household heads, which has a column for number of "Negroes," 24 June 1776, and Draft Letter, Gideon Hawley to Governor Hancock, 8 July 1791, Gideon Hawley Letters, MHS; Gideon Hawley to Jedidiah Morse, 16 Sept. 1800, SPG.

42. On Mingo's Narragansett roots, see "Joseph Mingo Dead," *Vineyard Gazette*, 10 Apr. 1913; "Samuel G. Mingo."

43. Emanuel Joseph, 18 Jan. 1864, Deaths, Tisbury, MAVR, gives his birthplace as Western Islands (Azores).

44. Herndon and Sekatau, "Right to a Name"; Melish, "Racial Vernacular."

45. John Brooks to Gentlemen of the Senate and Gentlemen of the House of Representatives, 27 Jan. 1820, rl. 1, Unpassed Legislation, Indian Affairs, MSA.

46. Earle, 109–10.

47. "An Act for the Better Regulation of the Indian, Mulattoe and Negro Proprietors in Marshpee," Acts 1788, chap. 2, approved 12 June 1788; "An Act for the Better Regulating of the Indian, Mulatto, and Negro Proprietors and Inhabitants of the Plantation Called Marshpee," Acts 1788, chap. 38, approved 30 Jan. 1789; "An Act for the Better Regulation, Instruction, and Government of the Indians and People of Colour in the County of Dukes County," Acts 1827, chap. 114, approved 10 Mar. 1828, MAR.

48. Bird, 30.

49. John A. Spencer estate inventory, 2 June 1854, rl. 10, Dukes County Probate Records, MSA.

50. Two-thirds of the Christiantown and Chappaquiddick annual accounts from 1828 to 1869 are on rl. 2, Indian Guardian Papers, and the remaining, with a few missing years, on rl. 1, Dukes County Probate Records, MSA. Tucker, 1830, 1832, Dukes County Probate; Williamson, 1828, and Spencer, 1847, Indian Guardian Papers. Williamson was born in Baltimore, according to crew list, ship *Congress* of Nantucket, 1832–1835, MVM.

51. Earle, 22, 64, iii. Earle's appendix, ii–lxxviii, distinguishes individuals as Indians or "foreigners" and further categorizes Indians by tribal affiliations such as Gay Head or Herring Pond. Bird, 6, tabulated the number of "foreigners" in its summary statistics of each community but did not identify non-Indians in its roll of individuals. Bird's statement "Under the head of foreigners, we include all, one or both of whose parents are not of Indian blood," must be a mistake; the number of "foreigners" is so small at each place, it must mean those who had no "Indian blood."

52. Zaccheus Howwoswee to John Milton Earle, 27 Jan. 1860 and 12 Sept. 1860, Earle Papers.

53. O'Brien, *Dispossession by Degrees*, 44–51, 101–19; Levy, *Town Born*; Herndon, *Unwelcome Americans*.

54. Silverman, *Faith and Boundaries*, ch. 7; Mandell, *Tribe, Race, History*; for late twentieth century, see Cramer, *Cash, Color, and Colonialism*, ch. 8.

55. Bird, 54, 12.

56. Plane and Button, "Massachusetts Indian Enfranchisement Act"; Rosen, *American Indians and State Law*, ch. 6.

57. Rhode Island and Providence Plantations, *Report of Commission on the Affairs of the Narragansett Indians*; Boissevain, "Detribalization of the Narragansett Indians."

58. Commonwealth of Massachusetts, *Hearing before the Committee on Indians, at Marshpee*, 4–5, 20, 25. Godfrey's birthplace: 25 Dec. 1896, Deaths, Mashpee, MAVR.

59. Vanderhoop, Petition for Naturalization granted May term, 1872, Superior Court Records for the Commonwealth of Massachusetts, vol. 2, pp. 280–82, Superior Court Clerk's Office, Dukes County Courthouse, Edgartown, Mass. See similar phrasing in earlier petitions in vol. 1, 114–15, 309–12; John P. Randolph Petition for Naturalization and admission to citizenship, May term, 1872, Superior Court Records for the Commonwealth of Massachusetts, vol. 2, pp. 299–301.

60. "Superior Court, May Term," *Vineyard Gazette*, 31 May 18722; "Respected Citizen Dead," *Worcester Daily Spy*, 30 Sept. 1893.

61. Commonwealth of Massachusetts, *Hearing before the Committee on Indians, at Marshpee*, 34.

62. Earle, 34.

63. "Last of Narragansett Chiefs," *Providence Journal*, 4 Dec. 1899.

64. Rhode Island and Providence Plantations, *Report of Commission on the Affairs of the Narragansett Indians*, 64, also 3–4, 59–60.

65. Deaths, 1862, and Births, Marriages, and Deaths, 1870–1889, Gay Head, MAVR.

66. Gay Head, Mass., U.S. manuscript census, 1870, 1880, 1900 (1890 manuscripts no longer exist); Davis, household 327, Edgartown; Hillman, household 46, Chilmark, 1880; Vanderhoop, household 24 in 1870, 135 in 1880, and 31 in 1900; Foster, household 16, and Cook, household 19, Gay Head, Mass., in 1900; U.S. manuscript census, www.ancestry.com.

67. "Martha's Vineyard Pays Final Honors to Edwin D. Vanderhoop," *Boston Globe*, 31 Jan. 1923; Mary Vanderhoop's birthplace, household 31, Gay Head, Mass., 1900 U.S. manuscript census, www.ancestry.com.

68. Vanderhoop, "Gay Head Indians," 25 June 1904.

69. Tantaquidgeon, "Notes on the Gay Head Indians," 26.

Chapter 10

1. Quoted in Kugler, *William Allen Wall*, 23.

2. Strother, "Summer in New England," 448; "The Marshpee Indians," *New Bedford Mercury*, 13 Dec. 1833.

3. Tudor, *Letters on the Eastern States*, 287–88.

4. "Marshpee Indians"; Strother, "Summer in New England," 452.

5. "Marshpee Indians."

6. Bird, 7, 37.

7. Earle, 34, 63.

8. Leavitt Thaxter to John Milton Earle, 3 Feb. 1860, Earle Papers.

9. Hallett, *Rights of the Marshpee Indians*; William Apess on "Indian Nullification," in O'Connell, *On Our Own Ground*, part IV. In petitions, Indians often refer to their dependent status; for a petition in which they embraced their status as "minors" to contest land sales, see Indian Inhabitants and Proprietors of Sundry Tracts of Lands Lying in the Towns of Plymouth and Sandwich, 6 Aug. 1783, rl. 1, Unpassed Indian Legislation, MSA. See also Silverman, *Faith and Boundaries*; Mandell, *Tribe, Race, History*; Calloway, *After King Philip's War*; John A. Strong, *Montaukett Indians*.

10. B. C. Marchant, to J. M. Earle, 31 Dec. 1859, Earle Papers; Bird, 12, also mentions that "A few are now voters, being taxed for lands, which they own in Edgartown." Jethro Daggett, grantor, to Peter Belain, grantee, 25 July 1825, vol. 23, p. 140; David G., Isaiah, George, Joseph, and William Belain, grantors, to Theodate Goodridge, grantee, 14 Apr. 1847, Land Records, vol. 31, pp. 502–5; George Belain, grantor, to David Belain, grantee, vol. 31, p. 506; Isaiah Belain, grantor, to David J. Belain, grantee, vol. 31, p. 507; John Vinson, grantor, to Isaac Joab, grantee, 7 Jan. 1848, vol. 38, pp. 208–10; John Vinson, grantor, to Isaac Joab, grantee, 5 Apr. 1850, vol. 38, pp. 210–11; Land Records, Registry of Deeds, Dukes County Courthouse, Edgartown, Mass.

11. Crew list, schooner *Gleaner Packet* of Edgartown, 1828–1828, MVM.

12. Daniel Croud, in Charles Endicott to John Milton Earle, 19 Mar. 1860, Earle Papers.

13. On the long tradition of this benevolent discourse, see Stevens, *Poor Indians*; Mielke, *Moving Encounters*.

14. Bird, 48.

15. Earle, 11, 128, 136–37; for native opposition to changes in their status, see Earle, 24, 29, 43, 64.

16. Bird, 7; for population tables including those "At sea," see Bird, 13, 18, 25, 41.

17. Strother, "Summer in New England," 448, 451–52.

18. Todd, *In Olde New York*, 220–22. These voyages match the DPTs except for Todd claiming that Lee was first mate on the *Florida* in 1870, when more likely that would have been later in his career, perhaps in 1879. On the crew list, bark *Abraham Barker* of New Bedford, 1871–1875, WSL, 23 May 1871, Lee was still only a boatsteerer. For schooner *Abbie Bradford* of New Bedford, 1880–1881, see WSL, 11 May 1880, and "Died," 12 Sept. 1881; for ship *Nassau* of New Bedford, see crew list, WSL, 8 Dec. 1863, and its capture by the *Shenandoah*, in "Further Destruction of Whaleships," WSL, 29 Aug. 1865.

19. Todd, *In Olde New York*, 222–23.

20. "Obituary Notices."

21. "Visit to the Elizabeth Islands," 320.

22. Joseph Thaxter to Governor John Brooks, 22 Sept. 1818, Indian Guardian Papers, MSA.

23. Avery, *History of the Town of Ledyard*, 260. See also Fithian, "Shinnecock Reservation," 102–3.

24. Gideon Hawley to Reverend J. Freeman, 15 Nov. 1802, Hawley Letters, MHS.

25. Bird, 13, 19. The report adopts this perspective from the Chappaquiddick and Christiantown guardian Leavitt Thaxter, whose 28 Dec. 1848 letter is reprinted in the report, 72–76.

26. Earle, 6, 63.

27. Leavitt Thaxter in Bird, 75.

28. David Wright to Rev'd Messrs Walker & Parkman, 9 Apr. 1839, Society for Propagating the Gospel Among the Indians and Others in North America Records, MHS.

29. For Massachusetts generally, see Vickers, *Young Men and the Sea* and *Farmers and Fishermen*.

30. Wright to Walker & Parkman, 9 Apr. 1839.

31. O'Connell, *On Our Own Ground*, 155.

32. Ebenezer Skiff to Paul Cuffe, Oct. [1816], Paul Cuffe Papers, NBL.

33. Paul Cuffe to Joel Rogers, 3 Nov. 1816, in Wiggins, *Captain Paul Cuffe's Logs and Letters*, 474.

34. Commonwealth of Massachusetts, *Hearing before the Committee on Indians, at Marshpee*, 17–18, 34.

35. Ibid., 10–11. Amos was first mate on bark *Pamelia* of New Bedford, 1855–1858: crew list, WSL, 5 June 1855.

36. Commonwealth of Massachusetts, *Hearing before the Committee on Indians, at Marshpee*, 25.

37. Mitchell, "Cape Cod," 658; "Reminiscences of Daniel Webster," 22.

38. "Last of Narragansett Chiefs," *Providence Journal*, 4 Dec. 1899; SHP, ship *Emma C. Jones* of New Bedford, 1849–1852.

39. On Hammond, see Deyo, *History of Barnstable County*, 709, 716; "Reminiscences of Daniel Webster," 21; I have found Hammond on only one whaling voyage, DPT, ship *Liverpool II* of New Bedford, 1851–1853, but Earle, xxv, lists his occupation as "mariner" in 1861. For Vanderhoop, see "Martha's Vineyard Pays Final Honors to Edwin D. Vanderhoop," *Boston Globe*, 31 Jan. 1923; George F. Andrews, *Commonwealth of Massachusetts, 1888*, 57.

40. "Joseph Mingo Dead," *Vineyard Gazette*, 10 Apr. 1913; and "Historic Church," Alton Tilton Scrapbook, MVM; see also "Samuel G. Mingo."

41. Poole, "Full Circle"; "Deaths and Funerals: Man Who Killed 'Moby Dick,' Amos Smalley, Dies at 84," *Boston Globe*, 8 Mar. 1961.

42. Smalley, "I Killed 'Moby Dick.'"

43. "'Moby Dick' Premiere in New Bedford July 4," *Boston Globe*, 3 Mar. 1956; Eleanor Sayre, "Gay Head Indians Open Their Museum," *Boston Globe*, 28 Aug. 1958.

44. For more contemporary native perspectives, see the oral histories in Shoemaker, *Living with Whales*, chs. 6–7.

45. Elizabeth Thunder Bird Haile, in Shoemaker, *Living with Whales*, 171; see in same volume the photograph on p. 172 and oral histories of Holly Haile Davis, 177–78, and David Bunn Martine, 189.

46. Shoemaker, *Living with Whales*, 178.

Appendix A

1. "A New Feature," WSL, 1 June 1852.

Appendix B

1. Others existed, but their current whereabouts are unknown. Ramona Peters and Elizabeth James Perry know of some that had been in their families at one time; see Shoemaker, *Living with Whales*, 145–46, 157. For another Samuel G. Mingo journal, while he was fourth mate on the bark *Andrew Hicks* of Westport from 1879 to 1881, see Gale Huntington, *Songs the Whalemen Sang*, 323; and "Songs That Resounded in the Fo'castles and Cabins," *Vineyard Gazette*, 11 May 1956.

2. Shifting pronouns ("his" and "my") and boosterish promotion of central New York's economic potential suggest that Cuffe was not the author. More telling, the Connecticut Historical Society copy has at the top of the title page, in what appears to be nineteenth-century script, "written by Dr. Henry T. Sumner of Stockbridge, New York." Sumner was a hotel keeper, household 139, Stockbridge, New York, U.S. census manuscript, 1850, www.ancestry.com. Some of Cuffe's Wainer relatives had moved to the Stockbridge area; Wiggins, *Captain Paul Cuffe's Logs and Letters*, 471, 475.

3. Lewis and Murakami, *Ranald MacDonald*; Schodt, *Native American in the Land of the Shogun*.

4. Smalley, "I Killed 'Moby Dick.'"

5. Poole, "Full Circle." Poole says the voyage was in 1905–1907 (p. 128), but Captain Andrew D. West's journal, bark *Josephine* of New Bedford, 1907–1909, ODHS 895, NBW, reports the death of Madison's cousin Luther on 14 April 1908, an event that Madison also recounted.

6. Murray, *To Do Good to My Indian Brethren*, 84, 92; "Bits from Book of Jeremiah Pharoah," *Sag Harbor Express*, 31 July 1924, clipping, East Hampton Public Library, East Hampton, N.Y. Occom kept a diary for many years and may have inspired Johnson and Pharoah; for his diary, see Brooks, *Collected Writings of Samson Occom*.

7. Wiggins, *Captain Paul Cuffe's Logs and Letters*, 100–106.

8. When put up for sale by a San Francisco auction house in 2002, this journal did not sell, and the gallery did not later know its whereabouts: e-mail correspondence with Shannon Kennedy, PBA Galleries, 14 Dec. 2009; "Manuscript Log Book of the Ship Barclay," Item 115034, PBA Galleries, San Francisco, Calif., www.pbagalleries.com/search/item 115034.php?&PHPSESSID=eeb941, 11 Dec. 2009.

9. Most whale sightings in this journal have no name written alongside, so the frequency of Pells's name is not due to his having raised the most whales. Pells's signature is on the "Indian Petition of Isaac Wickams & twenty seven others in aid of the Pet. Of Phineas Fish," District of Marshpee, 25 Jan. 1841; on the counterpetition, the "Petition of Mashpee Proprietors against the Petition of Phineas Fish" [1842?]; and the "Petition of Isaac Wickums & 41 other Indians of Marshpee praying for aid to build a House of Worship," 28 Jan. 1848; in Unpassed Indian Legislation, MSA. Pells is on the "List of persons entitled to an allotment of land from the common lands of the district of Marshpee, under the provisions of the Act of March 3rd, 1842," Mashpee Book 1, p. 3, Registry of Deeds, Barnstable County Courthouse, Barnstable, Mass. The probate records of Pells's son, also named James F. Pells, give his father's death date as 1848, which explains why Pells Sr. was not in Bird or Earle; Probate Record 9304 (1886), Probate Office, Barnstable County Courthouse, Barnstable, Mass.

10. This quote from Ammons appears at the front of his first volume, Log 792, MSM.

11. Bark *Mercator* of Westport, 1850–1852, Log 838, NBW; bark *Lagoda* of New Bedford, 1860–1864, NBL.

12. Sherman, *Voice of the Whaleman*, 25–45; Sherman, Downey, Adams, and Pasternack, *Whaling Logbooks and Journals*. For a list of known whaling voyages and the locations of surviving logbooks, see Lund. Whaling captains' wives kept close to the logbook form but for an occasional entry about sewing, tending to husbands and children, and their isolation as the only woman in a seaborne community of men; see Springer, "Captain's Wife at Sea"; Garner, *Captain's Best Mate*; Druett, *"She Was a Sister Sailor."*

Bibliography

Archival Collections

Australia
    Mitchell Library, Sydney
        James S. Royce Diary (microform)

Fiji Islands
    National Archives of the Fiji Islands, Suva
        Land Claims Commission Records

New Zealand
    Akaroa Museum, Banks Peninsula
        Robert Gilbert Memoir
    Archives of New Zealand, Wellington
        Land Claims of South Island Half Castes
        South Island Maori Land Court Records Minute Book (microform)
    Hocken Library, Dunedin
        J. W. Barnicoat, Diary
        James Herries Beattie Papers
        Edward Shortland Papers
        Henry Devenish Skinner Papers
        George Craig Thomson Papers
    Alexander Turnbull Library/National Library of New Zealand, Wellington
        Mantell Family Papers (microform)
        J. F. H. Wohlers Papers (typescript)
        James Watkin Journal (photocopy)
        Weller Brothers Papers (photocopies)

United States
    California
        Huntington Library, San Marino
            Logbooks
    Connecticut
        Colchester Town Clerk's Office, Colchester
            Land Records
            Town Records, 1797–1805
        Connecticut State Library, Hartford
            Barbour Collection
            Colchester Town Records (microform)
            Hartford Land Records (microform)

Records of the Judicial Department, County Court of New London County
and New London County Superior Court, Papers by Subject:
Indians, and Indian Overseers' Reports, in Records of the
Secretary of the State.

G. W. Blunt White Library, Mystic Seaport Museum, Mystic
Charles W. Morgan Collection
Logbooks and Journals
Miscellaneous Volumes
Records of the Holmes's Shipyard

Hawai'i
Hawaiian Mission Children's Society Library, Honolulu
Damon Papers
Journal Collection
Missionary Letters Collection

Maryland
National Archives at College Park
Records of Foreign Service Posts. Consular Posts. Honolulu,
Hawai'i

Massachusetts
American Antiquarian Society, Worcester
John Milton Earle Papers
Barnstable County Courthouse, Barnstable
Probate Office
Records of the Court of Common Pleas
Registry of Deeds
Boston Public Library, Boston
Holbrook Research Institute Microfiche Collection
Newspaper Collection
Congregational Library, Boston
Gideon Hawley Journals and Letters
Dukes County Courthouse, Edgartown
Dukes County Land Records
Falmouth Historical Society, Falmouth
Maritime Collection
Houghton Library, Harvard University, Cambridge
Daniel B. Fearing Logbook Collection
Martha's Vineyard Museum, Edgartown
Alton Tilton Scrapbook
Indian Papers
U.S. Customs Office Records

Massachusetts Historical Society, Boston
  Gideon Hawley Letters
  John Richards Child Papers
  Miscellaneous Bound Manuscripts
  Society for Propagating the Gospel Among the Indians and Others in
    North America Records
Massachusetts State Archives, Boston
  Dukes County Probate Records (microform)
  Executive Records (microform)
  Indian Guardian Papers (microform)
  Passed Legislation Packets
  Unpassed Indian Legislation (microform)
Nantucket Historical Association Research Library, Nantucket
  Edouard A. Stackpole Collection
  Ships' Log Collection
  Ships' Papers Collection
National Archives at Boston, Waltham
  Barnstable Port Records
  Edgartown Port Records
  New Bedford Port Records
  Newport Port Records
  *Records of the Collector of Customs for the Collection District New
    London, Connecticut, 1789–1938*, Microcopy Collection M-1162
    (departure crew lists, reels 53–57; return crew lists, reels 47–52)
    (microform)
  Records of the U.S. District Court of Massachusetts
New Bedford Free Public Library, New Bedford
  Crew Lists and Shipping Articles (microform)
  J. & W. R. Wing Papers (microform)
  Logbooks and Journals (usually microform)
  Paul Cuffe Papers
  Voyage Accounts of C. R. Tucker (microform)
New Bedford Whaling Museum, New Bedford
  Aiken & Swift Records
  Charles Waln Morgan Papers
  Cummings Family Papers
  Logbooks and Journals (microform and manuscript)
  Rotch Collection
  Whaling and Marine Manuscript Archives/International Marine
    Manuscript Archives (microform)

        Wood & Nye Papers
    New England Historic Genealogical Society, Boston
        Massachusetts Vital Records, 1841–1910 (online database)
        Shattuck Collection
    Phillips Library, Peabody Essex Museum, Salem
        John B. Williams Papers
        Logbooks and Journals
        Society for Propagating the Gospel among the Indians and Others in
            North America Records
New York
    East Hampton Public Library, East Hampton
        Crew Lists and Shipping Articles
        Long Island Collection
        New York State Manuscript Census for 1865 (microform)
    Rush Rhees Library, University of Rochester, Rochester
        William Roy Vallance Papers
Rhode Island
    Providence Public Library, Providence
        Nicholson Whaling Collection
    Rhode Island Historical Society, Providence
        U.S. Custom House Records, Port of Bristol/Warren
Washington, D.C.
    U.S. National Archives
        General Records of the Department of State, RG59, *Despatches from
            United States Consuls in Apia, Samoa, 1843–1906*, Microcopy
            Collection T27; *Bay of Islands and Auckland, New Zealand, 1839–1906*,
            T49; *Fayal, Azores, Portugal, 1795–1897*, T203; *Lauthala, Fiji Islands,
            1844–1890*, T25; *Levuka and Suva, 1891–1906*, T108; *Paita, Peru,
            1833–1874*, T600; *Tahiti, Society Islands, French Oceania, 1836–1906*,
            M465; *Valparaiso, Chile, 1812–1906*, M146; *Zanzibar, Zanzibar,
            British Africa, 1836–1906*, M468 (microform) *Letters Received by the
            Secretary of the Navy from Commanders, 1804–1886*, Microcopy 147
            (microform)
        Records of the Bureau of Naval Personnel, RG 24

Selected Websites

Ancestry.com. www.ancestry.com.
"Early American Newspapers." www.readex.com
Mystic Seaport Museum. "New London Crew Lists: 1803–1879." http://library
    .mysticseaport.org/initiative/CrSearch.cfm
National Library of Australia. *Trove.* http://trove.nla.gov.au/
National Maritime Digital Library. http://nmdl.org/wsl/wslindex.cfm

New Bedford Free Public Library. Whaling Archives. http://www.newbedford-ma
    .gov/Library/Whaling/Whaling.html
New Bedford Whaling Museum. "Whaling Crew List Database." www.
    whalingmuseum.org/online_exhibits/crewlist/
Oxford English Dictionary Online. http://dictionary.oed.com
Otago Nominal Index. University of Otago, New Zealand. http://marvin.otago.ac.nz/oni
Pacific Manuscripts Bureau. Australian National University, Canberra. http://
    asiapacific.anu.edu.au/pambu/
PapersPast. paperspast.natlib.govt.nz/cgi-bin/paperspast
State Library of Massachusetts. "Acts and Resolves." www.archives.lib.state.ma.us
    /handle/123456789/2
Yale Indian Papers Project. www.library.yale.edu/yipp/

Selected Newspapers

Barnstable Patriot and Commercial Advertiser
Connecticut Herald (New Haven, Conn.)
Dunedin Evening Star
Empire (Sydney)
Friend (Honolulu)
Greenfield Gazette
Nantucket Inquirer
New Bedford Evening Standard
New Bedford Gazette
New Bedford Mercury
Otago Daily Times
Otago Witness
Pacific Commercial Advertiser
Providence Journal
Sag Harbor Corrector
Salem Gazette
Sandwich Islands Gazette
Sandwich Observer
Vineyard Gazette
The Whalemen's Shipping List and Merchants' Transcript

Printed Primary Sources

Alexander, Mary Charlotte. *William Patterson Alexander in Kentucky, the
    Marquesas, Hawaii.* Honolulu: privately printed, 1934.
Andrews, George F. *Commonwealth of Massachusetts, 1888, State Government:
    Biography of Members, Councillor, Senate, and House Committees, and Organiza-
    tion of Departments.* Framingham, Mass.: Lakeview Press, 1888.
Andrews, Lorrin. *A Dictionary of the Hawaiian Language, to Which Is Appended an
    English-Hawaiian Vocabulary and a Chronological Table of Remarkable Events.*
    Honolulu: Henry M. Whitney, 1865.

Ashley, Clifford W. *The Yankee Whaler*. Boston: Houghton Mifflin, 1926.

———. *The Yankee Whaler*. 2nd ed. 1942; reprint, New York: Dover, 1991.

Avery, John. *History of the Town of Ledyard, 1650–1900*. Norwich, Conn.: Noyes & Davis, 1901.

Bangs, Jeremy Dupertuis. *Indian Deeds: Land Transactions in Plymouth Colony, 1620–1691*. Boston, Mass.: New England Historic Genealogical Society, 2002.

Barber, John Warner. *Historical Collections, Being a General Collection of Interesting Facts, Traditions, Biographical Sketches, Anecdotes, &c., Relating to the History and Antiquities of Every Town in Massachusetts, with Geographical Descriptions*. 1839; reprint, Worcester, Mass.: Warren Lazell, 1848.

Beaglehole, J. C., ed. *The Journals of Captain James Cook on His Voyages of Discovery*. 4 vols. Cambridge, Mass.: Hakluyt Society, 1955–1974.

Beane, J. F. *From Forecastle to Cabin: The Story of a Cruise in Many Seas, Taken from a Journal Kept Each Day, Wherein Was Recorded the Happenings of a Voyage around the World in Pursuit of Whales*. New York: Editor's Publishing, 1905.

Beasley, Delilah L. *The Negro Trail Blazers of California: A Compilation of Records from the California Archives in the Bancroft Library at the University of California, in Berkeley; and from the Diaries, Old Papers, and Conversations of Old Pioneers in the State of California. It Is a True Record of Facts, as They Pertain to the History of the Pioneer and Present Day Negroes of California*. Los Angeles: n.p., 1919.

Beattie, J. Herries, ed. *The First White Boy Born in Otago: The Story of T. B. Kennard*. 1939; reprint, Christchurch, New Zealand: Cadsonbury Publications, 1998.

Belknap, Jeremy, ed. "The Discovery and Description of the Islands Called the Marquesas, in the South Pacific Ocean, with a Farther Account of the Seven Adjacent Islands, Discovered First by Capt. Joseph Ingraham, and since by Capt. Josiah Roberts. Compiled from Dalrymple's Collection of Discoveries; Cooke's Second Voyage, and the Journals and Log-Book of the Ship Jefferson, of Boston." *Collections of the Massachusetts Historical Society for the Year 1795*. 1795; reprint, Boston: John H. Eastburn, 1835: 238–46.

Bicknell, Thomas Williams. *The History of the State of Rhode Island and Providence Plantations: Biographical*. Vol. 8. New York: American Historical Society, 1920.

Bill, Erastus. *Citizen: An American Boy's Early Manhood Aboard a Sag Harbor Whale-Ship Chasing Delirium and Death around the World, 1843–1849, Being the Story of Erastus Bill Who Lived to Tell It*. Edited by Robert Wesley Bills. Anchorage: O. W. Frost, 1978.

Bingham, Hiram. *A Residence of Twenty-One Years in the Sandwich Islands; or the Civil, Religious, and Political History of Those Islands; Comprising a Particular View of the Missionary Operations Connected with the Introduction and Progress of Christianity and Civilization among the Hawaiian People*. 2nd ed. Hartford: Hezekiah Huntington, 1847.

Bird, F. W., Whiting Griswold, and Cyrus Weekes. *Report of the Commissioners Relating to the Condition of the Indians in Massachusetts*. Massachusetts House Document 46. Boston: n.p., 1849.

"Bits from Book of Jeremiah Pharoah." *Sag Harbor Express*. 31 July 1924. Clipping. East Hampton Public Library, East Hampton, N.Y.

Bodfish, Hartson H. *Chasing the Bowhead*. Edited by Joseph C. Allen. Cambridge, Mass.: Harvard University Press, 1936.

Bougainville, Louis-Antoine de. *Écrits sur le Canada: Mémoires—Journal—Lettres*. Sillery, Québec, Canada: Septentrion, 2003.

Brooks, Joanna, ed. *The Collected Writings of Samson Occom, Mohegan: Leadership and Literature in Eighteenth-Century Native America*. New York: Oxford University Press, 2006.

Brower, Charles D. *Fifty Years below Zero: A Lifetime of Adventure in the Far North*. New York: Dodd, Mead, 1942.

Browne, J. Ross. *Etchings of a Whaling Cruise*. Edited by John Seelye. Cambridge, Mass.: Harvard University Press, 1968.

Browning, Robert Lee-Wright. "The Cruise of the United States Sloop-of-War 'Vincennes,' Circumnavigating, 1833–1836." *The United Service: A Monthly Review of Military and Naval Affairs* 13 (Nov. and Dec. 1885): 576–85, 717–28; 14 (Jan., Feb., and Mar. 1886): 81–88, 194–210, 265–78.

Bullen, Frank T. *The Cruise of the Cachalot: Round the World after Sperm Whales*. 1898; reprint, New York: Grosset & Dunlap, 1913.

Burgess, Edward S. "The Old South Road of Gay Head or Musings on Discontinued Byways." *Dukes County Intelligencer* 12 (Aug. 1970): 1–35.

Burns, Walter Noble. *A Year with a Whaler*. New York: Outing Publishing, 1913.

Calkin, Milo. *The Last Voyage of the Independence: The Story of a Shipwreck and South Sea Sketches, 1833 to 1836*. San Francisco: Weiss Printing Company, 1953.

Calvert, James. *Fiji and the Fijians: Mission History*. Edited by George Stringer Rowe. 1858; reprint, Suva, Fiji: Fiji Museum, 2003.

Camp, Mortimer M. *Life and Adventures of a New England Boy*. New Haven, Conn.: Frederic W. Cone, 1893.

Cargill, David. *The Diaries and Correspondence of David Cargill, 1832–1843*. Edited by Albert J. Schütz. Canberra: Australian National University Press, 1977.

Cary, William S. *Wrecked on the Feejees*. 1928; reprint, Fairfield, Wash.: Ye Galleon Press, 1972.

Cheever, Henry T. *The Whale and His Captors; or, The Whaleman's Adventures, and the Whale's Biography, as Gathered on the Homeward Cruise of the "Commodore Preble."* New York: Harper & Brothers, 1850.

Clark, Joseph G. *Lights and Shadows of Sailor Life, as Exemplified in Fifteen Years' Experience, Including the More Thrilling Events of the U.S. Exploring Expedition, and Reminiscences of an Eventful Life on the "Mountain Wave."* Boston: John Putnam, 1847.

Clarke, Cyrene M. *Glances at Life upon the Sea, or Journal of a Voyage to the Antarctic Ocean, &c., &c.* Middletown, Conn.: Charles H. Pelton, 1854.

Clarke, George. *Notes on Early Life in New Zealand*. Hobart, Australia: J. Walch and Sons, 1903.

Cloud, Enoch Carter. *Enoch's Voyage: Life on a Whaleship, 1851–1854*. Edited by
Elizabeth McLean. Wakefield, R.I.: Moyer Bell, 1994.

Coan, Titus. *Life in Hawaii: An Autobiographic Sketch of Mission Life and Labors,
1835–1881*. New York: Anson D. F. Randolph, 1882.

Cole, J. R. *History of Washington and Kent Counties, Rhode Island*. New York: W. W.
Preston, 1889.

Commonwealth of Massachusetts. *Acts and Resolves Passed by the General Court of
Massachusetts, in the Years 1843, 1844, 1845: Together with the Rolls and
Messages*. Boston: Dutton and Wentworth, 1845.———. *Acts and Resolves Passed
by the Legislature of Massachusetts, at Their Second Session in the Year 1842:
Together with the Rolls and Messages of Both Sessions*. Boston: Dutton and
Wentworth, 1842.

———. *Documents Relative to the Marshpee Indians*. Massachusetts Senate Document
14. Boston: Dutton and Wentworth, 1834.

———. *Hearing before the Committee on Indians, at Marshpee, Tuesday, February 9,
1869*. Boston: Wright & Potter, 1869.

———. *Resolves of the General Court of the Commonwealth of Massachusetts, Passed at
the Several Sessions, Commencing January, 1835, and Ending April, 1838*. Boston:
Dutton and Wentworth, 1838.

Comstock, William. *The Life of Samuel Comstock, the Terrible Whaleman, Containing
an Account of the Mutiny, and Massacre of the Officers of the Ship Globe, of
Nantucket, with His Subsequent Adventures, and His being Shot at the Mulgrave
Islands, Also, Lieutenant Percival's Voyage in Search of the Survivors*. Boston:
James Fisher, 1840.

———. *A Voyage to the Pacific, Descriptive of the Customs, Usages, and Sufferings on
Board of Nantucket Whale-Ships*. Boston: Oliver L. Perkins, 1838.

Cook, John A. *Pursuing the Whale: A Quarter-Century of Whaling in the Arctic*.
Boston: Houghton Mifflin, 1926.

Crapo, Henry H. *The New-Bedford Directory*. New Bedford: J. C. Parmenter, 1836.

Crapo, Thomas. *Strange, but True: Life and Adventures of Captain Thomas Crapo
and Wife*. New Bedford, Mass.: Author, 1893.

"Cruise of the Vincennes, (by a Ward Room Officer)." *Army and Navy Chronicle*
(7 July 1836): 24–25.

Cuffe, Paul, Jr. *Narrative of the Life and Adventures of Paul Cuffe, a Pequot Indian;
During Thirty Years Spent at Sea and in Travelling in Foreign Lands*. Vernon,
N.Y.: Horace N. Bill, 1839.

Dana, Richard Henry, Jr. *The Seaman's Friend: Containing a Treatise on Practical
Seamanship, with Plates; A Dictionary of Sea Terms; Customs and Usages of the
Merchant Service; Laws Relating to the Practical Duties of Master and Mariners*.
6th ed. Boston: Thomas Groom, 1851.

———. *Two Years before the Mast: A Personal Narrative of Life at Sea*. Edited by
Thomas Philbrick. 1840; reprint, New York: Penguin Books, 1981.

Davis, William M. *Nimrod of the Sea; or, the American Whaleman*. 1874; reprint,
North Quincy, Mass.: Christopher Publishing House, 1972.

Delano, Reuben. *Wanderings and Adventures of Reuben Delano, Being a Narrative of Twelve Years Life in a Whale Ship!* Worcester, Mass.: Thomas Drew Jr., 1846.

Densmore, D. C. *The Halo: An Autobiography of D. C. Densmore*. Boston: Voice of Angels Publishing House, 1876.

De Varigny, Charles. *Fourteen Years in the Sandwich Islands, 1855–1868*. Translated by Alfons L. Korn. Honolulu: University Press of Hawai'i, 1981.

Drake, Samuel Gardner. *The Book of the Indians*. 9th ed. Boston: Benjamin B. Mussey, 1845.

———. *Indian Biography, Containing the Lives of More than Two Hundred Indian Chiefs*. Boston: Josiah Drake, 1832.

Druett, Joan, ed. *"She Was a Sister Sailor": Mary Brewster's Whaling Journals, 1845–1851*. Mystic, Conn.: Mystic Seaport Museum, 1992.

Dunmore, John, trans. and ed. *The Pacific Journal of Louis-Antoine de Bougainville, 1767–1768*. London: Hakluyt Society, 2002.

D'Urville, Jules-Sébastien-César Dumont. "On the Islands of the Great Ocean." Translated by Louise Ollivier, Antoine de Biran, and Geoffrey Clark. *Journal of Pacific History* 38 (September 2003): 163–74.

Dwight, E. W. *Memoirs of Henry Obookiah: A Native of Owhyhee, and a Member of the Foreign Mission School, Who Died at Cornwall, Conn., Feb. 17, 1818, Aged 26 Years*. New Haven, Conn.: Religious Intelligencer Office, 1818.

Earle, Augustus. *A Narrative of a Nine Months' Residence in New Zealand in 1827; Together with a Journal of a Residence in Tristan d'Acunha, an Island Situated between South America and the Cape of Good Hope*. London: Longman, Rees, Orme, Brown, Green, and Longman, 1832.

Earle, John Milton. *Report to the Governor and Council, Concerning the Indians of the Commonwealth, under the Act of April 6, 1859*. Massachusetts Senate Document 96. Boston: William White, 1861.

Eber, Dorothy Harley. *When the Whalers Were up North: Inuit Memories from the Eastern Arctic*. 1989; reprint, Norman: University of Oklahoma Press, 1989.

Ely, Ben-Ezra Stiles. *"There She Blows": A Narrative of a Whaling Voyage, in the Indian and South Atlantic Oceans*. Edited by Curtis Dahl. Middletown, Conn.: Wesleyan University Press, 1971.

Endicott, William. *Wrecked among Cannibals in the Fijis: A Narrative of Shipwreck and Adventure in the South Seas*. Salem, Mass.: Marine Research Society, 1923.

Fithian, Jon. "Shinnecock Reservation." *Tenth Annual Report of the Superintendent of Public Instruction, of the State of New York*. Albany: Comstock & Cassidy, 1864: 101–3.

Freeman, James. "Notes on Nantucket" (1807). *Collections of the Massachusetts Historical Society*. 2nd ser. Vol. 3 (1815): 19–38.

Gardner, Edmund. *Captain Edmund Gardner, of Nantucket and New Bedford: His Journal and His Family*. Edited by John M. Bullard. New Bedford, Mass.: John M. Bullard, 1958.

Garner, Stanton, ed. *The Captain's Best Mate: The Journal of Mary Chipman Lawrence on the Whaler* Addison, *1856–1860*. Hanover, N.H.: University Press of New England, 1966.

Gaul, Theresa Strouth, ed. *To Marry an Indian: The Marriage of Harriet Gold and Elias Boudinot in Letters, 1823–1839*. Chapel Hill: University of North Carolina Press, 2005.

Gelett, Charles Wetherby. *A Life on the Ocean: Autobiography of Captain Charles Wetherby Gelett: A Retired Sea Captain Whose Life Trail Crossed and Recrossed Hawaii Repeatedly*. Honolulu: Hawaiian Gazette, 1917.

Goode, George Brown, and Joseph W. Collins. *The Fishermen of the United States*. Section IV of *The Fisheries and Fishery Industries of the United States*. Washington, D.C.: Government Printing Office, 1887.

Gordon, Ross S., ed. *Waikouaiti and Dunedin in 1850: Reminiscences of John McLay, an Early Settler*. Dunedin, New Zealand: Ross S. Gordon, 1998.

Guernsey, A. H. "A Cruise after and among the Cannibals." *Harper's New Monthly Magazine* 7 (Sept. 1853): 455–75.

Haley, Nelson Cole. *Whale Hunt: The Narrative of a Voyage by Nelson Cole Haley, Harpooner in the Ship Charles W. Morgan, 1849–1853*. New York: Ives Washburn, 1948.

Hall, Basil. *Extracts from a Journal, Written on the Coasts of Chili, Peru, and Mexico, in the Years 1820, 1821, 1822*. 3rd ed., 2 vols. Edinburgh: Archibald Constable, 1824.

Hall, Charles Francis. *Life with the Esquimaux: The Narrative of Captain Charles Francis Hall, of the Whaling Barque "George Henry," from the 29th May 1860, to the 13th September 1862*. 2 vols. London: Sampson Low, Son, and Marston, 1864.

Hallett, Benjamin F. *Rights of the Marshpee Indians: Argument of Benjamin F. Hallett, Counsel for the Memorialists of the Marshpee Tribe, before a Joint Committee of the Legislature of Massachusetts; Messrs. Barton and Strong of the Senate and Dwight of Stockbridge, Fuller of Springfield and Lewis of Pepperell, of the House, to Whom the Complaints of the Indians for a Change of Government and Redress of Grievances Were Referred, Published at the Request of Isaac Coombs, Daniel Amos and William Apes, the Marshpee Delegation, March 1834*. Boston: J. Howe, 1834.

Hawkesworth, John. *An Account of the Voyages Undertaken by the Order of His Present Majesty for Making Discoveries in the Southern Hemisphere*. 3 vols. London: W. Strahan and T. Cadell, 1773.

Hawley, Gideon. "Biographical and Topographical Anecdotes Respecting Sandwich and Marshpee, Jan. 1794." *Collections of the Massachusetts Historical Society* 3 (1794): 188–93.

Hazen, Jacob A. *Five Years before the Mast, or Life in the Forecastle, Aboard of a Whaler and Man-of-War*. 2nd ed. Philadelphia: Willis P. Hazard, 1856.

Hocken, Thomas Morland, ed. *Contributions to the Early History of New Zealand (Settlement of Otago)*. London: Sampson Low, Marston, 1898.

Holden, Horace. *A Narrative of the Shipwreck, Captivity and Sufferings of Horace Holden and Benj. H. Nute; Who Were Cast Away in the American Ship Mentor on the Pelew Islands in the Year 1832; and for Two Years Afterwards Were Subjected to*

Unheard of Sufferings among the Barbarous Inhabitants of Lord North's Island.
1836; reprint, Cooperstown, N.Y.: E. & H. Phinney, 1841.

Ingraham, Joseph. "An Account of a Recent Discovery of Seven Islands in the South
Pacific Ocean, by Joseph Ingraham." *Collections of the Massachusetts Historical
Society, for the Year 1793.* Vol. 2. 1793; reprint, Boston: Munroe & Francis, 1810:
20–24.

Jarves, James J. *Scenes and Scenery in the Sandwich Islands, and a Trip through
Central America: Being Observations from My Note-Book during the Years
1837–1842.* Boston: James Munroe, 1843.

[Jones?]. *Life and Adventure in the South Pacific, by a Roving Printer.* New York:
Harper & Brothers, 1861.

Jones, Silas. "Narrative of Captain Silas Jones, from the Log of the Awashonks."
Atlantic Monthly 120 (Sept. 1917): 313–22.

Lightcraft, George. *Scraps from the Log Book of George Lightcraft, Who Was More
than Twenty Years a Sailor. An Account of the Whale Fishery, with Many
Thrilling Incidents in the Life of the Author.* 2nd ed. Detroit: F. P. Markham &
Bro., 1850.

Kamakau, Samuel M. *Ruling Chiefs of Hawaii.* Rev. ed. Honolulu: Kamehameha
Schools Press, 1992.

Kaplanoff, Mark D., ed. *Joseph Ingraham's Journal of the Brigantine HOPE on a
Voyage to the Northwest Coast of North America, 1790–92.* Barre, Mass.: Imprint
Society, 1971.

Kendall, Edward Augustus. *Travels through the Northern Parts of the United States,
in the Years 1807 and 1808.* 3 vols. New York: I. Riley, 1809.

Kenny, Robert W, ed. *The New Zealand Journal, 1842–1844, of John B. Williams
of Salem, Massachusetts.* Portland, Maine: Anthoensen Press, 1956.

Kiryaku, Hyoson. *Drifting toward the Southeast: The Story of Five Japanese
Castaways, as Told to the Court of Lord Yamauchi of Tosa in 1852 by John
Manjiro.* Translated by Junya Nagakuni and Junji Kitadai. New Bedford, Mass.:
Spinner Publications, 2003.

Lamb, Jonathan, Vanessa Smith, and Nicholas Thomas, eds. *Exploration &
Exchange: A South Seas Anthology, 1680–1900.* Chicago: University of Chicago
Press, 2000.

Lay, William, and Cyrus M. Hussey. *A Narrative of the Mutiny, on Board the Ship
Globe, of Nantucket, in the Pacific Ocean, Jan. 1824 and the Journal of a Residence
of Two Years on the Mulgrave Islands; with Observations on the Manners and
Customs of the Inhabitants.* New London, Conn.: Authors, 1828.

Leavitt Thaxter, Administrator vs. Lawrence Grinnell & Others, Supreme Court of
Massachusetts, Bristol and Plymouth, 43 Mass. 13 (1840).

Lewis, William S., and Naojiro Murakami, eds. *Ranald MacDonald: The Narrative of
His Early Life on the Columbia under the Hudson's Bay Company's Regime; of his
Experiences in the Pacific Whale Fishery; and of his Great Adventures to Japan;
with a Sketch of His Later Life on the Western Frontier, 1824–1894.* Portland:
Oregon Historical Society, 1990.

Liholiho, Alexander. *The Journal of Prince Alexander Liholiho: The Voyages Made to the United States, England and France in 1849–1850*. Edited by Jacob Adler. Honolulu: University of Hawai'i Press, 1967.

Lucett, Edward. *Rovings in the Pacific from 1837 to 1849; with a Glance at California, by a Merchant, Long Resident at Tahiti*. 2 vols. London: Longman, Brown, Green, and Longmans, 1851.

Lyman, Chester S. *Around the Horn to the Sandwich Islands and California, 1845–1850, Being a Personal Record Kept by Chester S. Lyman*. Edited by Frederick J. Teggart. New Haven, Conn.: Yale University Press, 1925.

Martin, Kenneth R., ed. *"Naked and a Prisoner": Captain Edward C. Barnard's Narrative of Shipwreck in Palau, 1832–1833*. Sharon, Mass.: Kendall Whaling Museum, 1980.

Melville, Herman. *Moby-Dick*. 1851; reprint, New York: Oxford University Press, 1999.

———. *Typee*. 1846; reprint, New York: New American Library, 1964.

Miller, Hunter, ed. *Treaties and Other International Acts of the United States of America*. Vol. 7. Washington, D.C.: Government Printing Office, 1942.

Mitchell, F. "Cape Cod." *Century Magazine* 26 (Sept. 1883): 643–58.

Munford, James Kenneth, ed. *John Ledyard's Journal of Captain Cook's Last Voyage*. Corvallis: Oregon State University Press, 1964.

Murray, Laura J., ed. *To Do Good to My Indian Brethren: The Writings of Joseph Johnson, 1751–1776*. Amherst: University of Massachusetts Press, 1998.

Nevens, William. *Forty Years at Sea; or a Narrative of the Adventures of William Nevens, Being an Authentic Account of the Vicissitudes, Hardships, Narrow Escapes, Shipwrecks and Sufferings in a Forty Years' Experience at Sea*. Portland, Maine: Thurston, Fenley, 1846.

Newhall, Charles L. *The Adventures of Jack; or, a Life on the Wave*. Southbridge, Mass.: Author, 1859.

Nordhoff, Charles. *Nine Years a Sailor: Being Sketches of Personal Experience in the United States Naval Service, the American and British Merchant Marine, and the Whaling Service*. 3 vols. Cincinnati: Moore, Wilstach, Keys, 1957.

"Obituary Notices." *Piscataqua Evangelical Magazine*. July/August 1805: 159.

O'Connell, Barry, ed. *On Our Own Ground: The Complete Writings of William Apess, a Pequot*. Amherst: University of Massachusetts Press, 1992.

Olmsted, Francis Allyn. *Incidents of a Whaling Voyage to Which Are Added Observations on the Scenery, Manners and Customs, and Missionary Stations, of the Sandwich and Society Islands*. 1841; reprint, Rutland, Vt.: Charles E. Tuttle, 1969.

Osborn, John Burr. *Reminiscences of a Voyage around the World in the Forties*. Union City, Mich.: Union City Register, 1892.

Paddack, William C. *Life on the Ocean, or Thirty-Five Years at Sea, Being the Personal Adventures of the Author*. Cambridge, Mass.: Riverside Press, 1893.

Page, Harlan. *Memoir of Thomas H. Patoo, a Native of the Marquesas Islands, Who Died June 19, 1823*. New York: American Tract Society, 1825.

Page, Walter Gilman. "A Descendant of Massasoit." *New England Magazine* 3 (Jan. 1891): 642–44.

Parke, William C. *Personal Reminiscences of William Cooper Parke, Marshal of the Hawaiian Islands, from 1850 to 1884, Rewritten and Arranged by His Son, William C. Parke.* Cambridge, Mass.: University Press, 1891.

Paulding, Hiram. *Journal of a Cruise of the United States Schooner Dolphin, among the Islands of the Pacific Ocean; and a Visit to the Mulgrave Islands, in Pursuit of the Mutineers of the Whale Ship Globe.* New York: G. & C. & H. Carvill, 1831.

Pease, Jeremiah. "Jeremiah Pease's Diary (Continued)." *Dukes County Intelligencer* 19 (Aug. 1977).

Pease, Richard L. *Report of the Commissioner Appointed to Complete the Examination and Determination of All Questions of Title to Land, and of All Boundary Lines between the Individual Owners, at Gay Head, on the Island of Martha's Vineyard.* Boston: Wright and Potter, 1871.

Peirce, Ebenezer W. *Indian History, Biography, and Genealogy; Pertaining to the Good Sachem Massasoit of the Wampanoag Tribe, and His Descendants, with an Appendix.* North Abington, Mass.: Zerviah Gould Mitchell, 1878.

Perkins, Edward T. *Na Motu: or, Reef-Rovings in the South Seas. A Narrative of Adventures at the Hawaiian, Georgian, and Society Islands.* New York: Pudney & Russell, 1854.

Perkins, Thomas, ed. *A Whaling Voyage in the Bark "Willis," 1849–1850: The Journal Kept by Samuel Millet.* Boston, Mass.: privately printed, 1924.

Poole, Dorothy Cottle. "Full Circle." *Dukes County Intelligencer* 10 (Nov. 1968): 121–45.

Porter, David. *A Voyage in the South Seas, in the Years 1812, 1813 and 1814, with Particular Details of the Gallipagos and Washington Islands.* London: Sir Richard Phillips, 1823.

Pratt, Addison. *The Journals of Addison Pratt: Being a Narrative of Yankee Whaling in the Eighteen Twenties, a Mormon Mission to the Society Islands, and of Early California and Utah in the Eighteen Forties and Fifties.* Edited by S. George Ellsworth. Salt Lake City: University of Utah Press, 1990.

Prince, Thomas *A Chronological History of New England in the Form of Annals: Being a Summary and Exact Account of the Most Material Transactions and Occurrences Relating to This Country, in the Order of Time Wherein They Happened, from the Discovery by Capt. Gosnold in 1602, to the Arrival of Governor Belcher, in 1630.* Boston: Kneeland & Green for S. Gerrish, 1736.

Quinn, David B., and Alison M. Quinn, eds. *The English New England Voyages, 1602–1608.* London: Hakluyt Society, 1983.

Reilly, Kevin S., ed. *The Journal of George Attwater: Before the Mast on the Whaleship Henry of New Haven, 1820–1823.* New Haven, Conn.: New Haven Colony Historical Society, 2002.

"Reminiscences of Daniel Webster: Being an Authentic Account of His Mashpee Fishing Trips." *Cape Cod Magazine* 1 (June 1915): 21–23.

Reynolds, J. N. *Address on the Subject of a Surveying and Exploring Expedition to the Pacific Ocean and South Seas, Delivered in the Hall of Representatives on the Evening of April 3, 1836*. New York: Harper & Brothers, 1836.

Reynolds, Stephen. *Journal of Stephen Reynolds*. Edited by Pauline N. King. Vol. 1: 1823–1829. Honolulu and Salem, Mass.: Ku Pa'a and Peabody Museum of Salem, 1989.

Reynolds, William. *The Private Journal of William Reynolds: United States Exploring Expedition, 1838–1842*. Edited by Nathaniel Philbrick and Thomas Philbrick. New York: Penguin Books, 2004.

Rhode Island and Providence Plantations. *Report of Commission on the Affairs of the Narragansett Indians, Made to the General Assembly, at Its January Session, 1881*. Providence: E. L. Freeman, 1881.

Ricketson, Annie Holmes. *The Journal of Annie Holmes Ricketson on the Whaleship A. R. Tucker, 1871–1874*. Edited by Philip F. Purrington. New Bedford, Mass.: Old Dartmouth Historical Society, 1958.

Robbins, Charles Henry. *The Gam: Being a Group of Whaling Stories*. Rev. ed. Salem, Mass.: Newcomb & Gauss, 1913.

Ross, W. Gillies, ed. *An Arctic Whaling Diary: The Journal of Captain George Comer in Hudson Bay, 1903–1905*. Toronto: University of Toronto Press, 1984.

Salisbury, Neal, ed. *The Sovereignty and Goodness of God: With Related Documents*. Boston: Bedford Books, 1997.

Sampson, Alonzo. *Three Times around the World: Life and Adventures of Alonzo D. Sampson*. Buffalo: Express Printing, 1857.

"Samuel G. Mingo." *The Narragansett Dawn* 1 (Jan. 1936): 222–23.

Scidmore, George H. "Report of Mr. George H. Scidmore, Special Agent of the Department of State to Investigate Claims of American Citizens to Lands in Fiji." In "Message from the President of the United States . . . " U.S. Serial Set 3350 (1895–1896). 54th Cong., 1st sess., doc. 126.

Seemann, Berthold. *Viti: An Account of a Government Mission to the Vitian or Fijian Islands in the Years 1860–61*. Cambridge, U.K.: Macmillan, 1862.

Shortland, Edward. *The Southern Districts of New Zealand; A Journal, with Passing Notices of the Customs of the Aborigines*. London: Longman, Brown, Green, & Longmans, 1851.

Simmons, William S., and Cheryl L. Simmons, eds. *Old Light on Separate Ways: The Narragansett Diary of Joseph Fish, 1765–1776*. Hanover, N.H.: University Press of New England, 1982.

Smalley, Amos. "I Killed 'Moby Dick.'" As told to Max Eastman. *Reader's Digest*. June 1957: 172–80.

[Smythe, Sarah]. *Ten Months in the Fiji Islands by Mrs. Smythe*. Oxford, U.K.: John Henry and James Parker, 1864.

Starke, June, ed. *Journal of a Rambler: The Journal of John Boultbee*. Auckland, New Zealand: Oxford University Press, 1986.

Stewart, C. S. *Journal of a Residence in the Sandwich Islands, during the Years 1823, 1824, and 1825 Including Descriptions of the Natural Scenery, and*

Remarks on the Manners and Customs of the Inhabitants: An Account of Lord Byron's Visit in the British Frigate Blonde, and of an Excursion to the Great Volcano of Kirauea in Hawaii. Edited by William Ellis. 2nd ed. New York: John P. Haven, 1828.

———. *A Visit to the South Seas*. London: Fisher, Son & Jackson, 1832.

Stone, John. *Stones Otago & Southland Directory*. Dunedin, New Zealand: John Stone, 1887.

Strother, D. H. "A Summer in New England." *Harper's New Monthly Magazine* 21 (Sept. 1860): 442–61.

Tantaquidgeon, Gladys. "Notes on the Gay Head Indians of Massachusetts." *Indian Notes* 7 (Jan. 1930): 1–26.

Taylor, Nathaniel W. *Life on a Whaler, or Antarctic Adventures in the Isle of Desolation*. Edited by Howard Palmer. New London, Conn.: New London County Historical Society, 1929.

Taylor, William Arthur. *Lore and History of the South Island Maori*. Christchurch, New Zealand: Bascands, 1950.

Thompson, A. C. C. *Incidents of a Whaling Voyage: Being a True Account of the Voyage and Shipwreck of the Author*. 1859; reprint, n.p., n.d.

Thompson, Harold W., ed. *The Last of the "Logan": The True Adventures of Robert Coffin, Mariner, in the Years 1854 to 1859*. Ithaca, N.Y.: Cornell University Press, 1941.

Thompson, John. *The Life of John Thompson, a Fugitive Slave; Containing His History of 25 Years in Bondage, and His Providential Escape, Written by Himself*. Worcester, Mass.: John Thompson, 1856.

Todd, Charles Burr. *In Olde New York: Sketches of Old Times and Places in Both the State and the City*. New York: Grafton Press, 1907.

Torrey, William. *Torrey's Narrative: Or, the Life and Adventures of William Torrey*. Boston: A. J. Wright, 1848.

Truth, Sojourner. *Narrative of Sojourner Truth, a Northern Slave, Emancipated from Bodily Servitude by the State of New York, in 1828*. Boston: J. B. Yerrinton & Son, 1850.

Tudor, William. *Letters on the Eastern States*. 2nd ed. Boston: Wells and Lilly, 1821.

U.S. Congress. "An Act Concerning the Navigation of the United States." 1 Mar. 1817. U.S. Statutes at Large. 14th Cong., sess. II, ch. 31, sec. 3.

———."An Act for the Regulation of Seamen on Board the Public and Private Vessels of the United States." 3 Mar. 1813. U.S. Statutes at Large. 12th Cong., sess. II., ch. 42, sec. 1.

———. "An Act Repealing Certain Provisions of Law Concerning Seamen on Board Public and Private Vessels of the United States." 28 June 1864. U.S. Statutes at Large. 38th Cong., sess. I, ch. 170.

———. "Sloop of War 'John Adams' at Fejee Islands." U.S. Serial Set 859 (1855–56). 34th Cong., 1st sess. House of Representatives Ex. Doc. 115: 5–76.

U.S. Department of State. *Memorandum on Fiji Land Claims*. Washington, D.C.: Government Printing Office, 1902.

Vanderhoop, Mary A. Cleggett. "Gay Head Indians: Their History and Traditions." *New Bedford Evening Standard*, weekly series, 25 June 1904 through 13 Aug. 1904.

"Visit to the Elizabeth Islands." *North American Review and Miscellaneous Journal* 5 (Sept. 1817): 313–324.

Wakefield, Edward Jerningham. *Adventure in New Zealand, from 1839 to 1844; with Some Account of the Beginning of the British Colonization of the Islands.* 2 vols. London: John Murray, 1845.

Wallis, Mary D. *Life in Feejee, or, Five Years among the Cannibals, by a Lady.* Boston: William Heath, 1851.

Warriner, Francis. *Cruise of the United States Frigate Potomac, Round the World, during the Years 1831–34.* New York: Leavitt, Lord, 1835.

Waterhouse, Joseph. *The King and People of Fiji.* Honolulu: University of Hawai'i Press, 1997.

West, Ellsworth Luce. *Captain's Papers: A Log of Whaling and Other Sea Experiences.* As told to Eleanor Ransom Mayhew. Barre, Mass.: Barre Publishers, 1965.

Whitecar, William B., Jr. *Four Years Aboard the Whaleship, Embracing Cruises in the Pacific, Atlantic, Indian, and Antarctic Oceans, in the Years 1855, '6, '7, '8, '9.* Philadelphia: J. B. Lippincott, 1864.

Wiggins, Rosalind Cobb, ed. *Captain Paul Cuffe's Logs and Letters, 1808–1817: A Black Quaker's "Voice from within the Veil."* Washington, D.C.: Howard University Press, 1996.

Wilkes, Charles. *Narrative of the United States Exploring Expedition during the Years 1838, 1839, 1840, 1841, 1842.* 5 vols. Philadelphia: Lea & Blanchard, 1845.

Williams, Harold, ed. *One Whaling Family.* Boston: Houghton Mifflin, 1964.

Williams, John. *A Narrative of Missionary Enterprises in the South Sea Islands: with Remarks upon the Natural History of the Islands, Origin, Languages, Traditions, and Usages of the Inhabitants.* London: J. Snow, 1837.

Williams, John G. *The Adventures of a Seventeen-Year-Old Lad and the Fortunes He Might Have Won.* Boston: Collins Press, 1894.

Williams, Roger. *A Key into the Language of America.* London: Gregory Dexter, 1643.

Williams, Thomas. *Fiji and the Fijians: The Islands and Their Inhabitants.* Edited by George Stringer Rowe. 1858; reprint, Suva, Fiji: Fiji Museum, 1982.

Williams, William. *A Dictionary of the New Zealand Language, and a Concise Grammar; to Which Is Added a Selection of Colloquial Sentences.* 2nd ed. London: Williams and Norgate, 1852.

Woodhouse, James H. *Autobiography of James H. Woodhouse: Compiled between Dec. 3rd, 1896, and Dec. 10th, 1896, Principally from Memory, but with Facts and Dates Verified by Reference to the Author's Journals and Ship Logs.* New Haven, Conn.: W. H. Hale, 1897.

Zollers, George D. *Thrilling Incidents on Sea and Land: The Prodigal's Return.* 7th and rev. ed. Elgin, IL: Brethren Publishing House, 1909.

Other Printed Sources

Abrams, Ann Uhry. "Benjamin West's Documentation of Colonial History: *William Penn's Treaty with the Indians*." *Art Bulletin* 64 (March 1982): 59–75.

Alsultany, Evelyn. "Los Intersticios: Recasting Moving Selves." In *This Bridge We Call Home: Radical Visions for Transformation*, edited by Gloria E. Anzaldúa and Analouise Keating, 106–10. New York: Routledge, 2002.

Altick, Richard Daniel. *The Shows of London*. Cambridge, Mass.: Harvard University Press, 1978.

Anderson, Atholl. *Race against Time: The Early Maori-Pakeha Families and the Development of the Mixed-Race Population in Southern New Zealand*. Dunedin, New Zealand: Hocken Library, 1991.

Anderson, Charles Roberts. *Melville in the South Seas*. New York: Columbia University Press, 1939.

Andrews, Edward E. *Native Apostles: Black and Indian Missionaries in the British Atlantic World*. Cambridge, Mass.: Harvard University Press, 2013.

Anzaldúa, Gloria. *Borderlands/La Frontera: The New Mestiza*. 2nd ed. San Francisco: Aunt Lute Books, 1999.

Baker, Lee D. *From Savage to Negro: Anthropology and the Construction of Race, 1896–1954*. Berkeley: University of California Press, 1998.

Ballantyne, Tony. "Te Anu's Story: A Fragmentary History of Difference and Racialisation in Southern New Zealand." In *Rethinking the Racial Moment: Essays on the Colonial Encounter*, edited by Alison Holland and Barbara Brookes, 49–73. Newcastle upon Tyne, U.K.: Cambridge Scholars, 2011.

Ballard, Chris. "'Oceanic Negroes': British Anthropology of Papuans, 1820–1869." In *Foreign Bodies: Oceania and the Science of Race, 1750–1940*, ed. Bronwen Douglas and Chris Ballard, 157–201. Canberra, Australia: ANU E Press 2008.

Banner, Stuart. *Possessing the Pacific: Land, Settlers, and Indigenous People from Australia to Alaska*. Cambridge, Mass.: Harvard University Press, 2007.

Barsh, Russel Lawrence. "'Colored' Seamen in the New England Whaling Industry: An Afro-Indian Consortium." In *Confounding the Color Line: The Indian-Black Experience in North America*, edited by James F. Brooks, 76–107. Lincoln: University of Nebraska Press, 2002.

Basson, Lauren L. *White Enough to Be American? Race Mixing, Indigenous People, and the Boundaries of State and Nation*. Chapel Hill: University of North Carolina Press, 2008.

Bell, Leonard. "Augustus Earle's *The Meeting of the Artist and the Wounded Chief Hongi, Bay of Islands, New Zealand, 1827*, and His Depictions of Other New Zealand Encounters: Contexts and Connections." In *Voyages and Beaches: Pacific Encounters, 1769–1840*, edited by Alex Calder, Jonathan Lamb, and Bridget Orr, 241–64. Honolulu: University of Hawai'i Press, 1999.

Bentley, Trevor. *Pakeha Maori: The Extraordinary Story of the Europeans Who Lived as Maori in Early New Zealand*. Auckland, New Zealand: Penguin, 1999.

Berkhofer, Robert F., Jr. *The White Man's Indian: Images of the American Indian from Columbus to the Present*. New York: Alfred A. Knopf, 1978.

Binney, Judith. "'In-Between' Lives: Studies from within a Colonial Society." In *Disputed Histories: Imagining New Zealand's Pasts*, edited by Tony Ballantyne and Brian Moloughney, 93–117. Dunedin, New Zealand: Otago University Press, 2006.

Blum, Hester. *The View from the Masthead: Maritime Imagination and Antebellum American Sea Narratives*. Chapel Hill: University of North Carolina Press, 2008.

Bockstoce, John R. *Whales, Ice, and Men: The History of Whaling in the Western Arctic*. 2nd ed. Seattle: University of Washington Press, 1995.

Boissevain, Ethel. "The Detribalization of the Narragansett Indians: A Case Study." *Ethnohistory* 3 (Summer 1956): 225–45.

Bolster, W. Jeffrey. *Black Jacks: African American Seamen in the Age of Sail*. Cambridge, Mass.: Harvard University Press, 1997.

Bradburn, Douglas. *The Citizenship Revolution: Politics and the Creation of the American Union, 1774–1804*. Charlottesville: University of Virginia Press, 2009.

Braginton-Smith, John, and Duncan Oliver. *Cape Cod Shore Whaling: America's First Whalemen*. Charleston, S.C.: History Press, 2008.

Breen, T. H. *Imagining the Past: East Hampton Histories*. Athens: University of Georgia Press, 1995.

Brown, Barbara W., and James M. Rose. *Black Roots in Southeastern Connecticut, 1650–1900*. Detroit: Gale Research, 1980.

Brown, Stanley. *Men from under the Sky: The Arrival of Westerners in Fiji*. Rutland, Vt.: Charles E. Tuttle, 1973.

Busch, Briton Cooper. *"Whaling Will Never Do for Me": The American Whaleman in the Nineteenth Century*. Lexington: University Press of Kentucky, 1994.

Calloway, Colin G., ed. *After King Philip's War: Presence and Persistence in Indian New England*. Hanover, N.H.: University Press of New England, 1997.

Camino, Mercedes Marota. *Exploring the Explorers: Spaniards in Oceania, 1519–1794*. Manchester, U.K.: Manchester University Press, 2008.

Campbell, I. C. *"Gone Native" in Polynesia: Captivity Narratives and Experiences from the South Pacific*. Westport, Conn.: Greenwood Press, 1998.

Cash, Floris Barnett. "African American Whalers: Images and Reality." *Long Island Historical Journal* 2 (Fall 1989): 41–52.

Cesarini, J. Patrick. "Sources and Interpretations: John Eliot's 'A Breif History of the Mashepog Indians,' 1666." *William and Mary Quarterly*. 3rd ser. 65 (Jan. 2008): 101–34.

Chappell, David A. *Double Ghosts: Oceanian Voyagers on Euroamerican Ships*. Armonk, N.Y.: M. E. Sharpe, 1997.

——. "Shipboard Relations between Pacific Island Women and Euroamerican Men, 1767–1887." *Journal of Pacific History* 27 (Dec. 1992): 131–49.

Christie, John. *History of Waikouaiti*. 2nd ed. Christchurch, New Zealand: Christchurch Press Company, 1929.

Christopher, Emma. *Slave Ship Sailors and Their Captive Cargoes, 1730–1807*. Cambridge, U.K.: Cambridge University Press, 2006.

Church, Ian. *Karitane by the Sea: Whalers, Traders and Fishermen.* Port Chalmers, New Zealand: Ian Church, 2010.

"Church Records of Preston, Connecticut." *New England Historical and Genealogical Register* 45 (Jan. 1891): 24–27.

Clark, Geoffrey, ed. "Dumont D'Urville's Divisions of Oceania: Fundamental Precincts or Arbitrary Constructs?" *Journal of Pacific History.* Special Issue. 38 (Sept. 2003).

Clark, Geoffrey. "Dumont d'Urville's Oceania." *Journal of Pacific History* 38 (Sept. 2003): 155–61.

Colley, Linda. *Captives.* New York: Pantheon Books, 2002.

Cramer, Renée Ann. *Cash, Color, and Colonialism: The Politics of Tribal Acknowledgment.* Norman: University of Oklahoma Press, 2005.

Creighton, Margaret S. "Davy Jones' Locker Room: Gender and the American Whaleman, 1830–1870." In *Iron Men, Wooden Women: Gender and Seafaring in the Atlantic World, 1700–1920,* edited by Margaret S. Creighton and Lisa Norling, 118–37. Baltimore: Johns Hopkins University Press, 1996.

———. *Rites and Passages: The Experience of American Whaling, 1830–1870.* New York: Cambridge University Press, 1995.

Davis, Lance E., Robert E. Gallman, and Karin Gleiter. *In Pursuit of Leviathan: Technology, Institutions, Productivity, and Profits in American Whaling, 1816–1906.* Chicago: University of Chicago Press, 1997.

Degler, Carl N. *Neither Black nor White: Slavery and Race Relations in Brazil and the United States.* New York: Macmillan, 1971.

Deloria, Philip J. *Indians in Unexpected Places.* Lawrence: University Press of Kansas, 2004.

Demos, John. *The Heathen School: A Story of Hope and Betrayal in the Age of the Early Republic.* New York: Alfred A. Knopf, 2014.

Dening, Greg. *Islands and Beaches: Discourse on a Silent Land, Marquesas, 1774–1880.* Chicago: Dorsey Press, 1980.

Derrick, R. A. *A History of Fiji.* Vol. 1. Rev. ed. 1950; reprint, Suva, Fiji: Government Press, 2001.

Deyo, Simeon L., ed. *History of Barnstable County, Massachusetts.* New York: H. W. Blake, 1890.

Diamond, Marion. "Queequeg's Crewmates: Pacific Islanders in the European Shipping Industry." *International Journal of Maritime History* 1 (Dec. 1989): 123–40.

Dippie, Brian W. *The Vanishing American: White Attitudes and U.S. Indian Policy.* Middletown, Conn.: Wesleyan University Press, 1982.

Dodge, Ernest S. *Islands and Empires: Western Impact on the Pacific and East Asia.* Minneapolis: University of Minnesota Press, 1976.

Dolin, Eric Jay. *Leviathan: The History of Whaling in America.* New York: W. W. Norton, 2007.

Dominguez, Virginia R. "Exporting U.S. Concepts of Race: Are There Limits to the U.S. Model?" *Social Research* 65 (Summer 1998): 369–99.

Dorrance, John C. "John Brown Williams and the American Claims in Fiji." Thesis, University of Hawaii, 1966. microfilm rl. 27. Pacific Manuscripts Bureau. Australian National University.

Douglas, Bronwen. *"Novus Orbis Australis"*: Oceania in the Science of Race, 1750–1850." In *Foreign Bodies: Oceania and the Science of Race, 1750–1940*, edited by Bronwen Douglas and Chris Ballard, 99–155. Canberra, Australia: ANU E Press, 2008.

——. "Slippery Word, Ambiguous Praxis: 'Race' and Late-18th-Century Voyagers in Oceania." *Journal of Pacific History* 41 (June 2006): 1–29.

Druett, Joan. *Hen Frigates: Wives of Merchant Captains under Sail.* New York: Simon & Schuster, 1998.

——. *In the Wake of Madness: The Murderous Voyage of the Whaleship Sharon.* Chapel Hill, N.C.: Algonquin Books, 2003.

Dunmore, John. *Storms and Dreams: The Life of Louis de Bougainville.* Fairbanks: University of Alaska Press, 2007.

——. *Visions & Realities: France in the Pacific, 1695–1995.* Waikanae, New Zealand: Heritage Press, 1997.

Edmond, Rod. *Representing the South Pacific: Colonial Discourse from Cook to Gauguin.* New York: Cambridge University Press, 1997.

Ellingson, Ter. *The Myth of the Noble Savage.* Berkeley: University of California Press, 2001.

Ellis, Richard. *Men and Whales.* New York: Alfred A. Knopf, 1991.

Entwisle, Peter. *Behold the Moon: The European Occupation of the Dunedin District, 1770–1848.* Dunedin, New Zealand: Port Daniel Press, 1998.

Evison, Harry C. *The Ngai Tahu Deeds: A Window on New Zealand History.* Christchurch, New Zealand: Canterbury University Press, 2006.

——. *Te Wai Pounamu, the Greenstone Island: A History of the Southern Maori during the European Colonization of New Zealand.* Christchurch, New Zealand: Aoraki Press, 1993.

Fabian, Ann. *The Skull Collectors: Race, Science, and America's Unburied Dead.* Chicago: University of Chicago Press, 2010.

Farr, James. "A Slow Boat to Nowhere: The Multi-Racial Crews of the American Whaling Industry." *Journal of Negro History* 68 (Spring 1983): 159–70.

Fisher, Linford D. *The Indian Great Awakening: Religion and the Shaping of Native Cultures in Early America.* New York: Oxford University Press, 2012.

Forbes, Jack D. *Africans and Native Americans: The Language of Race and the Evolution of Red-Black Peoples.* Urbana-Champaign: University of Illinois Press, 1993.

Forster, Honore, ed. *More South Sea Whaling: A Supplement to the South Sea Whaler, an Annotated Bibliography of Published Historical, Literary, and Art Material Related to Whaling in the Pacific Ocean in the Nineteenth Century.* Canberra: Research School of Pacific Studies, Australian National University, 1991.

——. *The South Sea Whaler: An Annotated Bibliography of Published Historical, Literary and Art Material Relating to Whaling in the Pacific Ocean in the Nineteenth Century.* Sharon, Mass.: Kendall Whaling Museum, 1985.

France, Peter. *The Charter of the Land: Custom and Colonization in Fiji*. Melbourne: Oxford University Press, 1969.

Frank, Stuart M. *Dictionary of Scrimshaw Artists*. Mystic, Conn.: Mystic Seaport Museum, 1991.

Fredrickson, George M. *White Supremacy: A Comparative Study in American and South African History*. New York: Oxford University Press, 1981.

Fullagar, Kate. *The Savage Visit: New World People and Popular Imperial Culture in Britain, 1710–1795*. Berkeley: University of California Press, 2012.

Geiger, Jeffrey. *Facing the Pacific: Polynesia and the U.S. Imperial Imagination*. Honolulu: University of Hawai'i Press, 2007.

Geoffrey, Theodate. *Suckanesset, Wherein May Be Read a History of Falmouth, Massachusetts*. 1930; reprint, West Barnstable, Mass.: Falmouth Historical Society, 1992.

Gibson, Arrell Morgan. *Yankees in Paradise: The Pacific Basin Frontier*. With John S. Whitehead. Albuquerque: University of New Mexico Press, 1993.

Gibson, Gregory. *Demon of the Waters: The True Story of the Mutiny on the Whaleship Globe*. Boston: Little, Brown, 2002.

Gilje, Paul A. *Liberty on the Waterfront: American Maritime Culture in the Age of Revolution*. Philadelphia: University of Pennsylvania Press, 2004.

Glenn, Myra C. *Campaigns against Corporal Punishment: Prisoners, Sailors, Women, and Children in Antebellum America*. Albany: State University of New York Press, 1984.

———. *Jack Tar's Story: The Autobiographies and Memoirs of Sailors in Antebellum America*. New York: Cambridge University Press, 2010.

Grandin, Greg. *The Empire of Necessity: Slavery, Freedom, and Deception in the New World*. New York: Henry Holt, 2014.

Gray, Edward G. *The Making of John Ledyard: Empire and Ambition in the Life of an Early American Traveler*. New Haven, Conn.: Yale University Press, 2007.

Greer, Richard A. "Trouble on the Waterfront." *Hawaiian Journal of History* 22 (1988): 20–32.

Gross, Ariela J. *What Blood Won't Tell: A History of Race on Trial in America*. Cambridge, Mass.: Harvard University Press, 2008.

Grover, Kathryn. *The Fugitive's Gibraltar: Escaping Slaves and Abolitionism in New Bedford, Massachusetts*. Amherst: University of Massachusetts Press, 2001.

Hagan, William T. "Squaw Men on the Kiowa, Comanche, and Apache Reservation: Advance Agents of Civilization or Disturbers of the Peace?" In *The Frontier Challenge: Responses to the Trans-Mississippi West*, edited by John G. Clark, 171–202. Lawrence: University Press of Kansas, 1971.

Haines, David. "In Search of the 'Whaheen': Ngai Tahu Women, Shore Whalers, and the Meaning of Sex in Early New Zealand." In *Moving Subjects Gender, Mobility, and Intimacy in an Age of Global Empire*, edited by Tony Ballantyne and Antoinette M. Burton, 49–66. Urbana: University of Illinois Press, 2009.

Harmon, Alexandra. *Rich Indians: Native People and the Problem of Wealth in American History*. Chapel Hill: University of North Carolina Press, 2010.

Hau'ofa, Epeli. "Our Sea of Islands." In *A New Oceania: Rediscovering Our Sea of Islands*, edited by Eric Waddell, Vijay Naidu, and Epeli Hau'ofa, 2–16. Suva, Fiji: School of Social and Economic Development, University of the South Pacific in association with Beake House, 1993.

Hawaiian Mission Children's Society. *Missionary Album: Portraits and Biographical Sketches of the American Protestant Missionaries to the Hawaiian Islands*. Enlarged ed. Honolulu: Hawaiian Mission Children's Society, 1969.

Heartfield, James. *The Aborigines' Protection Society: Humanitarian Imperialism in Australia, New Zealand, Fiji, Canada, South Africa, and the Congo, 1836–1909*. New York: Columbia University Press, 2011.

Heffernan, Thomas Farel. *Mutiny on the Globe: The Fatal Voyage of Samuel Comstock*. New York: Penguin, 2003.

Heflin, Wilson. *Herman Melville's Whaling Years*. Edited by Mary K. Bercaw Edwards and Thomas Farel Heffernan. Nashville: Vanderbilt University Press, 2004.

Herbert, T. Walter, Jr. *Marquesan Encounters: Melville and the Meaning of Civilization*. Cambridge, Mass.: Harvard University Press, 1980.

Herndon, Ruth Wallis. *Unwelcome Americans: Living on the Margin in Early New England*. Philadelphia: University of Pennsylvania Press, 2001.

Herndon, Ruth Wallis, and Ella Wilcox Sekatau. "The Right to a Name: The Narragansett People and Rhode Island Officials in the Revolutionary Era." In *After King Philip's War, Presence and Persistence in Indian New England*, edited by Colin G. Calloway, 114–43. Hanover, N.H.: University Press of New England, 1997.

Hiroa, Te Rangi (Peter H. Buck). *Explorers of the Pacific: European and American Discoveries in Polynesia*. Honolulu: Bishop Museum, 1953.

Hodes, Martha. "Fractions and Fictions in the United States Census of 1890." In *Haunted by Empire: Geographies of Intimacy in North American History*, edited by Ann Laura Stoler, 240–70. Durham, N.C.: Duke University Press, 2006.

———. "The Mercurial Nature and Abiding Power of Race: A Transnational Family Story." *American Historical Review* 108 (Feb. 2003): 84–118.

———. *The Sea Captain's Wife: A True Story of Love, Race, and War in the Nineteenth Century*. New York: W. W. Norton, 2006.

Hohman, Elmo Paul. *The American Whaleman: A Study of Life and Labor in the Whaling Industry*. 1928; reprint, London: MacDonald and Jane's, 1974.

Huntington, Gale. *Songs the Whalemen Sang*. 3rd ed. Mystic, Conn.: Mystic Seaport, 2005.

Hutchins, Francis G. *Mashpee: The Story of Cape Cod's Indian Town*. West Franklin, N.H.: Amarta Press, 1979.

Igler, David. *The Great Ocean: Pacific Worlds from Captain Cook to the Gold Rush*. New York: Oxford University Press, 2013.

Ignatiev, Noel. *How the Irish Became White*. New York: Routledge, 1995.

Jacobson, Matthew Frye. *Whiteness of a Different Color: European Immigrants and the Alchemy of Race*. Cambridge, Mass.: Harvard University Press, 1998.

"John Douglas Bemo." *The Church at Home and Abroad* 9 (1891): 329–30.

Johnson, Donald D. *The United States in the Pacific: Private Interests and Public Policies, 1784–1899.* With Gary Dean Best. Westport, Conn.: Praeger, 1995.

Johnson, Robert Erwin. *Thence Round Cape Horn: The Story of United States Naval Forces on Pacific Station, 1818–1923.* Annapolis: United States Naval Institute, 1963.

Jolly, Margaret. "Imagining Oceania: Indigenous and Foreign Representations of a Sea of Islands." *Contemporary Pacific* 19 (Fall 2007): 508–45.

Jones, Jane. "The Purchase of the Southern Blocks: Changing Colonial Attitudes towards Land and Māori." In *When the Waves Rolled in upon Us: Essays in Nineteenth-Century Māori History,* edited by Michael Reilly and Jane Thomson, 54–74, 194–96. Dunedin, New Zealand: University of Otago Press, 1999.

Joyce, Barry Alan. *The Shaping of American Ethnography: The Wilkes Exploring Expedition, 1838–1842.* Lincoln: University of Nebraska Press, 2001.

Kame'eleihiwa, Lilikalā. *Native Land and Foreign Desires: Pehea LA E Pono Ai? How Shall We Live in Harmony?* Honolulu: Bishop Museum Press, 1992.

Kaplan, Sidney. *American Studies in Black and White: Selected Essays, 1949–1989.* Amherst: University of Massachusetts Press, 1996.

Kardell, Caroline Lewis, and Russell A. Lovell. *Vital Records of Sandwich, Massachusetts to 1885.* 3 vols. Boston: New England Historic Genealogical Society, 1996.

Karttunen, Frances Ruley. *The Other Islanders: People Who Pulled Nantucket's Oars.* New Bedford, Mass.: Spinner Publications, 2005.

Kashay, Jennifer Fish. "Competing Imperialisms and Hawaiian Authority: The Cannonading of Lāhainā in 1827." *Pacific Historical Review* 77 (Aug. 2008): 369–90.

Kelly, John D. "Gordon Was No Amateur: Imperial Legal Strategies in the Colonization of Fiji." In *Law & Empire in the Pacific: Fiji and Hawai'i,* edited by Sally Engle Merry and Donald Brenneis, 61–100. Santa Fe, N.M.: School of American Research Press, 2003.

Kettner, James H. *The Development of American Citizenship, 1608–1870.* Chapel Hill: University of North Carolina Press, 1978.

King, C. Richard. "De/Scribing Squ*w: Indigenous Women and Imperial Idioms in the United States." *American Indian Culture and Research Journal* 27, no. 2 (2003): 1–16.

Kugler, Richard C. *William Allen Wall: An Artist of New Bedford.* New Bedford, Mass.: Trustees of the Old Dartmouth Historical Society, 1978.

Kuykendall, Ralph S. *The Hawaiian Kingdom.* Vol. 1. *Foundation and Transformation, 1778–1854.* 1938; reprint, Honolulu: University of Hawai'i Press, 1968.

Kverndal, Roald. *Seamen's Missions, Their Origin and Early Growth: A Contribution to the History of the Church Maritime.* Pasadena, Calif.: William Carey Library, 1986.

Lake, Marilyn, and Henry Reynolds. *Drawing the Global Colour Line: White Men's Countries and the International Challenge of Racial Equality.* Cambridge: Cambridge University Press, 2008.

Langdon, Robert. *Where the Whalers Went: An Index to the Pacific Ports and Islands Visited by American Whalers (and Some Other Ships) in the 19th Century*. Canberra: Pacific Manuscripts Bureau, Australian National University, 1984.

Leavitt, John F. *The Charles W. Morgan*. Mystic, Conn.: Mystic Seaport Museum, 1998.

Lebo, Susan A. "Native Hawaiian Seamen's Accounts of the 1876 Arctic Whaling Disaster and the 1877 Massacre of Alaskan Natives from Cape Prince of Wales." *Hawaiian Journal of History* 40 (2006): 99–129.

———. "Native Hawaiian Whalers in Nantucket, 1820–60." *Historic Nantucket* 56 (Winter 2007): 14–16.

———. "Two Hawaiian Documents Shed New Light on the Loss of Nineteen Native Hawaiian Seamen aboard the Hawaiian Whaling Barque *Desmond*." *International Journal of Maritime History* 18 (Dec. 2006): 257–81.

Legge, J. D. *Britain in Fiji, 1858–1880*. New York: St. Martin's Press, 1958.

Lepore, Jill. *The Name of War: King Philip's War and the Origins of American Identity*. New York: Knopf, 1998.

Levy, Barry. *Town Born: The Political Economy of New England from Its Founding to the Revolution*. Philadelphia: University of Pennsylvania Press, 2009.

Linebaugh, Peter, and Marcus Rediker. *The Many-Headed Hydra: Sailors, Slaves, Commoners, and the Hidden History of the Revolutionary Atlantic*. Boston: Beacon Press, 2000.

Little, Elizabeth A. "The Female Sailor on the Christopher Mitchell: Fact and Fantasy." *American Neptune* 54 (Fall 1994): 252–56.

———. "The Indian Contribution to Along-Shore Whaling at Nantucket." *Nantucket Algonquian Studies* 8 (1981).

———. "The Indian Sickness at Nantucket, 1763–1764." *Nantucket Algonquian Studies* 11 (1988).

López, Ian F. Haney. *White by Law: The Legal Construction of Race*. New York: New York University Press, 1996.

Lund, Judith Navas. *Whaling Masters and Whaling Voyages Sailing from American Ports: A Compilation of Sources*. Gloucester, Mass.: Ten Pound Island Book Co., 2001.

Lyons, Paul. *American Pacificism: Oceania in the U.S. Imagination*. New York: Routledge, 2006.

Malloy, Mary. "The Sailor's Fantasy: Images of Women in the Songs of American Whalemen." *Log of Mystic Seaport* 49 (Autumn 1997): 34–43.

Mancini, Jason R. "Beyond Reservation: Indians, Maritime Labor, and Communities of Color from Eastern Long Island Sound, 1713–1861." In *Perspectives on Gender, Race, Ethnicity, and Power in Maritime America: Papers from the Conference Held at Mystic Seaport, September 2006*, edited by Glenn S. Gordinier, 23–44. Mystic, Conn.: Mystic Seaport Museum, 2008.

Mandell, Daniel R. *Behind the Frontier: Indians in Eighteenth-Century Eastern Massachusetts*. Lincoln: University of Nebraska Press, 1996.

———. "The Saga of Sarah Muckamugg: Indian and African American Intermarriage in Colonial New England." In *Sex, Love, Race: Crossing Boundaries in North American History*, edited by Martha Hodes, 72–90. New York: New York University Press, 1999.

———. *Tribe, Race, History: Native Americans in Southern New England, 1780–1880*. Baltimore: Johns Hopkins University Press, 2008.

Maude, H. E. *Of Islands and Men: Studies in Pacific History*. Melbourne: Oxford University Press, 1968.

McCormick, E. H. *Omai: Pacific Envoy*. Auckland, New Zealand: University of Auckland Press, 1977.

McIntyre, W. D. "Anglo-American Rivalry in the Pacific: The British Annexation of the Fiji Islands in 1874." *Pacific Historical Review* 29 (Nov. 1960): 361–380.

McNab, Robert. *The Old Whaling Days: A History of Southern New Zealand from 1830 to 1840*. 1913; reprint, Auckland, New Zealand: Golden Press, 1975.

Mehta, Uday Singh. "The Essential Ambiguities of Race and Racism." *Political Power and Social Theory* 11 (1997): 235–46.

Melish, Joanne Pope. "A Racial Vernacular: Contesting the Black/White Dyad in 19th-Century New England." In *Race, Nation, and Empire in American History*, edited by James T. Campbell, Matthew Guterl, and Robert G. Lee, 17–39. Chapel Hill: University of North Carolina Press, 2007.

Mielke, Laura L. *Moving Encounters: Sympathy and the Indian Question in Antebellum Literature*. Amherst: University of Massachusetts Press, 2008.

Moment, David. "The Business of Whaling in America in the 1850's." *Business History Review* 31 (Autumn 1957): 261–91.

Morison, Samuel Eliot. *The Maritime History of Massachusetts, 1783–1860*. Boston: Houghton Mifflin, 1921.

Morton, Harry. *The Whale's Wake*. Honolulu: University of Hawai'i Press, 1982.

New Bedford Whaling Museum. "New Bedford: The City That Lit the World" [poster map]. New Bedford, Mass.: New Bedford Whaling Museum, 2012.

New England Historic Genealogical Society. *Vital Records of Chilmark, Massachusetts, to the Year 1850*. Boston: New England Historic Genealogical Society, 1904.

———. *Vital Records of Edgartown, Massachusetts, to the Year 1850*. Boston: New England Historic Genealogical Society, 1906.

———. *Vital Records of New Bedford, Massachusetts to the Year 1850*. 3 vols. Boston: New England Historic Genealogical Society, 1932–1941.

———. *Vital Records of Tisbury, Massachusetts, to the Year 1850*. Boston: New England Historic Genealogical Society, 1910.

New Zealand Parliament. *Appendix to the Journals of the House of Representatives*. Wellington, New Zealand: Government Printer, 1858–1899.

Nicholas, Mark A. "Mashpee Wampanoags of Cape Cod, the Whalefishery, and Seafaring's Impact on Community Development." *American Indian Quarterly* 26 (Spring 2002): 165–97.

Nightingale, Carl H. "Before Race Mattered: Geographies of the Color Line in Early Colonial Madras and New York." *American Historical Review* 113 (Feb. 2008): 48–71.

Nobles, Melissa. *Shades of Citizenship: Race and the Census in Modern Politics.* Stanford, Calif.: Stanford University Press, 2000.

Norling, Lisa. *Captain Ahab Had a Wife: New England Women & the Whalefishery, 1720-1870.* Chapel Hill: University of North Carolina Press, 2000.

O'Brien, Jean M. *Dispossession by Degrees: Indian Land and Identity in Natick, Massachusetts, 1650-1790.* New York: Cambridge University Press, 1997.

———. *Firsting and Lasting: Writing Indians out of Existence in New England.* Minneapolis: University of Minnesota Press, 2010.

Omi, Michael and Howard Winant. *Racial Formation in the United States: From the 1960s to the 1990s.* 2nd ed. New York: Routledge, 1994.

Orange, Claudia. *The Treaty of Waitangi.* Wellington, New Zealand: Allen & Unwin, 1987.

Pálsson, Gísli. "Race and the Intimate in Arctic Exploration." *Ethnos* 69 (Sept. 2004): 363–86.

Pascoe, Peggy. *What Comes Naturally: Miscegenation Law and the Making of Race in America.* New York: Oxford University Press, 2009.

Paterson, Lachy. "*Hāwhekaihe*: Māori Voices on the Position of 'Half-Castes' within Māori Society." *Journal of New Zealand Studies* 9 (2010): 135–56.

Pearce, Roy Harvey. *Savagism and Civilization: A Study of the Indian and the American Mind.* Berkeley: University of California Press, 1988.

Philbrick, Nathaniel. *Abram's Eyes: The Native American Legacy of Nantucket Island.* Nantucket, Mass.: Mill Hill Press, 1998.

———. *Away off Shore: Nantucket Island and Its People, 1602-1890.* Nantucket, Mass.: Mill Hill Press, 1994.

———. *In the Heart of the Sea: The Tragedy of the Whaleship* Essex. N.Y.: Penguin Books, 2000.

———. *Sea of Glory: America's Voyage of Discovery, the U.S. Exploring Expedition, 1838-1842.* New York: Penguin, 2003.

Philbrick, Nathaniel, and Thomas Philbrick, eds. *The Loss of the Ship* Essex, *Sunk by a Whale: Thomas Nickerson, Owen Chase, and Others.* New York: Penguin Books, 2000.

Phillips, Clifton Jackson. *Protestant America and the Pagan World: The First Half Century of the American Board of Commissioners for Foreign Missions, 1810-1860.* Cambridge, Mass.: East Asian Research Center and Harvard University Press, 1969.

Pierce, R. Andrew. "Joseph Daggett of Martha's Vineyard, His Native American Wife, and Their Descendants." *New England Historical and Genealogical Register* 161 (Jan. 2007): 5–21.

Plane, Ann Marie. *Colonial Intimacies: Indian Marriage in Early New England.* Ithaca, N.Y.: Cornell University Press, 2000.

Plane, Ann Marie, and Gregory Button. "The Massachusetts Indian Enfranchisement Act: Ethnic Contest in Historical Context, 1849-1869." In *After King Philip's War: Presence and Persistence in Indian New England,* edited by Colin G. Calloway, 178–206. Hanover, N.H.: University Press of New England, 1997.

Putney, Martha S. *Black Sailors: Afro-American Merchant Seamen and Whalemen prior to the Civil War*. New York: Greenwood Press, 1987.

Pybus, T. A. *Maori and Missionary: Early Christian Missions in the South Island of New Zealand*. Wellington, New Zealand: A. H. & A. W. Reed, 1954.

Quanchi, Max. *Atlas of the Pacific Islands*. Honolulu, Hawai'i: Bess Press, 2003.

Raffety, Matthew Taylor. *The Republic Afloat: Law, Honor, and Citizenship in Maritime America*. Chicago: University of Chicago Press, 2013.

Ralston, Caroline. "Changes in the Lives of Ordinary Women in Early Post-Contact Hawaii." In *Family and Gender in the Pacific: Domestic Contradictions and the Colonial Impact*, edited by Margaret Jolly and Martha MacIntyre, 45–64. New York: Cambridge University Press, 1989.

——. *Grass Huts and Warehouses: Pacific Beach Communities of the Nineteenth Century*. Honolulu: University Press of Hawai'i, 1978.

Rapito-Wyppensenwah, Philip. "Eighteenth & Nineteenth Century Native American Whaling of Eastern Long Island." In *The History & Archaeology of the Montauk*, edited by Gaynell Stone, 437–44. 2nd ed. Stony Brook, N.Y.: Suffolk County Archaeological Association and Nassau County Archaeological Committee, 1993.

Rediker, Marcus. *Between the Devil and the Deep Blue Sea: Merchant Seamen, Pirates, and the Anglo-American Maritime World, 1700–1750*. New York: Cambridge University Press, 1987.

——. *The Slave Ship: A Human History*. New York: Viking, 2007.

Reeves, Randall R., Jeffrey M. Breiwick, and Edward D. Mitchell. "History of Whaling and Estimated Kill of Right Whales, *Balaena glacialis*, in the Northeastern United States, 1620–1924." *Marine Fisheries Review* 61, no. 3 (1999): 1–36.

Richards, Rhys. *Murihiku Re-Viewed: A Revised History of Southern New Zealand from 1804 to 1844*. Wellington, New Zealand: Lithographic Services, 1995.

——. "On Using Pacific Shipping Records to Gain New Insights into Culture Contact in Polynesia before 1840." *Journal of Pacific History* 43 (2008): 375–82.

Ricketson, Daniel. *The History of New Bedford, Bristol County, Massachusetts: Including a History of the Old Township of Dartmouth and the Present Townships of Westport, Dartmouth, and Fairhaven, from Their Settlement to the Present Time*. New Bedford, Mass.: Daniel Ricketson, 1858.

Riles, Annelise. "Division within the Boundaries." *Journal of the Royal Anthropological Institute* 4 (Sept. 1998): 409–24.

——. "Law as Object." In *Law and Empire in the Pacific: Fiji and Hawai'i*, edited by Sally Merry and Donald Brenneis, 187–212. Santa Fe, N.M.: School of American Research Press, 2003.

Rockman, Seth. *Scraping By: Wage Labor, Slavery, and Survival in Early Baltimore*. Baltimore: Johns Hopkins University Press, 2009.

Rodríguez, Clara E. *Changing Race: Latinos, the Census, and the History of Ethnicity in the United States*. New York: New York University Press, 2000.

Roediger, David R. *The Wages of Whiteness: Race and the Making of the American Working Class*. New ed. New York: Verso, 2007.

————. *Working toward Whiteness: How America's Immigrants Became White: The Strange Journey from Ellis Island to the Suburbs*. New York: Basic Books, 2005.

Rosen, Deborah A. *American Indians and State Law: Sovereignty, Race, and Citizenship, 1790–1880*. Lincoln: University of Nebraska Press, 2007.

Ross, W. Gillies. *Whaling and Eskimos: Hudson Bay, 1860–1915*. Ottawa, Canada: National Museum of Man, 1975.

Rouleau, Brian J. "Maritime Destiny as Manifest Destiny: American Commercial Expansionism and the Idea of the Indian." *Journal of the Early Republic* 30 (Fall 2010): 377–411.

Routledge, David. *Matanitū: The Struggle for Power in Early Fiji*. Suva, Fiji: University of the South Pacific, 1985.

Rubertone, Patricia E. *Grave Undertakings: An Archaeology of Roger Williams and the Narragansett Indians*. Washington, D.C.: Smithsonian Institution, 2001.

Russell, Lynette. "'A New Holland Half-Caste': Sealer and Whaler Tommy Chaseland." *History Australia* 5, no. 1 (2008): 1–15.

Ryan, Tom. "'Le Président des Terres Australes': Charles de Brosses and the French Enlightenment Beginnings of Oceanic Anthropology." *Journal of Pacific History* 37 (Sept. 2002): 157–86.

Sahlins, Marshall. *Anahulu: The Anthropology of History in the Kingdom of Hawaii*. Vol. 1. *Historical Ethnography*. With the assistance of Dorothy B. Barrère. Chicago: University of Chicago Press, 1992.

Salesa, Damon Ieremia. *Racial Crossings: Race, Intermarriage, and the Victorian British Empire*. New York: Oxford University Press, 2011.

————. "Samoa's Half-Castes and Some Frontiers of Comparison." In *Haunted by Empire: Geographies of Intimacy in North American History*, edited by Ann Laura Stoler, 71–93. Durham, N.C.: Duke University Press, 2006.

Salmond, Anne. *Aphrodite's Island: The European Discovery of Tahiti*. Berkeley: University of California Press, 2009.

Sánchez-Eppler, Karen. "Copying and Conversion: An 1824 Friendship Album 'from a Chinese Youth.'" *American Quarterly* 59 (June 2007): 301–39.

Schell, Jennifer. *"A Bold and Hardy Race of Men": The Lives and Literature of American Whalemen*. Amherst: University of Massachusetts Press, 2013.

Schmitt, Robert C. "Early Crime Statistics of Hawaii." *Hawaii Historical Review* 2 (July 1966): 325–32.

Schodt, Frederik L. *Native American in the Land of the Shogun: Ranald MacDonald and the Opening of Japan*. Berkeley, Calif.: Stone Bridge Press, 2003.

Scruggs, Marc. "Anthony D. Allen: A Prosperous American of African Descent in Early 19th Century Hawai'i." *Hawaiian Journal of History* 26 (1992): 55–93.

Seed, Patricia. *Ceremonies of Possession in Europe's Conquest of the New World, 1492–1640*. New York: Cambridge University Press, 1995.

Segel, Jerome D., and R. Andrew Pierce. *The Wampanoag Genealogical History of Martha's Vineyard, Massachusetts*. Vol. 1. Rev. ed. Baltimore: Genealogical Publishing, 2003.

Shannon, Timothy J. "Queequeg's Tomahawk: A Cultural Biography, 1750–1900." *Ethnohistory* 52 (Summer 2005): 589–633.

Sherman, Stuart C. *The Voice of the Whaleman, with an Account of the Nicholson Whaling Collection*. Providence: Providence Public Library, 1965.

Sherman, Stuart C., Judith M. Downey, Virginia M. Adams, and Howard Pasternack. *Whaling Logbooks and Journals, 1613–1927: An Inventory of Manuscript Records in Public Collections*. New York: Garland, 1986.

Shoemaker, Nancy, ed. *Living with Whales: Documents and Oral Histories of Native New England Whaling History*. Amherst: University of Massachusetts Press, 2014.

———. "Mr. Tashtego: Native American Whalemen in the Antebellum Period." *Journal of the Early Republic* 33 (Spring 2013): 109–32.

———. "Race and Indigeneity in the Life of Elisha Apes." *Ethnohistory* 60 (Winter 2013): 27–50.

Silverman, David J. *Faith and Boundaries: Colonists, Christianity, and Community among the Wampanoag Indians of Martha's Vineyard, 1600–1871*. New York: Cambridge University Press, 2005.

———. "The Impact of Indentured Servitude on the Society and Culture of Southern New England Indians, 1680–1810." *New England Quarterly* 74 (Dec. 2001): 622–66.

Sluby, Paul E. *The Family Recollections of Beulah A. Shippen and Mabel S (Shippen) Hatcher*. Long Island, N.Y.: B. A. Shippen, 1994.

Smedley, Audrey. *Race in North America: Origin and Evolution of a Worldview*. 3rd ed. Boulder, Colo.: Westview Press, 2007.

Smith, Bernard. *Imagining the Pacific: In the Wake of the Cook Voyages*. New Haven, Conn.: Yale University Press, 1992.

Smits, David D. "The 'Squaw Drudge': A Prime Index of Savagism." *Ethnohistory* 29 (Fall 1982): 281–306.

Spicer, Edward H. *Cycles of Conquest: The Impact of Spain, Mexico, and the United States on the Indians of the Southwest, 1533–1960*. Tucson: University of Arizona Press, 1962.

Spoehr, Anne Harding. "George Prince Tamoree: Heir Apparent of Kauai and Niihau." *Hawaiian Journal of History* 15 (1981): 31–49.

Springer, Haskell. "The Captain's Wife at Sea." In *Iron Men, Wooden Women: Gender and Seafaring in the Atlantic World, 1700–1920*, edited by Margaret S. Creighton and Lisa Norling, 92–117. Baltimore: Johns Hopkins University Press, 1996.

Stackpole, Edouard A. *The Sea-Hunters: The New England Whalemen during Two Centuries, 1635–1835*. Philadelphia: J. B. Lippincott, 1953.

———. "The Story of David Whippey of Nantucket." *Historic Nantucket* 34 (July 1986): 16–20.

Starbuck, Alexander. *History of the American Whale Fishery*. 1878; reprint, Secaucus, N.J.: Castle Books, 1989.

Stein, Douglas L. *American Maritime Documents, 1775–1860, Illustrated and Described*. Mystic, Conn.: Mystic Seaport Museum, 1992.

Stepan, Nancy. *The Idea of Race in Science: Great Britain, 1800–1960*. Hamden, Conn.: Archon, 1982.

Stevens, Laura M. *The Poor Indians: British Missionaries, Native Americans, and Colonial Sensibility*. Philadelphia: University of Pennsylvania Press, 2004.

Stoler, Ann Laura. "Racial Histories and Their Regimes of Truth." *Political Power and Social Theory* 11 (1997): 183–206.

Stone, Gaynell, ed. *The Shinnecock Indians: A Culture History*. Lexington, Mass.: Ginn Custom Publishing, 1983.

Strauss, W. Patrick. *Americans in Polynesia, 1783–1842*. East Lansing: Michigan State University Press, 1963.

Strong, John A. *The Algonquian Peoples of Long Island from Earliest Times to 1700*. Interlaken, N.Y.: Empire State Books, 1997.

———. *The Montaukett Indians of Eastern Long Island*. Syracuse, N.Y.: Syracuse University Press, 2001.

———. "The Pigskin Book: Records of Native American Whalemen." *Long Island Historical Journal* 3 (Fall 1990): 17–28.

———. "Shinnecock and Montauk Whalemen." *Long Island Historical Journal* 2 (Fall 1989): 29–40.

———. *The Unkechaug Indians of Eastern Long Island: A History*. Norman: University of Oklahoma Press, 2011.

Strong, Warren P., ed. "The Wharves of Plymouth." *Pilgrim Society Notes* 3 (15 Mar. 1955): 1–8.

Strong, William Ellsworth. *The Story of the American Board*. 1910; reprint, New York: Arno Press, 1969.

Sweet, John Wood. *Bodies Politic: Negotiating Race in the American North, 1730–1830*. Philadelphia: University of Pennsylvania Press, 2003.

Tcherkézoff, Serge. *"First Contacts" in Polynesia: The Samoan Case (1722–1848): Western Misunderstandings about Sexuality and Divinity*. Canterbury, New Zealand: MacMillan Brown Centre for Pacific Studies, 2004.

———. "A Long and Unfortunate Voyage towards the 'Invention' of the Melanesia/Polynesia Distinction, 1595–1832." *Journal of Pacific History* 38 (Sept. 2003): 175–96.

———. *Polynésie/Mélanésie: L'Invention Française des "Races" et des Régions de l'Océanie (XVIe–XXe Siècles)*. Tahiti: Au Vent Des Isles, 2008.

———. "A Reconsideration of the Role of Polynesian Women in Early Encounters with Europeans: Supplement to Marshall Sahlins' Voyage around the Islands of History." In *Oceanic Encounters: Exchange, Desire, Violence*, edited by Margaret Jolly, Serge Tcherkézoff, and Darrell Tryon, 113–59. Canberra, Australia: ANU E Press, 2009.

———. *Tahiti–1768, Jeune Filles en Pleurs: La Face Cachée des Premiers Contacts et la Naissance du Mythe Occidental*. Tahiti: Éditions Au Vent des Îles, 2004.

Tehranian, John. "Performing Whiteness: Naturalization Litigation and the Construction of Racial Identity in America." *Yale Law Journal* 109 (Jan. 2000): 817–48.

Tent, Jan, and Paul Geraghty. "Exploding Sky or Exploded Myth? The Origin of *Papalagi*," *Journal of the Polynesian Society* 110 (June 2001): 171–214.

Thomas, Lamont D. *Rise to Be a People: A Biography of Paul Cuffe*. Urbana: University of Illinois Press, 1986.

Thomas, Nicholas. *In Oceania: Visions, Artifacts, Histories*. Durham, N.C.: Duke University Press, 1997.

———. *Marquesan Societies: Inequality and Political Transformation in Eastern Polynesia*. Oxford, U.K.: Clarendon Press, 1990.

———. "'On the Varieties of the Human Species': Forster's Comparative Ethnology." In Johann Reinhold Forster, *Observations Made during a Voyage Round the World*, edited by Nicholas Thomas, Harriet Guest, and Michael Dettelbach, xxiii–xl. Honolulu: University of Hawai'i Press, 1996.

Tobin, Beth Fowkes. "Native Land and Foreign Desire: *William Penn's Treaty with the Indians*." *American Indian Culture and Research Journal* 19, no. 3 (1995): 87–119.

Tompkins, E. Berkeley. "Black Ahab: William T. Shorey, Whaling Master." *California Historical Quarterly* 51 (Spring 1972): 75–84.

Tønnessen, J. N., and A. O. Johnsen. *The History of Modern Whaling*. Translated by R. I. Christophersen. London: C. Hurst, 1982.

Tripp, William Henry. *"There Goes Flukes": The Story of New Bedford's Last Whaler*. New Bedford, Mass.: Reynolds Printing, 1938.

Tucker, Louis Leonard. *Clio's Consort: Jeremy Belknap and the Founding of the Massachusetts Historical Society*. Boston: Massachusetts Historical Society and Northeastern University Press, 1990.

U.S. Census Bureau. *Measuring America: The Decennial Censuses from 1790 to 2000*. Washington, D.C.: Government Printing Office, 2002.

U.S. National Archives Project. *Ship Registers of New Bedford, Massachusetts*. 3 vols. Boston: National Archives Project, 1940.

Usner, Daniel H., Jr. *Indian Work: Language and Livelihood in Native American History*. Cambridge, Mass.: Harvard University Press, 2009.

Vaughan, Alden T. *Transatlantic Encounters: American Indians in Britain, 1500–1776*. New York: Cambridge University Press, 2006.

Veracini, Lorenzo. *Settler Colonialism: A Theoretical Overview*. New York: Palgrave Macmillan, 2010.

Vickers, Daniel. *Farmers and Fishermen: Two Centuries of Work in Essex County, Massachusetts, 1630–1850*. Chapel Hill: University of North Carolina Press, 1994.

———. "The First Whalemen of Nantucket." *William and Mary Quarterly*. 3rd ser. 40 (Oct. 1983): 560–83.

———. "Nantucket Whalemen in the Deep-Sea Fishery: The Changing Anatomy of an Early American Labor Force." *Journal of American History* 72 (Sept. 1985): 277–96.

———. *Young Men and the Sea: Yankee Seafarers in the Age of Sail*. With Vince Walsh. New Haven, Conn.: Yale University Press, 2005.

Viola, Herman J., and Carolyn Margolis, eds. *Magnificent Voyagers: The U.S. Exploring Expedition, 1838–1842*. Washington, D.C.: Smithsonian Institution Press, 1985.

Wallace, Lee. *Sexual Encounters: Pacific Texts, Modern Sexualities*. Ithaca, N.Y.: Cornell University Press, 2003.

Wang, Lu-in. *Discrimination by Default: How Racism Becomes Routine*. New York: New York University Press, 2006.

Wanhalla, Angela. *In/visible Sight: The Mixed-Descent Families of Southern New Zealand*. Wellington, New Zealand: Bridget Williams Books, 2009.

Ward, Alan. *An Unsettled History: Treaty Claims in New Zealand Today*. Wellington, New Zealand: Bridget Williams Books, 1999.

Ward, R. Gerard. "Land Use and Land Alienation in Fiji to 1885." *Journal of Pacific History* 4 (1969): 3–25.

———. "The Pacific *Bêche-de-Mer* Trade with Special Reference to Fiji." In *Man in the Pacific Islands: Essays on Geographical Change in the Pacific Islands*, edited by R. Gerard Ward, 91–123. Oxford, U.K.: Clarendon Press, 1972.

Warrin, Donald. *So Ends This Day: The Portuguese in American Whaling, 1765–1927*. North Dartmouth: Center for Portuguese Studies and Culture, University of Massachusetts Dartmouth, 2010.

Weierman, Karen Woods. "'For the Better Government of Servants and Slaves': The Law of Slavery and Miscegenation." *Legal Studies Forum* 24, no. 1 (2000): 133–55.

Weintraub, Elaine Cawley. *Lighting the Trail: The African-American Heritage of Martha's Vineyard*. West Tisbury, Mass.: African American Heritage Trail History Project, 2005.

Wolfe, Patrick, "Land, Labor, and Difference: Elementary Structures of Race." *American Historical Review* 106 (June 2001): 866–905.

Wood, Virginia Steele. *Live Oaking: Southern Timber for Tall Ships*. Boston: Northeastern University Press, 1981.

Woods, Karen M. "A 'Wicked and Mischievous Connection': The Origins of Indian-White Miscegenation Law." *Legal Studies Forum* 23, nos. 1–2 (1999): 37–70.

Worth, Henry B. "Voyages of Ship 'Bartholomew Gosnold.'" *Old Dartmouth Historical Sketches* 44 (3 Apr. 1916): 11–12.

Young, John. *Adventurous Spirits: Australian Migrant Society in Pre-Cession Fiji*. St. Lucia, Australia: University of Queensland Press, 1984.

Index

Bristol, R.I., whaleships of, 114, 199

Brooks, John, 171

Brower, Charles, 52

Brower, Isaac Mills, 142–43

Brown, John, 114

Brown, Sarah, 26

Browne, J. Ross, 45

Bruce, W. H., 142

Bunn, David W., 72, 204

Bunn, Russell, 221 (n. 2)

Bunn, William, 221 (n. 2)

Burns, Walter Noble, 49–50

Burt, G. Rodney, 141, 143

Cakobau, 133–35, 138–41, 144

Calder, 133

California, 120, 130

California, 15, 62, 208

Callao, 24, 70, 72, 131, 187, 208

Calvert, James, 136–37

Camp, Mortimer, 72–73

Canada, 85, 88

Cannibals, 86–87, 106, 112, 114–15, 132

Canton, Mass., 184

Cape Cod, 10–12, 42, 93, 96, 100, 163, 191

Cape Horn Pigeon, 67, 94

Cape Poge, 96

Cape Verde Islands, 16, 32, 46. *See also* Intermarriage: Native Americans and foreigners to U.S. citizens; Portuguese whalemen; Whaling labor: diversity of

Captivity narratives, 80

Caribbean, 90, 167; Bermuda, 69; Cayman Islands, 4; Haiti, 175; Jamaica, 174

Caroline Islands, 89

Catharine, 114

Censuses: collected by missionaries and guardians, 43, 170, 200; federal, 4, 41, 169, 176–77, 200; in New Zealand, 153–54, 158

Certificates of protection, 41–42, 46–47, 164, 199

Champlin, Mary A. ("Chamblin"), 3

Chappaquiddick, 22, 26, 69, 95–98, 131–32, 164, 167, 172, 183–84, 186; whalemen of, 28, 32, 37, 95, 208

Chappell, David A., 110

Chappell, William H., 52–53

Charles Doggett, 105

Charles W. Morgan, 54, 94, 131

Chaseland, Tommy, 151, 153

Cheever, Henry, 37

Chelsea, 48

Cherokee, 31, 94

Cherokees, 88–89, 102

Chile, 53; St. Mary's, 34; Santiago, 34; Talcahuano, 17, 32, 34; Valparaiso, 17, 32, 80–82; vessels of, 34, 119

Chili, 51

Chilmark, Mass., 176

China trade, 12, 26, 88, 93, 113, 132, 164

Chinese, 88–89

Chinook, 203

Choctaws, 88

Christiantown, 22, 30–31, 37, 69, 165–66, 172, 17, 183, 192; whalemen of, 3, 23, 27, 30–31, 37–38, 63–64, 67, 208

Christie, John, 161

Christopher, Emma, 5

Christopher Mitchell, 72

Chummuck, Lydia, 164

Cicero, 94

Circassian, 187

Citizenship: of New Zealand, 131; of United States, 41, 47, 137, 139, 142, 169, 174–75, 184–86, 191

Clark, Uriah, 71

Clarke, Cyrene, 47–48

Clensy, Robert, 70

Clipperton Island, 121

Cloud, Enoch Carter, 48

Coan, Titus, 117

Colburn, George Lightcraft, 64–65, 72, 74

Colchester, Conn., 146

Cole, John A., 67

Coleman, Ellinwood B., 58

France, 108; vessels of, 12, 114, 116, 119, 130, 135, 149
Francis, James, 60, 219 (n. 65)
Freeman, Percival, 22
Friendship, 104
Futuna, 49

Galapagos Islands, 1, 16, 22
Gams, 1, 51–53, 205
Gardner, William, 107
Gay Head, 98
Gay Head, 9, 29–30, 37, 131, 163, 165–68, 170, 173–78, 186, 188–90, 192–93, 200; cliffs, 37, 112, 193; whalemen of, 1–4, 23–24, 29–31, 34, 40, 42–43, 50–74 passim, 120, 122–23, 130–31, 207–8, 221 (n. 2), 226 (n. 30)
Gender, 51–56. *See also* Manhood, expressions of; Sexuality; Women
George, 94
George, Peter, 147
George, Sally, 147
George Washington, 32, 94
Germany, vessels of, 119, 149
Gershom, Anstress, 1, 3
Gershom, Rosannah, 3
Gershom, Sarah, 1
Gershom, Temperance, 1, 3
Gilbert, Robert, 148–49, 151–52
Gilbert, William, 148–49, 151–52
Gilbert Islands, 106
Globe, 79–83, 93–94, 117
Gloucester, Mass., 167
Godfrey, Samuel, 174
Golden City, 26
Goodall, Charles, 165
Goodridge, Eleanor, 169
Goodridge, Philip, 60
Goodridge, Samuel P., 22
Goodridge, Simeon, 32, 60
Goodridge, Theodate, 32
Gordon, Arthur, 140
Gosnold, Bartholomew, 95–97, 181
Gouch, Young, 174
Grant, Joseph, 64

Great Mahele, 108
Greeks, 85, 88
Greene, Toby, 114
Greenough, John, 171
Grinnell, Lawrence, 22
Groton, Conn., 85, 146–48
Guam, 67
Guardians of Indians, 9, 21–23, 69, 97, 100, 102, 145, 162–63, 170, 172, 183–84, 188–90
Gulf Stream, 32

Haberfield, William, 160
Hammond, Watson F., 192, 219 (n. 67), 221 (n. 2)
Harper, William, 158
Harpooner. *See* Boatsteerers
Hartford, Conn., 85, 146
Haskins, Amos, 24, 25 (ill.), 26–27, 31–32, 42, 60–61, 72, 98
Haskins, Elizabeth P., 31
Haskins, Samuel, 3, 42
Hawai'i: Captain Cook's death at, 86; ships stopping at, 1, 48, 52, 65, 72–73, 80, 103–4, 106, 111–12; whaling's impact on, 93, 108, 116–20. *See also* Intermarriage: Native Americans and foreigners to U.S. citizens; Missionaries: of American Board of Commissioners of Foreign Missions; Pacific Islanders: as whaling laborers; Women: and prostitution
Hawaiian language, 49, 87
Hawksworth, John, 84
Hawley, Gideon, 21, 164, 170, 175, 188
Helen, 219 (n. 67)
Hendricks, Isaac F., 219 (n. 67), 221 (n. 2)
Henry, 44, 94, 219 (n. 67)
Henry, Benson Robert, 143
Henry Kneeland, 48
Hercules, 74, 94
Hero, 32–34
Herschel Island, 122
Herring Pond, 30, 164

Mungi, 122
Mutinies, 67–69, 79–82, 148
Mye, John, 107

Nantasket, 119
Nantucket, 94
Nantucket, Mass., 10, 12, 16, 24, 26, 28,
  58; whalemen of, 67, 131–32, 167;
  whaleships of, 12, 21, 22, 24, 32, 42,
  54, 79–83, 104, 110–14, 207; whaling
  records of, 199
Napoleon, 61
Narragansett, 94
Narragansett reservation (Charlestown, R.I.), 9, 47, 88, 120, 174–76, 192,
  200; whalemen of, 107, 170. *See also*
  Ammons, Gideon; Ammons, Joseph
Native Americans: in New England,
  9–10, 13; and non-whaling occupations, 9, 26, 29–30, 120, 145–46,
  188–89; and survival, 9, 14, 99,
  193–94. *See also* Guardians of Indians;
  Memory; *specific communities*
Native American whalemen: as captains,
  24–25, 60–61, 70, 72; and community
  leadership, 30, 175–76, 192–93;
  database of, 18, 199–202; and desertion, 66–70, 72, 80, 131; and families,
  1–3, 18, 22, 26, 28–31, 131; importance
  to native communities of, 14, 189,
  193–94; importance to whaling
  industry of, 13–14, 182; life course of,
  1–3, 15, 22–23, 28–30, 189; motivations
  of, 27–36, 98; as officers, 14–15, 17, 21,
  23, 27, 34–39, 47, 58–76, 118; and
  professionalism, 3, 5, 34, 38, 111, 118,
  120, 205; as ship owners, 26–27; as
  world travelers, 5–6, 110, 112, 129–32,
  194, 203. *See also* Journals; Logbooks;
  Memoirs; Whaling labor; Women
Native of Marshpee, 26
Naturalization, 169, 174–75
Navarch, 52, 122
Navigation, 38, 130, 187, 190–91
Nevers, Absalom, 67

Nevers, Daniel, 67, 69
New Bedford, 94
New Bedford, Mass., 12–14, 16, 24, 31,
  96, 111, 167, 177, 181, 189, 192; whalemen of, 136; whaleships of, 1–2, 12, 14,
  15, 22–24, 27, 29–31, 46, 60, 72–74, 95,
  111, 123, 131, 147, 165, 188, 201, 207–8;
  whaling records of, 199–200
New England, 26, 36, 55, 94, 120
New England, 8–14, 88–89, 102, 188–89;
  in seventeenth century, 90, 94, 97, 100
New Haven, Conn., whaleships of, 16, 44
New London, Conn.: whaleships of, 16,
  41, 44, 48, 55, 67, 72, 107, 119, 124, 145;
  whaling records of, 199
Newport, R.I., whaleships of, 130, 199
New Zealand, 8, 88; Arowhenua, 153;
  Auckland, 131; Bay of Islands, 17, 131,
  136; Cook Strait, 153; Dunedin, 160;
  Karitane, 145, 148, 156; Matanaika,
  150; Otago, 148–51, 158, 160; Puket-
  eraki, 148, 150, 152, 156, 159; sheep
  industry of, 154, 156; shorewhaling
  industry of, 149–50, 153–54; Waik-
  ouaiti, 145, 148–51, 153–54, 157–61;
  Wanganui, 48; whaling grounds, 28,
  112, 149, 165. *See also* Apes, Elisha;
  Maori
Ngai Tahu, 148–51, 153, 159
Niagara Falls, 108
Niger, 58, 131, 167–68, 208
Noble savage, 86, 88
Nordhoff, Charles, 38–39
Norfolk Island, 131, 167
Norling, Lisa, 31
North America, 44
Northwest Coast, 16
Norway, 14
Norwich, Conn., whaleships of, 147

Oak Bluffs, Mass., 192
Oakley, James A., 67–69
Occom, Samson, 85, 88
O'Connell, Barry, 145
Oeno, 28

Portuguese whalemen, 1, 6, 46–50, 165–66, 169, 171. *See also* Azores; Cape Verde Islands; Whaling labor: diversity of

Potomac, 104, 106

Pratt, Addison, 42

Pratt, Thomas (Tame Parata), 154, 158

Preston, Conn., 146

Prince, Thomas, 95

Protection, 24

Provincetown, Mass., whaleships of, 191, 202

Punahere, Mata (Caroline Apes), 153–54, 156–58

Punkapog, 184

Quallah Battoo, Sumatra, 104

Queequeg, 37

Quippish, John, 60

Race: and categorization, 4–5, 8, 18, 41–43, 87, 127, 143–47, 152, 157–58, 160–61, 163, 170, 176–78; and complexion, 41–42, 48, 86–87, 90, 147, 152, 161, 176, 201; contingency of, 3–9, 17, 21, 42, 51, 59–61, 73–76, 86, 91–92, 120, 125–26, 129, 144, 162, 182, 186, 191, 195–98; as identity, 18, 86, 125–26, 129, 136, 144, 171, 175, 177; and nationality, 41, 47–50, 168–69; and science, 17, 87.

Rambler, 42

Randolph, John P., 175

Rebecca, 12

Rediker, Marcus, 59

Redsdale, Evelina, 167–68, 177 (Evelina Cook)

Reindeer, 75

Religion, 9, 46, 48–49, 64, 79, 85, 100, 107, 119–20, 132, 136–37, 145, 183–84, 192. *See also* Missionaries

Reservations: in New England, 8–9, 13, 64, 97–98, 125, 162, 171–74, 181–86, 189–90; in New Zealand (reserves), 151, 162. *See also* Guardians of Indians; *specific communities*

Respect, 14, 34–36, 61, 70–71, 73, 75, 87, 182, 189–94, 197

Revolutionary War, 10, 163

Reynolds, Jeremiah, 105

Reynolds, William, 106, 108

Rhode Island, 47, 147, 174–76, 192, 200

Ridge, John, 89

Rio de Janeiro, 67, 101

Rising States, 24

Roanoke, 94

Roberts, Josiah, 113

Rogers, James L., 227–28 (n. 55)

Roman, 60, 118–21, 207

Rose, Isaac, 176

Rounds, Charles, 136

Rousseau, 67

Royce, James, 139

Russell, Joseph, 181

Sac, John, 106

Sachems, 95, 98–100

Sag Harbor, N.Y., 16, 199, 203

Sag Harbor Whaling Museum, 26

Sailors: conceptions of, 74, 120; and riots, 118–19

St. Helena, 8, 16, 69–70, 167–68

St. Lawrence Island, 122

Salem, Mass., 138; vessels of, 104–5

Sally, 80

Salisbury, Beulah, 167

Salsbury, Druzilla, 3

Salsbury, Emily, 3

Salsbury, Jophanus, 3, 130

Salvary, Emanuel, 171

Samoa, 17, 103–7, 142

Sampson, William, 101

Samuel & Thomas, 1, 23, 207

Samuel Robertson, 60

Sandwich, Mass., 100

San Francisco, Calif., 14, 66; whaleships of, 25, 49, 63, 122, 131, 166, 187

Sarah, 94

Saratoga, 52

Sassacus, 95

Schmitt, Robert C., 117

Webquish, Levi L., 23, 37, 73
Webquish, Nathan S., 23, 37, 95–98
Webquish, Solomon, 26
Webquish, William S., 23, 32, 37
Webquish surname, 200–201
Weeks, Jeremiah, 165
Weeks, Tristram A., 63, 176, 208
Weeks, William, 221 (n. 2)
Weller Brothers, 149–51, 153
West, Benjamin, 96, 99
West, Ellsworth Lewis, 72, 75
Westport, Mass.: whalemen of, 23–25, 130; whaleships of, 27
Whalemen's Shipping List and Merchants' Transcript, 61, 68, 200
Whales: bowhead, 12–13, 118–19; humpback, 13, 131; right, 10, 12–13, 34, 35 (ill.), 149; sperm, 2 (ill.), 12–14, 34, 35 (ill.), 36, 42, 67, 90, 103–4; stranded, 10
Whale stamps, 1, 2 (ill.), 35 (ill.), 206
Whaling: grounds, 16, 112, 119; hunting and processing methods, 1–2, 10, 12–13, 28, 34, 61–63, 73, 118; literature of, 17, 45–46, 90–91; before nineteenth century, 9–13; ports, 11–12; in twentieth century, 14, 29
Whaling industry: expansion and decline, 12–14, 21; profitability of, 24, 26–27, 40; and ship owners, 12, 22, 39–40, 59, 66, 69, 94–95, 99, 102. *See also* Native American whalemen; Whaling; Whaling labor
Whaling labor: demand for, 6, 13, 21, 47, 69, 71; diversity of, 6–7, 13, 40–41, 46–51, 59, 69, 147; and free-labor ideology, 23; and hiring practices, 21–22, 28, 43–48, 50; and income, 9, 22, 29–31, 36, 107, 188–89, 194; and law, 22–23, 40–41, 45, 47, 56, 66–69, 71; and nationality, 40, 46–51, 163; and

nicknames, 49–50, 55, 61; and race, 21, 23–24, 27–28, 36–45, 48–51, 55–59, 66, 71–73; and rank, 6–7, 12–13, 21, 38–45, 58–76; and risk, 22, 29–34, 38, 194. *See also* Lay
Wheelock, Eleazar, 85, 88
Whippy, David, 132–34, 136, 140–43, 197
Whippy, David, Jr., 133
White, William Allen, 89
Whitecar, William B., 56
Whiteside, Joseph A., 52
Whiteness, 5, 23, 38–39, 43, 45, 49, 56–57, 71, 74, 79, 81, 91, 151–52, 181, 185
Wilkes, Charles, 105–6, 134
William Lewis, 72
William Penn, 99, 103–4, 106–7
Williams, John B., 134–40, 142–43, 152, 197
Williams, Martha, 164
Williamson, James, 172
Winnebagoes, 91
Wisconsin, 177
Women: as captains' wives, 17, 44, 52, 69, 143, 205; as cross-dressers on whaleships, 52; and prostitution, 53–54, 115–18, 121, 124, 189; as servants, 189; as whalemen's relatives, 1–3, 22, 52; as whalemen's wives and sweethearts, 3, 15 (ill.), 30–32, 52–55, 64
Wood & Nye, 73
Wood's Hole, Mass., 99
Worth, William, 104
Wright & Long, 149

Yap, 133
Yarmouth Indians, 171
Young Phenix, 72

Zanzibar, 166
Zollers, George, 147